Our Every Day Life is not a scholarly book—it wasn't meant to be. It's a practical book, as it was meant to be. In the pages you will find godly advice that's drawn from God's Word. Sit at the feet of man who has walked with the Lord for decades and listen as he reads Scripture, pulls out gems, and gives practical advice for every day living.

Tim Rupp, D.Min.
Founder of the Strong Blue Line Foundation
TheStrongBlueLine.org

As a first responder, we deal everyday with issues such as death, anger, hurts, relationships, possessions, work, betrayals, hopes, and love. "Our Every Day Life" will use the Bible, a true source of light, to help address these different topics. From our personal live to our professional engagements with the community members in times of need, this will bless you personally and professionally!

Jake Skifstad
Founder Shield 616
Shield616.org

Sometimes I have a difficult time finding a daily devotional to engage with. Some are just too shallow and others attempt to dig so deep that they end up in the realm of academia. What Pastor Paul Verhoeven has done with Our Every Day Life, is refreshing. Here we have an exemplary balance of something that feels, 'just right.' Paul present daily thoughts and challenges, prefaced and seasoned with Scripture, engaging and meaty enough to start (or finish) our daily walk with Christ.

James Runcorn, D.Min.
Lead Pastor, Hope Church in Spencer, IA

There are, of course, many ways to read and understand the Bible... most of them are wrong. They are usually wrong because of the preconceived notions of the reader. Theologians love to apply their "approved grid" to help God fit into their man-made conventions. How refreshing it is to read the observations from my very good friend, Pastor Paul Verhoeven, as he simply allows God's Word to be, well, God's Word. Each day, Paul applies the balm of the Word, allowing it to soothe, mend, heal, and guide. Enjoy this book, unencumbered from the theological bias, free to simply hear from your Heavenly Father regarding your every day life.

David Coleman
Family Pastor, Watersprings Church in Idaho Falls, ID

Paul Verhoeven is a man of faith and integrity. His faith reflects a heart that has delved deeply into the grace of God. His devotionals flow from his personal experience of intimacy and dependence on the Word of God He hares from what he has both learned and lived. You will be blessed by this book.

Aaron Hale
Lead Pastor, Calvary Chapel Foothill Ranch in Lake Forest, CA

I've enjoyed reading and meditating on Paul's daily devotionals. I find them uplifting and inspiring, just what I need each day to face the challenges that come my way. Paul does a great job sharing the context of the daily verse to help us better understand the passage and the true meaning behind it. I've drawn closer to God by reading these each day. I encourage you to read this devotional book to grow in your daily walk with God.

Brian Chandler
Senior Pastor, Trinity Baptist Church in Healdsburg, CA

I'll tell you what Paul has done here. He has put to paper his own devotional discoveries. You can feel that he didn't so much set out to write a daily devotional as he did simply record the journey he himself went on after considering a passage. It's genuine, in other words. We need more of that, don't you think?

Gene Pensiero
Senior Pastor, Calvary Hanford in Hanford, CA

The Word of God is powerful and alive. This book will help anyone grow in their faith.

Pastor Dan Finfrock
Founder Intensive Care Ministries
icmbible.com

"I'll tell you what Paul has done here. He has put to paper his own [illegible] didn't so much [illegible] [illegible] record [illegible] [illegible]. It's [illegible] [illegible] more of that [illegible]?"

[illegible]

[illegible] Landlord of [illegible]

[illegible] This [illegible] will help [illegible]

[illegible]

[illegible] Founder [illegible]

Our Every Day Life

A One-Year Devotional

Paul Verhoeven

ISBN 979-8-218-37179-1

This book is dedicated to my good friend Patrick Egle, the author of "Renovating the Mind." Thank you for your friendship and encouraging me to begin writing devotions with you back in 2009.

Also, to Dr. Tim Rupp of the Strong Blue Line Foundation. I appreciate your friendship, your service, and all the encouragement and help that you have given me to make it possible to get this book and "Traveling Through The Gospels" published.

Our Every Day Life

A One-Year Devotional

January 1

"For I am the least of the apostles, unworthy to be called an apostle, because I persecuted the church of God. But by the grace of God I am what I am, and His grace toward me was not in vain."
1 Corinthians 15:9-10a

Perfection! It is a trait that most of us strive to reach even though we know that it is impossible. We often are guilty of placing unrealistic goals and ideals on ourselves, and then become upset and/or depressed when we do not achieve those unrealistic goals or ideals. That is crazy.

Why do we expect so much from ourselves, and others, and then have a completely different set of standards for what is considered great? Look at professional athletes as an example. A baseball player will not get a hit 2 out of every three times he steps up to bat, and for being successful only one-third of the time he will make millions of dollars per year. In fact, with that average they will most likely end of in the Hall of Fame. A basketball player who can make half of his shots will be an All-Star and end up in the Hall of Fame.

We allow "professionals" to get by with much less than what we expect from ourselves and those we work with. That is crazy. Why do we have such a critical spirit towards those we personally know, and ourselves too? Instead of always being critical of others we need to project a spirit of grace. Grace is what God gives, as the apostle Paul reminds us. Paul had been a Pharisee, and was guilty of persecuting, and even killing, members of the church. In spite of this flagrant failure before God, the apostle Paul still received grace from God, and is considered one of the greatest preachers and teachers of the gospel in the history of the world. God used this "failure" to greatly impact the world; and his impact is still felt today.

May we extend grace towards those we have contact with today.

May we show God's love and grace to others, not because they deserve it, but because "You received without paying; give without pay" (Matthew 10:8). God has freely given grace to us, so we can do the same for others. We do it not because others are better than us and deserve it, but because we received God's grace when we did not deserve it too. Bible scholar Donald Barnhouse said, "Love that goes upward is worship; love that goes outward is affection; love that stoops is grace." May we live a life of grace towards others.

January 2

"But none of these things move me; nor do I count my life dear to myself, so that I may finish my race with joy, and the ministry which I received from the Lord Jesus, to testify to the gospel of the grace of God." NKJV
Acts 20:24

Even though the apostle Paul had been warned numerous times that trouble awaited him in Jerusalem, he responded by saying "none of these things move me." Paul did not look at life the same way most of us do. Self-preservation wasn't his top priority; obedience was. He even admits this when he said, "nor do I count my life dear to myself." Paul acts like an accountant. He has two columns in front of him: credits and expenses. As he looks over these two columns and compares them to each other, he finds that the credits of following Jesus are worth far more than the expenses of his own life. Therefore, there is no reason for him to count his own life as dear. God is worth far more, and it is much more beneficial to serve God than to try to preserve his own life. Paul embraced the words of Jesus, when He said, "If anyone would come after me, let him deny himself and take up his cross daily and follow Me" (Luke 9:23).

Paul's goal in life was to "finish my race with joy." Paul saw himself as a runner running a race, the race of life. When you run in a race, there is a course that must be followed. Paul's desire is to follow that course and finish the race with joy. God set the course and Paul was following what God set before him until his race was done.

This is not an easy task to do. Those of you who run long distance races know the difficulties of finishing the race. There is that point when you "hit the wall." You are so tired that you don't think you can run any more. You are sore, tired, and ready to give up. This is true in life as well as long distance races. The author of Hebrews provides us with the secret to continue, even when you want to give up. "...run with endurance the race that is set before us, looking to Jesus, the founder and perfecter of our faith, who for the joy that was set before him endured the cross, despising the shame, and is seated at the right hand of the throne of God" (Hebrews 12:1b-2). When things are tough, when you are tired, when you want to give up and stop, that is when it is important to make sure your focus isn't on the race you are running, but on Jesus. Did Paul do this? Yes. At the very end of his life he wrote, "I have fought the good fight, I have finished the race, I have kept the faith" (2 Timothy 4:7).

January 3

"And he said to him, 'What is your name?' And he said, 'Jacob.' Then he said, 'Your name shall no longer be called Jacob, but Israel, for you have striven with God and with men, and have prevailed.'"
Genesis 32:27-28

When asked what his name was, he had to say Jacob. This most likely brought him a sense of shame, as he had to admit that he was a sneaky conman, because that is what Jacob means. But this was an important step, because before we can become more like God, we have to admit who we are in ourselves. From what is recorded for us in the book of Genesis, the last time Jacob was asked this question he lied, he said to his father Isaac, "I am Esau your firstborn" (Genesis 27:19). This time he shamefully admits who he is.

God didn't ask Jacob his name for information because He obviously already knew who Jacob was. When God asked what his name was, He was asking "Are you going to continue to live up to your name, deceiving yourself and others; or will you admit what you are and allow Me to change you?"

When a person received a new name in the Bible, it was to signify a new beginning in their life. Jacob's name is now changed to Israel, which means "he who rules, or prevails, with God." Even though Jacob lost the battle, he did win the victory. How did that happen? He was weakened and not able to rely on himself, so he surrendered to God and allowed God to rule over him. This is how he became victorious. It is also how we can become victorious. When we stop trying to rule our own lives, and instead allow God to "break" us, to conquer us, and rule over us. When we realize our own weakness and our need for God in our life, then we are victorious.

The apostle Paul learned this lesson in his life also. When he did, this is what he wrote about it, "'My grace is sufficient for you, for my power is made perfect in weakness.' Therefore I will boast all the more gladly of my weaknesses, so that the power of Christ may rest upon me. For the sake of Christ, then, I am content with weaknesses, insults, hardships, persecutions, and calamities. For when I am weak, then I am strong" (2 Corinthians 12:9-10).

January 4

"So whether we are at home or away, we make it our aim to please Him."

2 Corinthians 5:9

The apostle Paul is talking about his goal in life. Each of us has goals for our lives. Most people's goal is to earn a good living to provide themselves with comfort and ease; to avoid problems and pain. They want money in both checking and savings accounts, to have a nice car, and to go on a nice vacation each year. The goal that the apostle Paul had was to please God in everything that he did. The Living Bible translates this verse very clearly, "So our aim is to please Him always in everything we do, whether we are here in this body or away from this body and with Him in Heaven."

Too often we make choices and decisions in our life based on how others will view our choice. We allow others to influence our decisions based on how we think they will respond, or what we think they will approve. Often this is based on our assumptions of them; but even if we know it to be true, it is still catering to their desires instead of making a decision to please God. When we make decisions to please God first and foremost, there will be times that other people will not approve of our decisions. It is ok that other people do not agree with what God is calling and/or the direction He is leading, because they're not who you are aiming to please, God is. The idea behind this word "please" is "to devote oneself zealously to a cause." When you zealously devote yourself to God, what others think will not carry enough weight to change your mind. God then becomes the overriding factor in all decisions that you make. How God is affected by the decision now directs your thoughts, instead of how another person will be affected.

Keep in mind that one of those "other" people that take a back seat to God is you. Decisions are made by whether or not they please God. This will lead you to make decisions that may bring discomfort into your life. The apostle Paul realized this, and even knew that it could lead to his physical death. No matter, he made a conscious decision in his mind that he would rather die and go to Heaven than make a choice that displeases God to help himself here on earth. Wow! Think about that for a minute.

Who is influencing your decisions? Are you willing to make a decision that others will not agree with and will not please them, but you know that God is leading you to make? The question is are we are willing to make decisions that will remove comfort from our lives in order to bring God glory?

January 5

"You shall not add to the word that I command you, nor take from it, that you may keep the commandments of the LORD your God that I command you."
Deuteronomy 4:2

Most people enjoy eating at cafeteria style restaurants because of the choices. You can get as much of what you like, and if you don't like a type of food, you can avoid it and not eat it. It's great. You can even "pig out" on those tasty and enjoyable desserts. That's ok to do once in a while, but if that is your regular habit of eating, you will not be healthy.

How we approach the Bible is the same way. Too often people approach the Bible like it is cafeteria-style. I love the Psalms, so I'll take a large helping of that. Some of the Proverbs encourage me, so I'll take some of those. Philippians is nice to read, give me that. You can keep Romans, Hebrews, and Ephesians; those books are too heavy for me. You can also keep Revelation; it is too difficult to understand and too controversial. People think it's ok to keep the sections of the Bible they "enjoy," while not reading, listening, and applying the sections of Scripture they do not like. This is because those other sections may be more difficult to understand; but most likely it is because they are convicting.

When the Bible convicts me of the wrongness of my actions and/or attitudes, then I need to change. If I do not want to change then it is easier to change the Bible so that my thoughts, actions, or attitudes are no longer wrong. To do this I just need to ignore the sections that convict me, re-write them, or question their validity. These are the steps that false religions take. Groups like Mormons and Jehovah Witnesses change Scripture to fit their own doctrines. The Jesus Seminar hold "scholarly" meetings to question whether Jesus really said what the Bible claims He did. According to them only 18% of what the Bible says Jesus said is true while 82% of what Jesus said in the Bible is false.

God makes it very clear that we are not to add or subtract from what the Bible says. In case it wasn't understood here in the Law, it was repeated a few more times. "Do not add to His words, lest He rebuke you and you be found a liar" (Proverbs 30:6). In Revelation 22:18-19: "I warn everyone who hears the words of the prophecy of this book: if anyone adds to them, God will add to him the plagues described in this book, and if anyone takes away from the words of the book of this prophecy, God will take away his share in the tree of life and in the holy city, which are described in this book." God wants to make sure that there is no misunderstanding; God's Word (the Bible) is true, complete, and accurate. We need to accept it and believe on Him. He shared His love letter with us because He loves us and wants us to know His truth.

January 6

"And Samuel said, 'Has the Lord as great delight in burnt offerings and sacrifices, as in obeying the voice of the Lord? Behold, to obey is better than sacrifice, and to listen than the fat of rams.'"
1 Samuel 15:22

Going to church on Sunday. Going to church during the week. Teaching Sunday School or attending a mid-week Bible Study. Giving a portion of my paycheck back to God or helping out a family that is in need. Going on a mission trip, or street witnessing. Giving up my time off to help at Vacation Bible School. These are activities that we as Christians are involved in and will actively do. Sometimes we look at the different things that we do and begin to congratulate ourselves on the many different things that we are doing for the Lord. It is easy for us to get caught up in the worldly mindset and attitude that doing more and always being busy makes us a better Christian. That is false! It's not how much we do, or how many different ministries that we are involved in that's important.

Some people look at the different ministries they are involved in as sacrifices. The more we "sacrifice" for God, the better we believe that we are doing. That is not true. God is not going to reward a person for the number of things that they have done for Him. The idea of being rewarded for doing more than others is a worldly idea and concept. In fact, oftentimes we work so hard at trying to be involved in more things than we should that we cause ourselves to be busier than we should, which leads to being tired, worn out, and ineffective. It also can lead to a sense of pride because of all that we are doing for God.

What is it that God looks for from us? He looks for obedience. God doesn't give out awards for the person who is involved in the most ministries. God simply wants us to be obedient to what He has called us to do. That doesn't change at all; whether God calls you to do one thing or more than one thing, God wants you to be obedient to His calling.

King Saul thought he could impress God by keeping some of the best animals to sacrifice to God, but that wasn't what God wanted him to do. God wasn't impressed by this, even though the sacrifices were to be made to Him. God instructed Saul to kill all the animals, along with the Amalakites, because of their disobedience to Him. Saul failed to do this, and because of that he was rejected as king. "For rebellion is as the sin of divination, and presumption is as iniquity and idolatry. Because you have rejected the word of the Lord, He has also rejected you from being king" (1 Samuel 15:23).

Failure to obey God is sin. So, whatever God has called you to do, then do it. It's not about how "much" you do. It is all about being obedient to whatever God calls you to do. Do that!

January 7

"...walk in a manner worthy of the calling to which you have been called, with all humility and gentleness, with patience, bearing with one another in love, eager to maintain the unity of the Spirit in the bond of peace."
Ephesians 4:1b-3

I love team sports. They are fun to watch, and even more enjoyable to participate in. I have been astounded watching teams with only average talent defeat more talented teams. Now don't misunderstand what I am saying, talent is important, but it is even more important for a team to work together. For victory to be achieved, there needs to be unity. Unity is critical.

In addition to sports teams, this same analogy applies to the church. When church members aren't united, the church becomes weak and ineffective. In fact, unity within the church is even more important than unity on sports teams. Unity is vital to the health of a church. That means every single church member, including you, must contribute to the unity of the church.

The apostle Paul reminds us of the responsibility that each of us has in fostering unity within the church instead of being divisive. This means that we need to accept others in the church that aren't like us, even those that are "different" than us. This doesn't mean we have to agree with them all the time, but we must be willing to sacrifice our personal preferences to keep unity within the church.

What we need most in our life to contribute to unity is love. Love is the opposite of gossip. Romans 1:29 reminds us that gossip is a tool used by unrighteous people. Gossip is destructive and will tear a church apart and leave it powerless. This is the opposite of what love does to a church. This is why the apostle Peter said, "Whoever desires to love life and see good days, let him keep his tongue from evil and his lips from speaking deceit" (1 Peter 3:10).

To help the church be effective in fulfilling its purpose, individual church members have the responsibility to love one another and to watch their tongues so the words they speak don't tear down others, but instead build each other up in God's grace. Don't tear down, but instead be a unifier and help build the church into a unified, effective body that spreads God's love to this world that so desperately needs it.

January 8

"...but in your hearts honor Christ the Lord as holy, always being prepared to make a defense to anyone who asks you for a reason for the hope that is in you; yet do it with gentleness and respect..."
1 Peter 3:15

A funny fact of life is that we need to always be ready for the unexpected. This is not how most people live. The majority of people live day in and day out simply going through the motions. Too often we live disengaged from things as a way to cope and get through the day. This is not how Jesus wants His children to live. Instead of being disengaged, Jesus desires for His children to be engaged, ready, and prepared. What do we need to be ready and prepared for? To give a defense of the hope that we have. What does this mean? It does not mean that we have to be ready and prepared at all times to defend a theological position. To have a four-point presentation in our mind ready to be unleashed at a moment's notice. What it does mean is that we are prepared to share very simply what Jesus has done in our life. You see, Jesus is our hope. It is important that we are ready to share Jesus with others. Who He is, what He has done, and how He has changed your life.

All too often people say that faith is a personal matter and needs to be kept to yourself. Not true! Peter does remind us of how we are to share with others, "with gentleness and respect." Don't go around beating people over the head with your Bible (both figuratively or literally) or being obnoxious about what you believe. Remember that you are also a sinner saved by grace, which means you are no better than the person you are sharing with, so be gracious to them. Peter is writing this letter to the church body, not just to pastors. This means that Peter is directing these words to the church body. It isn't the job of only the pastor or pastor at church to share about Jesus with others. This is the responsibility of every single believer. Peter experienced this often in his own life (see Acts 2:14-39; Acts 3:11-26; Acts 4:8-12; and Acts 5:29-32). How did Peter prepare for this unexpected sharing of the Gospel? He spent time daily in the Word, but most importantly he relied on the power of the Holy Spirit to help give him the necessary words to share. The Holy Spirit will do the same for you when you rely on Him for wisdom and direction. Jesus told the disciples "do not be anxious about how you should defend yourself or what you should say, for the Holy Spirit will teach you in that very hour what you ought to say" (Luke 12:11b-12).

January 9

"And when they had entered, they went up to the upper room, where they were staying, Peter and John and James and Andrew, Philip and Thomas, Bartholomew and Matthew, James the son of Alphaeus and Simon the Zealot and Judas the son of James. All these with one accord were devoting themselves to prayer, together with the women and Mary the mother of Jesus, and his brothers."
Acts 1:13-14

The eleven remaining disciples returned to Jerusalem to wait for the gift of the Holy Spirit, along with Jesus' earthly mother Mary and her sons, plus the women who followed Jesus. It is interesting that Mary's sons, including James and Judas, were with this group. While Jesus was on earth they didn't believe Him and wanted nothing to do with

Him or His ministry (see John 7:5). But His resurrection proved to them that He truly was the Messiah, and they believed Him and became followers of Jesus too.

In the next verse, Acts 1:15, we are told that this group numbered about 120 people. What a diverse group this was. There were men and women, apostles, and unknown "ordinary" people. They were there together as one group. The eleven disciples weren't elevated above the others, and neither was Mary or her children. Either of these groups could have tried to elevate themselves above the rest because of their close association to Jesus, but they didn't. Instead, there was unity among the entire group.

We know this because verse 14 tells us "these with one accord were devoting themselves to prayer." This means there were no divided interests. The group of disciples that were continually bickering and fighting when Jesus was here, were now unified and in agreement with each other. They were no longer striving against each other for recognition or advancement. What caused this change? Their differences were still there, but the reality of Jesus' resurrection brought them together because it was greater than their differences.

Unity is so important to the church. We are made up of many different individuals. We have different tastes, ideas, likes, temperaments, etc. Each of those areas are important, but not nearly as important as the truth that Jesus died for our sins, rose from the dead, and sits at God's right-hand interceding on our behalf. That is our hope, and it overrides every difference that we may have. Think about music to help you understand what it means to be continually united. Music is made when many different notes are played at the same time. Even though they are different, they harmonize together in pitch and tone, making a beautiful sound. Every person in God's church is an instrument that plays a different sound. We all play our sounds together under the direction of the conductor, who is Jesus. As we follow Him, we blend together in harmony to create a beautiful and pleasing sound.

These 120 followers of Jesus did this as they prayed together.

Jesus told them to wait in Jerusalem, and as they were waiting, they spent their time together in prayer. I also believe that their spending time together in prayer is part of what caused their unity. When we pray together with others, we find ourselves being united with them. This happened here as these 120 followers of Jesus persevered together in prayer while waiting for the Holy Spirit to be given to them.

January 10

"Every good gift and every perfect gift is from above, coming down from the Father of lights, with whom there is no variation or shadow due to change."
James 1:17

One of the most frustrating things that can happen to us is when someone tells us something, we believe what they tell us, and later we find out that it is not true. This is especially true if it was done on purpose. The reason this is so frustrating and heart-breaking is because someone meant to deceive you, to purposefully mislead you. This deception is also a favorite tool of Satan's. In fact, it is the very first tool that he used since the beginning of time. Even though it is an old tool, Satan is very good at it, and he continues to deceive people today. He should be good at it, since he has been deceiving people for at least 6,000 years. When Satan approached Eve in the Garden of Eden, he planted the seed in her mind that if God was really good, He would allow her and Adam to eat from any tree that they wanted to, including the forbidden tree. It worked. Satan's deception of Eve led to Adam and Eve sinning, and every person born since that time has been born with a sin nature. Satan also used this same tool with Jesus. Jesus had been in the desert, fasting, for forty days. There was no question that Jesus was hungry, so Satan approached Him and tried to plant the thought in Jesus' mind that if God the Father really loved Him, then He wouldn't be hungry. Satan was doing then what he continues to do today: questioning the goodness of God.

Satan, our enemy, wants to convince us that God isn't good, that He is withholding things that we need from us. This would then mean that God isn't good, and that He doesn't really love us. Is this true? Absolutely not! God is good. He does love us and care for us. This is why James answers that question be reminding us that every good thing we have is a gift from God. Not only does God give us good gifts, but He also doesn't change. God is "the same yesterday and today and forever" (Hebrews 13:8). This also means that God's goodness is constant. It doesn't change from day to day, or year to year, or even century to century. God has always been good, and He will always be good. He isn't like humans are. God isn't moody. He doesn't have a good day one day, and then a bad day the next day. He's not generous one day, and then grouchy the next day. God is constant, and He is constantly good. Since God is constantly good, He also doesn't respond to us according to how we act towards Him. This is because even when "we are faithless, He remains faithful" (2 Timothy 2:13).

January 11

"So Israel took his journey with all that he had and came
to Beersheba, and offered sacrifices to the God of his father Isaac."
Genesis 46:1

There is only one constant in life, and that is change. Yet many find change to be exceedingly difficult. The older we get the more resistant most people become to change. They yearn for the way things used to be instead of embracing the changes that have occurred. It is easy to understand why. When we are surrounded by familiarity (surrounding, habits, practices, people, etc.), we tend to be much more comfortable and experience feelings of safety. Change, or even the threat of change, can upset all that and bring with it feelings of fear. This is exactly what Jacob was dealing with at this time. He had lived here in Canaan for many years, surrounded by family. It would not be easy to leave, yet he willingly left. Jacob, or Israel, knew that God was in control of his life and to resist where God was leading him would have been detrimental. Even though Canaan was the land of promise, he knew that if God was calling him out of that land for a period of time, He had to have a good reason to do so. I love this trust that Israel has in God. Instead of focusing on the here and now, or his feelings or personal desires, he exhibited a trust in God to go and follow Him, even when he didn't know what to expect, or even why he was being called to do so.

As he travels south towards Egypt to live through an invitation by royalty, he didn't allow royalty to cloud his vision. Instead of being in awe of royalty, Israel kept his focus on God. This is why he stopped in Beersheba. He stopped to offer sacrifices to God, in other words, he worshipped and praised God before leaving the land of promise. Before he enters this new phase of life, he stops and makes sure that God is with him and leading him. Change is the only constant we have in life, which means that each of us will experience new phases of life. Learn from Israel, stop to worship and praise God. Trust Him. Know that God has a divine plan and purpose for what is happening in your life, even when you don't know what is happening, or why it is happening. The good news is we don't have to know or understand, we just need to trust God and continue following Him, just as Israel is doing here.

January 12

"...with whom the kings of the earth have committed sexual immorality, and with the wine of whose sexual immorality the dwellers on earth have become drunk."
Revelation 17:2

Karl Marx very famously said that "Religion is the opiate of the masses." As with all lies, there is an element of truth in that saying. It is built within every person to worship because God created us to worship Him. Those that reject to worship God will find themselves worshipping something else in His place because we are made to worship. Sadly, many choose to worship created things instead of the Creator. This is why we see people worshipping nature, earth, animals, work, money, relationships, power, etc. People will worship just about anything. There is a God shaped vacuum inside each person, and it will be filled with the worship of whatever god a person chooses to worship.

This isn't a new idea but has existed since the time of Adam and Eve at the beginning of creation. Due to sin, man-made and man-centered religion has seduced people, especially leaders, around the world. Throughout history world leaders have willingly followed Satan to gain power, whether it be in politics, society, religion, economics, military, etc. At the end of the tribulation period, rulers from around the world will be so seduced by the antichrist and false prophet that they will gladly follow them in their false religion. This system will be popular around the world, have an appearance of being religious, and will appear attractive to follow. But it will be false and very immoral.

It is so important that Jesus remains the object of our worship. He is Who we were created to worship. Don't allow popular opinions, trends, or any other pressures to move your worship to anything other than Jesus. Other things are important, things like nature, the earth, etc., but not important enough to worship. Only Jesus is worthy of worship. As Lenny LeBlanc wrote in his song Born To Worship, "I was born to worship the Lord, that is why I sing, to give Him praise and lift up my voice is such a natural thing." We have been created to worship God. It is a natural thing, so let His worship flow.

January 13

"Whatever you do, work heartily, as for the Lord and not for men."
Colossians 3:23

Football season just ended. Many people enjoy spending their Sunday afternoon watching these athletes play their game. The players are some of the best athletes in the world. They spend countless hours working to get themselves in prime condition, and to improve on the immense talents given to them by God. If you watched the Super Bowl, you noticed that these players gave everything they had to win.

That was for the Super Bowl. If you watched games the other weeks you wouldn't always see that. Professional team sports have gotten to the point that many of the athletes go all out and give their best only when the game really matters. If there is no chance to make the playoffs, you will see many of the greatest players in the world not give it 100%. They know they are still getting their large paychecks, so they just "clock in" and go through the motions, but don't really play with heart.

As Christians we can get into that same mindset. If we aren't careful, we treat "large" events as more important than witnessing to an individual that no one else sees us doing. The apostle Paul is reminding us that everything that we do needs to be done to please God, not men. This includes the work that we do to earn a living, but also what we do the rest of the time too. Whether we are a pastor, a housewife, collect garbage, a salesman, a contractor, a janitor, a government employee, or a boss; we need to give a 100% effort in what we do. There is no time to "slack off" and just do what is expected. We need to give everything we do a wholehearted effort. We don't work to please our boss; or work differently when we know they can see us.

This attitude isn't just for work, but also for our leisure time and what we do at home. This doesn't mean we should never rest or take it easy, in fact, it's the opposite of that. When it's time to rest, we should do that wholeheartedly, just as we do our work. Our goal, as Christians, is to bring pleasure and glory to God in *whatever* we do.

January 14

"I perceived that whatever God does endures forever; nothing can be added to it, nor anything taken from it. God has done it, so that people fear before Him."
Ecclesiastes 3:14

Forever is a very long time; more than our human minds are truly able to comprehend. We see things on the earth that have existed for a long time, but in reality the time is not that long. For example, there are buildings that men have created that are magnificent, true creations of beauty. But they all fade and pass away as they decay and fall into ruin. I think of the Parthenon in Greece, it is over 2000 years old, but in ruins. Nothing man has ever made was more beautiful than Solomon's temple, but it no longer is standing. Even relationships that we make with other people will end; even the best of them will end because we die. There are no works that man can do which will last forever. Only God can do things that last forever.

What has God done? God gives us His love, "For God so loved the world, that He gave His only Son, that whoever believes in Him should not perish but have eternal life" (John 3:16). God's love is so great that He was willing to have His only Son die a cruel death on a cross to pay the penalty for our sin, so that we can be saved and live with Him forever. The price that Jesus paid was complete; it lasts forever, and never needs to be paid again. What Jesus did for us will last forever, and He has also promised to be with us forever too. God has also promised that He will be with us forever, "It is the Lord who goes before you. He will be with you; He will not leave you or forsake you. Do not fear or be dismayed" (Deuteronomy 31:8). Not only will God remain with us forever, but He has also promised to protect us forever, and not allow us to be destroyed by the enemy, "I give them eternal life, and they will never perish, and no one will snatch them out of My hand" (John 10:28). God has also promised that His grace and mercy are enough for us and will last forever. "The steadfast love of the LORD never ceases; His mercies never come to an end; they are new every morning; great is Your faithfulness." (Lamentations 3:22-23). "But He said to me, 'My grace is sufficient for you, for My power is made perfect in weakness.'" (2 Corinthians 12:9).

What an amazing God we serve. We are in awe of Him because what God does lasts forever. That is why we are to look to Him, and to rest in what He has done instead of our own works, which will not last. One day we will all stand before God and our works will be tested by fire. What we have done will go up in a cloud of smoke because nothing we can do will last forever; only God's work is permanent. Praise God.

January 15

"His divine power has granted to us all things that pertain to life and godliness, through the knowledge of Him who called us to His own glory and excellence..."
2 Peter 1:3

Chances are good that you have watched the television advertisement that has the famous line stating, "but wait, there's more...". Advertisers love to use this idea that you are getting such a great deal, but wait, it's so good because there's even more. Sadly, this is seen in false religions too. Religions will tell you all they have to offer, and that they have a "special doctrine" that adds even more to your life. The apostle Peter informs us here that this idea that there is something more is false. You see, when a person accepts Jesus Christ as their Lord and Savior, making Him King of their life, they are born again, and just like a newborn baby, they have everything they need. When a child is born, they have all the "equipment" that they need for life. What they need to do is grow and mature into what they already have. The same is true for the believer. When a person is born again, they have everything that they need, they will grow and mature into what God has already given to them, which is "all things that pertain to life and godliness."

As a believer grows and matures, they will grow in their "knowledge of Him." How does a person grow in their knowledge of God? The first step in growing in the knowledge of God means that we know who He is. "For the Lord gives wisdom; from His mouth come knowledge and understanding" (Proverbs 2:6). How does God speak to us today? He gave us His Word so that we can know Him. His Word is the Bible, and the apostle Paul reminds us that "all Scripture is breathed out by God and profitable for teaching, for reproof, for correction, and for training in righteousness, that the man of God may be complete, equipped for every good work" (2 Timothy 3:16-17). In addition to the Bible, we also grow in our knowledge of God through prayer and community with other believers. We need God alone, and nothing else, but God doesn't just meet us in our "aloneness", but in the community of other believers. It is important for the believer to be in fellowship with God's people, fellow believers.

January 16

"Now when Sanballat and Tobiah and Geshem the Arab and the rest of our enemies heard that I had built the wall and that there was no breach left in it (although up to that time I had not set up the doors in the gates), Sanballat and Geshem sent to me, saying, 'Come and let us

meet together at Hakkephirim in the plain of Ono.' But they intended to do me harm."
Nehemiah 6:1-2

When a person is doing a great work there is also great temptations and attacks that they will experience. There are many people who do not want to see others accomplish great things, and they will do everything within their power to derail that great work from being finished. Read through the Bible and you will find many examples of this happening. Think of Joseph. He was sold by brothers as a slave, but in Egypt he was faithful to God and began to experience some promotions. What happened to him next? He was greatly tempted to sin by Mrs. Potiphar, his boss' wife. David was a successful soldier and had never lost a battle, so he decided to stay home and rest when he should have been at war, and he met Bathsheba. Just before Jesus began His earthly ministry He was first driven to the desert and experienced 40 days of temptation by the devil. Just before great things were going to be done Satan tried with everything he had to derail, or stop, those great things from happening.

Nehemiah and his crew have finished rebuilding the wall around the city of Jerusalem, and his enemies, Sanballat and Geshem, try to lure him away from the work before he can hang the doors and gates. They are tools of Satan, and they are trying to keep him from completing the work God has called him to do. Until the work is finished, they will not stop trying to keep it from being finished. They have made fun of, mocked, and threatened Nehemiah and the people, but none of that worked, so now they come to Nehemiah and say, "Hey, let's be friends. Let's forget the past and let bygones be bygones. Can't we all get along?" They tell Nehemiah that they want to start over and be friends, but Nehemiah has a gift from God, which is called discernment. He knows that they are lying. The world will continually try to draw you away from God, wanting to be your friend. Pray to God for discernment to know what is real and what is an attempt to lead you astray. We receive discernment when are in close fellowship with God. As Jesus told us, "Abide in me, and I in you. As the branch cannot bear fruit by itself, unless it abides in the vine, neither can you, unless you abide in me. I am the vine; you are the branches. Whoever abides in me and I in him, he it is that bears much fruit, for apart from me you can do nothing" (John 15:4-5).

January 17

"And the Lord said to Paul one night in a vision, 'Do not be afraid, but go on speaking and do not be silent, for I am with you, and no one will attack you to harm you, for I have many in this city who are My people.'"
Acts 18:9-10

God appears to Paul in a vision one night with a message that Paul needs to hear. God says, "Do not be afraid." I believe that God says this to Paul because he was afraid. After all, since Paul had been obedient to the Macedonian vision (Acts 16:6-10), Paul had been run out of every town he had gone to; in some he was even physically abused. Paul was human, so it's no wonder that he was afraid. Paul wasn't some sort of super-hero that was never scared, and neither was he a masochist that enjoyed being beaten and hurt. No! Paul is afraid, so God comes to encourage him.

This is what God does. He comes and speaks to us when we need Him the most. When God tells us "Fear not," even the wildest storm we can imagine instantly becomes calm. Read through the Bible and you will see that God consistently responds to His children this way. He did it with Abraham in Genesis 15:1; Isaac (Genesis 26:24); Jacob (Genesis 46:3); King Jehoshaphat (2 Chron.20:15-17); Daniel (Daniel 10:12); Mary (Luke 1:30); and Peter (Luke 5:10). So, when you are discouraged and you feel like giving up, remember what God says: "I will never leave you nor forsake you" (Deuteronomy 31:6).

That wasn't just a promise in the Old Testament, because "Jesus Christ *is* the same yesterday, today, and forever" (Hebrews 13:8).

God promised Paul that He was with him, so he wasn't to stop preaching the Good News that Jesus is the Messiah. God doesn't just tell Paul to not be afraid, but He also gives him the reason why. Paul doesn't have to be afraid because "I am with you." God was with him. Not only that, but God had many other children in the city. We need to remember that Paul was in Corinth; a city known for its wickedness and debauchery. In the midst of this, God was working. God also promised that the opposition would not be successful. Yes, people would oppose Paul, but they wouldn't be successful in hurting him. God is reminding Paul that He is in charge, and His plan and purpose will be accomplished no matter what! That is good news!

January 18

"You shall also make a basin of bronze, with its stand of bronze, for washing. You shall put it between the tent of meeting and the altar, and you shall put water in it, with which Aaron and his sons shall wash their hands and their feet."
Exodus 30:18-19

God is giving Moses the instructions for setting up the Tabernacle and its courtyard. One of the implements that was outside the Tabernacle was this bronze laver, which the priests used to wash and clean themselves. This wasn't done just for ceremonial sakes, but it was a necessity. The priests would get very bloody and dirty as they served, especially from offering sacrifices; it was not a clean job. God knew this and made preparations to keep the priests clean.

Today we do not offer sacrificial animals to God, but we do need to present ourselves clean to Him. God is a holy God and He is not able to be in the presence of anyone or anything that is not holy. How do we do that? Too often we think as long as we live a pure life we will remain clean. As long as we continue to endure through tribulations and trials that we have, we will remain clean before God. That is not the case. We also need to be cleansed by water.

For us the water is the Word of God. We are washed, sanctified, and spiritually cleansed as we spend time in God's Word. As we submit ourselves and our conduct to God's Word, we will be cleansed and purified. The apostle Paul wrote about this to the Ephesian church, speaking about Jesus' sacrifice for the church: "that He might sanctify her, having cleansed her by the washing of water with the word, so that He might present the church to Himself in splendor, without spot or wrinkle or any such thing, that she might be holy and without blemish" (Ephesians 5:26-27).

While we live on this earth, we will continue to get sullied and dirty from this world. This is why we need to continue to be in God's Word, and to be cleansed and refreshed by God's Word. If we would run to God's Word when we are tempted, we would discover that the sin and temptation that is hampering us will often go away. Too often though, we entertain the sin and temptation instead of going to God's Word. Run to God. He is waiting for you, and He will cleanse you and refresh you as you enter into His presence.

January 19

"No longer will there be anything accursed, but the throne of God and of the Lamb will be in it, and His servants will worship Him."

Revelation 22:3

People often want to know what places are like that they have not been to. Heaven is one of those places. People want to know what Heaven will be like. Some people have had either near-death experiences, or their heart stopped beating for a period of time, and after it has been revived, they will tell what they experienced during their "death." We don't have to wonder what it will be like because God told the apostle John what it will be like. The greatest aspect of Heaven is that the curse of sin will be gone. Ever since the Garden of Eden, when Adam and Eve committed the first sin, the entire world, both man and creation, has had to deal with the effects of sin. What effects are those? "To the woman he said, 'I will surely multiply your pain in childbearing; in pain you shall bring forth children. Your desire shall be contrary to your husband, but he shall rule over you.' And to Adam he said, 'Because you have listened to the voice of your wife and have eaten of the tree of which I commanded you, "You shall not eat of it," cursed is the ground because of you; in pain you shall eat of it all the days of your life; thorns and thistles it shall bring forth for you; and you shall eat the plants of the field. By the sweat of your face you shall eat bread, till you return to the ground, for out of it you were taken; for you are dust, and to dust you shall return" (Genesis 3:16-19). There will be no more sorrow and pain for women in childbirth, no friction, and battles between the two sexes, and no more burdensome work struggling to survive. But the greatest thing that will be gone is death.

So, you may wonder, what then will we do in Heaven. No, we won't be sitting around on clouds strumming guitars and shooting arrows like little cupids. We will have a purpose in what we do in Heaven. That purpose is to worship, or serve, our Lord and Savior, Jesus. This is not the same as the toil of work that we have here on earth now due to the curse, but we will experience the true blessedness of serving and worshipping Jesus. The point of us being in Heaven is to worship and serve Jesus. Everything that we need will already be there. We will have no worries about food, clothing, or shelter. In fact, we will have no worries at all. What we will do is worship and serve Jesus. How wonderful Heaven will be.

January 20

"Do all things without grumbling or disputing."

Paul Verhoeven

Philippians 2:14

Recently I read about a study done in a university by the psychology department. They had two groups of students wired for audio that were then given time to freely converse with each other. One group knew they were being monitored to measure the amount of complaining that occurs in a normal conversation, the other group did not. At the end of the time both groups were shocked at how much they complained during the conversations. The group that knew what was being measured complained almost as much as the group that was unaware.

Whether we like to admit it or not, each of us are complainers. It is part of our sin nature and is as old as time. Where did complaining begin? Back in the Garden of Eden. "The man said, 'The woman whom You gave to be with me, she gave me fruit of the tree, and I ate'" (Gen 3:12). Instead of owning up to his mistake Adam complained to God and tried to deflect responsibility away from himself. This nasty habit of complaining didn't stay in the Garden either. "And the people complained in the hearing of the LORD about their misfortunes, and when the LORD heard it, his anger was kindled, and the fire of the LORD burned among them and consumed some outlying parts of the camp" (Numbers 11:1). This is just one of numerous times that the children of Israel complained while they spent 40 years wandering in the desert. God dealt very severely with the children of Israel because of their complaining.

God hears every utterance that we make, even if no one else does. Just because complaining has been around forever, that does not make it right. We need to choose not to actively participate in complaining. Why shouldn't we complain? Because complaining is a poison. The person who complains becomes poisoned and polluted by their complaints and the person who hears the complaints also becomes polluted. If complaining has all these problems with it, why do we complain? Recently I had a person complaining to me and they acknowledged they shouldn't be complaining, but they had to because "if they didn't no one else would and nothing would ever change." They expected something positive to come from their negative words. It didn't. So, what happened? The person was angry even though they got all these "problems" off their chest. I also became angry because of how they were speaking and dealing with the situation. Instead of focusing and working on a solution to the problem, the focus was on the complaining and nothing productive was accomplished. This is what happens when we complain. Instead of having constructive dialogue over a problem, the exchange becomes heated and angry and that is where the focus stays. The complainer continues to be brought down by their complaints, and the target of their complaint becomes focused on the complainer instead of fixing the problem. This is why Solomon said, "A soft answer turns away wrath, but a harsh word stirs up anger" (Proverbs 15:1).

When we have a problem with another person, how we approach them can determine if it creates more problems or brings resolution to the problem. Approach people with respect and kind words; trying to be part of the solution instead of the problem. This is not how the world operates, which is why it is also effective because it is how God designed it to work. "Do all things without grumbling or disputing, that you may be blameless and innocent, children of God without blemish in the midst of a crooked and twisted generation, among whom you shine as lights in the world" (Philippians 2:14-15).

January 21

"As the LORD, the God of Israel, lives, before whom I stand, there shall be neither dew nor rain these years, except by my word."
1 Kings 17:1

We see in the life of Elijah that he was obedient to God during his entire life. He remained obedient, even in very difficult and challenging times. In fact, we can say he lived up to his name. The name Elijah means "Yahweh is my God." Even the mention of Elijah's name spoke truth in the middle of a time that was very much like today; truth was scarce.

God called Elijah into the public arena and commanded him to go speak to wicked King Ahab and his evil wife Jezebel. We read this in 1 Kings 17:1, where Elijah said to King Ahab, "As the LORD, the God of Israel, lives, before whom I stand, there shall be neither dew nor rain these years, except by my word." Think about that for a moment. Elijah came from a small, unknown town in the desert, had no experience in national politics or speaking to large groups, and God directs him to go speak a word of rebuke to the king of Israel. Wow! That is not an easy thing to do. But he was obedient and did exactly what God called him to do.

Ahab was known for introducing the worship of the false god Baal to Israel and was the most evil king in the history of Israel. His wife was from Sidon and was also known for her wickedness and evil. Listen to how the Bible describes the life of Ahab: "And Ahab the son of Omri did evil in the sight of the LORD, more than all who were before him. And as if it had been a light thing for him to walk in the sins of Jeroboam the son of Nebat, he took for his wife Jezebel the daughter of Ethbaal king of the Sidonians, and went and served Baal and worshiped him. He erected an altar for Baal in the house of Baal, which he built in Samaria. And Ahab made an Asherah. Ahab did more to provoke the LORD, the God of Israel, to anger than all the kings of Israel who were before him" (1 Kings 16:30-33).

After confronting and rebuking Ahab, Elijah did a crazy thing. He left the city and went out to live by a small creek. Ahab didn't appreciate what Elijah had to say to him and wanted to kill him. So, God protected Elijah by removing him to a remote location. A drought was going on, but there was water in this creek, so Elijah was able to survive. It took great faith to go eastward into the desert to live by a creek. It took faith to believe that in the middle of a drought that the creek would continue to flow with water for him to drink. While there, God directed ravens to bring Elijah food every morning and every evening. You can read about this in 1 Kings 17:3-6. This didn't make human sense, but Elijah had faith in God, trusted Him, and was obedient to the Word of God. God responded to Elijah's faith by providing for him.

Eventually the creek did dry up, and Elijah continued to live with faith and obedience. When this happened, God directed him to go to Zarephath in Sidon (see 1 Kings 17:8-15). This was another step of faith. Widows weren't known for having great resources, and this lady didn't. She was so poor that she was preparing to make the last meal for her and her son, and then they would die. Elijah instructed her to make him a loaf of bread first, and if she did so she would never run out of flour or oil during the drought. She obeyed, and this is exactly what happened.

God continued to lead Elijah one step at a time. God did not lead Elijah to the brook in Cherith until after he delivered the message of drought to Ahab. God did not tell him he would go to Zarapheth until after the brook dried up. God continued to lead Elijah one step at a time; and Elijah followed God one step at a time by faith.

January 22

"We ourselves are Jews by birth and not Gentile sinners; yet we know that a person is not justified by works of the law but through faith in Jesus Christ, so we also have believed in Christ Jesus, in order to be justified by faith in Christ and not by works of the law, because by works of the law no one will be justified."

Galatians 2:15-16

This is one of the clearest teachings the apostle Paul gives about being saved by faith and not by keeping the law. No matter how hard we may try to keep the law, we will fail. There is no human being alive who can keep the entire law. This is a problem, because in order to be saved by the law, a person has to continually keep every single aspect of the law; this means twenty-four hours a day and seven days a week. As soon as one part of the law is broken, that person is condemned as guilty; there is no hope for that person to be saved any longer by the law.

There is only one way for every single person on earth to be saved, and that is by faith in Jesus Christ. To have faith in Jesus Christ means that we trust in the redemptive work that Jesus accomplished through His death on the cross and His rising from the grave. Jesus says the person who does this is then justified. What does it mean to be justified? That is a legal term, which means "to be declared righteous." In other words, when we are justified, that means all our sins and mistakes are wiped away as if they never happened. Believers are justified by the shed blood of Jesus. This is the source of our salvation, there is nothing else.

No one can be saved by the law. If we could be saved by the law, then Jesus died for no reason. "I do not nullify the grace of God, for if righteousness were through the law, then Christ died for no purpose" (Galatians 3:21). If a person was able to keep the entire law, they would have reason to brag over those who were saved by God's grace. This is another reason why every single person can only be saved by God's grace; it is all about Him and what He did, not what any one of us is able to do. "For by grace you have been saved through faith. And this is not your own doing; it is the gift of God, not a result of works, so that no one may boast" (Ephesians 2:8-9).

Thank You God for the gift of grace that You so freely give to us, allowing us to be saved through our faith in You and what You have done for us.

January 23

"And Israel stretched out his right hand and laid it on the head of Ephraim, who was the younger, and his left hand on the head of Manasseh, crossing his hands (for Manasseh was the firstborn)."
Genesis 48:14

Traditions are all around us. They can be a good thing, but there can also be a danger with traditions. Sometimes traditions continue simply because they are traditions, even when people have no idea why they began. This is when traditions can become dangerous. This is why sometimes people attempt to remove many traditions, especially those that there isn't a good reason or explanation for why they are practiced. An ancient tradition that used to be practiced is that the first-born son received a greater inheritance than all other children born to the father. The first-born son became the primary heir and would be the one responsible for leading the family. Another ancient tradition is that the right hand is the strong hand. This is where the saying, my right-hand man, came from. Your strongest person would be the person on your right, so that you were well protected. Both these traditions are dealt with by Israel as he blesses Joseph's two sons, Ephraim and Manasseh.

Manasseh was the oldest son, so Joseph placed him by Israel's right hand. Ephraim was the younger son, so he was placed by Israel's left hand. This would have been expected and customary. Imagine how shocked and surprised Joseph would have been when he realized his father had crossed his arms, and his left hand was on Manasseh and his right hand rested on the head of Ephraim. This was backwards. It was wrong. This meant that the customary blessing and double portion of inheritance would be placed on the younger son, Ephraim. This is exactly what Israel meant to do. He crossed his hands on purpose. He purposefully chose to go against cultural expectations, traditions, and the customs of the time. This happened because he was being led by God. God does not always follow cultural expectations, traditions, or customs. How do we receive God's blessing today? The same way Abraham received it. Abram "believed the Lord, and He counted it to him as righteousness" (Genesis 15:6). In other words, Abraham had faith. The same is true for us today. If we want to receive God's blessing, like Abraham and Ephraim did, it is received by faith, not traditions or customs. God does not reward His children because it is expected of Him. He blesses His children through faith. "And without faith it is impossible to please Him, for whoever would draw near to God must believe that He exists and that He rewards those who seek Him" (Hebrews 11:6).

January 24

"...casting all your anxieties on him, because he cares for you."
1 Peter 5:7

Anxiety is a sense of uneasiness, distress, or dread, that a person feels before an event, especially an important event. There is a certain level of anxiety that keeps a person alert and aware of their surroundings. But any level of anxiety above that becomes a heavy burden, weighing down and sometimes even bringing a person to the point of incapacitation. What causes a person's level of anxiety to grow beyond what they can handle? Oftentimes it is a refusal to let go of what causes their anxiety. Why won't a person let go? Generally, it is because of pride. This is the opposite of what Peter has been reminding the believer that they need to be, which is humble. Whenever a burden arises in our life it is not for us to grasp on to it and hold on to it, but to give it over to God by faith.

God is good. He loves you. In fact, God loves His children, which is why He willingly takes every single burden that we allow Him to take. God doesn't fight or argue with us and force a burden out of our grasp. But, if we are willing to hand it over to Him, He will take it for us.

I heard a story about an old lady who lived in a small town. Not only had she never owned a car before, but she hadn't even ever ridden in a car. One day she was walking home from town, carrying a heavy basket on her head. A rich man drove by in his car, when he stopped beside her and offered her a ride home. She accepted his offer and climbed into his car but kept her basket on her head. When the driver realized this, he told her that she should lay her basket down on the seat and rest herself. The old lady was shocked by this and told him that while she appreciated the car carrying her home, it was too much for her to ask that the car also carry the burden of her basket. We may laugh at her response, but how often do we behave the same way? We look to God to carry us, but we hold on to our burdens, the things that cause us anxiety, refusing to allow God to carry them, because, after all, He's already carrying us, and we don't want to burden Him with our anxieties too. Relax, lay down your burdens, and allow God to carry them as He already carries you.

January 25

"The house of the wicked will be destroyed, but the tent of the upright will flourish."
Proverbs 14:11

What does Solomon mean when he writes about a wicked person? He is speaking about a person who is morally wrong, a person who is condemned and guilty because of their sin. Their heart is not right with God. On the outside they might appear to be an all-American person, but if they haven't humbled themselves before God, they are guilty in His sight. Solomon refers to them as a house. When I think of a house it suggests thoughts of comfort, security, happiness, and permanence. The person who is storing up their treasures here on earth is trying to accomplish that in this life. Any person who is not living for God, what they have here on earth is the best that they will get. This is why there is so much focus on earthly items. Now don't get me wrong, there is nothing wrong with nice items here on earth. It is ok to make our home nice. But that can't be our sole focus, because if Jesus is our Savior we won't be living here forever.

Solomon compares the upright person to a tent. I do enjoy camping in a tent, but it speaks of something temporal; not permanent. While a tent is enjoyable, after a few days, or even a week, it is nice to come back to a house with four walls and a roof. You see, a tent becomes uncomfortable after a while; they get hot in the summer, they leak when it rains. Tents are not designed for permanence. This is a reminder to us Christians that this world is not our home. God does not want us getting too comfortable here on earth because He has a much better home for us. The home that God is building for us is one of permanence; it will last for eternity.

It is easy to get caught up in this life and to become so engrossed in it that we forget the "big picture." We are sojourners here on earth, we are just passing through. This means that our focus is not to be just on this earth and the pleasures that it can bring to us, but our focus needs to be on eternity. Our hope is not in this world. Our hope is in Jesus and the future that He provides for us. This world is one of illusion, or smoke and mirrors. It appears to offer hope and permanence, but it is like an old western movie town; it appears good up front, but when you look behind the walls you see it has no substance; it is a false front building. Jesus offers us true hope and permanence. He provides us with a future, to spend eternity with Him in Heaven. That is our hope, and when our focus remains on Him, He will give us the strength to persevere through this world.

January 26

"...but God raised Him on the third day and made Him to appear, not

to all the people but to us who had been chosen by God as witnesses, who ate and drank with Him after He rose from the dead. And He commanded us to preach to the people and to testify that He is the one appointed by God to be judge of the living and the dead. To Him all the prophets bear witness that everyone who believes in Him receives forgiveness of sins through His name."
Acts 10:40-43

Peter clearly expresses the power of the Gospel, and the source of our hope. Jesus rose from the dead, thereby defeating sin and death. This wasn't something done in secret either; Jesus was seen by hundreds, if not thousands, of witnesses. Jesus gave His followers the command to share this message with all people. Part of this message is that Jesus is "appointed by God to be judge of the living and the dead." Jesus shared this with the disciples when He said, "the Father, in fact, judges no one but has given all judgment to the Son" (John 5:22). The apostle Paul reminded us of this when he wrote, "Christ Jesus, who is to judge the living and the dead, and by His appearing and His kingdom" (2 Timothy 4:1).

It is only through Jesus that a person can have their sins forgiven and receive salvation. Notice though, who Peter says this is for; "everyone who believes in Him." It doesn't matter if you're a Jew or a Gentile. Black, white, or brown. Rich or poor. Highly educated or have no education at all. Tall or short. Skinny or heavy. All that matters is that you believe in Jesus, that you place your faith and trust in Him.

There is a reason why forgiveness of sins can only come through the name of Jesus. It is because Jesus Christ is the only person that took care of the problem that keeps our sin from being forgiven. What's the problem that keeps us from being forgiven? What keeps us from God? It is sin! Jesus dealt with sin when He died on the cross and rose from the grave. There is an unpassable chasm that separates sinful people from sinless God. Jesus is the bridge between mankind and God; He makes it possible for us to have forgiveness of sins and to be able to come into the presence of God.

January 27

"Joseph wept when they spoke to him."
Genesis 50:17b

Joseph wept when his brothers came to him telling him that their dad said he should forgive them. Why would this cause Joseph to weep? When we remember how poorly they had treated Joseph and everything they had done to him, it makes sense that they would need to be forgiven by him. But the reason Joseph weeps when they say this to him is because he has already forgiven them. He forgave them 17 years earlier and proved it through both his words and actions for the past 17 years. It is now obvious that his brothers didn't believe him. They thought he was simply holding a grudge against them and waiting for their dad to die so he could release all the anger and hatred he had towards them. Anyone who has been completely misunderstood like Joseph can understand why he is weeping. He has forgiven his brothers, and they don't believe that his forgiveness is true. This is terrible.

God also understands this because too often we respond the same way Joseph's brothers did. We may have completely blown it, again, and begin to wonder if God can really forgive us, or even accept us, after the things we have done. Anyone who questions whether God will accept them or forgive them doesn't truly know God or understand how great His love is for them. Read through the Gospels and you will see that Jesus' focus when He was here on earth was for the person who was hurting, rejected, the outcast. He spent His time reaching out for and touching those who were sick, ill, hurt, and even dead. His touch brought healing to them. He reached out and touched those because He loves them. He died on the cross to pay the penalty for our sin because He loves us. Reach out for God. He loves you just the way you are. He loves you so much that He accepts you the way that you are, but then He will change you from the inside out. You don't have to clean yourself up for Him to accept you. Remember, "there is therefore now no condemnation for those who are in Christ Jesus. For the law of the Spirit of life has set you free in Christ Jesus from the law of sin and death" (Romans 8:1-2).

January 28

"Then it happened one evening that David arose from his bed and walked on the roof of the king's house. And from the roof he saw a woman bathing, and the woman was very beautiful to behold."
NKJV
2 Samuel 11:2

David, as king of Israel and commander of the army, should have been leading his troops in battle, but he chose to stay home. While he remained at home, he got himself in lots of trouble, which often happens when we allow ourselves to be where we aren't supposed to be. During this time David took a nap, and when he awoke, he was wandering around on the roof of the palace and looking over the city. While wandering around he notices a beautiful woman taking a bath. The fact that David noticed her beauty is not a problem. As Billy Graham says, "the first look is free, but it's the second look that will kill you." Here is where David went wrong, he continued to look. He should have looked away and gone back inside when he saw what was happening, but he continued to look at her. He continued to look and gaze at her.

This was not the battle he was supposed to be in, but here he was in a battle. The battle is all around us. It is what we look at and gaze upon because that helps determine what we fill our minds with and what we think about. That battle goes on daily from what we look at on TV and the internet, to the billboards we see as we drive, and how we look at people.

Job understood this, and that is why he made a covenant with his eyes that he would not look lustfully at another woman (Job 31:1). David learned his lesson from this episode and later in life wrote that "he would set nothing wicked before his eyes" (Psalm 101:3a NKJV). By continuing to look at Bathsheba, he allowed himself to get sucked deeper and deeper into this battle; one that leads to death. Because of this we need to be militant about what we allow to pass through our eyes. We need to post a squadron of military police over our eyes so they will not allow anything through that shouldn't be seen.

But notice where David was when this happened. He was at home where you let down your guard and relax, because it is supposed to be a safe place. And our home should be a place of safety, where we can let our guard down and relax. At least it should be physically and mentally, but not spiritually. You are prepared for the battle where it is expected, such as at work, while you are driving, or any other place out in the world. In these places we are prepared to have struggles and temptations. We must also be prepared to fight while we are home. This is especially true today, with the garbage that is so easily available via the internet and TV. Don't relax spiritually at home, the battle is just beginning. Be vigilant about what you allow to pass through your eyes and remember to keep it holy and glorifying to God. Do not fill your eyes, and therefore your mind and heart, with garbage.

January 29

"So also the tongue is a small member, yet it boasts of great things. How great a forest is set ablaze by such a small fire! And the tongue is a fire, a world of unrighteousness. The tongue is set among our members, staining the whole body, setting on fire the entire course of life, and set on fire by hell."

James 3:5-6

You may have heard the saying that bigger is better, but that's not always true: sometimes smaller is much more powerful. That is especially true with the tongue. Look at how small the tongue is in relation to our bodies, but what great power it holds. Our tongue can be used to build up, to encourage, or to speak words of comfort, hope, love, and strength. But the tongue can also be used to break down, to destroy, or simply to cut a person to pieces. Many children have been taught the rhyme that says, "Sticks and stones may break my bones, by words will never hurt me." That's a lie! Words can hurt, and they do hurt. We would be wise to heed the words of King Solomon, who wrote "Like a madman who throws firebrands, arrows, and death is the man who deceives his neighbor and says, 'I am only joking!'" (Proverbs 26:18-19).

This is why James relates the tongue to a fire. Fire is a wonderful thing when it burns under control. When a fire is in a woodstove or a fireplace, it is beautiful, even romantic. It provides heat and is very beneficial. But take that fire away from its constraints, and it is not beautiful, and definitely not romantic. When that fire is outside, it quickly causes much destruction, heartache, and loss. Fire will spread as long as it has fuel to keep it burning, and the more fuel it has, the quicker and hotter it burns. This means we need to remove fuel from the fire. How do we do that? To do this, our "speech [must] always be gracious, seasoned with salt" (Colossians 4:6). To help us in this, we need to "take every thought captive to obey Christ" (2 Corinthians 10:5). Once our thoughts are taken captive, then we need to change what we think about and focus on. "Finally, brothers, whatever is true, whatever is honorable, whatever is just, whatever is pure, whatever is lovely, whatever is commendable, if there is any excellence, if there is anything worthy of praise, think about these things" (Philippians 4:8).

January 30

"So the Lord dispersed them from there over the face of all the earth, and they left off building the city."
Genesis 11:8

By confusing their language and scattering them over all the earth, God graciously spared their lives and gave them opportunity to return to Him. He could have destroyed the builders, their city, and their tower; but He chose to let them live. God scattered mankind and separated them from each other so that each group of people would be able to seek God on their own. They were driven away and divided so that God could draw them to Himself.

That might sound inconsistent to us, but the apostle Paul tells us that is how God operates. "And he made from one man every nation of mankind to live on all the face of the earth, having determined allotted periods and the boundaries of their dwelling place, that they should seek God, and perhaps feel their way toward him and find him. Yet he is actually not far from each one of us" (Acts 17:26-27). God still operates this way today.

When the Communists were taking over China, they were concerned with the Christians in the villages. They noticed that they met together and assumed that this gave them their strength to resist communism. To combat this, the communist leaders decided to separate the Christians; no village was able to have more than one Christian in a village. The result of this action was that Christians were now spread throughout the country, and into every village. Unknowingly, the communist leaders became tools for God in helping spread His Word throughout the country. God allowed these believers to be separated to draw more people to Him.

God has called us to be lights in this dark world that we live in. Every believer is a light. Think of them as streetlights. If your town placed every streetlight in the parking lot of the local church, that church would be well lit up. It would be very bright and everyone there would be able to see well. But leave the church and go into the local neighborhood and it would be very dark. It would be difficult to see. The farther away you got from the church the more difficult it would be to see. We are that light. We go to church to spend some time there learning and serving. Then we are to go out into the world. God separates us from each other in order that we will reach others and draw them to Him too. Go out and let your light shine brightly.

January 31

"And Peter directed his gaze at him, as did John, and said, 'Look at us.' And he fixed his attention on them, expecting to receive something from them. But Peter said, 'I have no silver and gold, but what I do have I give to you. In the name of Jesus Christ of Nazareth, rise up and walk!'"
Acts 3:4-6

Peter and John could have easily walked right by this man. They could have made a number of excuses for avoiding him, like "I'm on my way to pray, so I can't stop now," or "I have a very tight schedule today. Stopping now will mess it up." But they didn't do that. They were sensitive to the leading of the Holy Spirit and recognized that God wanted them to do something special for this man. So, Peter directed this lame man to look at him.

Amazingly, this man did look at Peter. He looked directly at Peter, and he was ready to receive something from Peter. He was expecting a coin or two, but Peter had something much better for him. That's how God operates. We have our minds fixed on what we expect, or what we think we need. But God has plans and thoughts for us that are so much better for us. God's plans exceed our own thoughts and plans for ourselves. This guy wanted a few coins, God wanted to heal him and completely transform his life. Plus, Peter and

John didn't have any coins to give to him. In Acts 2:44-45, Luke told us that everyone in the church pooled their resources and gave what they had to help those that didn't have enough. This is very possibly why Peter and John had no money. Of course, it also could be something as simple as they simply didn't bring any money with them that day.

It really doesn't matter, because while they didn't have any money, they did have what this man needed. They didn't have money, but they did have authority from Jesus to heal people. Too often we focus on what we don't have, but the real question is "are we willing to share the things we do have." Peter and John didn't let the fact that they didn't have money mean they couldn't give to this man. They willingly gave to him what they had. That is so important. God doesn't ask us to share with others what we don't have, but He does ask us to share what we do have. Don't hold on to our possessions with a death grip; be willing to let go.

I also find it interesting that Peter and John didn't have any money. This is such a difference from the Prosperity/Name it and Claim it preachers that we see too often today. The world is so concerned about having money, but it isn't money that we need. It's Jesus. Peter and John had Jesus, and they were willing to "share" Him with this man.

The story is told that Pope Innocent II was counting the church's riches when Thomas Aquinas walked into the room. The Pope pointed to the chests full of gold and jewels and said, "Thomas, no longer can we say, 'silver and gold I do not have.'" Thomas Aquinas looked at the pope and said, "Neither can you say, 'in the name of Jesus Christ of Nazareth, rise up and walk.'" The power we need is not in money, but in the name of Jesus.

February 1

"Arise, go to Nineveh, that great city, and call out against it, for their evil has come up before Me."
Jonah 1:2

God called Jonah to go to the city of Nineveh and preach to them that they were about to be destroyed because of their wickedness. Jonah was more than willing to do that because Assyria was the leading world power of that day, and they were an enemy of Israel's. The Assyrian's represented everything that Jonah, as a good Jew, hated. They were very cruel, barbaric, and intent on ruling the entire world. Listen to the words of one of their kings, Ashurnasirpal II, describe themselves: "I stormed the mountain peaks and took them. In the midst of the mighty mountains I slaughtered them; with their blood I dyed the mountain red like wool... The heads of their warriors I cut off, and I formed them into a pillar over against their city; their young men and their maidens I burned in the fire... their leader I flayed, his skin I spread upon the wall of the city..." God wanted Jonah to go there?

Assyria is modern-day Iraq. It would be like sending a missionary to Baghdad today. Or it would be like asking a Holocaust survivor to become a missionary in Germany, or a white-supremist to share the Gospel in Africa. Jonah had a problem with God's word to him because he was prejudiced. Jonah loved God, but he hated the Ninevites. Racial prejudice, or bigotry, is very irrational and highly offensive to God! Bigotry and prejudice limits God's grace; it places restrictions upon God and narrows His grace. Prejudice is the ultimate selfishness because it narrows God's grace down to one group of people; people just like me and no one else. Prejudice says that if you're not just like me that you are inferior since you don't have the same skin color or national heritage or whatever. It is foolishness, and it is sin!

Even though Jonah knew God and loved God, he could not fathom that God could love Gentiles as much as He loved Jews. He refused to accept that God could love the cruel and hated Assyrians the same way that He loved the Jews. But, before we come down too hard on Jonah, how many of us have similar sentiments? We know that God loves us and others that belong to our political party, but how could He love the others? We know that God loves us as Americans but have a more difficult time accepting that He also loves the Arabs, Russians, and Mexicans, and every other nationality just as much.

February 2

"...to those who are elect...according to the foreknowledge of God the Father..."
1 Peter 1:1a, 2a

There is a group of children standing in a line on the playground. Two of them are chosen as captains, and step in front of the rest of the group. One of them chooses someone to be on their team, and then the other captain chooses. One by one the line of kids decreases as each team grows. After a few minutes the line is down to one kid, and neither team wants that kid on their team. What an awful feeling that is. That kid feels bad because they are "not chosen." For whatever reason they aren't chosen, the feeling of not being chosen hurts. When we are chosen, that means there was a choice to choose us or not, and we were chosen. The apostle Peter reminds us that he is writing to believers who were chosen by God. There was a time when only the Jews could claim that they were chosen by God, but because Jesus died on the cross and rose from the grave, both Jews and Gentiles alike are chosen by God. God wants us. We belong to Him. How wonderful is that?

Not only does God choose us, but He does so according to His foreknowledge. We weren't chosen by luck, or even by random chance. God choosing us was an informed decision that He made. The foreknowledge of God is based upon His omniscience. What is omniscience? It simply means that God is all-knowing, or that He knows all things. This includes how you and I would one day respond to the Gospel. The fact that Jesus knew all things is mind blowing. This means that He knew what He would encounter here on earth, including His death on the cross, and He still chose to come to earth and live here confined within the body of a man. Jesus even explained this to His disciples after He rose from the dead. Jesus said, "'These are my words that I spoke to you while I was still with you, that everything written about Me in the Law of Moses and the Prophets and the Psalms must be fulfilled.' Then He opened their minds to understand the Scriptures, and said to them, 'Thus it is written, that the Christ should suffer and on the third day rise from the dead, and that repentance for the forgiveness of sins should be proclaimed in His name to all nations, beginning from Jerusalem'" (Luke 24:44-47). We can take comfort in the fact that Jesus knows the end from the beginning, so nothing happening on earth is a shock to Him. He knows what is going on, and He remains in control.

February 3

"There is nothing better for a person than that he should eat and drink and find enjoyment in his toil. This also, I saw, is from the hand of God, for apart from Him who can eat or who can have enjoyment?"
Ecclesiastes 2:24-25

Solomon was the wisest man to ever live, even though he made many foolish choices and decisions in life. He attempted to live life to its fullest, but without God. At the end of his life, he realized the mistake he had made, and wrote about it here in the book of Ecclesiastes. Solomon is writing about what he has learned regarding the futility of living a life without God, and warning others so they do not make the same mistake.

The first two chapters of Ecclesiastes are Solomon telling people about the futilities that life brings. Life under the sun, or without God, will not bring any happiness or satisfaction to people. The Rolling Stones were right, you can't get no satisfaction. Solomon had more resources than anyone else who has ever lived, and he used them to find satisfaction, and it couldn't be done. Solomon was a master architect and builder; he accomplished great works but wasn't satisfied. Solomon poured himself into his work, having the largest animal herds in the world, running the world's largest corporation, and having more money than anyone who has ever lived; but it wasn't satisfying. Solomon threw himself into entertainment and had the world's best bands and entertainers on his staff performing at his will; but they did not satisfy. He then pursued academic endeavors, seeking intellectual satisfaction in wisdom; but that did not satisfy either. Solomon had the resources to try everything, more than any of us could ever do, but nothing worked.

Finally, in verse 24 Solomon imparts the first statement of the true message of this book. Life is not a meaningless event that turns all of us into jaded and cynical people, but it is a gift from God. It is funny that the more we pursue the pleasures of life, the more they elude us. But, when we accept the free gift of life from God, we are more blessed than we can ever imagine. That is what Solomon is telling us. Even with all his resources, he could find no satisfaction in life until he humbled himself before God and received from Him. If earthly possessions and works could bring satisfaction, no one would have been more satisfied than Solomon, but it didn't work. The same thing still applies today. Work, entertainment, intellectual pursuits, earthly possessions, none of these will bring satisfaction and enjoyment into our lives. For us to be truly satisfied, we must understand and accept that all things come from God.

Solomon is not saying "Eat, drink and be merry, for tomorrow we die!" What he is saying is that we need to thank God for what we do have, and to enjoy what He has given us. That is the key to a satisfying life; understanding that it comes from God.

These are the two things Solomon wanted everyone to know. First, we need to know that everything we own is a gift from God; without this there will be no satisfaction. Second, no person is able to extract enjoyment from life on their own; that is a gift from God. God shares that with all who come to Him and ask Him to come and lead their life. A relationship with God is the only thing that will satisfy. Look to God, not anything on this earth, if you want to be truly satisfied.

February 4

"Then they laid their hands on them and they received the Holy Spirit."
Acts 8:17

These Samaritan believers were saved, but as of this time they had not received the power of the Holy Spirit. So, when Peter and John arrived, they prayed for these believers, and then laid hands on them to receive the Holy Spirit. The believers had been baptized, which identified them with Jesus in His death and resurrection. Now, Peter and John prayed for them to receive the Holy Spirit, and His power.

In the Greek language there are three different prepositions that describe the three kinds of relationships we have with the Holy Spirit.

1. With (para, meaning "with," or "alongside"). This is the kind of relationship the Holy Spirit has with the majority of people in the world; He is the One "alongside" them. This is the "Comforter" that Jesus spoke of in John 14:6.
2. In (en). When a person accepts Jesus as their Lord and Savior, the Holy Spirit no longer remains alongside them, but He lives inside them. You are now a temple of the

Holy Spirit (1 Corinthians 6:19), and He lives inside of you (John 14:7c).

3. Upon (epi). There is an even closer relationship with the Holy Spirit than His living in us. This is when the Holy Spirit comes upon us, filling us with His power and giving us the ability to live the Christian life as God desires. This is what we see here in Acts 8:17.

The Holy Spirit came upon the Samaritan believers when the apostles laid their hands upon them. Hands are laid upon something to be identified with something else. In the Old Testament the sinner would identify with his offering by laying hands upon it. Then, when the offering was slain, it would symbolize that he had been slain. So, when Peter and John laid their hands upon the Samaritan believers, they were identifying themselves, the rest of the apostles, and all the Jewish believers with these new believers. There was only one church; they were unified. There was only one Lord, one faith, one baptism.

February 5

"...and they said to them, 'The Lord look on you and judge, because you have made us stink in the sight of Pharaoh and his servants, and have put a sword in their hand to kill us.'"
Exodus 5:21

The leaders of Israel blame all their problems and the added bondage and work they are dealing with on Moses. They are telling Moses that he has literally made them stink before Pharaoh. What really happened is that Pharaoh now knows that Israel is no longer a docile servant for him, and he responds harshly, as would be expected. When Israel was a docile servant, Pharaoh seemed like their friend, even though that's the furthest thing from the truth. The children of

Israel are blaming their problems on Moses simply because he's the "new guy" in town, the one that God is using to bring about God's perfect plan. The people are failing to see that Pharaoh is the problem, as he has been the entire time.

We can see this same thing in our own lives. When we compromise and engage in sin, Satan appears to be our friend, and very friendly to us. But, when we reject him and follow God, then he reveals his true colors by opposing us and trying to enslave us by making our lives difficult too. There is nothing new in Satan's playbook. Everything he does to us is exactly what he has done to others throughout history.

When Moses came back to Egypt, he shared with the people of Israel what God had shown him in the desert by the burning bush. Remember how the people responded to Moses? "And the people believed; and when they heard that the Lord had visited the people of Israel and that he had seen their affliction, they bowed their heads and worshiped" (Exodus 4:31). The faith, excitement, and worship has disappeared pretty rapidly. Reality has set in. They were filled with joy when things were easy, but it is much more difficult to have joy and contentment when engaged in a battle, or spiritual warfare. It takes a spiritually mature person to find joy in the midst of a battle.

All of this could have been avoided if the leaders of Israel had not brought their complaints to Pharaoh. If instead they had come to Moses and Aaron and set up a time of prayer to God for all the people, they could have received comfort and strength from God to prepare them and help them endure through this battle. May we learn from their mistake and take our problems and concerns directly to God so that we can find joy and contentment, even in the midst of a battle.

February 6

"And I was with you in weakness and in fear and much trembling,

and my speech and my message were not in plausible words of wisdom, but in demonstration of the Spirit and of power."
1 Corinthians 2:3-4

The adage "power corrupts, and absolute power absolutely corrupts" is true. Despite this warning, many people are still consumed with power and put lots of effort into getting power and work diligently to make sure they have no apparent weaknesses to others. That is the way of the world, but the apostle Paul tackles this head-on, showing that it is not how he lived and operated. He tells the believers in Corinth that when he came to them, he was weak, not powerful. This was done on purpose! He didn't want to be filled with over-confidence, but desired to rely on the strength of God through the Holy Spirit. This is where many people stumble and fail today, even Christians. They rely on themselves and their own strength instead of relying on God through the Holy Spirit. Self-reliance is a poison that stumbles, hurts, and even destroys, many people.

The apostle Paul was a very wise and intellectual person, but he willingly chose to NOT impress people with his wisdom and intellect. When he preached, he chose to speak to people in simple, common, everyday language. The reason for this was so the message was the focus, and not the messenger. Some have taken this approach and concluded that words don't matter. That is the exact opposite of the truth. Paul chose the words that he used carefully. He chose words that would get the message across with words that the audience would understand. All too often preachers and speakers like to use words that impress people with how vast their vocabulary is, the richness and depth of their intellect, or to confound them with their philosophy or logic that is beyond what others grasp or understand. You see, the words we use are very important. Paul's desire was for people to grasp and understand the message of the Gospel. The words Paul used was the Gospel, sharing who Jesus is, what He did for them, and how much He loves them. The Gospel is powerful, even when simple words are used. Simple words of the Gospel are more powerful than the wisest and most persuasive words man can design. Follow the example of the apostle Paul and rely on the power of the Holy Spirit to help you share the Gospel with others.

February 7

"Now when Sanballat heard that we were building the wall, he was angry and greatly enraged, and he jeered at the Jews. And he said in the presence of his brothers and of the army of Samaria, 'What are these feeble Jews doing? Will they restore it for themselves? Will they sacrifice? Will they finish up in a day? Will they revive the stones out of the heaps of rubbish, and burned ones at that?'"
Nehemiah 4:1-2

An important lesson we must learn is that if we are going to serve the Lord, then we will face opposition from our enemies. They will do everything they can to stop us from serving the Lord. This is what Nehemiah and the Israelites are facing. They are doing the work of rebuilding the walls of Jerusalem, and Sanballat, and others, are opposed to the work they are doing. As soon as the people of Jerusalem came together and began to rebuild the walls, notice what Sanballat's response was; he became "angry and greatly enraged." His anger can be likened to a fire that is burning out of control. He was consumed with rage over what was happening.

Notice what Sanballat did with his rage; he made fun of the Jews and the work they were doing. He didn't make fun of the work they were doing, he made it personal by making fun of the workers. This is a tactic that the devil loves to use because it is so successful. This was an easy thing for him to do. After all, the people rebuilding the walls weren't professionals. It is possible that the people didn't know what they were doing, or because they weren't professionals that they took a long time doing what could have been done in a short period of time. But Sanballat made sure that the people knew he was mocking them and their abilities because that is a tool Satan loves to use. When Satan tries to stop the work that a person is doing for the Lord, he will point out every weakness of that person he can and belittle the work that has been done. For most people this causes them to question themselves and their ability to do the work they are attempting. This is exactly what Satan wants to happen. He does this so that the Lord's work will be stopped. That is the devil's goal. We will see that Nehemiah was wise to this and he did the wisest thing possible: he ignored these taunts. Believer don't listen to or buy into the lies that Satan tells you. Continue to serve God.

February 8

"And the angel whom I saw standing on the sea and on the land raised his right hand to heaven and swore by Him who lives forever and ever, who created heaven and what is in it, the earth and what is in it, and the sea and what is in it, that there would be no more delay..."'
Revelation 10:5-6

In the interval between the sixth and seventh trumpets sounding this angel descends from Heaven. It is a large angel. John tells us that he planted his right foot in the waters and his left foot on land. This is significant. An angel is an emissary of God and is sent to do His work. He comes to announce that God's judgment will fall upon everything under God's control, which is everything under his feet. Remember, his feet are upon both water and land, which means God has authority over all creation. This angel then raises his right hand toward Heaven. This is the same thing that witnesses do when they are in a court of law. Why does a witness raise their right hand? When they raise their right hand, the right hand is a symbol of strength, and it is raised toward Heaven, where God dwells and all authority comes from. So, raising your right hand toward Heaven signifies that the person makes a solemn vow to tell the truth.

That is exactly what this angel is doing. Notice that his vow is in the name of God. Almost all of verse six is devoted to telling us about God, more so than what the angel says. What the angel says is that God's judgment is coming, and there won't be a delay any longer. But he declares an awful lot about God. The first thing he says about God is that He is eternal; He "lives forever and ever." In addition to being eternal, God is also the Creator. He created the Heavens and everything in them. This is enormous. Scientists tend to believe that in the Milky Way galaxy there are some 200 billion stars. God created all of them. In addition to this there are more universes too. That is a lot of creation. God also created the earth and everything in it. From the tallest mountains to the canyons, to the microscopic animals; God created all of them. God also created the seas, oceans, and every living thing they contain. Every created thing that lives was created by God. Everything was created for a purpose, which is to bring honor and glory to God. Sin has stopped this from occurring. This is the reason for God's judgment. The Creator is perfectly just in judging His own creation. Before the time comes for God's judgment to be released upon the earth, may we bring glory and honor to God through our life, our words, our actions, and our thoughts.

February 9

"Honor the Lord with your wealth and with the firstfruits of all your produce; then your barns will be filled with plenty, and your vats will be bursting with wine."
Proverbs 3:9-10

This one is difficult for most people because we live in a material world, and we are material people. If we are honest with ourselves, we would admit that God has given us more than what we need.

There is a problem with having too many things; we think that they belong to us. In reality, they all belong to God; He has entrusted them to us to use for His glory. One day we will stand before God and give Him an accounting of how we took care of the resources entrusted to us. It's not about how many things we have, but how we are using them.

There is a concept seen throughout the Bible known as "firstfruits." This is how it worked; when a farmer harvested his crops, he gave the first produce he harvested to the Lord as an offering. He gave to the Lord at the beginning. That's generally not how we do it here in America. The first thing we do when we get paid is pay our rent/mortgage. Then we feed our tummies. After that there is a long list of things we pay for: fuel for vehicles, car payments, credit cards, cable TV, utilities, etc. Then, after everything is paid, we look at our checkbook and if there's anything left, we give some of it to God. When we do that, we are saying that these things are more important to us than God. The principle of firstfruits is that we give to God first. Why would we do that? Because it all belongs to Him anyway. When we give back to God first, we are honoring Him with the possessions He has entrusted to us. I encourage you to try this. Give back to God first. Then, pay your rent/mortgage, buy groceries, and all those other things. Know what you're going to find out? You will be able to pay all your obligations.

The difference is that God is now being honored when you give to Him first. When you honor the Lord with the possessions that He entrusts you with, you will find that you begin to think more about God's kingdom than your own little kingdom. You will begin to look at your possessions differently, because you will realize that you are a conduit for God's blessings to flow through to bless others. You will begin to own your possessions instead of your possessions owning you.

February 10

"But Elymas the magician (for that is the meaning of his name) opposed them, seeking to turn the proconsul away from the faith."
Acts 13:8

The name Elymas is an interpretation of the word "sorcerer." His name was Bar-Jesus (see acts 13:6), but Luke refused to call him by that name. Why would Luke refuse to call this man by his name? Because of what he was doing! His actions were completely contrary to the name Jesus.

Elymas had heard Barnabas and Saul preaching, and it scared him. He knew that if his boss, Sergius Paulus (the governor of Cyprus), heard these men that he could easily lose his influence and power over the people. So, what we have here is a man that is jealous of the power that Barnabas and Saul possess, and he wants to make sure no one else hears about it, so he begins to speak out about how awful they are and does everything he can within his power to keep people from listening to Barnabas and Saul; especially his boss Sergius Paulus.

This is a scary thing to do. In fact, Jesus gave a very harsh warning against people doing exactly what he is doing. Jesus said, "whoever causes one of these little ones who believe in Me to sin, it would be better for him to have a great millstone fastened around his neck and to be drowned in the depth of the sea. Woe to the world for temptations to sin! For it is necessary that temptations come, but woe to the one by whom the temptation comes!" (Matthew 18:6-7). It is a very serious offense to try and keep people away from Jesus.

Why would a person do that? Because Jesus has the power and the ability to radically change a person's life; and to change it for the better. There are people who hold power over others and don't want to see them changed for the better. That is what Elymus is doing here. He is playing with fire, and he is going to get burned. Learn a lesson from him; don't try to keep people away from Jesus. Instead, do everything you can to bring people to Jesus so that He can change them.

February 11

"Then He said to me: 'Son of man, go to the house of Israel and speak My words to them.'"
Ezekiel 3:4

Ezekiel was given the command to go and speak God's Word to the people of Israel. God told Ezekiel that *he* needed to go out. He wasn't to go and send someone else to represent him; he was the one to go out and share God's Word. It wasn't left up to just the pastor of the church, the elders of the church, or a special committee of select individuals that are to evangelize; Ezekiel had a personal responsibility himself. God gave Ezekiel a specific job to do, and an audience to go to. God also gave Ezekiel a particular message for that audience.

Notice that God didn't say, "Zeke, go and speak *some* words." God didn't say, "Zeke, just speak what's on your mind." No! God told him to go and speak God's Word. The specific message that God was telling Ezekiel to share was God's Word, in other words, the truth. Ezekiel wasn't to share with the people what they wanted to hear, what would make them feel good, or what pleased Ezekiel; he was to only share with them God's Word.

When we share with others, we need to make sure that it is God's Word that we are sharing. Don't go around sharing your thoughts or opinions. Opinions are a dime a dozen, and they are worth even less than that. We want to make sure that we are sharing God's Word, because God's Word will stand forever. "The grass withers, the flowers fade, but the word of our God will stand forever" (Isaiah 40:8). The apostle Peter also reminds us of this truth: "...All flesh is like grass and all its glory like the flower of grass. The grass withers, and the flower falls, but the word of the Lord remains forever." (1 Peter 1:23-25).

Ezekiel was given the responsibility to share a specific message to a specific audience. He wasn't allowed to change any of it; not who delivered the message, the message itself, or the audience. This is the same responsibility that each of us Christians still have today. The power to change lives is not in what we think, but in God's Word, which is why we need to share God's Word with others.

February 12

"Draw near to God, and He will draw near to you."
James 4:8a

Here is one of the greatest promises from God. He promises that if we draw close to Him, then He will draw close to us. He does not say that He *might* draw close to us, or that *sometimes* He will draw close to us. He does not say that if we do enough good things then He will draw close to us. NO, He promises that He WILL draw close to us. This is an unconditional promise from God. So, what does this mean if God is not close to me right now? Then you are not drawing close to Him. It is too easy to blame God and believe that we are drawing close to Him and He just isn't drawing close to us. But that is a lie; because God promises He WILL draw close to us when we do draw near to Him. So, how do we draw close to God?

James offers five good ways to draw close to God. First, we are to submit to God (James 4:7a). When we submit, we surrender, humble ourselves before, or throw yourself down at His feet. It means we acknowledge that God is our Lord, and we are His humble servant. We serve and obey Him, doing His will and not our own will, or trying to please others. Second, we are to resist the devil (James 4:7b). We are not to be enticed by sin, and that which we know is contrary to God and His Word. This means that we keep our guard up and do not relax, allowing the devil to infiltrate our lives. Third, cleanse your hands...and purify your hearts (James 4:8b). We are to lead a pure life, not knowingly participating in sin, but continually seeking God and getting rid of the junk in our lives. Fourth, we are to be miserable and mourn and weep (James 4:9a). This does not mean that we cannot have any fun or joy in our life, but that we are truly and sincerely sorry for the sin in our life. Also, that we have the same heart as Jesus when we see sin; that our hearts would be broken over sin. Finally, we are to humble yourselves before the Lord, and He will exalt you (James 4:10). Desire to lead a life that pleases God, and any promotions or exalting will come from Him. Too often we seek to be exalted by others and remind them who we are and what we have done. Our goal and aim should be to please God, not what others think of us.

As we incorporate these five things in our life, we will draw closer to God, and as He promised, He will draw close to us. What a great God we serve.

February 13

"So the first angel went and poured out his bowl on the earth, and harmful and painful sores came upon the people who bore the mark of the beast and worshiped its image."
Revelation 16:2

Sometimes the decisions and choices that we make seem to be particularly good and wise. But we either miss something or fail to listen to advice that we have been given and we later suffer and deal with the consequences of our choice because the decision, after all, was not a good one. What we have to deal with can be painful and not pleasant at all. This will continue to be true, and many people during the Tribulation will experience this very thing.

Today we have people pushing to have everyone microchipped.

They say that it is safer for everyone. You don't have to worry about carrying your wallet with you. You won't need a checkbook, or even credit cards. Stolen identities will be a thing of the past. Having a microchip implanted in the back of your hand will even improve security. A person who doesn't have the correct encoding on their microchip will not be able to enter buildings, including your own home. The safety and convenience of this concept sounds very enticing, which is why companies are encouraging its use right now. But this is not a good idea. Do not allow a microchip to be implanted on your body.

We have been warned not to accept this, and even during the time of the Tribulation the 144,000 Jewish evangelists will be warning people not to accept the mark of the Beast. People will not listen to this wise council and people worldwide will allow this mark, or chip, to be placed upon their bodies. When these angels in Heaven begin to pour out God's wrath upon the earth, every person who accepted the mark of the Beast will wish they hadn't done it. Every person who receives the mark of the Beast will be marked by God with these foul sores which will cover their bodies. This will be a direct result of their not listening to the words of God. Disobedience always brings negative consequences. That's how sin works, and this will be no exception. This is why we are wise when we do everything within our power to live a life of obedience to God and His Word. Read the Bible. Know it. Obey it. Live it. Instead of painful sores and bad consequences, obedience to God's Word brings joy, peace, and most importantly, eternal life.

February 14

"Be not wise in your own eyes; fear the Lord, and turn away from evil. It will be healing to your flesh and refreshment to your bones."
Proverbs 3:7-8

I love this definition of humility: "humility is not thinking less of yourself but thinking about yourself less." A.W. Tozer was a theologian back in the earlier 1900's, He spoke about humility this way: "In the heart of every believer there is a cross and a throne. For many believers, we leave Jesus on the cross so that we can sit on the throne. But in the Spirit-filled believer we take the cross and we let Jesus take the throne." Jesus said much the same thing here on earth, "If anyone would come after Me, let him deny himself and take up his cross and follow Me" (Mark 8:34). We need to remember that when Jesus said this, the cross wasn't seen as a piece of jewelry; it was an instrument of death. That is what Jesus was saying: we need to die to self and allow God to live in us. That is humility. It is saying, "God, I want you to be exalted, so I will humble myself so you can be." John the Baptist said it so well, God "must increase, but I must decrease" (John 3:30). Being humble is a key to growing spiritually. That is why the apostle Paul reminds us, "Do not be haughty, but associate with the lowly. Never be wise in your own sight" (Romans 12:16).

You may be wondering, "how does a person become humble?" There is only one way: come into the presence of God. Anytime a person comes into the presence of God there is an observable humility that happens. We see this with Isaiah. When he came into the presence of God, the first words out of his mouth were, "Woe is me! For I am lost; for I am a man of unclean lips" (Isaiah 6:5). The apostle Peter experienced this too. Peter was a professional fisherman, but after a night of fishing he had caught nothing. Jesus told him to throw his net on the other side of the boat. I am sure that Peter's first response was to laugh. After all, he was the professional, not Jesus. But to humor Jesus, he did. What happened? Their net was so full of fish that it began to break. What was Peter's response to Jesus? He said, "Depart from me, for I am a sinful man, O Lord." (Luke 5:8). The more time we spend in the presence of Jesus, the humbler we will become.

February 15

"Like newborn infants, long for the pure spiritual milk, that by it you may grow up into salvation..."
1 Peter 2:2

Being the father of three children, I have noticed that they share a common desire with other children, that is to grow up. Not only my children, but all children have this desire in them. If there is an older sibling, the child will want to grow up and be like them or the child will want to grow up and be like their parents. They don't want to stay where they are but want to grow and do things that they aren't yet able to do. This is true in a physical sense, but it is also true spiritually. Once a person has been born again, they become a spiritual babe and have the same desire that a child has in wanting to grow up and be like their older siblings, or more importantly their Father. One of the things that a child needs to help them grow is milk. A healthy baby does not need to be coerced into drinking milk because it is something that they naturally desire. This is true both physically and spiritually.

When a believer is healthy, they will have a desire for God's Word because this is what will help them grow and become more mature. No matter where we are in our spiritual journey, we need to have a desire for more and more of God's Word. When a mother breastfeeds her young baby, it is important that she takes care what she ingests into her body because anything that she ingests will affect the quality of her milk. Again, this is also true on a spiritual level. Each of us needs to monitor what we allow to be ingested into our body, whether it is into our mind or into our heart. We must be careful because there are many things in the world that will spoil our appetite for God's Word, things that will distract us and keep us away from God's Word. Remember that the Bible is filled with great and simple truths that we need no matter how old or mature we are.

What about you? Do you crave God's Word? Spend some time in His Word and continue to seek after God and watch how the more time you spend in His Word the closer you will grow to Him.

February 16

"In the month of Nisan, in the twentieth year of King Artaxerxes, when wine was before him, I took up the wine and gave it to the king. Now I had not been sad in his presence."
Nehemiah 2:1

One of the most difficult things in life to learn is to wait. Think about what it was like as a child knowing that Christmas was coming. It was just as difficult for your birthday. Tom Petty was right. The waiting is the hardest part. What do you do while you wait? The anticipation while waiting is difficult. This is what Nehemiah experienced. He heard what the conditions in Jerusalem were like, and he was heartbroken over it. He began to pray to God for help and for direction. This began around the beginning of December, and now it is around April, four months later. He has been praying this entire time and has not yet received an answer or direction. What should he do?

When we are waiting for an answer from God, the waiting is not easy, but there is something for us to do. What do we need to do? Continue to pray. There are times when God has us wait for an answer, and He will do this for some good reasons. One reason is that waiting removes our emotion and refines our prayer. Nehemiah could have had an emotional response to the destruction of Jerusalem, but after four months that emotional response was gone, and he continued to pray because he had a broken heart over their condition. A second reason for a delayed answer is simply to keep us praying. God isn't a genie that simply responds immediately to our every request. Jesus explained this in Luke 18:6-8 when he taught his disciples about the persistent widow. A third reason is to provide us with time to plan. What did Nehemiah do these four months while he prayed while waiting for an answer? He made plans on what would be needed to rebuild the walls of Jerusalem. He didn't just pray and do nothing while waiting. A fourth reason for waiting is for God to prepare leaders, people, and to have needed things in place.

Hudson Taylor, the founder of Inland China Mission in the 1800's, experienced many trials while dealing with the Chinese government. Getting a straight answer proved to be almost impossible, opinions regularly changed, in addition to the regular problems dealing with bureaucracy. He prayed for wisdom on how to deal with the government. He didn't want to respond in the ways of the world and attempt to intimidate them, get angry, or resort to using threats. God revealed he simply needed to pray, so he did. He wrote, "I have learned it is possible to move men simply through prayer." May we learn the same.

February 17

"...for John baptized with water, but you will be baptized with the Holy Spirit not many days from now."
Acts 1:5

Jesus contrasted the baptism that John did with the baptism that He is going to do. John baptized with water, and it was John that did the baptizing. The element used was water, and the issue of this baptism is repentance from sin. It recognizes that the old life is dead and needs to be buried so you can live a new life in the Spirit. The issue for baptism by water is repenting from sin.

Contrast this with the baptism that Jesus is preparing to do. This is the baptism of the Holy Spirit, and it is Jesus who does the baptizing. The element of baptism is the Holy Spirit, and the issue is love because the fruit of the Spirit is love. When a person is baptized in the Holy Spirit, love is manifested in their life.

Jesus commanded the apostles to remain in Jerusalem because in a few days they would be baptized with the Holy Spirit. The word "baptize" means "to immerse." The origin of this word came from when a person had a piece of fabric and wanted to change its color. They would take the fabric and "baptize" it in a vat of dye. The fabric would be immersed in the dye, and when it was removed from the dye it would be changed. You take a white piece of fabric and "baptize" it in blue dye, when you remove it from the dye your white fabric will now be blue. It has been changed. Baptism signifies a change in a person.

Why did the disciples need to be baptized, or changed? Jesus had given the disciples a Great Commission, to "Go therefore and make disciples of all the nations, baptizing them in the name of the Father and of the Son and of the Holy Spirit, teaching them to observe all that I have commanded you" (Matthew 28:19-20), and this task was impossible for them to do in their own abilities. The disciples were willing to fulfill this commission, but their willingness wasn't enough. As they sat within the confines of the four walls of the upper room, they couldn't comprehend the stubborn unbelief of men, the strong opposition they would receive from religion, businesses, and government, or the level of persecution that awaited them. There was something else they needed, the "promise of the Father." John recorded this conversation Jesus had with the disciples, when Jesus said, "And I will ask the Father, and He will give you another Helper, to be with you forever" (John 14:16). This Helper is what they needed. The Helper Jesus promised that God the Father would give them was the Holy Spirit.

February 18

"But Moses' hands grew weary, so they took a stone and put it under him, and he sat on it, while Aaron and Hur held up his hands, one on one side, and the other on the other side. So his hands were steady

until the going down of the sun. And Joshua overwhelmed Amalek and his people with the sword."
Exodus 17:12-13

As long as Moses' hands were raised high the Israelites were winning the battle, but as soon as his hands lowered, they would begin to lose. This is a reminder to us that prayer is difficult work. You might think that fighting in the battle was hard work, which it was, but prayer was not the easy part. Prayer can be very difficult, but it is so important.

Moses' hands got heavy, he got tired, and he let his hands down. This is understandable. The problem with this is that when his hands were down victory was questionable. What could he do? Have you ever experienced this? You know that you should be praying more, with more frequency, or passion, or intensity. But the truth is, we're tired, and weary. What do we do? We need to do exactly what Moses did. Develop an Aaron and a Hur in your life. Everyone needs to have a couple of dependable friends in their life that they know they can count on. When they are in the midst of a battle, they can call, and their friends will be there to help. When you are weary and ready to "throw in the towel," develop friendships that you can call, and they will "lift you up" in prayer.

Not only do we need to have those Aaron and Hur's in your life, but you need to be an Aaron or Hur in someone's life too. Just as we need support, we also need to be supportive for others. God is looking for people who are willing to share in battles, to come alongside others and help life them up. You don't have to physically be in the middle of the battle to help fight the battle. Be on top of the mountain praying for strength for those in the battle. Be an intercessor for others.

Because Aaron and Hur came alongside Moses, Joshua and the Israelite army was able to defeat the Amalekites. They were victorious. If Moses, Aaron, and Hur had not persevered in prayer, Israel would have lost, and history would have been drastically changed. This passage reminds us how important prayer is. It also makes me wonder how many battles believers have been defeated in because they didn't pray, or stopped too soon?

February 19

"For this perhaps is why he was parted from you for a while, that you might have him back forever, no longer as a bondservant but more than a bondservant, as a beloved brother—especially to me, but how much more to you, both in the flesh and in the Lord."
Philemon 1:15-16

Paul reminds Philemon that God is still in control. Maybe God allowed Onesimus to run away from Philemon just for Onesimus' salvation. He is coming back to Philemon, not only as a slave, but also as a fellow believer, a brother in Christ.

It is interesting that Paul sends Onesimus back to become a slave again. I find this puzzling, because I would think that the freedom of Onesimus would be the most important thing for him, but it's not; his salvation is. Read through the New Testament and you will find that the church never tries to abolish the practice of slavery. This doesn't mean the church didn't believe slavery was wrong, but they never turned it into a political agenda. The church didn't become social activists and attempt to create governmental changes of slavery. There is no question that slavery is unbiblical and anti-Christian, but you never read about Paul or other church members picketing at slave markets. In fact, 1 Corinthians 7:21-24 tells new believers that are slaves to remain slaves unless they receive their freedom.

In modern times many believe everything can be achieved through legislative change. Strike down old laws with new laws and the desired social change will come about. Does this work? Slavery was made illegal almost 150 years ago, but how are we doing as a nation regarding racism? Bigotry, exploitation, and treating others cruelly still exist today. People that are supposedly free will continue to be exploited and manipulated by people who are stronger or smarter but lack love. These problems will continue to exist until the root of sin is removed from the heart of people. There is no law that can alter the human heart. The early church realized this. Problems like slavery and abortion are really symptoms of much deeper spiritual issues. When sin is only dealt with on a social level the problem won't be solved. For a problem to be solved, the heart has to be dealt with on an individual basis. This is why Paul and the early church didn't become social activists; they relied on a spiritual process.

The apostle Paul realized that the best way to change a person's heart was through the teaching of God's Word. Paul relied on the Holy Spirit to change people from the inside out. Paul relied on the power of love. Paul didn't force any law on Philemon to accept Onesimus back, he appealed to love.

There is also a deep spiritual meaning to this story. Just like Paul interceded on behalf of Onesimus, Jesus also interceded on our behalf. Jesus does this because every one of us is a runaway slave. Each and every one of us is unprofitable to God. We ran away from God for a while, but we are received back forever, not as slaves, but as family, co-heirs with Jesus. We belong at the feet of God, but He lovingly sits us around His table as His children. He loves our presence and watches us gobble up His provisions. What an amazing God!

February 20

"And Israel said, 'It is enough; Joseph my son is still alive. I will go and see him before I die.'"
Genesis 45:28

What a reunion this must have been. Jacob was reluctant to allow Benjamin to travel to Egypt with his ten older brothers, out of fear that he wouldn't return. He had already lost his favorite son, Joseph, and couldn't bear the thought of losing Benjamin too. But now, Benjamin had returned along with his ten older brothers, and all the food that they had purchased. That was all that Jacob wanted, but as his sons shared their experiences with him, Jacob was shocked and surprised. They were telling him that the Egyptian ruler who had ordered Benjamin to come with them was his long-lost son Joseph. This was too good to be true. Not only that, but both Joseph and Pharaoh told them all to move to Egypt to live with him, and so that all their needs could be supplied. As his sons continued talking to him, the reality of what they were saying began to sink in. His son was alive! This is why he cried out that this was enough. He could now die a contented man knowing Joseph was alive. He didn't need anything else. Very soon he would be on his way to see Joseph, something he didn't expect to happen before he died.

There is a lot of change happening in these last few verses. For the past several chapters Jacob has been called by his old name, Jacob. When Jacob was in charge, we see a man who is winy, manipulative, complaining, filled with self-pity and lacking faith. The first time his brothers returned from Egypt and told him they had to bring Benjamin with them when they returned, Jacob responded by complaining, "You have bereaved me of my children: Joseph is no more, and Simeon is no more, and now you would take Benjamin. All this has come against me." (Genesis 42:36). Now that he knows that Joseph is alive, he once again responds with faith. Notice that he is now referred to again by his new name, Israel. He is once again living by faith; he is Israel, governed by God. How about you? Are you living by your old nature, or living by faith? We will never be able to completely understand all the things that happen to us in our life, but we don't have to. God never calls us to know and understand everything but to trust Him. "For we walk by faith, not by sight" (2 Corinthians 5:7).

February 21

"All who dwell on earth will worship it, everyone whose name has not been written before the foundation of the world in the book of life of the Lamb who was slain."
Revelation 13:8

The antichrist, the final world dictator, will require the entire world populace to worship him. He will not be satisfied with anything less than complete and total submission to him from everyone, and he will receive it. Every person alive on earth that does not have their name written in the book of life will willingly submit to him and worship him. The question many ask is, what is this book of life? The prophet Malachi referred to it as the book of remembrance: "Then those who feared the Lord spoke with one another. The Lord paid attention and heard them, and a book of remembrance was written before him of those who feared the Lord and esteemed his name" (Malachi 3:16). In Philippians 4:3 the apostle Paul refers to fellow laborers of Jesus as those "whose names are in the book of life." Every person who has humbled themselves before God, receiving Him as their Lord and Savior, has their name written in the book of life. They have received God's free gift of salvation and mercy, thereby receiving eternal life. Those who reject God's free gift will experience the consequences of their choice. Their name will not be written in the book of life, and they will receive eternal damnation: "anyone's name was not found written in the book of life, he was thrown into the lake of fire" (Revelation 20:15).

How can you make sure that your name is written in the book of life? Repent of your sin and receive God's grace and forgiveness. "If you confess with your mouth that Jesus is Lord and believe in your heart that God raised him from the dead, you will be saved" (Romans 10:9). God's desire is for all to receive His free gift. This is what He is waiting for. "The Lord is not slow to fulfill his promise as some count slowness, but is patient toward you, not wishing that any should perish, but that all should reach repentance" (2 Peter 3:9). Once a person surrenders their life to God, they have complete assurance that they are saved. Jesus said this about those whose names are written in the book of life, "I give them eternal life, and they will never perish, and no one will snatch them out of My hand. My Father, who has given them to Me, is greater than all, and no one is able to snatch them out of the Father's hand. I and the Father are one." (John 10:28-30).

February 22

"And Solomon overlaid the inside of the house with pure gold, and he drew chains of gold across, in front of the inner sanctuary, and overlaid it with gold...In the fourth year the foundation of the house of the LORD was laid, in the month of Ziv. And in the eleventh year, in the month of Bul, which is the eighth month, the house was finished in all its parts, and according to all its specifications. He was seven years in building it."
1 Kings 6:21, 37-38

Chapters 6 and 7 of 1 Kings give us many details of the building of the Temple, its courtyard and surrounding buildings. Some of it is difficult to understand since it is technical architecture, which we do not completely know how it was built. But, in the midst of this there are two main points we can definitely understand and apply to our lives today.

First, Solomon held nothing back in building the Temple. He only used the finest woods, and then covered everything with gold. The interior of the Temple was covered with pure gold, and the items inside the Temple were made from pure gold. Only the best was given to God. There was nothing second rate, or inferior, that was given to God. This means that today we also need to give the best that we have to God. Too often God gets our leftovers. After we have paid our bills and done fun activities, then we give to God from what remains. To give God our best means we give to Him first, and then take care of our bills and fun afterwards. Same thing applies to our time. Do we make time for God? Or do we just fit Him in whenever possible? Setting aside time for God needs to be a priority in each of our lives.

Secondly, Solomon persevered in the building of the Temple. The construction of the Temple took around 7 ½ years to complete. The month of Ziv is approximately April, and the month of Bul is approximately October. Nowhere does it say that Solomon, or the workers, became complacent, bored, or just tired of what they were doing. They knew the goal, and they kept moving forward until it was complete. This does not mean they had no problems, but they did not allow the problems or frustrations they encountered to cause them to give up. Each of us has a goal in life too. We are to live our life for the glory of God, serving Him, getting to know Him, and becoming more like Him every day. We also will experience troubles, problems and frustrations in our life; but like Solomon, we need to continue moving forward. Do not allow anything to stop us, or sidetrack us, from living our life for God, and pleasing Him. Life is difficult at times, but God is with us every step of the way. He is guiding us home to Him. Do not give up but continue to give Him your best as you follow Him every day of the rest of your life.

February 23

"Peter, an apostle of Jesus Christ, to those who are elect exiles of the Dispersion in Pontus, Galatia, Cappadocia, Asia, and Bithynia..."
1 Peter 1:1

A desire that most people have is to fit in. People work diligently to fit in and to be a part of a group. This is an innate desire that resides in the heart of most people. It can be very good for the soul when a person finds a group that they fit in with, a place where they belong. When this happens, that person can fulfill their calling, or purpose in life. While this is nice to have, it is not a requirement. The apostle Peter is writing this letter to a group of believers whom he refers to as "elect exiles." Other translations of the Bible refer to them as "pilgrims." Now, many times when an American hears the word pilgrim, they begin to think of the English settlers who came to Plymouth Rock in the 1600's. Others think of John Wayne, who was fond of referring to people as pilgrim. The dictionary definition of the word pilgrim is "a person who journeys to a sacred place for religious reasons." In other words, a pilgrim is a person who lives as a temporary resident in a foreign land. Peter was writing to Jewish believers who had been forced to move away from Jerusalem and were now living in foreign lands.

The reason these believers were driven out of Jerusalem was because their beliefs were different than the culture that they lived in. Since they were different, they also stood out. Being different also caused them to be persecuted, which is why many moved to different places and became pilgrims. The result of the persecution is that the church left Jerusalem and spread throughout the Roman Empire. Persecution didn't stop the spread of the Gospel, in fact, it caused the Gospel to be introduced throughout the Roman Empire. The same holds true today. Christians are to have values and standards that are different from the world. This provides the believer an opportunity to be a witness, but also for the spiritual warfare that they will experience. Because we are not of this world, and its system, we will experience persecution. Jesus said this will happen. "In the world you will have tribulation. But take heart; I have overcome the world" (John 16:33). Persecution will happen. We don't have to be scared of it but realize that it is an opportunity given to us to spread the Gospel to a people, and a world, that is in desperate need of the hope that only God gives.

February 24

"And God blessed them. And God said to them, 'Be fruitful and multiply and fill the earth and subdue it, and have dominion over the fish of the sea and over the birds of the heavens and over every living thing that moves on the earth.'"
Genesis 1:28

God has created both man and woman, bringing them to the earth. Now that man and woman are on earth, God is going to bless them and give them their basic instruction, or commission, on what they are supposed to do.

Their first assignment is to be fruitful, multiply, fill the earth. There are some who have said that having children to fill the earth is God's main purpose for sex. I do not agree with that, because that would lower us to the same level as animals, and there are great differences between people and animals. Animals have sexual relations for the purpose of reproduction, but they also follow seasons of "heat" when the female is ovulating and stop when they are no longer able to reproduce. On the other hand, humans have sexual relations even when there is no ovulation in the female, have sex in private, and the pleasure and intensity of sex is stronger, which causes most to continue sexual relations even after the end of fertility. God created sex for the main purpose of bonding within a one-flesh relationship.

The second command He gave to man and woman was to subdue the earth and rule it. These are military terms, meaning to conquer and then to rule. Since there was no sin yet, there was nothing to conquer at this time. God gave them a command knowing what the future would be. We also have been commanded to conquer the earth. What must be conquered on this earth? That would be Satan. How do we subdue this earth from him? How can we protect our families, children, and our world from the enemy? We do it by being fruitful. "But the fruit of the Spirit is love, joy, peace, patience, kindness, goodness, faithfulness, gentleness, self-control" (Galatians 5:22-23). When we bear God's fruit in our life, we will conquer Satan. This will also help us fulfill the first assignment God gave man, which was to multiply. When we share God's love with others, we will lead them to God so He can change them. God shares His love with us through His Word, and when we share God's Word with others, we will see changed lives. As we share God's Word with our children, our co-workers, and our neighbors we will begin to see the earth being filled as Satan is being conquered.

February 25

"Strengthen the weak hands, and make firm the feeble knees. Say to those who have an anxious heart, 'Be strong; fear not! Behold, your God will come with vengeance, with the recompense of God. He will come and save you.'"
Isaiah 35:3-4

If we spend our time looking at society or listening to the news, it is easy to become fearful of the future. Our world is looking very bleak right now. The immorality that surrounds us is mind boggling. There is greed and corruption poisoning every level of business and government. This is causing the worst economic situation since World War 2, which has caused many people to lose their jobs, and even their homes. As Christians we can still be filled with hope, even in times like these, because our hope is in God and not this world.

We do not have to cower in fear. While fear can be a useful mechanism in our lives to heighten our awareness of danger, it also can cripple us into inactivity. Don't keep your focus on this world and all its problems because it will get you down. God has not called us to live a life of fear; in fact, He's called us to be the opposite. "For God gave us a spirit not of fear but of power and love and self-control" (2 Timothy 1:7).

During Biblical times God gave the Israelites an interesting command to those who were fearful. "Is there any man who is fearful and fainthearted? Let him go back to his house, lest he make the heart of his fellows melt like his own" (Deuteronomy 20:8). God knew that fear was contagious, so in time of battle He sent the fearful home so that they would not bring others down too. A fearful person can do much damage to others around them. So, God allowed the fearful to go home, which left the unafraid and committed left to fight. God will use those who are committed to Him and His ways, even when the fight looks overwhelming. John Wesley said, "Give me a hundred men who love God with all their hearts and fear nothing but sin, and I will move the world."

This is what God is doing today. He is creating an army of men and women who are not afraid, but instead are committed to Him. God will use this army to change the world. Through the battles and trials that we are in right now we are becoming refined and tested to accomplish great exploits for God.

Notice that the point of these verses is not for us to send home those who are fearful. We are to encourage those who are fearful. When we see our brothers and sisters immobilized by fear we are not to discard them or tell them to go home. Instead, we are to lovingly encourage them, share God's Word and hope with them to strengthen them. "Brothers, if anyone is caught in any transgression, you who are spiritual should restore him in a spirit of gentleness. Keep watch on yourself, lest you too be tempted. Bear one another's burdens, and so fulfill the law of Christ" (Galatians 6:1-2).

Each of us has a great opportunity to help encourage and build up the army of God, our brothers and sisters in the Lord. God has allowed us to be alive in this time of worldly and economic uncertainty. God can use us to share His love with a dying world that desperately needs Him. Let's not discard or send the fearful away, but instead we are to come alongside each other and build each other up in God's love. God is coming soon. Our hope draws near. This is greater than any fear the world gives us. Remind and encourage each other with this great news!

February 26

"We also take on ourselves the obligation to give yearly a third part of a shekel for the service of the house of our God: for the showbread, the regular grain offering, the regular burnt offering, the Sabbaths, the new moons, the appointed feasts, the holy things, and the sin offerings to make atonement for Israel, and for all the work of the house of our God."
Nehemiah 10:32-33

The children of Israel just recently completed rebuilding the walls around their city of Jerusalem. They had spent almost 100 years living in captivity in Babylon due to their neglecting of and disobedience of God's Word. Now that these children are back in their homeland, they have rebuilt both the temple and their city, and recommitted their life to living in ways that obey and honor God. In doing this the people recommit to following the laws of God at that time, which required daily sacrifices and a continual fire burning on the altar, "fire shall be kept burning on the altar continually; it shall not go out" (Leviticus 6:13). This was a commitment that required teamwork since no one person could afford or accomplish this task alone. The people committed to work together to get this done. Part of the reason why God decreed this was to get the people working together. The people needed each other. They relied upon each other and needed to learn how to depend upon others and work together. This is vitally important for the body of believers, both then and still today.

The people committed to do this together, and they did come together and "the people of Israel and the sons of Levi shall bring the contribution of grain, wine, and oil to the chambers, where the vessels of the sanctuary are, as well as the priests who minister, and the gatekeepers and the singers. We will not neglect the house of our God" (Nehemiah 10:39). As the children of Israel surrendered their lives to

God, they willingly gave everything they had to God. Not because they had to, but because they willingly chose to. You see, when you surrender your heart to God, He gets everything you have, including your checkbook. The people gave of their times, their resources, and their money to the temple because they were giving back to God. Today, we give to the church, Godly ministries, and people in need because of our love and commitment to God. Situations in life don't dictate what, when, or how we give. Love and commitment to God is why we give.

February 27

"And after Paul and Barnabas had no small dissension and debate with them, Paul and Barnabas and some of the others were appointed to go up to Jerusalem to the apostles and the elders about this question."
Acts 15:2

Paul and Barnabas most certainly disagreed with what these men said. Paul and Barnabas had seen God doing great and amazing things in the lives of Gentiles, and they weren't going to stand by idly while these "men from Judea" undermined the work of God.

What these men were teaching was dangerous because they were mixing law and grace. They were teaching that God's grace wasn't enough; you had to do something more in order to be saved. They were essentially doing what Jesus said not to do in Luke 5:36-39, which was to pour new wine into old wineskins. When Jesus died on the cross, the veil that separated the Holy of Holies was torn in two (Luke 23:45), these men were trying to sew it back together. By saying that a Gentile had to become a Jew in order to be saved, they were blocking the new and living way to God that Jesus had opened through His death on the cross; "Therefore, brothers, since we have confidence to enter the holy places by the blood of Jesus, by the new and living way that He opened for us through the curtain, that is, through His flesh" (Hebrews 10:19-20).

To follow their advice would be like moving out from the sunlight and living in the shadows. "Therefore let no one pass judgment on you in questions of food and drink, or with regard to a festival or a new moon or a Sabbath. These are a shadow of the things to come, but the substance belongs to Christ" (Colossians 2:16-17). In addition, if a Gentile has to become a Jew in order to be saved, that would mean that God only accepts Jews as His children, which would negate Galatians 3:26-29, which says, "For in Christ Jesus you are all sons of God, through faith. For as many of you as were baptized into Christ have put on Christ. There is neither Jew nor Greek, there is neither slave nor free, there is no male and female, for you are all one in Christ Jesus. And if you are Christ's, then you are Abraham's offspring, heirs according to promise." Paul and Barnabas took exception to what these men were saying because they were adding to God's Word. Salvation is completely by God's grace, through faith in Jesus Christ, plus nothing else!

February 28

"Come now, you rich, weep and howl for the miseries that are coming upon you. Your riches have rotted and your garments are moth-eaten. Your gold and silver have corroded, and their corrosion will be evidence against you and will eat your flesh like fire."
James 5:1-3a

Many Americans suffer with the idea of depending upon anyone for anything. Many of us were raised to be independent. That can be a very good thing, but for the believer, that is not how God wants us to live. Throughout this book James has been developing the idea of how the believer is to be completely dependent upon God. So, here at the beginning of chapter 5 he issues a rebuke towards those that are most likely to live independently from God; the rich. Now, please don't misunderstand what is being said here; it is wrong to live independently from God, but James is not saying it is wrong to be rich. Sadly, many who are rich do not live a life that is dependent upon God, but there are many wealthy individuals that are completely dependent upon God. Nowhere in the Bible is there any condemnation for a person to gather wealth and riches for themselves. The Bible does condemn wealth that is gained through illegal or unethical ways though. The point James is making here is not against the rich, but against those that aren't completely trusting God.

Here is where so many people fail to place their complete trust in God. So many people place their faith and trust in their riches instead of God; and sadly, this includes many believers also. There is a huge problem with placing your trust in riches, which is the fact that they don't last. Look at the stock market, and you can watch a person's wealth rise and fall by the hour. Other material wealth is ruined by rust, eaten by moths, and corroded by time. Any security riches and wealth can give you is fleeting. On the other hand, God is eternal. He does not rust away, cannot be eaten by moths, and neither can He corrode. God is eternal. He is trustworthy. Place your faith and hope in Him. "As for the rich in this present age, charge them not to be haughty, nor to set their hopes on the uncertainty of riches, but on God, who richly provides us with everything to enjoy" (1 Timothy 6:17).

February 29

"To those who are called, beloved in God the Father and kept for Jesus Christ."
Jude 1b

It appears that Jude writes this letter to three different groups of people: those who are called, those loved by God, and those kept by

Jesus Christ. While it may appear that way, that isn't the case. Jude is writing this letter to one person: believers. You see, a believer fits into each of these categories.

Those who are the called: A child of God is a privileged person, but they do not become a privileged person like other people who are privileged: by birth. No one becomes a child of God because of the family they are born into. The only way a person can become a child of God is because God has called them; which means they have been chosen by God. The word called refers to a person that is invited. That is the best news we could ever receive; God has chosen you, and me. The apostle Peter said we are "a chosen race" (1 Peter 2:9). Not only are we chosen, but we are also loved.

Those loved by God the Father: Some translations of the Bible translate the word "love" as "sanctified," which means "to separate from profane things and dedicate to God." Not only does God love us, but He separates His children from the world to do good works that bring glory and honor to Him. Think of people like plates. In your house you have special dishes that only come out for company, you also have normal, everyday dishes, and you also have paper plates for other occasions. They all serve the same function (to hold your food), but their purposes are very different from each other. God has set His children aside as "fine china."

Those kept for Jesus Christ: As children of God we are "kept" by Jesus, or "preserved" for Him. Jesus guards and takes care of His children. That means Jesus is watching over us, and nothing happens to His children that He doesn't allow to happen. This means as Christians that we can live a life of abandon for Jesus. Don't hold back; live to please Him because He is guarding you. Jesus gave the promise that "I give them eternal life, and they will never perish, and no one will snatch them out of My hand. My Father, Who has given them to Me, is greater than all, and no one is able to snatch them out of the Father's hand. I and the Father are One." (John 10:28-30).

God calls us, He sanctifies us, and Jesus guards and protects us.

How wonderful is that?

March 1

"Simeon and Levi are brothers; weapons of violence are their swords. Let my soul come not into their council; O my glory, be not joined to their company. For in their anger they killed men, and in their willfulness they hamstrung oxen. Cursed be their anger, for it is fierce, and their wrath, for it is cruel! I will divide them in Jacob and scatter them in Israel."
Genesis 49:5-7

Simeon and Levi are the second and third born sons of Jacob. They were paired together and received the same "blessing" for an evil act that they were involved with together. Their sister Dinah had been violated and their father did nothing about it at the time, so they decided to (see Genesis 34). They acted out of anger and deceived an entire town and in anger ended up killing every man in the town. In addition to that they also hamstrung all the oxen. This anger of theirs was sin since it was rooted in their own self-will. They chose to be violent and caused senseless damage out of their anger. This is the type of anger that the apostle Paul tells us that needs to be removed from our lives. "Let all bitterness and wrath and anger and clamor and slander be put away from you, along with all malice. Be kind to one another, tenderhearted, forgiving one another, as God in Christ forgave you" (Ephesians 4:31-32). Not all anger is sin. Anger can be righteous. The apostle Paul also reminds us "be angry and do not sin" (Ephesians 4:26). Jesus modeled this for us: "And making a whip of cords, he drove them all out of the temple, with the sheep and oxen. And he poured out the coins of the money-changers and overturned their tables. And he told those who sold the pigeons, 'Take these things away; do not make my Father's house a house of trade.'" (John 2:15-16). Jesus' anger was not personal, it was for a desire for purity in God's house. Too often our anger is personal, which was the case for Simeon and Levi.

Jacob's prophecy about them was completely fulfilled. Simeon's descendants became part of the tribe of Judah after entering the Promised Land (see Joshua 19:1). Levi's descendants didn't receive any land, instead they were appointed Priests and were scattered into 48 different cities spread throughout the land. We can learn much from these two men. Don't allow yourself to be consumed with anger. It causes much destruction in your life. King Solomon wisely reminds us that "Whoever is slow to anger has great understanding, but he who has a hasty temper exalts folly" (Proverbs 14:29).

March 2

"And night will be no more. They will need no light of lamp or sun, for the Lord God will be their light, and they will reign forever and ever."
Revelation 22:5

There are times, places, and events in our lives that we never want to stop. Times or places that are so wonderful that you would like that experience to continue forever, never to end. Here on earth that is not possible, but there is a time coming when that will happen. The apostle John tells us that this will be the experience in Heaven. God revealed to John certain aspects of Heaven to not only prepare us for Heaven, but also to whet our appetite for what it will be like there. When something good happens here on earth people tend to say it's like Heaven on earth. They are commenting on the fact of how good something is right now, and that Heaven is going to be filled with spectacular goodness. The greatest thoughts we can think of Heaven are nowhere as good as it really will be. Heaven is going to be grander and greater than we can possibly imagine with our limited and finite minds.

John tells us that there will be absolutely no darkness in Heaven. That's not because there are lights everywhere. In fact, there will be no artificial light in Heaven, including the sun. God Himself is the source of light, and in Heaven we will be in His presence so we will experience true all-encompassing light. This is something that our limited minds has difficulty comprehending.

One of the greatest things about Heaven is that those in Heaven will "reign forever and ever." God's people will have had lots of experience ruling already, as this is what they did during the Millennial Reign, but that reign was limited, and it will come to an end. There will be no end to Heaven. It will make the Energizer Bunny look like a flash in the pan, because it really will go on and on and on. One of the reasons for this is because God's Word never fails. In Revelation 3:21 God made the following promise, "The one who conquers, I will grant him to sit with me on my throne..." This will be completed in Heaven. This should give us the motivation we need to endure through our life here on earth, because as the apostle Paul reminds us, "if we endure, we will also reign with Him" (2 Timothy 2:12).

March 3

"But the LORD said to Samuel, 'Do not look on his appearance or on the height of his stature, because I have rejected him. For the LORD sees not as man sees: man looks on the outward appearance, but the LORD looks on the heart.'"
1 Samuel 16:7

Have you ever noticed that when a jeweler wants to show a beautiful piece of jewelry that they place that jewelry on a black surface? Look at art and you will find that artists often do the same thing. They use a dark background and then paint a beautiful object on that background. They do this because of contrast. The beauty of a diamond ring is contrasted with the dark background it rests on, and the beauty of the diamond stands out and is more clearly seen. The artist uses the dark background to contrast the object that they are painting. Contrast is a wonderful tool.

We see contrast here in 1 Samuel 16 when the prophet Samuel is directed by the Lord to go to the house of Jesse and anoint one of his sons as the future king of Israel. Saul has disobeyed God and followed his own heart, which led to God rejecting him, and the need for a new king to replace him. When Samuel arrives at Jesse's house, he is first introduced to Jesse's oldest son Eliab. He was tall, strong, dark, and handsome. Samuel took one look at him and knew that he had found Israel's next king. He was shocked when God said he was rejected. God rejected the next six sons of Jesse too. Finally, David was brought to Samuel, and God chose him to be Israel's next king. Why? Because of his heart.

David had a heart that sought to be more like God. In fact, God said, "I have found in David the son of Jesse a man after My heart, who will do all My will" (Acts 13:22). The goal and desire of David's heart was to please God, and to be like Him. Neither Saul nor any of David's brothers had this same heart desire. This is why none of them received the dynasty of kings that David did. The heart of David stands out in stark contrast to the heart of Saul and David's brothers. The darkness of their hearts helps us to see the beauty of David's heart. God has placed us in the midst of a dark world so that when our heart seeks after God's heart, the beauty of God will be seen by others, and God will be praised.

March 4

"The Lord passed before him and proclaimed, 'The Lord, the Lord, a God merciful and gracious, slow to anger, and abounding in steadfast love and faithfulness, keeping steadfast love for thousands, forgiving iniquity and transgression and sin.'"

Exodus 34:6-7a

Many people have incorrect views of God. People often describe God as an angry Father; like He is mad at people and wishing to inflict serious pain to them. This is not true. God is a loving God. God is not angry, but He is saddened by the choices of sin that people make. Sin brings separation from God. The result of sin is death. Those are brought about by the choices we make. God though, is not storming around Heaven in a rage of anger because He is mad at the behavior of people. The essence, or character, of God is love. As a person gets to know God better, they will find this to be true. God has been showing His graciousness and love to mankind since the beginning of time. This is what God did to Moses.

Moses was frustrated leading the Israelites across the desert towards the Promised Land. Moses cried out to God and said, "Please show me now Your ways, that I may know You in order to find favor in Your sight" (Exodus 33:13). God showed Moses His character, and what did Moses see? He saw the compassion and grace of God. Grace, compassion, and mercy are the essence of God; not anger.

The prophet Jonah knew God too. When God instructed Jonah to preach a message to Ninevah Jonah refused to go. The Ninevites were enemies of Israel, and Jonah wanted to see them destroyed. God performed miracles to get Jonah to Ninevah and he reluctantly shared God's message to the Ninevites. The people received Jonah's message and repented before God. God did not destroy them, and Jonah was upset. Why? Because he knew this was what would happen. "I knew that You are a gracious God and merciful, slow to anger and abounding in steadfast love, and relenting from disaster" (Jonah 4:2b).

As we get to know God more intimately, we know His mercy and compassion. As we receive that mercy and compassion, we are then to extend it to others too. "You received without paying; give without pay" (Matthew 10:8).

March 5

"And suddenly there came from heaven a sound like a mighty rushing wind, and it filled the entire house where they were sitting. And divided tongues as of fire appeared to them and rested on each one of them."
Acts 2:2-3

The first thing we need to realize about this event is that it wasn't an actual wind blowing; it was the sound "of a mighty rushing wind." People's hair wasn't getting messed up; no one ended up having a bad hair day. There weren't papers flying all over the place, and no lit candles were extinguished. The people heard the sound of the wind, but there was no effect from the wind blowing.

What was this sound of wind blowing? It was the presence of the Holy Spirit moving upon this group of believers that were gathered in unity. The Greek word for "wind" is *pneuma*; this is where we get the word pneumatic. It can also be translated as "breath," and is used to describe the Holy Spirit. This is a good definition, because the Holy Spirit is like wind, or breath. They each are invisible, but also can move to show great power. Neither wind nor the Holy Spirit can be cornered or contained by any special interest group, nor can either be commanded by anyone. While the Holy Spirit is here to serve mankind, He is not our servant but does what God wants Him to do, not what we want.

The sound of this wind "filled the entire house," but it wasn't heard outside the house. No one outside this house knew what was going on in the house at that moment. Even those inside the house couldn't *see* what was happening, they could only *hear* it. That is important, because "faith *comes* from hearing, and hearing through the word of Christ" (Romans 10:17). The people that heard the wind also couldn't *feel* the wind. This is to remind us that God's emphasis is not on feeling, but on faith. Feelings will mislead you, but faith in God will not.

First came the sound, and that was followed by sight. This is God's order. Hearing comes before sight. People often try to reverse this order and once they see God, then they will listen to Him. That's backwards. If you want to see God, first you must hear His Word. God's Word always comes before His work.

After the people heard the sound of rushing wind they saw what appeared to be flames of fire upon the heads of each believer. The fire is another symbol of the Holy Spirit. Fire begins with a small flame, and then it spreads and can cover a very large area.

Fire is also very important in the life of the believer. Fire is used to purify, as it removes dross, or sin, from the object it is applied to. Fire can also be used to burn away things that are temporary, while the things that are everlasting will remain. In the Old Testament, when both the tabernacle and the temple were dedicated, fire came down from Heaven and God consumed the sacrifices that were offered. On this day of Pentecost, a new temple is being dedicated. We see fire coming down from Heaven, and the sacrifice will also be consumed by God. What is being sacrificed? Those that are following Jesus. You see, the new temple is the church, which is made up of those that follow Jesus.

One last thing that we need to see is that these flames of fire were about every individual believer. This baptism of the Holy Spirit wasn't just for certain people, like Peter and John, but was given to every single believer there. God is no respecter of persons. This gift was given to the greatest individual believer, just as the same exact gift was given to the least known, unnamed believer in the group.

March 6

"But Joshua said to the people, 'You are not able to serve the Lord, for He is a holy God. He is a jealous God; He will not forgive your

transgressions or your sins. If you forsake the Lord and serve foreign gods, then He will turn and do you harm and consume you, after having done you good.'"
Joshua 24:19-20

Joshua had just challenged the people to serve God, they said they would, and now Joshua says, "You are not able to serve the LORD." Is Joshua trying to confuse the people? Is he trying to discourage them? No! He is causing them to consider the decision they are making so they don't take it lightly. Joshua is making sure they know what they're saying.

Joshua remembers their history; it helps that he was there and witnessed it. Just before God gave the Israelites the Ten Commandments God told them they were special to Him and were to be set apart for Him; they were commanded to obey His words. The Israelites responded by saying, "All that the LORD has spoken we will do" (Exodus 19:8). It wasn't very long after this that the people were bowing down and worshipping a golden calf (see Exodus 32). Joshua understood that it was easier to promise obedience than it was to obey.

Joshua is making sure that the people are not overconfident in their own words and abilities, but that they know the difficulty of following God and are willing to pay the price. It is too easy to say one thing but do something else. Jesus told a parable about this in Matthew 21:28-32. A father asked his son to go do some yardwork for him, and the son said he would. The father then went to his second son and asked him to do some yardwork, and the son said he wouldn't. The first son never followed through to do what he said he would, while the second son felt guilty and ended up doing what his father asked him to do. Jesus then asked which son did the will of his father. It was the second son. It wasn't because he gave the "right" answer, but because he obeyed. For us today, it is so important that we obey God. It is important to say the right things, but our actions are even more important. God wants us to be obedient to His Word, to do what He has called us to do. It is too easy for us to say that we are Christians, but are we really obeying God and doing what His Word says? That's most important!

March 7

"But he said, 'Far be it from me that I should do so! Only the man in whose hand the cup was found shall be my servant. But as for you, go up in peace to your father.'"
Genesis 44:17

Confrontation is not something that most people enjoy. In fact, many people do everything they can to avoid confrontation. There is one major problem with doing this, confrontation, though uncomfortable, is needed to bring growth to a person. If we are never confronted, we will fail to grow. Joseph loves his brothers enough to confront them and force them to make decisions that will cause them to move in one of two ways; either they will grow through these difficult choices, or they will remain where they are and continue to make the same choices they have previously made. The ten brothers didn't like Joseph, so they made the decision to abandon him and get rid of him. It was very uncomfortable for a while, especially since their dad mourned over his loss, but eventually they got over it. They had left Simeon here in Egypt as a prisoner to this Egyptian ruler, and they dad wasn't happy again, but that too passed. Now, this Egyptian ruler is once again causing them, through confrontation, to make a difficult decision. Are they going to abandon one of their brothers again, and deal with the consequences when they return home, or will they take a stand and not leave him behind? Taking a stand could cause all of them to remain in Egypt as slaves. Talk about tough decisions.

We are faced with these same difficult decisions in our own lives. Every one of us has family and/or friends who have areas in their lives where they are lacking. What do we do in those instances? Do we ignore the area they are lacking and hope and pray it gets dealt with? Or do we loving confront them, as Joseph here does, to help direct them towards making wise decisions and to overcome the area where they are lacking? Joseph knows from firsthand experience that his brothers are willing to abandon others in order to help themselves, so he lovingly confronts them to help them stop doing this. How about you? Are you willing to lovingly confront a loved one in whatever area they are lacking? Are you willing to confront the alcoholic to help them stop drinking? Or the person with anger issues to help them find ways to deal constructively with their anger? Confrontation is not a simple matter, but it is something that is needed. Pray to God for wisdom in how to lovingly confront those in your lives that need to be confronted.

March 8

"How can I save Israel?"
Judges 6:15

Gideon's faith isn't very strong it, but that doesn't hinder God. Gideon doesn't understand this yet because his vision hasn't been corrected yet. He wonders how he can deliver Israel from the Midianites, and the answer is, he can't! Gideon's problem is that his focus is on himself instead of God. Gideon is not yet a strong man of faith or courage, so God is going to patiently work with him to prepare him for what God has planned for him. God is always willing to work in us and change us into what He needs to accomplish His will when we surrender to Him. "For we are His workmanship, created in Christ Jesus for good works, which God prepared beforehand, that we should walk in them" (Ephesians 2:10). "For it is God who works in you, both to will and to work for His good pleasure" (Philippians 2:13). God chooses to use flawed people to accomplish His purposes. The apostle Paul reminds us in 1 Corinthians 1:26-29 that God uses the "weak things of this world" to accomplish great things, and to confound the "wise things of this world."

God uses inadequate people. There may be times that you feel inadequate, but God can use you. Moses felt inadequate, but God used him to lead Israel away from bondage, around the desert for forty years, and then led them to the Promised Land. Saul felt inadequate, but God raised him to be king of Israel and used him mightily until pride and arrogance got a hold of him. The prophets Isaiah and Jeremiah both felt inadequate, but they were each used mightily by God. This should help us to understand that feeling inadequate is not a bad thing. It means that we are in a place where God can use us, as long as we depend upon Him.

When we rely upon God, then He will work in us and change us to do the work He has called us to. God will never leave us where we are, but He will work in us until we become what He needs. "And I am sure of this, that He who began a good work in you will bring it to completion at the day of Jesus Christ" (Philippians 1:6).

March 9

"But you are a chosen race, a royal priesthood, a holy nation, a people for his own possession..."
1 Peter 2:9a

Most people describe their value or worth by the accomplishment that they have earned. Their success, their wealth, their knowledge; these are the things that most people use to determine their own worth, or to describe their worth to others. There is a problem with this though. It is not accurate, especially for Christians. For the Christian, our value comes from the fact that Jesus chose us as His very own. He did not choose us because we have so much to offer Him, but simply because He loves us. The fact that Jesus has chosen us as His very own is where we get our value from and not from any worldly success that we may have achieved. Not only did God choose us but He also gave three special privileges to us, His children.

The three special privileges that God gave to us are that we are His royal priesthood, a holy nation, and that we belong to Him, His special people. As priests for God, we have the special privilege of representing God to the people He has placed around us. We are set apart for Him. We are to be in this world, but we don't belong to it because we have been set apart for God. We are also His holy nation. No matter what country we live in, our citizenship is in Heaven, not here on earth. "But our citizenship is in heaven, and from it we await a Savior, the Lord Jesus Christ..." (Philippians 3:20). As a citizen of Heaven, that means our first allegiance, and our first priority is to follow the rules of our homeland, which is Heaven. In fact, God said that we "are to distinguish between the holy and the common, and between the unclean and the clean" (Leviticus 10:10). This means that we are to live our lives in a way that is obedient to God first and foremost. The reason we do this is because of the third privilege given to us: we belong to God. The fact that we belong to God gives us value and makes us unique in the world. Think of a museum. It is filled with mainly ordinary things, such as shoes, hats, tools, cars, etc. The reason we go see these items is because of who they belonged to. Someone famous either owned them or did something great and spectacular with them, which gives them value. That is true of us too. We are special because of Who we belong to: God. Don't forget that. You are special, a citizen of Heaven, because God has chosen you to be His child.

March 10

"Call to Me and I will answer you, and will tell you great and hidden things that you have not known."
Jeremiah 33:3

Remember when you were a child and you were scared, afraid, or overwhelmed? What did you do? Most children in one of those situations cry out for their parents. You can hear a loud sobbing child calling for their mommy or their daddy. I have been woken many times in the middle of the night by one of my children crying out for me because they had a bad dream or were scared by something. Whenever I heard that cry, I went to my child and comforted them, soothed them, and let them know everything was all right. To do that I sometimes had to explain things to them, things they did not know or understand. Why does a child call out for their parents? Because they do not have the answers and cannot take care of their current situation, they trust their parents. Children are not above admitting when they need help and cry out for that help. Instead of attempting to tackle the situation themselves, they let it be known that they cannot do it and want you to help.

Jesus said, "Truly, I say to you, whoever does not receive the kingdom of God like a child shall not enter it" (Mark 10:15). That is, we are to have a child-like faith in our lives, but we are not to act childish. We are to trust in and rely on Jesus the same way a child does their parents. When we are in a circumstance that we don't know how to deal with, like a child, we need to cry out to our Father in Heaven. No matter whether our problem is with a relationship, finances (or lack thereof), job related, concerns over decisions a child is making, or just being overwhelmed with life, we can cry out to God. He is our Father, and He waits for us to cry out to Him. He has promised that when we do, He will hear us and respond to us. An earthly parent will answer their child's cry, and God is better than any earthly parent. "What father among you, if his son asks for a fish, will instead of a fish give him a serpent; or if he asks for an egg, will give him a scorpion? If you then, who are evil, know how to give good gifts to your children, how much more will the heavenly Father give the Holy Spirit to those who ask Him!" (Luke 11:11-13). God is concerned for you and for me. When we call out to Him, He will answer us; He will comfort us, and as we listen to Him He will give us understanding to get us through what we are struggling with. God allows us to experience times of struggle to draw us closer to Him. Show Him that you trust Him and call out to Him, He is waiting for you. He will hear you and give you exactly what you need.

March 11

"Blessed is the man who remains steadfast under trial, for when he has stood the test he will receive the crown of life, which God has promised to those who love Him."
James 1:12

Most of us cringe at the word endure. It speaks of perseverance, or to remain firm during suffering or misfortune without yielding. This means not giving up but making it through to the other side. What is it that we endure? Trials or temptations. The root word for this is adversity, which speaks of a condition of suffering or affliction. Every one of us experiences this in our lives. The question is, how do we respond when these afflictions come into our life?

All too often when this happens, we get angry with God and ask why He is tempting us. But that is not the case. I have never entered a time of trial and said, "Thanks God, this is an area where I really need some growth in my life." I do not see the need for growth, until after I have endured through the trial and look back and review my life after the growth has already occurred. God knows beforehand where I need to grow, so He allows the temptations and trials to come into my life. God is allowing times of difficulty in my life to strengthen and grow me. God does this so that after we make it through the difficult times we will be approved and "will receive the crown of life, which God has promised to those who love Him."

Going through times of trial is not fun but is necessary. When those times come, we need to remember to not blame God for them. As James reminds us, "Let no one say when he is tempted, 'I am being tempted by God'; for God cannot be tempted by evil, and He Himself tempt no one" (James 1:13). God does not tempt us, instead He only gives us good. "Do not be deceived, my beloved brothers. Every good gift and every perfect gift is from above, coming down from the Father of lights, with whom there is no variation or shadow due to change" (James 1:16-17). Instead of God tempting us, He provides a way of escape for us, "No temptation has overtaken you that is not common to man. God is faithful, and He will not let you be tempted beyond your ability, but with the temptation He will also provide the way of escape, that you may be able to endure it" (1 Corinthians 10:13).

When times of difficulty come, do not blame God; instead draw closer to Him as He will lead you through these times to grow you, and prepare you for eternity with Him.

March 12

"But in the evening he took his daughter Leah and brought her to Jacob, and he went in to her. (Laban gave his female servant Zilpah to his daughter Leah to be her servant.) And in the morning, behold, it was Leah! And Jacob said to Laban, 'What is this you have done to me? Did I not serve with you for Rachel? Why then have you deceived me?'"
Genesis 29:23-25

Jacob has been waiting seven years for this day. Finally, he will be married and spend the night with his bride Rachel. Can you imagine how Jacob must have felt when he woke up and discovered he was married to Leah instead of Rachel? He most likely had to pinch himself to make sure he was awake, and not dreaming, or having a nightmare. Not only that, but there were still six days of celebrating to go through. I can imagine he wasn't really in the mood to be celebrating at that moment.

The first thing Jacob does is confront his father-in-law. It is interesting that he uses almost the exact same words that Pharaoh used to Abraham (Gen.12:18), that Abimelech used to Abraham (Gen.20:9), and that Abimelech used to Isaac (Gen.26:10). The shoe is now on the other foot; the deceiver has been deceived. Remember, those who choose to live by the sword also die by the sword. You reap what you sow, and it is an inescapable law of life; you cannot avoid it. Jacob had deceived his own father, and now he is deceived by his father-in-law. Jacob was the younger son, but had passed himself off as the elder, and he was to marry the younger daughter, but had the elder daughter passed off to him.

Jacob had learned how to deceive others, and now he experiences that same deception for himself. If we want others to treat us fairly and honestly, then we need to treat others fairly and honestly. As we teach our children, if you want others to be friendly to you, then you need to be friendly towards others. Dave Guzik also reminds us that "Though we can see this is God's correction upon Jacob, it in no way justifies Laban's deception. The fact God does work all things together for good never excuses the evil acts God works for good."

Lord, thank You that You are always faithful, and help us learn to treat others the way that we would like to be treated.

March 13

"Now to Him who is able to do far more abundantly than all that we ask or think, according to the power at work within us..."
Ephesians 3:20

When we are obedient to God it is easy for us to think that things should go smoothly, and when we encounter difficulties, we question whether we are really where God wants us to be. As nice as that sounds, it is a lie from the pit of hell.

My family and I followed the leading of the Lord and moved our family to a new state. Upon arriving there we found a nice house to rent. Things appeared to be going well. A few weeks later we were told the house sold and we had to find a new place to live. Shouldn't be a big deal, but where we moved, there aren't many houses for rent. Amazingly, God provided a house almost immediately. Two months later we received another phone call notifying us that we had to move again. What? We were moving for the third time in less than five months. This is how crazy this was, only three houses sold in our town during this time, and two of them were the ones we were living in. Is this really where God was leading and directing us?

After crying out to God and seeking Him, He began to show us how He was behind all of this. Moving is not fun, especially three times in five months, but it is truly amazing. You see, each time that we moved, the house we moved into was larger than the previous house. Not only that, but each house had lower rent than the others. None of the houses we moved into were available previously, but each came available when we had to move out of the previous house. Is that amazing or what? God is so good.

God continued to provide larger houses for us and saved us money each time too. God has continued to bless us beyond anything we could ever have thought of or imagined. That is how He operates. God has unlimited resources available to Him, and His desire is to bless our socks off with things that we haven't even thought of. These blessings that God has for us are not always for material things, but God has so many blessings in store for us. This is a reason why we can praise Him. We praise God because of His greatness. He gives us more than we deserve. He gives us more than we can imagine. He gives to us because He loves us so much! Thank You Jesus!

March 14

"He looked this way and that, and seeing no one, he struck down the Egyptian and hid him in the sand."

Exodus 2:12

Moses was certainly correct in stepping in to save the life of his fellow Hebrew, but he was also premature in his attempt to deliver his brethren from bondage. Moses was attempting to deliver Israel is a very logical manner. God placed him in this lofty and prestigious position so he could use it for the betterment of the Israelites. Moses figured God would use him and his position to deliver Israel. He failed to realize that God doesn't work according to man's wisdom and power. Why? Because God says, "For My thoughts are not your thoughts, neither are your ways My ways, declares the Lord. For as the heavens are higher than the earth, so are My ways higher than your ways and My thoughts than your thoughts" (Isaiah 55:8-9). Even though Moses was a prince, and very highly educated, he wasn't ready for God to use him. God had to take him out of Egypt, so he could take Egypt out of Moses. Moses had to learn to become a pastor, a shepherd, before he would be ready to lead Israel to their freedom.

Notice though, what Moses did. He wanted to serve God and help him, but he wanted to do it in his own way. He wanted to deliver Israel from Egypt, and he began it by him "this way and that way, and when he saw no one, he killed the Egyptian and hid him in the sand." In other words, Moses looked to the north, the east, the south, and to the west. There was no one watching them, so he killed the Egyptian, and then he hid his body so no one would know what he did. He was successful in what he did, but it backfired on him. Why? Because he failed to look up. He failed to look to God for any wisdom or direction. He did what he thought was right. He was like Frank Sinatra and did it his way. I easily relate to Moses and understand him right here, because I have made this same mistake in my own life. You might have done this too. We need to learn from Moses' mistake and learn to trust God instead of our own strength. That's why Solomon reminded us to "Trust in the Lord with all your heart, and do not lean on your own understanding" (Proverbs

3:5). Trust God. Look to Him for direction before stepping out. Follow His lead.

March 15

"If one member suffers, all suffer together; if one member is honored, all rejoice together."
1 Corinthians 12:26

Being a member of a Country Club comes with some privileges and perks. As long as your "dues" current, others will take care of you while you live a life of leisure. As a member of a Country Club, you are entitled to receive instead of giving, you are served instead of serving, you have rights instead of responsibilities, and entitlements instead of sacrifices. Sadly, many people have this same attitude about being a member of a church. Tithes and offerings given to the church keep their "membership" current, along with the privileges of membership, instead of it being an unconditional cheerful gift to the Lord.

Being a member of the church is a privilege, not a right. The giving of gifts and tithes does not secure, or purchase, our membership. The purchase that allows us to be a member of the church was paid by Jesus when He died on the cross. A church I attended at one time had a person who would send in a regular "gift," or "tithe," to the church. They never attended the church, but instead, regularly sent the church a check to keep their "membership" active. They had a misconception about what it meant to be a member of a church.

What does it mean to be a member of a church? It means that we belong to something that is much bigger than we are. As a member of the church, we have a role and a function to perform. Since the church is not a country club, we cannot pay our dues and have someone else do our work for us. We all have the responsibility to do our own work.

Every member of the church has a unique role suited to their gifts, abilities, and personality. The apostle Paul compared the church to the human body; some are hands, feet, eyes, or ears, etc. This means that we have to be unified and work together. If the body does not work together, it will not function well and will suffer. Eventually it will cease to function at all.

As a church member we should never ask the following question: "Should I be serving in the church?" The question we should be asking is, "How can I best serve my church?"

March 16

"And the day after the Passover, on that very day, they ate of the produce of the land, unleavened cakes and parched grain. And the manna ceased the day after they ate of the produce of the land. And there was no longer manna for the people of Israel, but they ate of the fruit of the land of Canaan that year."
Joshua 5:11-12

The nation of Israel has finally entered the Promised Land, and now they will experience many changes. The first change they encounter is right here. We see the change in the phrase "the manna ceased." For the past forty years God had provided all the food that the children of Israel needed to eat. Every morning they would exit their tent and the ground would be covered with food, which they called manna. This is explained in further detail in Exodus 16. Every morning for 40 years the 2-3 million people of Israel found this bread-like substance on the ground. They were to gather enough food for each person for that day. The only exception to this was the Sabbath. There was no food that day, because they took two days' worth of food the day before. If anyone tried this any other day, the extra food would spoil and be full of worms. God had the Israelites in a place where they literally relied on Him for their daily food.

Now that they are in the Promised Land that is changing. No longer will they find food on the ground every morning; instead, it is already growing there in the land. God provided fields of grain and trees of fruit for the people to eat. No longer was manna needed. God has changed the way He provides for them. He does that in our life too.

In Matthew 6:11 Jesus said, "Give us this day our daily bread." God still desires for us to rely on Him daily for our provisions. Too often we find other things to rely on instead of God. We rely on our paychecks, insurance, investments, etc. We look to the grocery store and supercenters for our food instead of looking to God. We do not want to be in a position of not knowing where our food, or provisions, will come from next. We do all we can to not need to live paycheck to paycheck. Instead of trusting in God we trust in the food, toilet paper and other items we have stockpiled in our homes.

The person who desires to be used by God will often find a change in the source of their provision. Often this will be our financial income, but it is not limited to this. When this occurs, it is difficult to go through. I will not lie and tell you it isn't, because it is. But when God dries up one source, He opens another source. This is what we see God doing for the children of Israel. He also does this for His children today. When the manna stops, look up to God and He will show you the produce of the land.

Why does God do this? Because He is Jehovah-Jireh, which means "the Lord will provide." God does provide all that we need, even though He doesn't always provide it the way we expect. God is faithful, and He has promised to provide and take care of His children as long as they walk on this earth. "Listen to Me, O house of Jacob, all the remnant of the house of Israel, who have been borne by Me from before your birth, carried from the womb; even to your old age I am He, and to gray hairs I will carry you. I have made, and I will bear; I will carry and will save" (Isaiah 46:3-4).

March 17

"Through Him then let us continually offer up a sacrifice of praise to God, that is, the fruit of lips that acknowledge His name."
Hebrews 13:15

We all have times in our life when we do not feel like worshipping God. We are tired, in a bad mood, or things are not going the way that we think they should be which causes us to not feel like worshipping God. This is why we don't allow our feelings to direct us. Feelings are fickle and we need to know when to override them. Our feelings are directly tied to the circumstances of our life; when things are going well our feelings are good, but when things are not good, our feelings will be let down.

Unlike us, God does not change. God is truth and is always the same. We are not. In fact, we go through seasons and cycles in our life. We have seasons of springtime in our life when we are growing in the Lord and our understanding of Him. Things are flourishing and exciting. Spring always leads to summer, which is a time of harvest. Summer leads to fall, when it gets a bit colder, and the leaves begin to fall off the trees. After fall we will experience winter when it is cold and silent. Winter seasons are often when we do not feel like worshipping God. We might even panic and begin to think that there is something wrong with us. No, we are just human. This is why God has called us to live a life of faith, and not just by what we can see (2 Corinthians 5:7).

We are not to panic when we don't feel like worshipping God, but we can understand that we ARE still to worship Him. That is why it is called "a sacrifice of praise", because our flesh is being sacrificed and put to death. God calls us to worship Him in spirit and in truth, not to worship Him when we feel like it. God is worthy of our praise all the time, and He is pleased when we live by faith. We were created to worship God and to bring Him praise, "Worthy are You, our Lord and God, to receive glory and honor and power, for You created all things, and by Your will they existed and were created" (Revelation 4:11). We are also called to obey God, "And by this we know that we have come to know Him, if we keep His commandments. Whoever says 'I know Him' but does not keep His commandments is a liar, and the truth is not in Him, but whoever keeps His word, in Him truly the love of God is perfected. By this we may know that we are in Him" (1 John 2:3-5). As we make the choice to worship God, even if we don't feel like it, we are obeying Him. We are then making a sacrifice of praise by putting our flesh to death and choosing to praise God with the words of our mouth.

March 18

"Then they said to one another, 'In truth we are guilty concerning our brother, in that we saw the distress of his soul, when he begged us and we did not listen. That is why this distress has come upon us.'"
Genesis 42:21

Have you ever done something wrong? Of course you have; we all have. When we have done something wrong, we also end up with the same result: guilt! Since we have done something that we know is wrong, it hangs over us like a wet blanket. It is stinky and it weighs us down. This is exactly what was happening to Joseph's brothers here in Egypt. They had beaten him and dropped him into an empty well because they were jealous that their father loved him more than them. Joseph cried out to them, but they ignored his cries. Eventually they sold Joseph as a slave. Joseph was no longer in their lives, but the memory of him crying out to them remained. That the thing about guilt, it doesn't go away with time. In fact, the longer it remains with you the heavier it can get, until it completely weighs you down.

It has been over twenty years since these brothers beat Joseph, dropped him in the empty well, and then sold him into slavery. Why is it that their guilt hasn't gone away? Why is their guilt still hanging on to them? Because there is only one way to get rid of guilt, and they hadn't dealt with it yet. The only way a person can get rid of their guilt is to repent of their sin. The word repent means "to turn away from sin." When we repent of our sin, we are saying that we agree what we did was wrong. Whom do we repent to? God. It is God that we have sinned against, so it is to Him that we must repent. When we repent to God for the sin that we have committed, what we are doing is confessing to God the sin in our life. Confession is very important.

How does God respond to us when we confess our sin to Him? "If we confess our sins, He is faithful and just to forgive us our sins and to cleanse us from all unrighteousness" (1 John 1:9). Joseph's brothers had failed to confess their sin to God and ask for forgiveness. If they had, they wouldn't have been burdened with the guilt of their previous actions. Don't allow guilt to weigh you down. Repent of the sin in your life. Confess it to God (He already knows about it anyway). Then God will forgive you and you won't be burdened by guilt.

March 19

"Was not Abraham our father justified by works when he offered up his son Isaac on the altar?"
James 2:21

Abraham was an amazing man, and he did some very extraordinary things in his life. One of the most amazing things was when God called him to offer his son, Isaac, as a sacrifice (see Genesis 22). This must have seemed very puzzling to Abraham, especially since God had promised that Abraham's descendants would be as numerous as the stars in the sky (see Genesis 15:4-5). In spite of this apparent contradiction, Abraham obeyed with obedience. Since Abraham responded with obedience by offering Isaac as a sacrifice, he proved that he really did trust God. His works were proof of his faith in God. But Abraham had been justified by God much earlier in his life. We see this when God first gave His promise to Abraham. At the time God told Abraham that his descendants would be as numerous as the stars in the sky, Abraham had no children, and he was in his mid-eighties at the time. All earthly evidence suggested that God's promise was impossible, but Abram "believed the Lord, and He counted it to him as righteousness" (Genesis 15:6). Abraham's faith and his works cooperated perfectly together. If he had never believed God, then he wouldn't have followed through and done the good work of obedience when God asked him to offer Isaac as a sacrifice. His faith was shown to be true, and therefore was completed, or made perfect, by his obedient works.

Since Abraham was a man of faith, and he obediently did what God called him to do, "Abraham believed God, and it was counted to him as righteousness"—and he was called a friend of God" (James 2:23). The word "credit" is a financial term, and it refers to "putting something into one's account." Abraham was a sinner, which means that his spiritual bank account was empty. We could even say that he was a bankrupt sinner. But he trusted God, and his trust in God allowed God to put righteousness into Abraham's spiritual bank account. His faith and trust in God meant he was no longer spiritually bankrupt. The righteousness that was put into his spiritual bank account was a gift from God; he hadn't earned it, and neither did he deserve it (see Romans 4:1-3). This was true for Abraham, and it remains true today for each one of us. When we act in obedience to God because we trust Him, we also have righteousness placed into our spiritual bank accounts.

March 20

"But Joshua commanded the people, 'You shall not shout or make

your voice heard, neither shall any word go out of your mouth, until the day I tell you to shout. Then you shall shout.'"
Joshua 6:10

This is a much more difficult task for the Israelites than it seems. Whenever we are told not to do something, we want to do that one thing even more. It may not appear to be that difficult to walk around a city one time in silence, but I believe that it was.

The first day the Israelites walked around the city the inhabitants of Jericho would have been curious about what they were doing. This was a new battle plan they had never seen before. The people of Jericho would have been lining the walls watching to see what the Israelites would do, and to be prepared for battle. After watching the people walk around the city and then go back to their camp the people of Jericho were most likely left scratching their heads in wonderment. Each day they witnessed this happening I could see the people of Jericho becoming more confident and beginning to yell down insults at the Israelites. They would be putting the Israelites down and making fun of them, making rude comments, and laughing at what appeared to be a foolish plan. Each day Israelites had to keep walking in silence, they were not allowed to utter a sound. That is very difficult.

Think of your own life, when someone begins to laugh at you or make fun of you or your beliefs, it hurts. A natural reaction is to strike back with words. I see it almost every day in the lives of children. They don't like what someone said to them, so they respond by saying something back to that person. Adults, just like children, do this naturally; we must be trained not to react that way. It was the same for the Israelites. When someone said they were stupid for walking around the city, they had to keep walking in silence. When they were called a name, or questioned why they would obey these "ridiculous" instructions, they could not respond at all, but had to keep walking in silence.

Why? Why didn't God allow them to defend themselves, or even

Himself? Why couldn't the people say anything? I believe it was to teach them discipline. The children of Israel needed to learn the discipline of holding their tongue, just as we do today. If we are not able to control what comes out of our mouth, we will be dealing with and cleaning up lots of messes. To avoid that we must learn to control our mouth, and what we speak. "So also the tongue is a small member, yet it boasts of great things. How great a forest is set ablaze by such a small fire! And the tongue is a fire, a world of unrighteousness. The tongue is set among our members, staining the whole body, setting on fire the entire course of life, and set on fire by hell" (James 3:5-6). It is a wise woman or man who learns to remain silent in the middle of adversity and allow God to handle the situation. There are times when we are to defend ourselves and speak up, but not always. It is better to wait and speak than to just blurt words out. By remaining silent the children of Israel showed their faith in God to work this out. It was not necessary for them to respond and speak back to the people of Jericho. What a comforting and burden-releasing realization this can be. Trust God and allow Him to take care of whatever situation or problem you may be experiencing right now. Don't spend time grumbling and complaining, or responding back whenever someone says anything unkind towards you. God can work through your silence and accomplish much more than we ever could by speaking. I wish I could tell you that this is easy, but it isn't. It isn't easy, but it is worthwhile. Trust God, He is faithful.

March 21

"And Jacob blessed Pharaoh and went out from the presence of Pharaoh."
Genesis 47:10

The world has a hierarchical system that is recognized everywhere you go. This is true for developed nations, third world countries, and everything in between. It is not a new phenomenon, but as old as time itself. It was true here in Egypt as well. Pharaoh was considered a god, and everyone else, no matter how well off they were, was considered to be a lesser person. This would especially be true for an old, crippled sheep herder. Everywhere you go, it is the lesser who receives a blessing from the greater. The Bible supports this to, "It is beyond dispute that the inferior is blessed by the superior" (Hebrews 7:7). Again, Pharaoh was considered to be the human embodiment of Ra, the sun god, so who could be greater than him? No one! So, how is it that Jacob (Israel), this crippled, old sheep herder blesses Pharaoh? And how did Pharaoh even allow this?

Jacob's grandfather, Abraham, was given a promise from God. "And I will make of you a great nation, and I will bless you and make your name great, so that you will be a blessing. I will bless those who bless you, and him who dishonors you I will curse, and in you all the families of the earth shall be blessed" (Genesis 12:2-3). We see this happening here. Pharaoh had exalted Joseph and been blessed greatly because of it. He also extended that exaltation to Joseph's family, and he also received a blessing from Joseph's dad. Pharaoh was greatly blessed by Israel and Joseph. In fact, we could say that Joseph saved the nation of Egypt and will make her kingdom even more prosperous by the end of this chapter. Egypt was also blessed by the presence of Israel in her land.

The world may have recognized Pharaoh as being greater than Jacob, but God doesn't see them that way. Jacob was a child of God. In God's sight he was the greater of the two. Jacob was God's treasure here on earth, as is every other believer. That remains true today. A believer is God's treasure, and therefore greater than every nonbeliever. The world does not see it that way, but it is true. This doesn't mean that we as believers are to lord it over nonbelievers, but that we are to be like Jacob here; to be a blessing to others. That is what we are to be also. We are to be a blessing to others. This means our neighbors, our co-workers, our boss, those in line next to us in stores, etc. We are to bring God's blessing everywhere we go.

March 22

"Then I saw another sign in heaven, great and amazing, seven angels with seven plagues, which are the last, for with them the wrath of God is finished."
Revelation 15:1

One of the reasons many people have difficulties understanding the book of Revelation is because it is written in a Hebrew style. Instead of writing how most Americans are used to, in chronological order, the apostle John writes in a Hebrew tradition where he describes events and then in later chapters gives additional details on the events previously written about. We see this in the creation story where we are given the overview in Genesis 1, and then in Genesis 2 we are given additional details and insights of what happened. This is what we see happening in Revelation 15. John has already described the seven trumpet judgments in Revelation 8:6–Revelation 11:15. Now John goes back to these events and gives us additional information and insights into what happened at that time.

When these seven trumpets are sounded God's judgment upon a Jesus-rejecting world will occur, and His judgment and wrath will be complete. The word John uses to describes God's wrath is the Greek word *thymos*. It describes a volatile and passionate anger. It is only used 11 times in the New Testament, and 10 of those times are in the book of Revelation. God's wrath, or anger, is volatile, but it is also controlled. It is executed, and once it is finished, it is also over. This is so different from the wrath of many people. Often when we get angry, we lose control of our emotions, thought processes, and even our actions. This isn't true of God. Even when He is executing His wrath He is in complete control of His emotions, thoughts, and actions. God has given the world and its inhabitants a long time to repent of their sins and turn to Him, but they have refused to do so. At this time, they will be reaping what they have sown, the consequences of their choices. God's judgment is a consequence of choices made. It is not irrational or executed in malice. It is controlled, just, and deserved. God, being just, cannot overlook and not deal with sin. As the apostle Paul reminds us that "the wages of sin is death" (Romans 6:23). Those that refuse to humble themselves before God will receive their judgment.

March 23

"And next to them the Tekoites repaired, but their nobles would not stoop to serve their Lord."
Nehemiah 3:5

Teamwork. That is a concept that every coach in a team sport works to instill into their players. A team with superstar talent but no teamwork can be beaten by a team with much less talent if they work together. That is what is seen in chapter 3 of the book of Nehemiah. As you read through this chapter you read that everyone, except the Tekoite nobles, willingly pitched in and worked together. People were not waiting for someone else to pick up the load or wait until the highly skilled or professionals showed up. No! Every single person willingly got involved themselves. Read through the chapter and you will see who was involved in doing the work. There were priests, goldsmiths, rulers, Levites, temple servants, foreigners, gatekeepers, merchants, and every imaginable type of everyday person, including the daughters. Everyone joined in the work. This doesn't mean that every person was trained or skilled, but they were still involved. The priests were the religious leaders of the nation, they weren't trained to do construction, but they were the first ones mentioned in doing the work because they were leaders, so they led by example.

No matter what skills or training we have received, we are prepared to be involved in ministry. This doesn't mean that we will be on stage preaching the message, but we can be involved in the work that God is doing. Think of the time when the Israelites were wandering though the wilderness and they were attacked by the Amalekites (see Exodus 17). Moses was leading the nation, and Joshua was his assistant. Moses had Joshua lead the army in battle, and God instructed Moses to lift up his arms, and as long as his arms were lifted the Israelites would be winning the battle. But after a time, Moses' arms became heavy, and they would begin to fall by his side. When this occurred, the Amalekites began to win the war. Aaron and Hur were on the top of the mountain with Moses, so when they saw his arms fall they came alongside him and lifted his arms back up so the Israelite army was victorious over the Amalekites. Like Aaron and Hur, we can come alongside others and assist them, bring them encouragement, or help as is needed. Nehemiah and the people were successful in rebuilding the walls of Jerusalem because everyone chose to work alongside each other. May we follow their example and willingly work alongside others in ministry too.

March 24

"But Peter said, 'Ananias, why has Satan filled your heart to lie to the Holy Spirit and to keep back for yourself part of the proceeds of the land?'"
Acts 5:3

Peter shows that he is filled with the Holy Spirit, and the Holy Spirit has given him the gift of discernment. There is absolutely no way that Peter could know that Ananias and Sapphira lied about giving the entire amount of the proceeds without having this information supernaturally revealed to him by God. When we are walking with God, filled with the Holy Spirit, He also will give us the gift of discernment when it is needed. Without knowing all the particulars about a situation, God can give us the inside information that is not known by others so that we have a clear understanding of what is going on.

This must have crushed Ananias. Here he was expecting to be praised for his generosity and willingness to sell his personal property to help others within the church. But, instead of being praised for his holy conduct, he is rebuked by Peter. The rebuke happened because his heart was filled with Satan instead of the Holy Spirit. He was following Satan's lead, looking for the praise from men instead of giving to God with a pure heart. This doesn't mean that Ananias was "possessed" by Satan, but that he had influence and power to direct the thoughts and actions of Ananias.

Peter then announced the heart of this deception by Ananias. He lied to the Holy Spirit. The Holy Spirit wasn't duped by the actions of Ananias. He was there with them when the property was put up for sale. He was there when a price for the land was agreed upon, when the deed was signed, and the money was transferred to complete the sale. The Holy Spirit was there when the money was deposited in the bank, and He knew exactly how much money was kept back. He knew how much money the couple had agreed to give back, and how much money they gave to the church. The Holy Spirit was present when Ananias left the house that morning and kissed his wife on the cheek. The Holy Spirit walked next to Ananias all the way to the church, prodding his conscience over his actions. He was even there while he gave the money to the church and lied to Peter.

Not only is this true about Ananias, but it is also true for each one of us. You see, God knows every mundane detail of our life. We can't hide anything from Him either. This can be very scary for some people, or it should motivate us to live a life that is pleasing to God. He knows everything that we do or think, so make sure that all we do is done to His glory.

March 25

"Therefore they set taskmasters over them to afflict them with heavy burdens. They built for Pharaoh store cities, Pithom and Raamses."
Exodus 1:11

The Egyptians made the Israelites into slaves attempting to intimidate and demoralize the nation of Israel. As slaves it would be much more difficult for them to achieve control of the nation, and at the same time, they would be used to strengthen the nation economically, and structurally. Egypt used the Israelite slave labor to build the storage cities of Pithom and Raamses, and historians tell us they also tended the fields surrounding these cities, in addition to digging canals. The Israelites were slaves doing both construction and farming to benefit the Egyptian people. The fact that this happened shouldn't be a surprise though since God prophesied this to Abraham in Genesis 15:13-14.

Why would Pharaoh and the Egyptians even want to turn the Israelites into slaves? After all, the Israelites weren't causing any trouble, and they were actually a blessing to the people of Egypt and their land. But they were foreigners, and because they were growing into such a large group of people, they were now considered to be a security risk. The Egyptians were afraid that the Israelites would either overrun their country or align with an enemy to destroy them. At least, this was the reason the Pharaoh and Egyptian leaders gave for their mistreatment of Israel, but there was a deeper reason for this. Whether or not Pharaoh even knew the real reason, it was a spiritual reason. We find the reason in Genesis 3:15, where God says, "I will put enmity between you and the woman, and between your offspring and her offspring." In other words, this was a conflict between the people of God and the people of Satan. This conflict continues to this very day. No nation in the world has ever suffered as much as the children of Israel have since the world began. God's promise to Abraham was "I will bless those who bless you, and him who dishonors you I will curse" (Genesis 12:3). God has kept this promise throughout the history of the world. Egypt and Babylon both mistreated Israel, and those nations received God's judgment for their actions. Even much more recently we have seen this same thing happen to Hitler's Germany and Stalin's Russia. God doesn't forget His promises, and nations that decide to persecute God's chosen nation will eventually be judged and punished for their actions. This promise still holds true today!

March 26

"Therefore, preparing your minds for action, and being sober-minded, set your hope fully on the grace that will be brought to you at the revelation of Jesus Christ."
1 Peter 1:13

Peter has reminded us of the importance of us living a life that is disciplined and balanced. While God has filled the pages of the Bible with promises of Jesus' Second Coming and events of the end times, that cannot be our only focus. We need to keep a balanced view and study of the Bible. This is because of our hope is not in the end times of even Jesus' Second Coming. What is our hope to be in? Peter tells us that our hope is in the grace that God so graciously gives to us. Reading through this letter from Peter we see how much God's grace impacted Peter's life. Peter began this letter with God's grace (1 Peter 1:2), then continued with how the prophets of the Old Testament prophesied about God's grace through Jesus (1 Peter 1:10). Now, Peter goes even further by telling us the grace that we receive when we realized and understood who Jesus is. It is God's grace that our hope rests upon. This begs the question, what is grace? Grace is the unmerited favor that God gives to us. We don't deserve it. In fact, instead of receiving what we deserve, God gives us not only what we don't deserve, but He gives good to us.

Grace is not just what God gave to us when we first surrendered our lives to him, and neither is it just for our life today. Now, it is both of those things. In fact, without God's grace we wouldn't be able to survive. God's grace is what allows us to stand and live in faith (see Romans 5:2). But grace is also about our future, and this is why it is on grace that our hope lies. Peter has been letting us know that Jesus is going to return to earth and bring His children back home to Heaven with Him. That is grace, since none of us deserve or can earn this wonderful blessing of spending eternity in Heaven with God. That future grace is not only promised to us, but we can rest assured that it is going to happen. This is our hope, it is what we live for and look forward to. It also means that we live with an eye to the future, since that is where our hope is. Think of a couple that is engaged to be married. All the plans that they are making is made with the thought and consideration of their upcoming wedding. We, as believers, are called to live in anticipation and expectation of Jesus coming to bring us home to Heaven with Him. That is the grace that our hope lies in, and what a glorious day that is going to be.

March 27

"The Lord said to Cain, 'Why are you angry, and why has your face fallen?'"
Genesis 4:6

Here we have a great picture of God's grace as He approaches Cain. As our Father God knows the inner workings of our heart, and He loves Cain too much to let him simmer and stew in his anger. God is lovingly confronting Cain and letting him know that he is not being rejected, there is still hope for him. God approaches Cain in a similar way as He approached Adam and Eve in the garden. He asks questions, not because He doesn't know the answers, but because He is allowing Cain an opportunity to confess his sin and let go of his anger.

We also see much wisdom in parenting by how God approached Cain. He could have compared him to Abel and asked why he wasn't more like his brother. This is easy to do, and too often parents do this. God did not do this. Instead, God pointed Cain back to the standard set by God, not his brother Abel. God brings him back to truth.

God does not condemn Cain for being angry, as some commentators do today. Anger is a God-given emotion and is not necessarily sin. In fact, the apostle Paul wrote "be angry and do not sin." There are times when it is ok to be angry. The important thing is the cause of the anger. In Mark 3 Jesus was angry. He was angry with the Pharisees because they were more concerned with keeping their man-made laws about working on the Sabbath than they were over the health of a man. In verse 5 of Mark 3 it says that Jesus "looked around at them with anger, grieved at their hardness of heart." Jesus' anger was over their insensitivity towards their fellow man, and this also caused Him sorrow. They held their rules in higher standing than the wellbeing of a person, and Jesus was angry. We see many injustices in the world today, and we are right to be angry over them. When we see innocent, unborn children being murdered inside the womb we have every right and reason to be angry. When we see the sanctity of an animal's life being held up as more important than a human's life, we have every right to be angry. But we also need to remember that Jesus was filled with sorrow. He became angry, but He did not attack the Pharisees. He healed the man with the withered hand. This is why Paul wrote to be angry, but do not sin. When we begin to attack those causing injustice, then that is when we sin. Righteous anger is ok, but all too often we become angry when we don't get our way, or when we are interrupted. We become angry because of our selfishness. That anger is sin.

March 28

"And the jailer called for lights and rushed in, and trembling with fear he fell down before Paul and Silas. Then he brought them out and said, 'Sirs, what must I do to be saved?' And they said, 'Believe in the Lord Jesus, and you will be saved, you and your household.'"
Acts 16:29-31

When the jailer verifies that it is true that none of the prisoners have escaped, he fell down before Paul and Silas, and he is trembling all over. He is overcome with emotion. He knew that they were in jail because of their preaching the gospel, so he asks them "what must I do to be saved?" He saw how different Paul and Silas were and wanted to be like them.

Paul and Silas gladly shared the gospel with this man. They simply told him that he needed to believe in Jesus and then he would be saved. This is the essence of the gospel; we are saved by God grace, and that is given through faith in Jesus Christ. There is nothing else that needs to be added to it; not the law, not works, nothing! We are saved by faith alone!

There are those who question this. Often, they will bring up a passage like James 2:26, which says: "For as the body apart from the spirit is dead, so also faith apart from works is dead." Does this mean the Bible contradicts itself? Does this mean that a person is saved by their works? No!, neither of those questions is correct. If they were, then Jesus is a liar. You see, Jesus told one of the thieves that hung on a cross next to Him, that "Truly, I say to you, today you will be with Me in paradise" (Luke 23:43). How could that be? This man had never done any good works, he hadn't been baptized, and he definitely never obeyed the Law (or Torah). How could Jesus say that he was saved and would be in Heaven? Jesus said that because the man believed in Jesus; he was saved by faith.

Then why is James saying that "faith without works is dead"?

James says that, not because a person can earn their faith through their works, but because a person's works are evidence of their faith. When a person surrenders their life to Jesus, through faith, God changes them from the inside out. That change is evident through the works of their life. They are not justified, or saved, by their works, but those works are proof of them being saved. In other words, works and faith don't contradict each other, they complement each other. Your works are a complement to your saving faith.

March 29

"You shall not steal."
Exodus 20:15

The eighth commandment prohibits stealing. To steal is simply to take and keep something that is not yours because it belongs to someone else. What this does is establish the right to personal property. This is an important part of the foundation of society. God has given people the right to possess things, and other people, or the government, are not allowed to take it away from them without the due process of law. Even though stealing is wrong, many people have no conscious problem stealing. This was clearly seen during a two-week long garbage strike in New York City. People's garbage was piling up since the garbage workers were out on strike, so one man put all his garbage in a box, wrapped it in nice wrapping paper, and then left it on the front seat of his car while he was at work. Every day he came back to his car and the package of garbage was gone.

Stealing is wrong. Why do people steal? Oftentimes it's because people are lazy and want to get something without having to work for it. That's not the right way to do it. In Ephesians 4:28 the apostle Paul says, "The thief must no longer steal. Instead, he must do honest work with his own hands, so that he has something to share with anyone in need." Stealing is wrong. If we want to have something, there are only two correct ways to get it: work for it or be blessed by someone giving it to you. Don't steal it.

It is possible for us to steal in many different ways than just taking the personal possessions of someone else. Not paying your taxes is stealing. Creative write-offs is also stealing. You can also steal from your employer by not doing your job or extending breaks. That is stealing just as much as taking home office supplies from work. Where did you get that box of paper clips? You can also steal from God. God blesses and trusts us with money, but if we hold it back from Him then we are stealing from Him. "Will man rob God? Yet you are robbing Me. But you say, 'How have we robbed you?' In your tithes and contributions" (Malachi 3:8). But it isn't just with money that we can be guilty of robbing God. We also rob God when we refuse to obey Him and completely give our lives to Him. We need to remember that "you were ransomed from the futile ways inherited from your forefathers, not with perishable things such as silver or gold, but with the precious blood of Christ..." (1 Peter 1:18-19). That means that we belong to God, because "you were bought with a price. So glorify God in your body" (1 Corinthians 6:20).

March 30

"...aspire to live quietly, and to mind your own affairs, and to work with your hands, as we instructed you, so that you may walk properly before outsiders and be dependent on no one."
1 Thessalonians 4:11-12

I read an article in which the author made the comment that too many young people today have the goal of being famous instead of being good at what they do. This happens all the time. Fame and fortune is the goal of many people today; both young and old. There are not enough people who care about what they do and try to be the best they can be at what they do.

Too often today people do not put enough emphasis on how they do their job, but they are concerned with being recognized by others for what they do. Instead of doing a good job because that is what God calls us to, the motivation for too many is to receive awards or recognition for what has been done. So instead of quality being accomplished, we have people striving to receive an Oscar, a Grammy, an Emmy, a Tony, or a Golden Globe. Being recognized for the work you have done is nice, but it is more important to be faithful to your work and doing it the best of your ability, whether you are recognized for it or not.

Jesus understands this. Jesus did not begin His earthly ministry until He was approximately 30 years old. Prior to entering the ministry, Jesus labored as a carpenter. According to the Christian apologist Justin Martyr, the farm plows that Jesus crafted were still being used in the second century; or over 100 years after He made them. That is good, quality work. No one recognized Him for what He did; He just focused on doing the best work He could do. Many people would consider manual labor as not being as important as spiritual work. Feeding 5000 men with a few fish and loaves of bread, raising the dead back to life, preaching to large groups of people, or healing the lame and sick are much more important than crafting plows for a farmer. Are we sure about that? Before Jesus performed any of His spiritual works or miracles, He spent many years crafting plows and yokes for farmers. He did the very best that He could, and God said He was well pleased with Jesus. Theologian Os Guinness commented on this in his book *The Call* when he wrote, "How intriguing to think of Jesus' plow rather than His cross – to wonder what it was that made His plows and yokes last and stand out." What made them last was quality. As Christians we need to ask ourselves what kind of work we are doing, and will it last? "Whatever you do, work heartily, as for the Lord and not for men" (Colossians 3:23).

March 31

"Then Jacob became angry and berated Laban. Jacob said to Laban, 'What is my offense? What is my sin, that you have hotly pursued me?... If the God of my father, the God of Abraham and the Fear of Isaac, had not been on my side, surely now you would have sent me away empty-handed. God saw my affliction and the labor of my hands and rebuked you last night.'"
Genesis 31:36, 42

Watching Laban search through all his family's belongings was too much for Jacob. Twenty years of pent-up frustration finally came to a head, and he spoke his true feelings from the heart. Jacob reminded Laban how faithfully he had served him these past twenty years, unlike how Laban had treated him.

Jacob had dealt so honestly with Laban, that if Laban lost a sheep to a wild animal, Jacob replaced that animal out of his own pocket. He didn't have to do that; losing a sheep or a goat to a wild animal was a hazard of the job, but Jacob reminds Laban that he did this so he can see how honest and faithful Jacob has been towards him.

Laban, on the other hand, had consistently mistreated and deceived Jacob, dealing with him in a very underhanded manner. In addition to those serious charges, Laban had even changed and altered Jacob's wages. Laban had dealt wrongly with Jacob, and if God hadn't intervened by speaking to him in a dream, he would be doing so again.

God has been very good to Jacob, even when Laban hadn't been. Jacob didn't deserve the blessing God had given him, but God did it because He had made a promise to Jacob twenty years earlier at Bethel. God is faithful and will always do what He has promised to do.

This has not changed. We may be mistreated and taken advantage of by the world. Yet, God continues to bless us. He watches over us and protects us because we are His children. The problems and setbacks we deal with have all been filtered by God, and they are allowed into our lives in order to shape us, mold us, and perfect us. God has not changed; He continues to take care of His children and fulfill His promises, and He will until He brings us home to Heaven to be spend eternity with Him.

April 1

"Count it all joy, my brothers, when you meet trials of various kinds..."
James 1:2

James writes very practically. The first thing he addresses in his letter is how we are to respond to trials. Most of us would admit that trials are not something we are fond of. In fact, I would dare say that most people would even say that they hate trials. James doesn't tell us to hate trials. How he tells us we are to respond to trials is completely opposite. James says that we are to "count it all joy." The word "count" is a financial term, and it means "to evaluate." The apostle Paul used this term many times in Philippians 3 to show the change in his life after he became a believer. As a new believer, Paul looked at the goals and priorities of his life, and he evaluated them now as a believer. Since he was a "new creation" (see 2 Corinthians 5:7), he now had new goals and priorities in his life. The things that were once important to him, he now considered those things to be worthless, or "garbage," because of his experience with Jesus Christ. James is telling us that when we face a trial in life, we need to evaluate it by what God is doing in our life. Then we can face it with joy.

The reason we can see trials with joy is due to our value system. Our values will determine how we evaluate things. If comfort is the most valuable thing to us, then trials will upset us. If we value character as important, then we can evaluate a trial with joy because of how this trial can cause us to grow. If we value the material and physical over the spiritual, then we will not be able to evaluate a trial with joy.

James knows that each one of us will experience trials in our life, that is why he wrote "when" and not "if" you experience trials. Trials are inevitable. God doesn't allow us to experience trials because He's mad at us, or because He doesn't like us. God's purpose in trials is not to destroy us, but to make us stronger. When we go through a trial, we realize how weak we really are. Our weakness will drive us towards God, so we can then see how strong He really is. This is why God will even deliberately allow you to get to your breaking point, so you will reach the end of yourself and realize your need and dependence upon God and His inexhaustible supplies. When we stop trusting in ourselves and our own resources, then we can learn to trust in God. He is not limited as we are. Trust Him.

April 2

"In those days there was no king in Israel. Everyone did what was right in his own eyes."
Judges 21:25

The book of Judges shows the inherent sinfulness in man. We do not need others to lead us astray; we naturally will go there on our own. It is so easy for us to blame others when we get into trouble, but the truth is we bring it on ourselves through the choices we make. I see this very often through children. When they are caught doing something wrong, their first response is to blame someone else for what they did. As adults we are no different. Even though we make the choice to do wrong, we try to blame others for what we have done.

Eight times in the book of Judges we see the phrase that "the children of Israel did evil in the sight of the LORD." Twice we see the phrase "everyone did what was right in his own eyes." How did this happen? Throughout the book of Judges, we see the people calling out to God and trusting in Him when things were difficult, or bad, in their life. After a while things were going well and they began to not rely on God any longer and began to think they had things under control. God's Word no longer was their basis for right or wrong; the people of Israel did not follow God's Word, but their own heart instead.

When we get to the point of thinking we have things under control and no longer need God, we are inviting trouble into our lives. Trust God more than your heart. God will not mislead you, but your heart will. Make sure that the choices you make are based on the truth and not your heart's desires. For that to happen we need to follow the truth. Truth does not change, and it is found in God's Word, the Bible. "All Scripture is breathed out by God and profitable for teaching, for reproof, for correction, and for training in righteousness, that the man of God may be complete, equipped for every good work" (2 Timothy 3:16-17). Make sure that God's Word is what you are following, that it is the basis for your choices and decisions, and not your heart. Your heart will mislead you, but God will never do that.

April 3

"But Moses said to God, 'Who am I that I should go to Pharaoh and bring the children of Israel out of Egypt?'"
Exodus 3:11

This is utterly amazing. God has spoken to Moses and told him that he is going to be God's tool in delivering the Israelites from their slavery in Egypt. How does Moses respond to this? Moses questions God's choice because he doesn't believe that he is the right choice. But it doesn't matter what Moses thinks about himself, or even what others think of Moses. All that matters is what God thinks, and God said that Moses is the person He has chosen.

We have what he said recorded for us, but what we don't have is how he said it. The way he answered God really determines whether what he said was valid or not. Wouldn't it be nice to have an audio recording of this conversation? It could be that Moses questions God's decision – directly to Him! Whoa! I realize that God says we are to come to Him with boldness (see Hebrews 4:16), but this is way beyond bold; it borders on arrogance.

But it also could be that Moses' arrogance had been broken; it all depends on the tone Moses used. Forty years earlier Moses thought he knew who he was: a prince of Egypt, a Hebrew, and the one that God was going to use to deliver Israel from their bondage. Now, after forty years of chasing sheep around the desert, that arrogant confidence is gone. Moses has been broken and humbled. If Moses was still the same way he was forty years earlier, he would have probably responded by saying something like, "It's about time You've called me to deliver Israel." The experiences of the past forty years have changed that. Instead of being brash, arrogant, and self-confident, Moses is now humble and broken. In other words, Moses is now prepared to be used by God.

All too often people today aren't used by God because they're not properly prepared. Many people are too strong for God to use them. That sounds strange, doesn't it? Worldly convention says you need to be strong to be used, but in the spiritual kingdom, being strong will keep God from using you. The apostle Paul understood this, which is why he reminded us that "when I am weak, then I am strong" (2 Corinthians 12:10). Both Moses and Paul understood that God can do amazing things through a vessel that is weak, and He does. He did with Moses, and He can do through you too.

April 4

"So Peter opened his mouth and said: "Truly I understand that God shows no partiality...""
Acts 10:34

Peter lays down the foundation of truth from God, which is completely contrary to the prevailing Jewish thought and practices. The truth is that "God doesn't show partiality." Was this a new thought? No! God said to Moses, "For the Lord your God is God of gods and Lord of lords, the great, the mighty, and the awesome God, who is not partial and takes no bribe" (Deuteronomy 10:17). God even repeated this to King Jehoshaphat in 2 Chronicles 19:7. So this wasn't anything new, except in practice. Over the centuries, through practice and teaching, the Jews had become nationalistically prideful and prejudiced against Gentiles. This drew a sharp line of contrasts between both groups. This wasn't God's heart, God's plan, or even His design. It came from the sinful hearts of men.

Through his earlier vision and the events that followed, Peter has finally realized that God doesn't look at or respond to people like we do. We respond to people based upon their nationality, their position, their possessions, their abilities, or their power. God doesn't do that. God doesn't look more favorably at a Jew than a Gentile. The apostle Paul admitted this when he wrote that in Christ "there is neither Jew nor Greek, there is neither slave nor free, there is no male and female, for you are all one in Christ Jesus" (Galatians 3:28 and Colossians 3:11). That is why there is only one thing that God looks at. It's not nationality (or ethnicity); it's the heart. What God looks at, and what concerns God has absolutely nothing to do with the "outside" of a person; it all has to do with what's "inside," their heart. God showed this to the prophet Samuel, when He said, "Do not look on his appearance or on the height of his stature, because I have rejected him. For the Lord sees not as man sees: man looks on the outward appearance, but the LORD looks on the heart" (1 Samuel 16:7).

This is why it is so important for us to commit our hearts to God, each and every day. We don't want our hearts to be distracted by earthly things or led away from God by other desires. May we instead make a daily commitment of our hearts to God!

April 5

"Then Joseph could not control himself before all those who stood by him. He cried, 'Make everyone go out from me.' So no one stayed with him when Joseph made himself known to his brothers. And he wept aloud, so that the Egyptians heard it, and the household of Pharaoh heard it."
Genesis 45:1-2

Joseph shows a great amount of restraint here as he sends everyone out of the room except for himself and his eleven brothers. He is understandably very emotional after all the difficult times he has experienced and dealt with the past years. He was rejected by these same brothers and sold as a slave. He was falsely accused of rape, sentenced to jail, and spent many years in jail. All this suffering was needless. It would be completely understandable for him to be filled with anger at his brothers for what they forced upon him. I know that I would be filled with anger if I was in his shoes. Anger isn't something new; it was just as common then as it is now. While anger is common, it is neither healthy nor beneficial. Holding on to anger can cause both physical and emotional damage. Ulcers, high blood pressure, heart problems, and emotional issues can all be caused by anger. The reality is that anger is really a disease. The good news is that just like other diseases, there is a cure.

The cure for anger is forgiveness. When we forgive a person, it means that we release, or set free, that person from the wrongs or injustices that have been done to us. This is what Joseph does. He had good reasons to be angry with his brothers. But he was able to recognize that God's hand was on his life, including the injustice that his brothers heaped on him. Joseph realized that God allowed those injustices to happen for a reason, which allowed him to forgive his brothers. Now, it is much easier to say, "you're forgiven," than it is to forgive. For Joseph this was really emotional. This is why he sent everyone that wasn't family out of the room. He was emotionally overcome, and the tears that he cried were real, and really loud. Forgiveness isn't easy, but it is worth it. Instead of Joseph being estranged from his brothers, he is about to be reconciled with them because he is willing to forgive them. Without forgiveness, reconciliation would not be possible. Who has done you wrong? Are you angry at them? Are you holding on to that anger? Follow the example of Joseph. Give it to God. Release them from the wrong they have done and forgive them. Reconciliation is so much better than estrangement.

April 6

"But it displeased Jonah exceedingly, and he was angry."
Jonah 4:1

This is a very strange response to God's mercy. After preaching a message to the people of Nineveh, they responded by repenting of their sin, and God forgave them. Generally, when a congregation repents of their sin, the preacher that God used is the most excited person around. That's not the case with Jonah. Instead of being excited, he is angry. The Hebrew word for "displeased" is very strong; it speaks of causing trembling, or shivering, due to aroused passion. Jonah wasn't just bummed that the people of Nineveh responded with repentance to his message and received God's grace. No! He was trembling with anger because they heard his message, repented, and God forgave them. His preaching was successful, and this bothered him tremendously. Why was Jonah so bothered by this?

The reason why Jonah was so angry is because of the idolatry in his life. Jonah had an idol in his life that he worshipped: himself. Jonah had this ideology in his head about how wicked and evil the Ninevites, and all Assyrians, were. They were wicked, cruel, barbaric people, and enemies of Israel, God's chosen people. Therefore, they deserved to be punished, even destroyed, by God. God failed to act the way that Jonah believed He should, and this is why Jonah was so angry. Jonah clung to his predisposed presupposition that Yahweh, God, was the exclusive God of Israel, and no other nation. Jonah's theology revolved around this idea of God being exclusive to Israel, and he wasn't willing to see God any other way. Jonah had an iron will, and he wasn't going to let anyone, or anything, change his theology; not even God Himself.

We need to make sure that we don't make the same mistake that Jonah did. We need to make sure that our views and theologies of God are consistent with God's Word, the Bible, and not our own thoughts and views. Too many people in America have the idea that God is American and refuse to accept God's will when it infringes upon their "American Dream." As believers, we need to be sensitive to God and His Word; ready to humble ourselves before Him and surrendering our own preconceived thoughts and notions to God. Don't hold on to them but allow God to change them so we are lined up with God and His Word.

April 7

"But Moses said to the LORD, 'Behold, I am of uncircumcised lips.
How will Pharaoh listen to me?'"
Exodus 6:30

God has already told Moses to go speak to Pharaoh, but that visit didn't go so well. In fact, the plight and work of the Israelites was increased because of his previous visit to Pharaoh. Because of this previous experience, Moses is reluctant to move forward in obedience. So, God reminds Moses of what his calling is; he is to go speak to Pharaoh and tell him to let Israel go. Notice, God even reminds Moses that the reason he is supposed to be obeying is because God is "the LORD," or Yahweh. This isn't just some random person speaking to Moses, it is God Himself; the One who spoke all creation into existence.

Notice Moses' response to God, he again makes excuses as to why he isn't being obedient. Yes, his task is not a pleasant one, and he has met quite a bit of resistance, but that is not a good reason to stop obeying. Moses says that the reason he can't go speak to Pharaoh is because of his "uncircumcised lips." What he means by this can be taken one of two ways. Number one, Moses is again immobilized because he thinks he has a speech impediment, or, number two, Moses realizes what a sinful man he is, and that makes him unworthy to be used by God. This second view would be similar to Isaiah's response to God after he was had seen a vision of God. Isaiah's response was, "Woe is me! For I am lost; for I am a man of unclean lips, and I dwell in the midst of a people of unclean lips; for my eyes have seen the King, the LORD of hosts!" (Isaiah 6:5). Moses may have felt like Isaiah did, knowing that the "center" of his sin was in his lips, that he wouldn't be able to speak and communicate in a way that would bring glory and honor to God. Here is the problem with this, that way of thinking is focused on himself, not God. God was more than able to overcome any of Moses or Isaiah's shortcomings, and in spite of themselves, God was able to use them to fulfill His plans and to bring both glory and honor to His Name. That is true for Moses and Isaiah, and it remains true for you and me today. No matter what shortcoming or imperfections we have, whether real or imagined, God can overcome them and use us for His glory. Don't limit God by focusing on yourself.

April 8

"But his servants came near and said to him, 'My father, it is a great word the prophet has spoken to you; will you not do it? Has he actually said to you, "Wash, and be clean"?' So he went down and dipped himself seven times in the Jordan, according to the word of the man of God, and his flesh was restored like the flesh of a little child, and he was clean."
2 Kings 5:13-14

Naaman was a commander in the Syrian army who had a skin disease, commonly believed to be leprosy. His wife had a Jewish servant girl who referred him to go see the prophet Elisha because she knew he was a prophet of God. Naaman was desperate to be healed and received permission from his king to go to this prophet in search of healing. Naaman was a leader in the nation and was accustomed to having people serve him. So, when he arrived at the home of Elisha, he was very upset when Elisha wouldn't even come greet him at the door. Instead, Elisha sent a servant to instruct him to dip himself into the Jordan River seven times, and then he would be healed. This was not what Naaman was expecting. The Jordan River was a dirty river, and not near as nice as the rivers back home. Naaman told his servant he would happily do this at a nicer river back in his home country.

We often can be like Naaman. We have a picture in our mind of the things we will do for God, and they are always great and wonderful things. Then when we are called to do something that no one else will even know about, we wonder if that is really God leading us. God calls us to be obedient to Him, and His calling can be humbling. Naaman struggled with this. He didn't want to go to the dirty Jordan River. God will lead us to places that are not understood by others and we may be embarrassed by where we are because it is not socially prominent or expected. In short, God will humble us in order to lead us to be obedient to Him. He does this because He seeks people who are obedient to Him. When we obey Him, He has great rewards in store for us. When Naaman obeyed he was healed.

God does not only call great people to spread His gospel to others. God is looking for people who will obey Him. His leading will not always make sense at the moment, but there is a purpose to it. In Acts 8 God called Philip to leave his thriving ministry in Samaria and to go to the desert in Gaza. Why? This made no sense at all. God had a reason and a purpose though, as Philip explained the gospel to an Ethiopian government official who accepted Jesus as His Savior and took the gospel to Ethiopia with him. Wow! Philip was obedient in a small and seemingly insignificant action, but it led to phenomenal results. That is the power of obedience. That is what God desires from each of us.

April 9

"And he carried me away in the Spirit into a wilderness, and I saw a woman sitting on a scarlet beast that was full of blasphemous names, and it had seven heads and ten horns. The woman was arrayed in purple and scarlet, and adorned with gold and jewels and pearls, holding in her hand a golden cup full of abominations and the impurities of her sexual immorality."

Revelation 17:3-4

The apostle John is carried away in the Spirit to a desert, which is an appropriate place for the vision of judgement that he is going to receive. The first thing John sees is a woman sitting astride this scarlet beast that has seven heads and ten horns. Of course, we have already seen this in Revelation 13:1, that this is the Antichrist and his dictatorship.

Who is this woman? She is organized religion. The fact that she is riding the beast shows that she has a dominant role, and she has at least some outward control of the beast. A second aspect of her riding the beast shows that she is also supported by the political power of the beast. The fact that she is covered with purple and scarlet clothing, and wearing gold, precious stones, and pearls, along with a gold cup in her hand, shows that the false religious system is not lacking for material wealth. Purple and scarlet are colors of nobility, royalty, and luxury (see 2 Samuel 1:24). It is also the color associated with sin and blood; "though your sins are like scarlet, they shall be as white as snow; though they are red like crimson, they shall become like wool" (Isaiah 1:18).

The Antichrist will arrogantly have others worship him, taking for himself names that only God is worthy of. These are some of the blasphemies that he will commit. He will blaspheme God through both his actions and words. People will worship him; he will be surrounded by earthly wealth and luxury. Everything will seem to be going will for him, at least until he receives God's judgment. This is a reminder for us. Be aware of the wealth and luxury that the world offers. It may appear to be inviting and even intoxicating for those who have taken a hold of it. But remember, it won't last. It isn't built on the truth of God or His Word, and it will lead to destruction.

April 10

"Issachar is a strong donkey, crouching between the sheepfolds. He saw that a resting place was good, and that the land was pleasant, so he bowed his shoulder to bear, and became a servant at forced labor."
Genesis 49:14-15

It is important that when we read the Bible that we don't interpret it through our 21st Century mind and ideas. The meanings of words and phrases often have completely different meanings today. For instance, here we have Jacob prophesying over his sons, and he calls one of his sons and his descendants' donkeys. What! Today, if you call someone a donkey you are putting them down with an insult. That is not a kind thing to call someone else. But Jacob was not insulting his son, nor was he putting him down. By calling him and his descendants' donkeys, he was prophesying two different facts about them.

The first fact is that a donkey is not their own boss. A donkey always works for someone else. Donkeys are animals, and they provide work for their owner. Historically this was also true of the tribe of Issachar. According to Numbers 26 they were the third largest tribe in Israel, and because of their size they were often the target of foreign countries when they invaded Israel to subdue and conquer them. In addition, the land they lived on was just south of the Sea of Galilee at the eastern end of the fertile Jezreel Valley. This area has often been referred to as the breadbasket of Israel due to the large amounts of crops that are grown there, even to this day. So, due to their size and the fertile ground that they worked diligently caused them to become the targets of invading foreign armies, which caused them to work and labor for others, like a donkey.

The second fact about donkeys is that they are a beast of burden; an animal that is known for its hard work. Work is often a word that many people think of as a dirty four-letter word, but it's not. God created us to work. All too often people are content to sit at home on their butts and receive some sort of government assistance. That's a travesty. Work is not a dirty word. In fact, God created Adam to work, and gave him work to do while he was in the Garden of Eden, even before sin (see Genesis 2:15). As believers we should follow this example and be hard workers. When the world looks at the life of a believer, they should see us being hard workers. The tribe of Issachar provides us with a great example to follow.

April 11

"So Philip ran to him and heard him reading Isaiah the prophet and

asked, 'Do you understand what you are reading?' And he said, 'How can I, unless someone guides me?' And he invited Philip to come up and sit with him."
Acts 8:30-31

Notice the enthusiasm of Philip. He doesn't yell after this man or just casually ask him a question. No! Philip ran to him. He eagerly obeyed God.

Since Philip had earlier responded to the Holy Spirit's leading, even though the directions weren't clear (see Acts 8:26), as he saw this man and heard him reading from the Scriptures, Philip clearly recognized this opportunity to share the Good News about Jesus. Now Philip saw the reason for his coming to this desert road. God cared about this Ethiopian man's soul, and He sent Philip to minister to him.

God wouldn't have sent Philip to this man without good reason. God knew this man was prepared to hear the Good News about Jesus. Philip recognized that God had presented him with an open door to share the Gospel, and he ran to that door while it remained open. Philip is an example to us of what we need to do. We need to be praying to God for open doors to share about Him, and then being sensitive to the leading of the Holy Spirit to recognize when an open door is presented to us for us to go through.

Philip asks this man if he understands what he is reading. He can read the manuscript with no problem, but he doesn't understand its message. He willingly admits to Philip that he needs help understanding what he's reading. This man has the correct attitude. There is absolutely nothing wrong with admitting that we don't understand something in Scripture. We need to be willing to do the same thing, and then look for someone to help us gain understanding. That's what's happening here.

This does bring up a good question. How do we get more understanding from our own reading of the Bible? To receive any understanding from the Bible, we have to plunge in. Butterflies wander over all the beautiful flowers in a garden without accomplishing anything. But bees plunge down into the flower, and they come away with essential food. We need to be like a bee; plunging into God's Word so we can come away with essential food and to be nourished by it.

April 12

"Be subject for the Lord's sake to every human institution."
1 Peter 2:13a

Submission is a word that many people have a difficult time with. Oftentimes people understand it to mean that they are beneath, or inferior, to whomever or whatever it is that they are in submission to. Sadly, that is how some people expect it to be followed, but it is not the true definition of the word. The word submission means "to rank under." It has to do with authority, not inferiority or superiority. When a person is in submission it means that they realize that there are proper levels of authority and that there are levels of authority above themselves. God has created and established levels of authority in society, the home, and the church. As a believer, it is important that we not only acknowledge, but follow and submit to the levels of authority that God has established.

Today it has become popular for people to defiantly disregard the authority of the government. It is important for us to realize that Peter is reminding us of the importance of submitting to the levels of authority in government, but not necessarily obeying every single law that has been passed by our government. It is possible for a person to submit to the government while disobeying that same governments' laws. For instance, Daniel and his three friends refused to follow the government's dietary laws, but they disobeyed in such a way that they still honored the king and showed respect to the government (see Daniel 1). As Peter is writing this, no doubt he remembers when he and his fellow apostles were in a similar position. The religious authorities had commanded that the apostles stop preaching in the name of Jesus. How did they respond? Did they argue about their rights? Did they protest and riot because they were being mistreated? No! They submitted themselves to the authority of the counsel but refused to stop preaching in the name of Jesus. "Whether it is right in the sight of God to listen to you rather than to God, you must judge, for we cannot but speak of what we have seen and heard" (Acts 4:19-20). There will be times when we, as believers, will be faced with situations like this. It is important for us to submit to the office, even if it is not possible for us to obey their laws. Cooperate as much as possible, but not if the law causes a person to violate of disobey God's Word.

April 13

"Do not love the world or the things in the world. If anyone loves the world, the love of the Father is not in him. For all that is in the world —the desires of the flesh and the desires of the eyes and pride of life —is not from the Father but is from the world. And the world is passing away along with its desires, but whoever does the will of God abides forever."

1 John 2:15-17

Our culture is defined by seeking pleasure. It is built on the concept of wanting more and more. Unfortunately, it also is designed to take our eyes off of God, and to place them on ourselves in our quest to satisfy our fleshly desires. Jesus said, "No one who puts his hand to the plow and looks back is fit for the kingdom of God" (Luke 9:62). This is the same tactic the devil used when Jesus was tempted in the desert (see Matthew 4:1-11).

I received a letter from some very good friends of mine who were missionaries in Africa. They sold everything they had to answer

God's call on them to be missionaries to Africa. Here is an excerpt of what they wrote:

"Baja Fresh, Del Taco, McDonald's, Domino's Pizza, Chipotle, Red Robin, Subway, Starbucks, Target, Wal-Mart. It troubles me that this is what comes to my mind when thinking about America. The delicious foods, the abundance of "things" at our fingertips, and everything that the world has to offer, "super-sized... There is almost too much selection, too many choices. In Africa, you eat to live, not live to eat. Style and fashion are no consideration when dressing for the day. God provides your daily bread, not a month's groceries, and you praise Him for it. I pray for contentment like that for my own country this holiday season... I wonder what it would be like for us Americans to experience life, and trust in the Lord for our daily needs, the way that the believers do where I live."

That is my prayer too. I do not want to be consumed with the lust of the flesh, the lust of the eyes and the pride of life; consumed with having more and more of this world and looking and being just like the world. May we keep our eyes on Jesus instead of the things of this earth. Trust in Him and stop craving, running after, and trying to keep up with acquiring more and more things.

April 14

"For to this you have been called, because Christ also suffered for you, leaving you an example, so that you might follow in his steps."
1 Peter 2:21

One of the most effective ways that we learn is through a process called modeling. A definition of modeling is "the acquisition of a new skill by observing and imitating that behavior being performed by another individual." Learning how to do something by observing another person doing it helps people learn, see, and understand how to do something they have never done before. Another word for this is "example." That's what Peter is talking about. Being an example for others to learn from, and to imitate in their own life. The Greek word Peter uses for example is *hupogrammos*, which is the combination of two Greek words, under and writing. This is how children learn. When a child is learning to write, they use pages that have the letters they are learning outlined on the paper for them, and they trace over those letters to learn how to write that particular letter. There is an example for them to follow, and they copy what is already on the page as closely as possible. Follow the example.

We also have an example given to us for us to learn from and to follow as closely as possible. Jesus is our example. He was unjustly punished and was treated unfairly for things He didn't deserve. Those are things that we may also experience in our lives, so we can learn from Jesus and how He responded so that we can respond as closely as possible the way that He did. How did Jesus respond to unfair treatment? Did He throw a fit? Get mad, angry, yell and make sure that people understood His point? Did He gather support for His side and try to overthrow those mistreating Him? No wait, He began an online smear campaign against those who were mistreating Him. Giving them a bit of their own medicine. No, He staged a protest, gathered a large and vocal mob around Him to make sure they were heard and damage and destroy property around them until they received the change and outcome they want to see. Jesus didn't do any of those things. "When He was reviled, He did not revile in return; when He suffered, He did not threaten, but continued entrusting Himself to Him who judges justly" (1 Peter 2:23). Jesus knew He was being treated wrongly, but instead of lashing out at His attackers He continued to trust God, draw closer to Him, and allow God to lead Him. That is not the way the world handles these situations, but it is how Jesus did, and He is the example God gave us to learn from and to model our behavior after.

April 15

"For the love of Christ controls us, because we have concluded this: that One has died for all, therefore all have died."
2 Corinthians 5:14

Motivation is so very important. It gives us the reasons why we do, or don't, do things. For example, I know of many reasons why I don't cheat on my wife Melanie. When I married Melanie, I married up. My wife is not only smoking hot, but she is smart and much better than I deserve. I've already got the best, so why would I go after someone else? Also, as a father, I wouldn't want to inflict pain or wound my children by such an action. In addition to that, as a pastor, cheating on my wife would bring disgrace upon God. I do not want to do that.

Each of these reasons are legitimate reasons for not cheating on my wife, but they're not the reason why I don't. Yes, each of these reasons are good and legitimate, but they're known as secondary motivators. They are good, but they're not the most important reason. The most important reason why I don't cheat on my wife Melanie is my primary motivator, and that is love. You see, I love my wife and I have absolutely no desire to be with any other woman than her. On top of that, I don't ever want to do anything that would hurt her or cause her pain. Why? Because I love her. This was especially true when we went through difficult times in our marriage. We have had times when we are mad at each other, and even had times when we didn't "like" each other. But we have always loved each other. That is the primary motivation that keeps us together, until death separates us.

We have the same thing in our relationship with God. That is what the apostle Paul is saying here. It is love that "compels" him. The word compels is sometimes translated as constrains, or drives. These are just other words for motivation, what drives us and moves us forward. Why do we go to church? Why do we serve others? Why do we help others? Our motivation should be because of our love for others. If love isn't our motivating factor, then we are just a loud noise and doing futile works. "If I speak in the tongues of men and of angels, but have not love, I am a noisy gong or a clanging cymbal. And if I have prophetic powers, and understand all mysteries and all knowledge, and if I have all faith, so as to remove mountains, but have not love, I am nothing. If I give away all I have, and if I deliver up my body to be burned, but have not love, I gain nothing" (1 Corinthians 13:1-3).

April 16

"...make every effort to supplement your faith with virtue..."
2 Peter 1:5b

We are saved by grace through faith. Peter is reminding us that we don't want to stop at faith, but we are to continue growing. In fact, we are to diligently pursue, to put every ounce of effort that we can muster into growing in our relationship with God, and the first characteristic, or virtue, for us to add on to our faith is virtue. Today this seems like such an old-fashioned word, that it is often ignored, and many don't realize what it really means. A literal translation of the word virtue means "a God-given ability to perform heroic deeds." A part of virtue is moral goodness, but it is more than just being moral. To have virtue means that you are courageous. Courage means to be willing and able to stand against the challenges that we face. Faith in God makes it possible for us to not run away from challenges that scare us or have the possibility of overwhelming us.

The Bible is filled with examples of believers being courageous because of their faith in God. A great example of this is the young shepherd boy David. The armies of Israel and the Philistines had been facing each other for forty days without a battle being engaged.

The reason there had been no battles was because the Israelites were scared. Why were they scared? Because the Philistines had a soldier by the name of Goliath who was over nine feet tall. David came to the battlefront and when he saw Goliath, he wondered why no one was willing to fight him. Was David scared? I am sure that he was. But he had more faith in God was greater than his fear over Goliath. So, David volunteered to go fight Goliath. He gathered five smooth stones for his slingshot and David said to Goliath, "You come to me with a sword and with a spear and with a javelin, but I come to you in the name of the LORD of hosts, the God of the armies of Israel, whom you have defied. This day the LORD will deliver you into my hand, and I will strike you down and cut off your head. And I will give the dead bodies of the host of the Philistines this day to the birds of the air and to the wild beasts of the earth, that all the earth may know that there is a God in Israel, and that all this assembly may know that the LORD saves not with sword and spear. For the battle is the LORD's, and He will give you into our hand" (1 Kings 17:45-47). God desires us to have the same courageous faith that David had, willing to face battles that seem overwhelming to us. Don't cower in fear, move forward in courage.

April 17

"The archers bitterly attacked him, shot at him, and harassed him severely."
Genesis 49:23

Too often people think that once they become a Christian that everything in life will go well. As a believer life will be one of daisies and sunshine, no problems at all. That is a lie from the pit of hell. Neither the Bible nor the pages of history prove that lie to be true. The life of Joseph is a perfect example. Even though Joseph now is in a position of power and prestige, his life has been filled with difficulties and tragedies. This is what Jacob is referring to when he says that "archers attacked him, shot at him." The imagery that Jacob uses gives us the idea of being in battle, or war. People in the midst of the battles of war experience intense suffering and hardship. This is exactly what Joseph experienced from his brothers and his masters in Egypt. King David took the image of arrows and likened them to bitter and hurtful words when he wrote that evildoers "who aim bitter words like arrows,

shooting from ambush at the blameless, shooting at him suddenly and without fear" (Psalm 64:3-4). Joseph had experienced many hurtful words being hurtled at him, such as the false claims by Potiphar's wife which put him in jail.

There is no doubt that Joseph experienced much difficulty in his life, but there is no record of mention of him every striking back at those who mistreated or abused him. This is very unusual. When I am mistreated, I want to get revenge and to see justice meted out to those needing it. We have no record of him striking back or even voicing his wish or desire for evil or harm to befall those who attacked him. In this, Joseph is an example of Jesus for us, when "He was oppressed, and He was afflicted, yet He opened not His mouth; like a lamb that is led to the slaughter, and like a sheep that before its shearers is silent, so He opened not His mouth" (Isaiah 53:7). Where did he get the strength to respond the way he did? It came from God. God tempered him so that he didn't immediately respond with anger or with revenge. The same God Who helped him respond this way is also here to help you respond the same way when today. Draw near to God, seek Him, and ask Him to help you respond wisely to the situations that you face so that like Joseph, you will bring honor and glory to God through the way you respond to difficult situations.

April 18

"But the woman was given the two wings of the great eagle so that

she might fly from the serpent into the wilderness, to the place where she is to be nourished for a time, and times, and half a time."
Revelation 12:14

We have seen in our study of this chapter that this woman is symbolic of the nation Israel. She is continually persecuted by Satan, until she is miraculously saved. John tells us that she "was given two wings of a great eagle." The term eagles' wings are a reference to how God saved Israel and delivered them from their Egyptian slavery. God told Moses "You yourselves have seen what I did to the Egyptians, and how I bore you on eagles' wings and brought you to Myself" (Exodus 19:4). Just as God did then, He will again provide a miraculous escape for the people of Israel. This time they will escape the persecution of Satan. Some wonder if the reference to eagles' wings refers to some sort of military plane evacuating the people in some sort of emergency situation. Some even see that the eagle represents the United States and see the U.S. helping to evacuate her allies.

What is clear is that the Israeli people will be miraculously preserved again, this time from the persecution from Satan. They will be brought into the wilderness to a place of safety and refuge. The time that they will be protected there is also told us. They will be there "for a time, times, and half a time." Each time is seen as one year. Therefore, times would be two years, and half a time is half a year. Add them together and you end up with a period of 3 and a half years. During this period God will supernaturally provide Israel with what is needed for survival. This is reminiscent of how God provided for Israel during her forty-year wilderness wanderings (see Deuteronomy 29:5) and Elijah during a time of famine at the Brook Cherith (see 1 Kings 17:1-6). It can be fun to discuss and try to figure out how God is going to provide for all these people, or even where it is that they will be hid and protected. But it is not necessary for us to do so. What is important for us to realize is that God cares for and provides for those that He uses to accomplish His purposes. This is true for the nation of Israel, but it is also true about you and me. God cares for us, and He provides for us. Maybe not in the way we think He should or expect Him to, but He does, and He will continue to.

April 19

"For this commandment that I command you today is not too hard for you, neither is it far off."
Deuteronomy 30:11

Have you ever asked how to do something and the person who answered you made you even more confused than you were before? For example, you ask someone what time it is, and they begin telling you the history of time, or how a watch is built. You may have noticed this already, but there are some people in this world who are more interested in showing you how great their intellect is, or how smart they are, instead of just answering your question. God knows that we don't need to be impressed with difficult answers that are beyond us, but by a simple answer that is reachable by every single person. That is what Moses is telling the Israelites. God is giving them a command that is not mysterious, too difficult for them, or beyond their reach or understanding.

This command that God is giving to them is a choice that they must make. What they choose will determine their eternal direction. God created us with a mind and an intellect. He didn't give us these capabilities to impress other people, but so that we can make an intelligent decision about whether to follow Him or not. You see, what God is asking us to choose, or to do, isn't so great and difficult that we have to send someone up into the heavens for the information, or even across the seas, a great distance away, to get the needed information. No! God gives us, right where we are, what we need to fulfill His command. The apostle Paul repeated what Moses was saying here. "But the righteousness based on faith says, 'Do not say in your heart, "Who will ascend into heaven?"' (that is, to bring Christ down) 'or "Who will descend into the abyss?"' (that is, to bring Christ up from the dead). But what does it say? 'The word is near you, in your mouth and in your heart' (that is, the word of faith that we proclaim); because, if you confess with your mouth that Jesus is Lord and believe in your heart that God raised Him from the dead, you will be saved" (Romans 10:6-9). This is what God is telling us to do. He is not calling us to impress, or confound, others with our intellect; it is about simply trusting Jesus.

April 20

"So speak and so act as those who are to be judged under the law of liberty. For judgment is without mercy to one who has shown no mercy. Mercy triumphs over judgment."
James 2:12-13

Freedom! Is there anything greater than a person who has been in bondage receiving their freedom? This is exactly what we, as believers, have experienced. No longer are we under the bondage of sin, because Jesus died on the cross and rose from the grave, we are now under the "law of freedom." Because of Jesus Christ, we have been set free. We are not under the law of Moses, because the law of Moses has never saved anyone, and never will. We are saved by faith in Jesus Christ, and that is what sets us free. Our faith in Jesus Christ brings us under a new law, the law of freedom, which is also referred to as the law of liberty. Under the law of liberty, we obey God, not to earn our salvation, but because He has saved us. We obey Him to please Him, not because we are forced or coerced to. God has saved us, and we show our gratitude to Him through our obedience to Him.

God has been very merciful to us; He has given us good, in spite of us not deserving it one iota. Since we are under the law of liberty, and we have been shown great mercy, we show our gratitude to God by extending mercy to others, not showing partiality or favoritism to them. James is contrasting different attitudes here: one who shows mercy, compared to the one who refuses to show mercy to others. Since God has been merciful to us, He also expects us to be merciful towards others. If we are not merciful to others, then God will not continue to be merciful towards us. But don't mistake this to mean that we earn God's mercy by being merciful towards others. That is not true! If it is earned, then it is not mercy. We show God our gratitude to Him and His mercy to us by our being merciful towards others. Neither should we make the mistake of thinking that mercy and justice are competitors. They're not, because God created both, and they both come from God. When a person is repentant, sorry for their sin, and faithful to God, then God can extend mercy towards that person. But, when a person is filled with rebellion towards God, and unbelief, then God has to give that person justice. The heart of the individual determines whether we receive God's mercy or His justice.

April 21

"For by the grace given to me I say to everyone among you not to think of himself more highly than he ought to think, but to think with sober judgment, each according to the measure of faith that God has assigned."
Romans 12:3

Walk into just about any bookstore in the United States and you will find several books relating to self-esteem. There are books bemoaning the problems of people with low self-esteem, and even more books describing the need for and importance of every person to raise their level of self-esteem. According to the "experts," most problems that people deal with are because they have low self-esteem. Just send them some money and they will tell you how to remove that problem. But the question we need to ask ourselves is, "is this Biblical?" What does Jesus say in the Bible about self-esteem?

As with most things, the Bible doesn't say the same thing the world is telling us. What the world tells us is the cure, the Bible says we need to be cured from. The problem is not self-esteem. In fact, every person has plenty of self-esteem. Ask anyone who they spend most of their time thinking about, and it will be themselves. We don't need more self-esteem, but we do need to think correctly about ourselves. Generally, we think too highly of ourselves. We look at the knowledge we have acquired, the abilities God has given us, and we use those as measuring sticks for how great we are. This is a travesty. God gives us gifts and abilities and has enabled us to learn things not to puff ourselves up with, but to help others. The world has completely turned this around, and we too easily follow the world's lead. Instead of taking what we have learned and helping others learn, understand, and apply to their lives, we spout off our knowledge to impress others with how much we know. This draws the focus to us, instead of helping others and bringing glory to God.

God does not need us to reach others, but He chooses to use us. To be more effective for Him we need to keep an accurate view of ourselves. We are nothing without Him. But, with God "I can do all things through Him who strengthens me" (Philippians 4:13). This is because it is not about me, but about God. It is about God using me, and the gifts and abilities He has blessed and equipped me with, to help and encourage others to grow in Him. We need to remember that it is all about God, and His working through us. "Not by might, nor by power, but by My Spirit, says the Lord of hosts" (Zechariah 4:6b).

April 22

"I also found out that the portions of the Levites had not been given

to them, so that the Levites and the singers, who did the work, had fled each to his field."
Nehemiah 13:10

History tends to repeat itself. The reason for this is because people tend to fail to learn from what happened previously. A main reason for this is that people tend to believe that they are more enlightened than those who lived before them, so they won't make the same mistakes that were made previously. That is a lie. When Nehemiah was leading the Israelites to rebuild the wall and to dedicate themselves to God, the people thrived, the priests led the people and had their needs taken care of and met by the people. But, once Nehemiah returned to Babylon strong spiritual leadership was lacking, and it didn't take long for the people to wander away from God. Instead of remaining faithful and committed to God, the people began to do their own thing, relying of their own abilities instead of relying on God. They stopped following God, and they stopped giving to God. This meant the priests were not only not listened to, but they were no longer provided for either. Instead of staying in the Temple and serving the Lord, they had to move outside the city and find jobs to provide for them and their families.

This is a truth that is repeated throughout history. Corrupt leadership will lead the people to a lack of faithfulness, a lack of commitment, and a lack of love for the things of God. This isn't the first time this happened; not even in Israel. There was a previous judge of Israel by the name of Eli. He was a godly man, but not a great leader. He failed to train and discipline his own sons, but still elevated them to positions of leadership within the nation of Israel. They misled the people, and through their corrupt leadership caused people to wander away from God. The people wandered away from God not because they hated God, but because they hated His representatives. Ouch! Today, God's representatives are you and me. It is so important that as believers we continue to seek after God, living lives that honor and glorify Him. We have people watching us and learning from us, whether we realize it or not. Look to God for wisdom and the strength to make sure that we don't mislead anyone or help to lead someone away from God.

April 23

"For consider your calling, brothers: not many of you were wise according to worldly standards, not many were powerful, not many were of noble birth. But God chose what is foolish in the world to shame the wise; God chose what is weak in the world to shame the strong."
1 Corinthians 1:26-27

An interesting aspect of social media is that many people believe they are more important and influential than they really are. People desire to be more than what they really are. Now it's not bad to have goals and to desire to be more than what you are, but the reality is that most people are ordinary. Not everyone is willing or able to accept this, which leads many to have a self-inflated ego. The apostle Paul could be fairly brash, and he was here in his writing to the Corinthians. He reminded them that according to the world's standards they weren't considered to be great. This was not a compliment to them, but it was accurate. Paul was reminding the church in Corinth that what they were was ordinary. They weren't rich, powerful, mighty, or such wonderful people that God couldn't get by without them. Yet, in spite of who they were, God still not only loved them, but called them to be His children. This is true today for you and me too. God not only loves us but calls us to be His children. Why?

Wouldn't God be more "successful" here on earth if He called leaders of nations, or successful businessmen to be His children? Why does God call ordinary people? God wants to show the world of their need for Him. While the world is impressed by social status, power, riches, fame; none of these things will bring a person eternal life. God uses what the world considers to be foolishness to be true wisdom. In other words, God takes the upside-down values of the world and turns them right side up to match His true, eternal values. Does this mean that God wants His followers to be unwise fools? No! It is a reminder to us that what the world considers to be valuable has no eternal, or spiritual, value because it cannot secure salvation for anyone. Only Jesus gives salvation. A second thing to remember is that there are way more ordinary people in the world, and God's desire is for them to be saved. Ordinary people can reach them much more effectively than the world's elite ever will.

April 24

"Whoever walks with the wise becomes wise, but the companion of fools will suffer harm."
Proverbs 13:20

It is important for us to watch who we are spending our time with. While it is true that we are to "Go into all the world and proclaim the gospel to the whole creation" (Mark 16:15), we also do need to be careful of who our best friends are; those we spend the most time with. Solomon is saying that we become like the people that we "hang out" with. This recalls the old saying "a rotten apple spoils the barrel." The people we hang out with will encourage us and help us to become better people, or they will bring us down. Either way you will become like the people you are closest to. I used to have an old boss who liked to say, "if you have a good hunting dog and a bad hunting dog and keep them in the same kennel, pretty soon you'll have two bad hunting dogs." That is so true. He wasn't a Christian, but he was right on. This is what Solomon is talking about.

As we look at this verse, we need to realize that there are really two sides to it. First off it is speaking of the people we are closest to, and how they influence us. Secondly, it is saying that we need to be people who influence others. Every one of us has people in our life that we influence. There are friends, co-workers, neighbors, spouses, children, and other family members. What type of influence are you being to them?

Think of King David and the people who hung around with him. "And everyone who was in distress, and everyone who was in debt, and everyone who was bitter in soul, gathered to him. And he became commander over them. And there were with him about four hundred men" (1 Samuel 22:2). This happened while David was running for his life from King Saul. Samuel had obeyed God and anointed David as the future king of Israel, but it hadn't happened yet. Saul was still king, and he wanted to kill David. So, David was running through the desert as a wanted man. The people who came to David were those who were stressed out, in debt, and unhappy. A pretty motley crew, and people who had nothing to offer David, but themselves. David proved to be a godly man, and as these men spent time with David they were influenced by his life. 2 Samuel 23:8-9 provides us a list of many of these men. By the end of David's life, they were known as David's Mighty Men. Read those verses and see the mighty and miraculous deeds that they performed.

How were stressed out, debt-ridden, unhappy men able to accomplish such feats? They spent their lives living with Godly people. They didn't just hear about Christianity, but they saw it lived out before them. By seeing David living his life for God, others began to become like him, a man after God's own heart (see Acts 13:22).

Instead of being concerned and worried about what others think about you, be concerned with what God thinks. Live your life to please God, to bring Him glory and honor and you will be a person who influences others to live the same way. God can use YOU, and He desires to use you to change and influence the lives of those He has placed in your everyday life.

April 25

"Now as he went on his way, he approached Damascus, and suddenly a light from Heaven shone around him. And falling to the ground, he heard a voice saying to him, 'Saul, Saul, why are you persecuting Me?'"
Acts 9:3-4

Saul is getting close to Damascus, which is about 130 miles from Jerusalem. He had lots of time to nurse his hatred of Christianity, or the Way. His heart and mind are set on the havoc that he is going to create within the city and remove these people from earth. There was no man that could stop him – at least no man on earth. There was a Man with nail scars in His hands and feet that was ready to introduce Himself to Saul.

As they were traveling along, suddenly a bright light from Heaven shone down on Saul and knocked him off his high horse. When the apostle Paul recounts this story in Acts 26:13, he reveals that this happened at midday when the sun shines at its brightest. The sun is bright but is nothing compared to this light from heaven.

It wasn't just about the light because there was also a voice that spoke to Saul. The voice said, "Saul, Saul, why are you persecuting Me?" God gets involved by speaking directly to Saul. He asks Saul why is he persecuting God? This had to be perplexing for Saul. After all, he wasn't persecuting God, he was helping God by getting rid of those blasphemous followers of the Way. At least he thought he was helping God, but in reality, it was God that he was persecuting. God didn't ask Saul why he was persecuting the church, because any persecution done to the church is against God. Saul is being confronted with the true nature of his crime. He is not persecuting blasphemous followers of the Way, he is persecuting God.

Sadly, this has been repeated many times in history. People have mistreated, tortured, and persecuted others thinking that they were helping God, when in reality they were mistreating, torturing, and persecuting God; just like Saul was doing here. This is a reminder to us that there is a link between the Head of the Church in Heaven (God) and the members of His church here on earth. Putting a hand on one here on earth is the same as putting a hand on God Himself. Saul never forgot this lesson, and may we learn it today too.

April 26

"Now in a great house there are not only vessels of gold and silver but also of wood and clay, some for honorable use, some for dishonorable. Therefore, if anyone cleanses himself from what is dishonorable,[d] he will be a vessel for honorable use, set apart as holy, useful to the master of the house, ready for every good work."
2 Timothy 2:20-21

Do you have a desire to be a vessel of honor for God? Too often when we think of honor, it causes us to think that God is honored by great and glorious works done in His name. Most of us are not involved in events that are considered great by the world. We are ordinary people, but through God we can do extraordinary things. What do we need to do to become a vessel of honor for God?

In verse 21 we are told that for us to be useful for the Master we need to be cleansed from the latter. What does this mean? The key to this is found a few verses earlier. The apostle Paul wrote "But avoid irreverent babble, for it will lead people into more and more ungodliness" (2 Timothy 2:16). We need to be careful with the words we speak. What we say needs to be glorifying to God, and not to just talk for the sake of talking. The apostle Paul states that babbling mouths and profane talk will lead us to ungodliness. So, what do we need to do then? "Do your best to present yourself to God as one approved, a worker who has no need to be ashamed, rightly handling the word of truth" (2 Timothy 2:15). This is saying we are to faithfully obey God in whatever He has called us to do.

God is not calling us to do things the world considers great, but to be obedient to what He calls us to do. What is done is not as important as obedience to God. 1 Samuel 15:22b says, "Behold, to obey is better than sacrifice." God desires our obedience. God has called each of us to love others. We can do this through the work that He calls us to, as a mechanic, a trash collector, an accountant, a teacher, an executive, etc. We also can do this through serving others. Teach a Sunday School class, help at a Bible study, usher at church, volunteer at a homeless shelter or food bank, do yard work for a sick or homebound neighbor, babysit the children of a single mom, pray for people when they share a need with you. None of these are considered "great" by worldly standards. But, in obedience to God, these acts of service are "vessels of gold and silver." As Jesus stated, "Then the righteous will answer Him, saying, 'Lord, when did we see You hungry and feed You, or thirsty and give You drink? When did we see You a stranger and take You in, or naked and clothe You? Or when did we see You sick, or in prison, and come to You?' And the King will answer and say to them, 'Assuredly, I say to you, inasmuch as you did it to one of the least of these My brethren, you did it to Me.'"

April 27

"Now Barnabas wanted to take with them John called Mark. But Paul thought best not to take with them one who had withdrawn from them in Pamphylia and had not gone with them to the work."
Acts 15:37-38

Paul and Barnabas both agreed on the importance of the trip, but not on whom to take with them. Barnabas was determined that his nephew, John Mark, would join them. There was no room for negotiation here; Barnabas continued to insist that John Mark be part of this team. We remember that he had joined Barnabas and Paul on their first missionary journey but left them in the middle of the journey and returned home. This wasn't a problem for Barnabas; he still wanted him to go with them. This also shouldn't be surprising to us, since Barnabas is an encourager. He wasn't one to let a previous failure hold someone back; he wanted to encourage John Mark by giving him another opportunity to prove himself.

Paul, on the other hand, was leery about John Mark. He was just as adamant about not taking John Mark with them as Barnabas was about bringing him along. John Mark's failure by abandoning them in the middle of the trip broke Paul's trust of him. He did not want to bring anyone along with them that he didn't trust. His desertion was a sign of weakness, and the work of the ministry was very difficult and demanding, so Paul didn't want an unreliable person coming along and leaving them when they would be needed.

They are at a stalemate. An impasse. So, the question is, "Who is right?" Well, they both were. Every single person fails at one point or another in their life, and therefore it is important for us to have an encourager to help restore us and to help us grow and mature. But it is also important for us to have trustworthy and reliable people by our sides.

At this point in time Paul's trust in John Mark was broken, but because Barnabas encouraged him and helped him grow, that trust was eventually restored. At the end of Paul's life while he was in prison again, he wrote, "Get Mark and bring him with you, for he is very useful to me for ministry" (2 Timothy 4:11). Failure is never the end, and this reminds us that even broken trust can be restored. If you find yourself in that place right now, don't give up hope. Continue to be faithful to what God has called you to do and remain so.

April 28

"Beloved, I urge you as sojourners and exiles to abstain from the passions of the flesh, which wage war against your soul."
1 Peter 2:11

We are in a war. The war is real, but it is a different war than most people think of. You see, the war we fight is not against other people, but the war we fight daily is against the passions that are within us. Every one of us has sinful passions, or lusts, that reside within us. Those passions could be sexual, for alcohol, for drugs, for power, and many other things. Sex is a good thing, when it follows the pattern that God designed it with, which is one man and one woman married to each other for the rest of their life. Drinks are not bad but when a person gets consumed with the desire for alcohol it will literally destroy them. This is why Peter reminds us that in this war we need "to abstain from the passions of the flesh." Satan lures and tempts us with these passions because he knows that they have the power to destroy us and keep us from fulfilling the calling that God has on our lives.

That is also the reason Peter reminds us that we are in a war. A war is made up of a series of battles. You don't simply fight one battle and declare victory. No! There are many battles that continue to be fought. The battles are constant, and we are bombarded with them daily. That is why Peter uses the word "war." It is the Greek word "*strateuomai*", which is where we get our English word "strategy" from. Our enemy, Satan, has a strategy to defeat you. That is his ultimate goal, your destruction. His strategy is not to immediately turn you into an addict, whether it be sex, drugs, alcohol, or power. No! A person in addiction turns people off, but many people continue to end up addicted because Satan's strategy works. Satan's strategy is to get you to compromise. He wants you to compromise, a little here and a little there, and pretty soon he has succeeded in getting control of your life. When you allow compromise into your life Satan will successfully wear you down. That is his goal. This is why Peter encourages us "to abstain from the passions of the flesh." Peter wants to see us living victorious lives, not living a defeated life. Remember that we are citizens of Heaven. We are just passing through this world. Don't become enslaved to the things of this world.

April 29

"Then he was afraid, and he arose and ran for his life and came to Beersheba, which belongs to Judah, and left his servant there. But he himself went a day's journey into the wilderness and came and sat down under a broom tree. And he asked that he might die."
1 Kings 19:3-4a

God has used Elijah to show the nation of Israel that God was the one and only true God. There was a spiritual revival in Israel because of these actions, and the 450 prophets of Baal were put to death. When this was over, Elijah prayed seven times, and after three years of no rain, rain returned to Israel. This should have been the greatest moment in Elijah's life. But it wasn't.

Queen Jezebel did not react very positively to the fact that not only were her "prophets" shown up, but they were put to death. She was so mad that she said to Elijah, "So may the gods do to me and more also, if I do not make your life as the life of one of them by this time tomorrow" (1 Kings 19:2). In other words, Jezebel told Elijah that within twenty-four hours he would be dead. She threatened him! What was Elijah's response to this? "Then he was afraid, and he arose and ran for his life and came to Beersheba, which belongs to Judah, and left his servant there. But he himself went a day's journey into the wilderness and came and sat down under a broom tree. And he asked that he might die" (1 Kings 19:3-4).

Elijah was depressed. Elijah was scared. He was very human;

just like you and me. I am sure that he was a little scared of Jezebel, but he wasn't afraid to die. He actually prayed that God would kill him. What scared Elijah the most was that he had been obedient to God, had trusted God, had placed his faith in God, but he wasn't seeing the results that he expected to see. He was disappointed in God, and he let God know it. Elijah is complaining to God; he is telling God that this is Your business, but the way You are running it, it will soon be a "non-prophet business." Elijah is the only prophet in Israel at the moment, and he is a wanted man; promised to be killed within the next twenty-four hours. How could God allow this to happen?

God is faithful to answer us when we cry out to Him. God doesn't leave us hanging. Things don't always work out the way we think they should, but that's because we have the wrong expectations; not because God isn't doing things the right way. God takes Elijah up to a mountain, meets with Him, and answers all his questions.

Hebrews 13:8 says, "Jesus Christ is the same yesterday and today and forever." That means that just as God showed Himself faithful to answer Elijah in his moments of doubt and depression, He will still do the same for us today.

April 30

"If he has wronged you at all, or owes you anything, charge that to my account. I, Paul, write this with my own hand: I will repay it—to say nothing of your owing me even your own self."
Philemon 1:18-19

Here is a true sign of friendship, money. Paul says he is willing to pay, out of his own pocket, any debt or lost revenue that Philemon is due. Paul is willing to pay a few bucks to help a brother.

Paul is doing for Onesimus exactly what Jesus already did for us. Every person has two problems: we can't live up to God's standards, and we aren't able to pay our debt from sin. Look at it from a business angle: on the asset side of life, we don't have enough merit, or stock, to gain God's favor. But on the liability side of life, we owe far more than we could ever pay off. Aren't you glad that Jesus, the accountant of grace, has the answer? Jesus adds to our assets by giving us His righteousness. This is why when we approach God, God sees us as His Son since we are covered by His righteousness. God sees us as Jesus, so we are accepted as family, and this is what allows us to boldly approach God's throne of grace.

Thankfully, Jesus doesn't stop there. Not only does He change our asset side of life, He also changes our liability side. When Jesus hung on the cross, all our sins were placed on His shoulders. Jesus paid the price we owed, and then He cleared all our debts off the books. The last words Jesus cried out when He was on the cross was "It is finished." That is an accounting term that means "paid in full." On the cross Jesus paid our debt of sin, and it has been paid in full. There is nothing due. This story of Paul, Philemon, and Onesimus beautifully model this.

Paul had a scribe write his letters, but at this point Paul took the pen in his own hand and wrote this himself. Philemon receives a personal IOU from Paul that he wrote out himself. When Paul signed this letter, his signature caused this letter to double as a promissory note. In other words, Paul is making this transaction legal.

Jesus did the same thing for us. Galatians 4:4 tells us that Jesus was born under the Law, and why He even suffered the indignity of the cross. Jesus came to earth to pay our penalty of sin because it couldn't just be "forgotten." No! Our penalty had to be dealt with legally in the court of God. Sin had to be blotted out, and Jesus' righteousness had to be transferred to us in a proper and legal way. It had to be done this way because God does things "by the book." Paul's signature is given to promise Onesimus's salvation just as Jesus' signature is on our own salvation.

May 1

"Trust in the LORD with all your heart, and do not lean on your own understanding. In all your ways acknowledge Him, and He will make straight your paths."
Proverbs 3:5-6

The word "trust" means "to lie helpless, facedown." It means that we have a total and complete dependence and faith in God. This is why the second half of the verse reminds us to not "lean on your own understanding." We can place all of our faith and trust in God because He has a great plan for your life, and He is carrying that plan out. To trust God means that we have complete confidence in God's wisdom, what He has done, and what He is currently doing. Let me ask you a question, has God ever let your down? The short answer to that is NO! In more than half a century I can assure you that God has never let me down. Have you ever let yourself down? Only on days that end in "y." It happens all the time. Have you ever been let down by someone else? Absolutely! No matter how long we have lived, God has never let us down, which is why He is worthy of us placing our total and complete faith and trust in Him. Since God has never let us down, and we continually let us down, it is complete foolishness to lean on our own understanding instead of placing all our faith and trust in God. When we place all our trust in God, we begin to understand that His wisdom is higher than ours, that His ways are higher than our ways. The psalmist reminds us of this in the middle verse in the entire Bible, Psalm 118:8, "It is better to take refuge in the LORD than to trust in man."

The second part of this is that we "acknowledge" God, or "think about Him in all your ways." When we acknowledge God, it means that we bring our questions to Him; we consult God. As a parent, I can attest how much parents like it when their children consult them with what is going on in their lives. God is no different; He loves it when we consult Him with what we are dealing with. There are two reasons for this: 1) the parent is pleased their child wants to spend time with them, and 2) that the child values and trusts them to receive guidance and wisdom from them. Here is something crazy to consider. We bless God when we bring our matters and questions to Him; when we consult Him with the issues we are dealing with in life. Have you ever considered that? You are able to bless God. How crazy is that. But it's true. God is blessed when we consult Him, when we value His wisdom over our own and seek Him out. We need to remember that the prophet Isaiah gave us some of the titles of God in Isaiah 9:6; one of them is "Wonderful Counselor." When we acknowledge God, it is impossible for us to receive any better wisdom, or counsel, than what He gives us. We can't get better wisdom from anyone else, any book, or smartphone, and definitely not from our own minds. We acknowledge God because He is a Wonderful Counselor. If we trust God and acknowledge Him, He then gives us a promise: He will "make straight your paths."

May 2

"...and they were singing a new song before the throne and before the four living creatures and before the elders."
Revelation 14:3a

These 144,000 evangelists of God's are standing on Mount Zion in Jerusalem with Jesus, and as they begin to sing a song of praise to God they are instantly transported to the throne of God in Heaven. Isn't that wonderful? That is the power of praise. John has already told us about this new song that they sang. In Revelation 5:9-10 John gave us the song lyrics, which are "You are worthy to take the scroll and to open its seals, because You were slaughtered, and You redeemed people for God by Your blood from every tribe and language and people and nation. You made them a kingdom and priests to our God, and they will reign on the earth." Notice that the focus of the song is on God, Who He is, and what He has done. This is the purpose of praise, it's all about God. The words of the songs we sing should be directed to and about God; not us. Sadly, too many songs sung in church are about us instead of God.

As these evangelists sang praises to God they were ushered into the presence of God. This is still true for you and me today. As we sing songs of praise to God, we are also brought before the throne of God, into His presence. This is why it is so important for us, as believers, to be worshippers of God. Songs of praise should flow off our lips as naturally and easily as water flows off the back of a duck. When we truly realize the debased sinner that we are, and that God still loves us and died for us so that we are saved, worship should be a natural response. Praising God can be, and needs to be, done no matter what our circumstances are. Remember, Paul and Silas were falsely beaten and imprisoned, yet that was exactly when they were singing songs of praise to God (see Acts 16:25). It doesn't matter whether things are going great, or we are in the midst of a trial, we can be ushered into the presence of God through singing songs of praise to Him. This is why the Psalmist reminds us to "Oh come, let us sing to the Lord; let us make a joyful noise to the rock of our salvation! Let us come into His presence with thanksgiving; let us make a joyful noise to Him with songs of praise! For the Lord is a great God, and a great King above all gods" (Psalm 95:1-3).

May 3

"And now do not be distressed or angry with yourselves because you sold me here, for God sent me before you to preserve life."
Genesis 45:5

One of the reasons that many people have difficulty in forgiving others is because their focus is on self. When we focus on the wrongs that have been done to us, forgiveness will not happen. Our eyes need to be taken off self. This is what Joseph does remarkably well. He sees the big picture. If he only saw what his brothers had done to him, he would never have forgiven them. But God gave him the ability to see how God would use this for His plans, and for good. You see, Romans 8:28 isn't just a verse that gives us hope in difficult times, it is true. Romans 8:28 reminds us that "And we know that for those who love God all things work together for good,[h] for those who are called according to His purpose." God has a purpose for all the wrongs that have been done to us, and the difficult times that we have experienced. When we go through those times it is important that we keep our eyes and focus on Jesus, not self, so that we can see what He is doing.

An important thing for us to remember is that this does not minimize the wrongs that are done to us. Nowhere in this chapter does Joseph minimize the sins of his brothers. What they did was wrong. But it is also important to see that when Joseph forgave his brothers he didn't focus on or bring attention to the sins of his brothers. He simply told them that they were forgiven. When he did that, he didn't minimize the wrongs they had done, but what he did was neutralize them by not focusing on them. This is exactly what Jesus is calling us to do. It is not easy. I would be lying if I told you it was, but it can be done. This is one of the purposes of Jesus confining Himself within the body of a man here on earth, so that He could experience the things that we do, but without sinning. That is why when Jesus unjustly hung on the cross, He cried out, "Father, forgive them, for they know not what they do" (Luke 23:34). When we take our focus off self and place it on Jesus, we also can forgive others as Jesus has done for us.

May 4

"So Barnabas went to Tarsus to look for Saul..."
Acts 11:25

Barnabas is excited by what he sees in the church at Antioch. As he observes what is going on here, the Holy Spirit speaks to him and places a burden on his heart. That burden is to find Saul and bring him back to Antioch. So, Barnabas leaves Antioch and travels to Tarsus. This is a trip of about 100 miles. That doesn't seem like much, but with the modes of transportation they had, it was a major undertaking.

Once Barnabas arrived in Tarsus, he took out his smartphone and "googled" Saul to find out where he was. No! That's not what happened. There were no internet search engines, there were no telephone booths with phone books in them. He searched throughout the city for Saul.

Dr. Luke tells us that Barnabas had to "search for Saul." The word for "search" is "anazateo," and it means to "search up and down, high and low." In other words, he had to hunt Saul. It speaks of a labor-intensive search. He didn't just sit at the local café with a cup of coffee waiting for Saul to stop in. No! He laboriously searched through every location he thought Saul might be in. If he wasn't there, he went to the next place, and after looking in every possible place there was, he went back over the places he had already stopped by. It carries the idea of a parent who is frantically and energetically searching for their lost child. There is a passion and purpose in Barnabas finding Saul.

Why would Barnabas search so diligently for Saul? Because he knew that God had a special calling upon Saul. God had gifted Saul with the needed abilities to bring God's gospel to the Gentile world. He had spent time in Antioch and saw what was happening. He wasn't seeking glory, otherwise he would have stepped up and tried to do it on his own, but he didn't do that. He knew that Saul was the man God had called and appointed for this work, and he did everything he could within his power to find Saul and encourage him to fulfill God's calling on his life. This is a common theme we see almost every time Barnabas is mentioned in the Bible; he is encouraging others. How are you doing in that area? Each one of us has so much that we can learn from Barnabas, so we can be encouragers of others too.

May 5

"And I said to the king, 'If it pleases the king, and if your servant has found favor in your sight, that you send me to Judah, to the city of my fathers' graves, that I may rebuild it.' And the king said to me (the queen sitting beside him), 'How long will you be gone, and when will you return?' So it pleased the king to send me when I had given him a time."

Nehemiah 2:5-6

God doesn't always answer our prayers immediately for different reasons. He wants us to be persistent in prayer, He uses that time to refine our prayers, and He prepares things and situations. In addition to those, He also wants to see us making plans and preparations while we wait. This is what Nehemiah did during the four months while he waited for an answer. This was important because when the king asked him what he needed, Nehemiah didn't stand there with a shocked looked on his face. He didn't respond, "Uhhh, I don't know. I have no idea." He did have an idea because he had been busy making plans while he prayed.

Another thing to notice about Nehemiah is that when the king asked him what he needed Nehemiah responded by simply telling him what was needed. He didn't try to "sell" the king on the benefits to him of giving Nehemiah what he asked for. Again, that is a tactic of the world. Nehemiah was trusting in and depending upon God, so he simply said what he would need. Did he know exactly what he would need? Probably not. Nehemiah was a cupbearer. He wasn't a contractor. He had no experience in building, or in organizing help from community members. How then did he know what he would need? He researched the situation, but most importantly he took this matter to God in prayer. God led and directed him to what he would need. Did he know exactly how long he would be gone? Most likely no. But he had an idea, so he shared that with the king. Nehemiah 5:14 tells us that he was gone for 12 years. Chances are very good that this was longer than he had anticipated, but he gave the king very practical answers. This is a good example for us to follow too. When we are faced with situations in life, pray over them, but make plans while waiting for an answer, and then when asked, give practical answers that you have received while you continue to pray.

May 6

"...and knowledge with self-control..."
2 Peter 1:6a

The apostle Peter continues his list of characteristics that the believer should possess after their faith. In addition to faith, Peter has mentioned that we need to possess virtue (or courage) and knowledge. Now he adds self-control to the list. It is interesting that self-control is the next characteristic added. You see, knowledge has a tendency to puff up a person. Knowledge has even been known to generate pride within the person who has knowledge. To balance knowledge, Peter recognizes that self-control is needed. But what exactly is self-control? It is the ability to master your passions and desires, not to be ruled by them, but to keep them in check and under control. In today's vernacular we could say that it means to "get a grip," and not let your passions and desires rule over yourself.

King Solomon said that a person with self-control is a very strong person. This is how King Solomon put it, "Whoever is slow to anger is better than the mighty, and he who rules his spirit than he who takes a city" (Proverbs 16:32). How can a person develop this skill of self-control? It does not sound very easy to do. It is not easy to do, and I would even go so far as to say that it cannot be done within our own power. This is why the apostle Paul says that self-control is a fruit of the Spirit (see Galatians 5:22-23). Self-control is achievable in a person when that person allows the Holy Spirit to fill them and empower them.

Once a person surrenders themselves to the Holy Spirit, allowing the Spirit to fill them and lead them, it then takes a willing determination from that person to continue to surrender themselves and allow the Spirit to continue to lead them. This requires great determination and stamina from the person who desires to see self-control being evident in their bodies. This requires great determination. To me it sounds like a world-class athlete, which is exactly how the apostle Paul describes it. "Every athlete exercises self-control in all things. They do it to receive a perishable wreath, but we an imperishable. So, I do not run aimlessly; I do not box as one beating the air. But I discipline my body and keep it under control, lest after preaching to others I myself should be disqualified" (1 Corinthians 9:25-27). Self-control does not come easily, but it is well worth the effort.

May 7

"I was very angry when I heard their outcry and these words. I took counsel with myself, and I brought charges against the nobles and the officials."

Nehemiah 5:6-7a

Nehemiah got angry. He was a man of God, and he got angry. This shocks many people today because too often we have the mistaken belief that being angry is a sin. That is false. The apostle Paul said, "be angry and do not sin" (Ephesians 4:26a). Being angry is not a sin in itself. We know this because Jesus never sinned, yet He became angry. Jesus was angry with how the Temple was being used, so He took a whip and drove out those selling sheep and oxen (see John 2:14-15 and Matthew 21:12). Jesus also was angry with His disciples (see Mark 10:14) when they tried to stop children from coming to Jesus. Anger itself is not sin, but why we get angry, and how we respond to anger can be a sin.

Why did Nehemiah get angry? Because people were disobeying God's law, which caused trouble for people and was stopping God's work from going forward. Nehemiah wasn't personally affected by this, but God's work was, and that is why he became angry. But notice how he responded to his anger. He didn't go off half-cocked and do something he would later regret. He was slow to anger and slow to speak, but quick to listen. The first person he spoke to was God. He was angry, but instead of rushing out into action he waited. While he waited, he prayed to God and thought through what was going on and how he would respond to this. That is a great response for us to follow.

After Nehemiah thought things over, he took action. Even though he was angry he remained in complete control of both his actions and his thought process. When the Bible says he "brought charges against the nobles and the officials", it is a reference to legal action. These were powerful people that Nehemiah was going against. They were the kind of people that could completely stop the work that had been happening. But Nehemiah was not depending upon people for God's work to be accomplished, he trusted God. Nehemiah chose to do what was right instead of what easiest for him to do. This meant going against the rich and powerful, knowing they wouldn't be pleased with his choice. This will be true for us also when we choose to obey God's Word. Choosing to obey God's Word has a cost to it, and it doesn't always please people, but it is the right thing, and the best thing, to do.

May 8

"But others mocking said, 'They are filled with new wine.'"
Acts 2:13

The world is always full of mockers. The word "mock" means "to tease or make fun of." We see this all around us today. People love to make fun of sin. When we make fun of sin, it seems to minimize the seriousness of it, and it doesn't appear to be so "bad." This is why so many people love to mock sin, Christians, and even God. Sadly, Christians who are weak in their faith can be held captive by this practice, and it has even kept people from Jesus. What enables a person to overcome and defeat the sin of mockery? Ironically, the very thing these people were mocking – being filled with the Holy Spirit. The Holy Spirit can make even the feeblest believer bold.

It is interesting that their form of mocking would claim that believers who were filled with the Holy Spirit would be compared to people that were drunk. There are some similarities to being filled with the Holy Spirit and being intoxicated with alcohol. Each will cause a change to a person's personality. They each will give a person a feeling of happiness, even causing them to go around singing songs.

That is where their similarities end. You see, the effects of alcohol or drugs and that of being filled with the Holy Spirit are not the same. In fact, you could say that the effects of drugs or alcohol are simply a counterfeit of the Holy Spirit. A counterfeit may look like the real thing, but it's nothing but a cheap imitation. In Ephesians 5:18 the apostle Paul contrasts the Holy Spirit with the effects of too much alcohol. He wrote, "do not get drunk with wine, for that is debauchery, but be filled with the Spirit." Here is the contrast between being under the control of alcohol, or drugs, compared to the Holy Spirit. When you are under the control of alcohol, you will lose control of your own actions and say things or do things that will later cause you great embarrassment, or long-lasting problems. But when you are filled with the Holy Spirit you have self-control and say and do things that bring glory and honor to God. Alcohol can make you feel good for a while, but once its effects wear off you are faced with reality. On the other hand, the Holy Spirit provides a deep satisfaction and everlasting joy. Don't be ripped off by an imitation; be filled with the original, the Holy Spirit.

May 9

"Thus says the Lord GOD concerning Edom: We have heard a report from the LORD, and a messenger has been sent among the nations: 'Rise up! Let us rise against her for battle!.'"
Obadiah 1

Obadiah was a prophet sent by God to pronounce the coming judgment and destruction of the nation Edom. Who is Edom? Edom is the nation that was founded by Esau, the twin brother of Jacob, the founder of the nation Israel. Even though Jacob and Esau were brothers, of the same family, or body, they did not work together. When Israel needed help, they looked to those related to them, Edom, but Edom ignored Israel and chose to ally themselves with Israel's enemies instead of helping. God did not create bodies, or families, to behave like this. There are consequences to every choice, and the result of these choices for Edom was coming judgment and destruction.

What Obadiah pronounces about Edom is also true for us today. The apostle Paul reminds us in 1 Corinthians 12:12-27 that as believers we are part of the same body. What is the purpose of that body? To work together to help each other and bring glory to God. If you have surrendered your life to Jesus, then you are part of the body of Christ. You are part of the body, whether you feel like it or not. It is a fact, not a feeling. This means, as part of the body, that we are to work together and to support our brothers and sisters in the Lord, no matter if we agree with them on every aspect or not. We cannot isolate ourselves and ignore others in the body. When a part of the body is truly isolated and not joined to the body, it means that that part of the body is amputated, dead, and useless. Therefore, to be spiritually alive means that we support and encourage other believers. We work together and we weep together because "If one member suffers, all suffer together; if one member is honored, all rejoice together " 1 Corinthians 12:26).

May 10

"But his father refused and said, 'I know, my son, I know. He also shall become a people, and he also shall be great. Nevertheless, his younger brother shall be greater than he, and his offspring shall become a multitude[d] of nations.'"
Genesis 48:19

Joseph is not pleased that his father, Jacob, has crossed his hands and placed his right hand, the hand of blessing, upon Ephraim, the younger son, instead of Manasseh, the older son. This went against the cultural norm, or tradition, of that day. Jacob resists his son and tells him that God has directed him to do this. The younger son will be more prominent than the older son. This does not mean that one son is better than the other, but that there is a greater plan for the younger than the older. The prophet Jeremiah spoke of this when he wrote, "I am a father to Israel, and Ephraim is My firstborn" (Jeremiah 31:9). Even though Ephraim wasn't Jacob's firstborn son, that was Reuben (he wasn't even Joseph's firstborn), God chose him to be the firstborn. This tells us that the firstborn isn't necessarily the first one to come from the mother's womb, it is a position of pre-eminence (priority or importance). We will see this later with King David. He was appointed King even though he was the youngest son (1 Samuel 16:11). This is also seen with Jesus. The apostle Paul tells us that Jesus "is the image of the invisible God, the firstborn of all creation" (Colossians 1:15). Jesus was not the first child to be born of a woman; in fact, He isn't even created. Yet God appointed Him to be the firstborn, or pre-eminent, of all beings.

History has proven that what Jacob prophesied came true. Manasseh was blessed, but Ephraim became the greater of the two. When Israel later became split into two nations, the ten northern tribes were also referred to as Ephraim, because Ephraim was the greatest of the ten tribes (Judah was the pre-eminent of the two southern tribes). Ephraim is just another example of God not following cultural tradition but reminding us that by blessing the younger instead of the eldest, that the best is yet to come. That is important for us to remember. As a believer, we need to remember that the best is yet to come. What are we looking forward to? "And we all, with unveiled face, beholding the glory of the Lord, are being transformed into the same image from one degree of glory to another. For this comes from the Lord who is the Spirit" (2 Corinthians 3:18).

May 11

"And I saw no temple in the city, for its temple is the Lord God the Almighty and the Lamb."
Revelation 21:22

We are often known for the things that we have. You may be known for the vehicle that you drive, or a collection of things that you have at home. The same is true for cities around the world. St. Louis is known for its Arch. Most large cities are known for their large skyscrapers. Toronto is known for the CN Tower, and London is known for Big Ben. Paris has the Arch de Triumph, while Rome has the Coliseum. In ancient times cities were known for the temples in their town. If you went to Jerusalem, the focal point of the city was its Temple, the Temple devoted to God. It was the largest building in the city, and it was covered with gold so that it stood out and could be seen from a far distance. The apostle John mentions that in the new Jerusalem this will be missing. This city is known for what isn't there, the Temple.

The reason there isn't a temple in the new Jerusalem is because there is no need for it. This is because God Himself and the Lamb are the temple. Here on earth the purpose for the temple was to point us to God for us to worship Him. In Heaven we won't need anything to point us to God because He will be right there in our presence. There will be no need for a building set aside for us to worship God in, because our life will be worship and worship will be life. You see, that is our entire purpose and intent in Heaven, to worship God. We will worship Him in everything that we do.

In Heaven it isn't just that the temple is removed, but it has been expanded. The temple was holy because that was where the presence of God was, but in Heaven it will be expanded because everything and everyplace will be holy and the place where God dwells. This is also a reason why there is no temple in Jerusalem today. God doesn't dwell only in one place. He is everywhere, and He dwells in the hearts of His people. The apostle Paul said, "do you not know that your body is a temple of the Holy Spirit within you, whom you have from God? You are not your own, for you were bought with a price. So, glorify God in your body" (1 Corinthians 6:19-20). God dwells in us as His children. This means that we also worship God everywhere we are and in everything that we do. Let's make sure that we live our lives in a way that brings glory and honor to God in everything that we do, say, and think.

May 12

"And David said to him, 'Do not fear, for I will show you kindness for the sake of your father Jonathan, and I will restore to you all the land of Saul your father, and you shall eat at my table always.'"

2 Samuel 9:7

The entire journey to see the king, Mephibosheth is convinced that this is his final trip. His doom has come. He knows he is about to die, which means there is only one thing left to do. Beg for mercy. As soon as he is brought into the presence of King David, he fell down on the ground before the king. He didn't even wait for the king to say anything. But, as soon as he fell on the ground, the king spoke. "You dirty, little scoundrel. Did you think you could hide from me?" No! That's not what David said. He called him by name. But, even more importantly, what kind of voice did he use? I am certain that it was a loving and tender voice. I imagine that as David called out to Mephibosheth, he was thinking in his mind, "You look just like your father. You're the spitting image of Jonathan." Mephibosheth came before the king as an image bearer. He was in front of the king, but all the king saw was his father. That's why he told Mephibosheth "Don't be afraid." He had nothing to be afraid of, because David was going to show him kindness for the sake of his father, Jonathan. He hadn't been brought here to be executed, but to be shown kindness. He was going to be shown God's kindness because of a covenant that was made before he had been born.

This is exactly how God's kindness comes to us. Jesus, the Lamb of God, was slain from the foundations of the world. This was determined by God because of a covenant that He made before any of us were ever born. So, the Lord went out and fetched us, just as David went out and fetched Mephibosheth. God sought us out in order to show us His kindness, and that kindness was based on a covenant that was made before we were born. Mephibosheth had an incorrect view of the king. He believed this because this is what others had told him about the king. He had no experience with the king. The same is true for the perceptions we had about God. We had incorrect perceptions about God because that is what others had told us. They were not based on fact, or truth. Once Mephibosheth met the king, his viewpoint and understanding of the king was radically changed. The same is true for our viewpoint and understanding of God. After meeting Him and getting to know Him, the truth about who He is is radically different from what we used to believe.

At the end of this meeting, David shares a great truth with Mephibosheth. Instead of killing him, he gives him a promise, which is a great benefit. David said, "you will always eat meals at my table." No longer will you live in obscurity, but instead you will dine at the king's table, as part of the king's family. This is how David is showing the kindness of God, by taking Mephibosheth in as part of his family. This promise is repeated three more times, in verses 10, 11, and 13. How is David showing the kindness of God by doing this? Because this is the same thing that God has done for you and for me. God has taken us, who have been crippled by a fall, and instead of giving us the death that we deserve, He has taken us in as part of His family. In Luke 22:30 Jesus promised that we will eat and drink at His table. This is also how we can show God's kindness to others.

May 13

"And there is salvation in no one else, for there is no other name under heaven given among men by which we must be saved."
Acts 4:12

Peter makes a very clear statement about Jesus. Jesus isn't only a way to salvation; He is the only way. Salvation cannot be received in the name of Buddha, or Allah, or Confucius, or Joseph Smith, not even Abraham, Moses, or David, or Elijah. The only name that can bring a person salvation is Jesus. This had to have irked these religious rulers. If there was one name that they hated, it was the name Jesus. By the name of Jesus this lame man had been healed, and now Peter is telling them that by the name of Jesus they could be saved. Them! If these men that had condemned Jesus to death would repent, even they could be saved. That is amazing grace!

What is it that they need to be saved from? The same thing every one of us need to be saved from, our sins! This has to do with much more than a lame man being healed. Peter is telling these religious rulers about eternal salvation; about being saved from the consequences of their sins. What is the consequence of sin? Romans 6:23 tells us that "the wages of sin *is* death." Fortunately, the verse doesn't end there! It continues by telling us that "the gift of God *is* eternal life in Christ Jesus our Lord." God looked down upon His creation and saw that we were separated from Him because of our sin. There was only one way to correct that situation: a perfect sacrifice had to be offered. That is why Jesus came to earth in human form; so that He could live a perfect life, die on the cross, and raise back to life. He paid the penalty for our sin, even though He didn't deserve it, so that we can now have both a relationship with Him, and even more importantly, eternal life. God offers to us the free gift of salvation. All we have to do is receive this free gift by believing in Jesus and surrendering our life to Him.

Some call this narrow-minded, but it's simply the truth. No one else has paid the penalty for your sins. To receive this free gift, all you have to remember is one name: Jesus!

May 14

"A man came from Baal-shalishah, bringing the man of God bread of the firstfruits, twenty loaves of barley and fresh ears of grain in his sack. And Elisha said, 'Give to the men, that they may eat.' But his servant said, 'How can I set this before a hundred men?' So he repeated, 'Give them to the men, that they may eat, for thus says the LORD, "They shall eat and have some left."' So he set it before them. And they ate and had some left, according to the word of the LORD."

2 Kings 4:42-44

God loves to do the impossible. He continually shows us that He is a miracle worker. He is able to take anything that is given to Him and stretch it into more than what was given. Here a man donated 20 loaves of bread to Elisha. They were given to him as a gift to God to be used anyway needed. Since it was a gift to God, there were no demands or instructions placed on how they were to be used. Elisha told the man working for him to give the bread to the people to eat. The attendant of Elisha looked at the gift in a purely physical way, and he completely missed the working of God. He only saw that this amount of bread would be able to feed about 100 men. Through Elisha God told him it would feed more than that many, and it did.

This is very similar to another miracle that God would perform through Jesus years later. "But Jesus said, 'They need not go away; you give them something to eat.' They said to Him, 'We have only five loaves here and two fish.' And He said, 'Bring them here to me.' Then He ordered the crowds to sit down on the grass, and taking the five loaves and the two fish, He looked up to Heaven and said a blessing. Then He broke the loaves and gave them to the disciples, and the disciples gave them to the crowds. And they all ate and were satisfied. And they took up twelve baskets full of the broken pieces left over. And those who ate were about five thousand men, besides women and children" (Matthew 14:16-21). God has a habit of taking the meager things we offer Him and stretching them to do greater things than we could imagine. God is not bound or limited by the same restraints that we are, therefore, He is able to use our little gifts to accomplish great works.

When we give to God, our focus is not to be on what can be done with what we are giving, but just to give obediently to God. He can take anything we give Him and stretch it beyond our human understanding. God does not do math the same way that we do, He adds exponentially. For us, 2 + 2 will always equal 4. But, with God 2 + 2 can equal 10, or 100. Give to God and see what He will do with your gifts. Remember, "Is anything too hard for the LORD?" (Genesis 18:14). The answer is NO!

May 15

"...you shall say, 'Your servants have been keepers of livestock from our youth even until now, both we and our fathers,' in order that you may dwell in the land of Goshen, for every shepherd is an abomination to the Egyptians."
Genesis 46:34

Most people desire to belong to, or gain acceptance into, what is considered the "right" group. Whether it is being popular, part of the "in" group, going to the "right" schools to become connected, or joining an association for connections. After becoming a part of the "right" group, a person can expect things to be much better for themselves. This is how the world operates, but not God. God specializes in using those with little to no social acceptance to accomplish His plans and purposes. The apostle Paul put it this way, "But God chose what is foolish in the world to shame the wise; God chose what is weak in the world to shame the strong; God chose what is low and despised in the world, even things that are not, to bring to nothing things that are, so that no human being might boast in the presence of God" (1 Corinthians 1:27-29). God specializes in using unlikely people in the most remarkable ways. Think about Jesus' birth. Instead of sending the Savior into the world in a position of prominence, He was born in a manger, and out-of-wedlock. God does not follow the world's way of doing things.

This is why Joseph instructed his brothers to tell Pharaoh that their occupation was as shepherds. In the Egyptian culture shepherds were despised; a job that no acceptable person would ever want to do. This kept the Israelites separated from and not intermingled with the Egyptians. God used this time and place to create a new, separate, and unique nation and culture. If they became a part of Egypt, their identity would be lost. The same thing is true for the believer today. We are called to stand out from, to be different than the world around us. Sadly, too often this is not the case. But, when you carry your Bible with you, put a Christian sticker on your vehicle, or wear clothing with a Christian message on it, the world takes notice, and you stand out from them. Be willing to stand out, to show that you are not part of this world. It won't always be appreciated, but it will make a difference. It isn't easy, in fact, it will be difficult. People will notice, and it will strengthen your resolve and grow your faith. Adversity has a way of causing us to grow. So, be bold. Take a stand for God.

May 16

"And Esther said, 'If it please the king, let the king and Haman come today to a feast that I have prepared for the king.' Then the king said, 'Bring Haman quickly, so that we may do as Esther has asked.' So the king and Haman came to the feast that Esther had prepared."
Esther 5:4-5

Esther skirted the king's question and did not give him a direct answer. Instead, she asked for a favor. This was very bold to do; especially to a man who has the power to separate your head from your shoulders. Why didn't she give him a direct answer? For one thing, it wasn't the right time. She didn't rush in because the Spirit was in control and knew the time was not right yet. If she had, it would appear that she was out to get Haman, and the king most likely would not believe her. Also, there were other people around, and word would get out to Haman once they heard her accusations. So, what did she do? She waited.

How often have you felt the need to say something to your spouse, a parent, a friend, or a co-worker, and you just rush out and say what's on your mind. If you speak immediately, how do they respond? Are they ready to hear what you have to say? Too often we speak without waiting and end up regretting what we said because the time is not right. Esther shows great wisdom in allowing the Spirit to lead her so she does not make this mistake.

Esther also was a wise woman, and she knew the way to a man's heart. It goes directly through the stomach. And as she figured, the king loved the idea and he immediately sent for Haman so they could fulfill this wish of the queens.

There is one thing we must notice here. The banquet was already prepared. Esther had prepared this feast ahead of time in faith. She worked out her faith by going in to see the king unannounced, but also by preparing this feast for him even before she asked him to attend it. Remember now, she has been fasting for three days. If you have fasted before you know how difficult it can be to be around others while they are eating when you are not. When you deprive your body if what it desires, your awareness of what it desires is heightened. Yet that did not stop her from preparing the feast. This was quite a feat for her to do. How did she do that? She relinquished control to the Spirit, and He was faithful to give her the needed strength to accomplish this task.

Esther also was willing to serve Haman, even though she knew he was her enemy and had written a law to destroy her and her people. In spite of that, she still served him. That reminds me of how Jesus Christ was willing to serve, and even wash the feet, of Judas Iscariot in John 13. This happened just before Judas went out to betray Jesus. He knew that, and He also was willing to serve His enemy. We are enemies of the world and those who do not believe in Jesus. Even though they are our enemies, we do not hate them, fight against them, or try to annihilate them. Instead, we are to follow the examples of Esther and Jesus by serving our enemies.

May 17

"So the people went out and brought them and made booths for themselves, each on his roof, and in their courts and in the courts of

the house of God, and in the square at the Water Gate and in the square at the Gate of Ephraim."
Nehemiah 8:16

One of the things the people of Jerusalem learned as they listened to Ezra read the law to them for six hours, was that the Feast of Booths, or the Feast of Tabernacles, was supposed to be celebrated every year. The people had not been doing this, so they made a decision to begin celebrating this festival right now. The instructions for the Feast of Booths is found in Leviticus 23:33-43. The people were instructed to construct a booth, or tent, out of tree branches and they and their family were to live in this tent for one week. This may seem weird to us today, but the purpose of this was to remind the people of how their ancestors lived after they were miraculously released from Egypt and how they lived as they wandered around the desert for forty years. This feast occurred in the fall, right after the harvest was completed, which was a reminder to the people of how faithful God had been to them, and how much He had blessed them by providing permanent homes for them and a bountiful harvest to feed them. Every family in the nation of Israel participated in this event. This included the leaders of the nation, as they and their family would "camp out" in a homemade booth for this week.

There were no instructions on how the booth was to be constructed. Does this make you think of school projects you did in elementary school? Some students created a project that looked like a small wind would knock it over, while other students' projects looked like an engineer had designed and built it, with everything imaginable in between. No doubt the booths were the same way. Some families constructed a booth that barely kept them covered, while other families built a booth that was solid, and possibly even had a front porch with a swing. The reason there weren't instructions on how the booths were to be built is because the booths weren't the focus of the celebration. God didn't reward the people for their architectural skills, but He rewarded those who were obedient to remember Him and how faithful He is. That is still true today. God rewards obedience, not how "pretty" your life appears to be. Live a life of obedience to God, to please Him and not anyone else.

May 18

"When Jacob finished commanding his sons, he drew up his feet into the bed and breathed his last and was gathered to his people."
Genesis 49:33

It is not common for both scientists and doctors to agree on things, but the majority are in agreement that 10 out of 10 people die. Death is one thing that every single person does experience. Social position, wealth, education, gender, ethnicity; none of these can save a person from death. So, as Jacob finished prophesying over his sons, he experienced the same thing that every person before him did, death. After his death we are told that he "was gathered to his people." One day this will happen to each of us too.

This raises a question. Who are his people? Who are your people? Since each of us will die, who will we be gathered to? We will be gathered to like-minded people. Eternity will be spent with people who made the same choices that we made. These people are either in hell or in Heaven. Too often people don't spend much time thinking about their future and have even joked that hell won't be too bad, after all, all my friends will be there. It may be true that their friends are there, but it will be bad. Hell is not like some people picture it. You won't be drinking your favorite beverage listening to your favorite music while playing poker with your best friends. Hell is dark. Hell is hot. Hell will be total and complete isolation.

If hell is so bad, some people wonder why God would send anyone there. The truth of the matter is God doesn't send anyone there. You receive what you want in your life. You see, God is light, but if you reject God then you choose to be in darkness. God is love, but if you reject God than you are choosing hate. God is Father, but if you reject God than you choose to be an orphan, in isolation. God doesn't send anyone to hell to torture them. Every person in hell is there because they rejected God, and His love and mercy.

God doesn't want anyone in hell. God wants you to receive His love, His mercy, and His forgiveness. God wants you in Heaven with Him. Don't reject God. Receive Him into your

life and live for Him.

May 19

"For it is written that Abraham had two sons, one by a slave woman and one by a free woman. But the son of the slave was born according to the flesh, while the son of the free woman was born through promise. Now this may be interpreted allegorically: these women are two covenants."

Galatians 4:22-24a

Abraham had two different sons, each of them from a different mother. Ishmael was born to Sarah's handmaiden (or slave) Hagar, while Isaac was the son of promise and born to Abraham's wife Sarah. The apostle Paul gives us spiritual insight here that these two women each represent different covenants. Hagar represents the covenant of the Law, or legalism and slavery; Sarah represents the covenant of grace, or freedom. These two women did not get along with each other; the same is true spiritually too. This is because these two covenants will never be able to get along with each other; one will always try to persecute the other.

We must remember that Abraham's first wife was Sarah, or grace. Hagar came along afterwards; she was added alongside Sarah. The same is true spiritually. God began with grace, and the law was added alongside grace. The law was temporary and added alongside what already existed. "Why then the law? It was added because of transgressions, until the offspring should come to whom the promise had been made, and it was put in place through angels by an intermediary" (Galatians 3:19). God began with grace; his relationship with Adam and Eve began with grace, not the law.

What then was the purpose of the law? "So then, the law was our guardian until Christ came, in order that we might be justified by faith. But now that faith has come, we are no longer under a guardian" (Galatians 3:24-25). The purpose of the law is to show us our need for a Savior; that we cannot keep the law on our own. Therefore, we need a Savior (Jesus) to save us. There is no way for us to achieve salvation on our own. Those that decide to live under the law become a child of Hagar, a slave. When they have a child, it will also be born a slave. Legalists are only able to produce slaves, they cannot produce freedom. Freedom is what God calls us to. "For freedom Christ has set us free; stand firm therefore, and do not submit again to a yoke of slavery" (Galatians 5:1). We can only become free through Jesus Christ.

May 20

"When you cry out, let your collection of idols deliver you! The wind will carry them all off,
a breath will take them away. But he who takes refuge in Me shall possess the land and shall inherit My holy mountain."
Isaiah 57:13

God gives us the choice of what we want to build the foundation of our lives upon. The foundation of our life is made from the things that we place our trust in. Many people have placed their trust in the things of this world. Things like money (checking accounts, investments, retirement accounts), power, jobs, the government (looking to them to provide for you), other people, and even the church, can be things people look to and trust in. None of these things are necessarily evil or wrong by themselves, but they are not the things we should build our lives upon because each of these items will fail us. For example, many people who have placed their trust and faith in money have been let down in recent years as many investments have lost lots of value. These things of earth are what God is here calling idols. An idol is anything that is worshipped. Every one of us has seen people worshipping each of these things. They may not bow down before them, but they have given their lives over to them. Jesus said that whatever we focus on, whatever we treasure in our hearts, is what we will worship. "Do not lay up for yourselves treasures on earth, where moth and rust destroy and where thieves break in and steal, but lay up for yourselves treasures in heaven, where neither moth nor rust destroys and where thieves do not break in and steal. For where your treasure is, there your heart will be also" (Matthew 6:19-21).

Jesus told us to set our treasures in Heaven because these earthly idols will not stand. A good gust of wind will blow them away. That explains why our investments have lost so much money these past few years; a wind blew them away. The only way to counteract that is to set our hearts to worship something that is solid and cannot be blown away. There is only one thing (or person) that is eternal and will never be blown away, fade away, or deteriorate. That is Jesus. The promise that Jesus gives us is that when we worship Him, and Him alone, then He will protect us and bring us security like no one else, or anything else, is able to. He also promised that we will possess His holy mountain. That is the New Jerusalem, which is in Heaven, and where Jesus will spend eternity with those who trust in Him and have asked Him to be Lord of their lives. Jesus is our security and a sure foundation. Look to Him and trust in Him alone.

May 21

"For they had previously seen Trophimus the Ephesian with him in

the city, and they supposed that Paul had brought him into the temple."
Acts 21:29

The apostle Paul was being hassled by a group of Jews from Asia (see Acts 21:27). Paul was accused of bringing a Gentile inside the temple area, and the Gentile that was supposedly with him was Trophimus, who was from Ephesus, which was the capital city of Asia. He would have been known to the Jews that were causing this commotion.

This group of Jews hated Paul and wanted to get rid of him. They knew he was in Jerusalem and had been inside the temple area. They had also seen Trophimus with Paul in Jerusalem. So, therefore, they concluded, Paul must have brought Trophimus into the temple with him, which was a major problem.

Why was it such a major problem if Paul had brought a Gentile into the temple? There were three sections to the Jewish temple: the outer court, the inner court, and the actual temple. Everyone was allowed in the outer court, Jews, Gentiles, men and women. Only Jewish men were allowed in the inner court, and only priests (Jewish males from the tribe of Levi) were allowed in the temple. At the entrance into the inner court there were large signs printed in both Greek and Latin, "No foreigner may enter within the barricade which surrounds the temple and enclosure. Anyone who is caught trespassing will bear personal responsibility for his ensuing death."

Notice that no one saw both Paul and Trophimus in the temple; they had been seen together in town, but not the temple. Instead of there being any witnesses to this, "they supposed" that Paul had brought Trophimus into the temple with him. This sure was convenient to their purposes in getting rid of Paul. Instead of verifying if this had really happened, this group of Jews allowed their prejudices to take over. They just figured it must have happened and began to stir up trouble based on their assumptions. This is a very dangerous thing to do. We need to learn from their mistake and not allow our personal prejudices to filter how we see things. Don't judge too quickly. That can allow our prejudices to mislead us. That is why Solomon reminded us, "If one gives an answer before he hears, it is his folly and shame" (Proverbs 18:13).

May 22

"In Judah it was said, 'The strength of those who bear the burdens is failing. There is too much rubble. By ourselves we will not be able to rebuild the wall.'"
Nehemiah 4:10

One of the most important aspects of a job is preparation. You can spend lots of time painting a room, but if you didn't take the time to wash the walls, fill in the holes, fix the cracks, etc., your paint job is not going to last, and quite possibly even look nice for any length of time. It isn't just for painting, but any project that you do. For a work to last and to be done correctly, preparation must be done first. This is what the residents of Jerusalem had to deal with as they were rebuilding the wall around the city. When the Babylonians had defeated them years earlier, one of the things they did was destroy the walls. The walls had remained in disrepair since they were broken. One of the difficult jobs they had to do before they could rebuild the wall was to remove all the rubble first. By removing the rubble, they could get down to the foundation and build the wall correctly so that it would be strong and provide protection for the city.

There is also an important spiritual lesson here for us to learn. The people had to remove the rubble to get to the foundation before they could begin to rebuild, this means they had to go down before they could go up. This is also true spiritually for us. We have to go down to the root of an issue before it can be corrected, and we move upward. Before we can bear fruit on the outside, we must bear fruit on the inside. What rubbish needs to be removed from your life? Do you have rubbish of pride, anger, unbelief, self-importance, or evil desires in your life? These need to be removed. They are part of your old self, which must be replaced with a new self. As the apostle Paul reminds us "to put off your old self, which belongs to your former manner of life and is corrupt through deceitful desires, and to be renewed in the spirit of your minds, and to put on the new self, created after the likeness of God in true righteousness and holiness" (Ephesians 4:22-24). This is a work of the Holy Spirit. Allow Him to work in your life and to change you from the inside out.

May 23

"And they worshiped the dragon, for he had given his authority to the beast, and they worshiped the beast, saying, "Who is like the beast, and who can fight against it?'"
Revelation 13:4

Things written in the book of Revelation have shocked and surprised people for many years. Reading through this book people have said they can't believe that these things will happen. They appear to be so far-fetched that it is difficult to imagine it occurring. Yet, every year these so-called far-fetched things become more and more reality. Today it doesn't take much to imagine these things happening because we see similar things happening daily. Years ago, it seemed preposterous that people would willingly bow down and worship the antichrist. Christianity was so accepted in the United States that it was a major component of the fabric of society. But today that is no longer the case. In fact, opposition to the Gospel becomes more common place every year. We don't even have to imagine what it would be like for people to willingly bow down and worship the antichrist because we see it happening around us every day.

The interesting thing about this is that some people will willingly and knowingly be worshipping Satan, other will unknowingly be worshipping him as they are ardent supporters of the antichrist.

Everything the antichrist does as he rises to power will succeed and he will appear to be invincible. He will impress people the entire world over, and this will cause many people to follow him to the point of adoring him and worshipping him. The people worshipping him may not realize it, but in doing so they are worshipping Satan since he is the one who has given antichrist his power and authority. This will please Satan because worship is something that he has always desired (see Matthew 4:8-10). As antichrist gains power he will call for and accept what Satan has always desired: worship. The apostle Paul tells us that antichrist "exalts himself against every so-called god or object of worship, so that he takes his seat in the temple of God, proclaiming himself to be God" (2 Thessalonians 2:4). It is so important that we are students of God's Word, so that we won't be deceived, or misled, by Satan or his followers. Trust God. Follow Him, and no one else.

May 24

"The LORD God took the man and put him in the garden of Eden to work it and keep it."
Genesis 2:15

Adam is in the middle of paradise, the Garden of Eden, but it is not what many of us envision paradise to be. When most people dream of paradise, they are lying on a hammock between two coconut trees, in the shade on a deserted island, with an ice-cold drink close by. In paradise most people dream they have absolutely no responsibilities or work to do; they are free to do as they please and there is no thought to any work. That is not what Adam found in paradise; he was given work to do. Work is not a curse, and it is not a dirty four-letter word either. Work is an opportunity for us to use our gifts and abilities to further God's kingdom as we are faithful stewards of His creation. Work is supposed to be a means of blessing and fulfillment that we can do unto the Lord. "Bondservants, obey in everything those who are your earthly masters, not by way of eye-service, as people-pleasers, but with sincerity of heart, fearing the Lord. Whatever you do, work heartily, as for the Lord and not for men, knowing that from the Lord you will receive the inheritance as your reward. You are serving the Lord Christ" (Colossians 3:22-24).

I read this story about a retired man who lived in the city who got tired of seeing an ugly vacant lot every morning as he took his walk. He asked the owner for permission to plant a garden there and received permission to do so. It took days to haul away the accumulated garbage, and even more time to prepare the soil for planting. The man worked hard though, and the following year the lot was filled with life and beauty. A visitor noticed the lot and commented, "God has certainly given you a beautiful piece of property," as he admired the flowers and landscaping. "Yes, He has," replied the busy gardener, "but you should have seen this property when God had it all by Himself."

The reply was a smart one and was not irreverent. God ordained for man to work, or tend, this earth. When it is not, then it is in sin, which leads to ruin and death. We must remember that work was created prior to sin. Work only became a toil and burdensome after sin, and the fall of man.

May 25

"He Himself bore our sins in His body on the tree, that we might die to sin and live to righteousness. By His wounds you have been healed."

1 Peter 2:24

Life is filled with paradoxes. What is a paradox? It is a statement that seems absurd, or even contradictory, but when thought upon it is found to be true. For example, "if you don't risk anything you risk everything." One I often say is, "the only constant is change." Another example is "the louder you are the less they hear." It isn't just life that has paradoxes, but Christianity does too. The cross that Jesus died upon has multiple paradoxes. Jesus was wounded on the cross so that we could be healed. Jesus died so that we can live. Because we died with Jesus, now we are dead to sin so we can live a new life filled with God's grace (see Romans 6). It seems absurd that Jesus had to die for us to live, but that is true. Of course, Peter isn't talking about physical life, but he is talking about spiritual life. Spiritually we are dead because of sin, but because Jesus once and for all paid the penalty of sin with His death on the cross, we can now be spiritually alive. What a wonderful paradox that is.

There is a reason why Jesus willingly died on the cross. He did it so that we can be healed. Peter quotes the prophet Isaiah when he says, "by His wounds you have been healed." This is a reference to Isaiah 53:5, which says, "He was pierced for our transgressions; He was crushed for our iniquities; upon Him was the chastisement that brought us peace, and with His wounds we are healed." This is also speaking of spiritual healing, but it can include physical healing as well. Here on earth, we may experience healing, but our healing will be fulfilled and complete when we are in Heaven, in His presence.

What does all this mean? To keep this verse in context with the chapter, we need to remember that Peter has been talking about submission to authorities, especially slaves to master, or for today, employees to employers. We submit even when we are being mistreated. Peter ends this section by reminding us that even if we are mistreated here on earth, or treated unjustly by authorities, we don't have to be afraid of what harm they may cause us because we have the assurance that we will be healed and restored because of what Jesus has already done for us. How wonderful that is. May we live in the confidence of that today.

May 26

"Morning by morning they gathered it, each as much as he could eat; but when the sun grew hot, it melted."
Exodus 16:21

The Christian life is about relationship, which is what God desires from us. He wants us to have a close and personal relationship with Him. There is only one way to develop a relationship, and that is by spending time together. This is what God wanted from the Israelites, and also what He wants from you and me today. Six days a week the Israelites had to go out early in the morning to gather their daily supply of manna. If they slept in, the sun would melt their manna and they wouldn't get to eat that day. Not only was God instilling a great work ethic in their lives, but He was establishing a great pattern to follow. We are wise to begin our day by feasting on spiritual food from God's Word, the Bible. Now some people get caught up in the word "early." Early could be 5 in the morning, but it could also be 10 in the morning. What early really means is first thing. Don't let the internet, emails, or social media be the first thing you look at in the morning. Start your day by reading and studying God's Word. What you begin your day with will determine your outlook and demeanor for the day. I have found that if I don't begin my day with God, very quickly I will find my day becoming cluttered with activities, or I will become distracted with other things; the end result is that if I don't begin my day with God and His Word, I most likely will not spend any time at all with Him and His Word.

The Bible is filled with people that met with God early, or first thing, in the morning. Moses (Genesis 19:27; 21:14; 22:3), Jacob (Genesis 28:18), Moses (Exodus 8:20; 9:13; 24:4), Joshua (Joshua 3:1), Samuel (1 Samuel 15:12), Job (Job 1:5), and Jesus (Mark 1:35). God included these events in the Bible for us to learn from, and as an encouragement for us to follow.

There is also a lesson for us to learn from the manna. We are not to hoard God's Word and attempt to live off of yesterday's spiritual nourishment. It is good for us to hear God's Word being taught on Sunday, but if we are to be a healthy believer, then we need to feast on God's Word every day. There is no substitute for daily time spent with God reading and studying His Word.

May 27

"And he said to me, 'Do not seal up the words of the prophecy of this book, for the time is near.'"
Revelation 22:10

Ask the average person on the streets, or even in the church, what the book of Revelation is about, and you will often hear the same answer. It is a book of mysteries. It is difficult to understand. Many churches will not even teach it, giving the reason that this book is too difficult to understand. That is wrong. In fact, that is a lie from Satan. He doesn't want people to read the book or to know what it contains. Often the difficulty in the book of Revelation is because it is filled with symbols from the Old Testament, and most people are not familiar enough with the Old Testament to grasp or understand the symbology that is presented. But, the outline of Revelation is given in the first chapter, and when it is understood the book becomes much easier to understand. The apostle John was told to write "the things that you have seen, those that are and those that are to take place after this" (Revelation 1:19). We can break the book down into the following segments:

- Jesus is resurrected (chapter 1)
- Church history (chapters 2-3)
- The Rapture (chapters 4-5)
- The Tribulation (chapters 6-19)

- The Millennium (chapter 20)
- New Heaven and new earth (chapters 21-22)

John makes it very clear that this book is NOT to be sealed up. It is meant to be taught and proclaimed so that everyone knows what is contained in it. In the Old Testament there was a time when this information was sealed: "The vision of the evenings and the mornings that has been told is true, but seal up the vision, for it refers to many days from now" (Daniel 8:26). But since Jesus has come to earth, died on the cross, risen from the grave (therefore defeating death and sin), and returned to Heaven, these prophecies and visions no longer need to be sealed. The reason we need to know and understand what is contained in the book of Revelation is to grow in us obedience to and worship of God. It is foolish to not read, study, and preach the book of Revelation. Any Christian who does not take the time to study and learn what is contained in this book hurts themselves. This is the only book in the Bible that promises a blessing to those that take the time and effort to study it and know. "Blessed is the one who reads aloud the words of this prophecy, and blessed are those who hear, and who keep what is written in it, for the time is near" (Revelation 1:3). Don't miss out on this blessing from God. Read Revelation, share it with others, and know the truths that are contained in this wonderful book.

May 28

"Judah, your brothers shall praise you; your hand shall be on the neck of your enemies;
your father's sons shall bow down before you. Judah is a lion's cub; from the prey, my son, you have gone up. He stooped down; he crouched as a lion and as a lioness; who dares rouse him?"
Genesis 49:8-9

John Wooden famously said, "Be more concerned with your character than your reputation, because your character is what you really are, while your reputation is merely what others think you are." This is very true, and it is also very applicable to Judah, the fourth son of Jacob. His reputation was not one that you would hold up for others to emulate. When he and nine brothers threw Joseph into a pit, Judah said, "'What profit is it if we kill our brother and conceal his blood? Come, let us sell him to the Ishmaelites, and let not our hand be upon him, for he is our brother, our own flesh.' And his brothers listened to him." (Genesis 37:26-27). He is the one that came up with the idea to sell their brother for a profit. Later he did not deal honestly with his daughter-in-law Tamar, and eventually he committed incest by sleeping with her, thinking that she was a prostitute (see Genesis 38). Some serious issues here. But his reputation shined through when he stepped up and offered himself as a substitute for his youngest brother because he told his dad he would guarantee his return home (Genesis 44:18-34). Because of his reputation, Jacob prophesies that he will be the son that receives praise, and the one that his brothers will bow down to. The double portion of the inheritance was given to Joseph, but the birthright is now given to Judah. His three older brothers disqualified themselves from this position, and Judah now is given this position.

Judah becomes the royal tribe, so it is fitting that his tribe becomes associated with a lion, the king of the beasts. From this tribe will also come the Lion of the Tribe of Judah, which is Jesus (see Revelation 5:5). The ruler from the tribe of Judah is the true King of the universe, and everyone in the entire world will one day bow before him, just as Jacob prophesied. You see, "at the name of Jesus every knee should bow, in heaven and on earth and under the earth, and every tongue confess that Jesus Christ is Lord, to the glory of God the Father" (Philippians 2:10-11).

May 29

"The fifth angel poured out his bowl on the throne of the beast, and its kingdom was plunged into darkness. People gnawed their tongues in anguish and cursed the God of heaven for their pain and sores. They did not repent of their deeds."
Revelation 16:10-11

As God's judgment continues upon the earth, this fifth angel pours out his bowl of judgment and it plunges the earth into darkness. Some people teach that this symbolizes political darkness that blinds people from the truth. That may be true, but we need to remember that the ninth plague on Egypt was a literal darkness. "Then the Lord said to Moses, 'Stretch out your hand toward heaven, that there may be darkness over the land of Egypt, a darkness to be felt.' So Moses stretched out his hand toward heaven, and there was pitch darkness in all the land of Egypt three days" (Exodus 10:21-22). This darkness was so intense it could be felt. That is literal. What this is is a preview of hell. In Matthew 25:30 Jesus described hell as "outer darkness. In that place there will be weeping and gnashing of teeth." Antichrist's kingdom, the entire earth, will be covered in darkness. The beast will be helpless, just like everyone on earth. God is in control, and He is more powerful than the beast.

The apostle John now shares with us the saddest part of what will happen at this time. The people on earth are encompassed in utter darkness, have been burned by intense heat from the sun, have no water to drink, and suffer from plagues and painful sores that cover their body. Surely this would cause them to bow down to God and confess their sins. No! Their hearts are so hardened against God, that even in the midst of His judgment, people refuse to repent and instead continue to blaspheme God. These people will be suffering the absolute worst conditions that have ever existed on earth, yet they will refuse to repent of their sin. How sad. God has written this for us to learn from. One day every person will bow down before Jesus and worship Him. We can either choose to voluntarily bow down and worship Him or have no choice when standing before Him. The choice is yours. What will you choose?

May 30

"'O Lord, let Your ear be attentive to the prayer of Your servant, and to the prayer of Your servants who delight to fear Your name, and give success to Your servant today, and grant him mercy in the sight of this man.' Now I was cupbearer to the king."
Nehemiah 1:11

Most kids in the United States hear the same thing when they are young. Get a good education and learn skills to help you later in life. There is a huge emphasis placed on getting training for what you will do when you are older. This is why there are so many colleges and universities, plus trade schools and technical colleges. In addition to all those, there are even apprentice programs where individuals receive on-the-job experience and training in various fields. The purpose of all these programs is to provide individuals with training and skills to make our work force more skilled and professional. This is a good model, and it has helped create many skilled workers. But it is important for us to realize that this is the world's model, and we need to realize that God does not always follow this.

Nehemiah prayed that God would give him success as he prepared to approach the king to request permission to go to Jerusalem and helped the rebuilding process. What Nehemiah was telling God was that he was willing to part of the solution. He wanted to be used by God. Not because he had any special training for what needed to be done. Being cupbearer to the king did not prepare him or train him to help rebuild the walls in the city. Neither did it prepare him for the construction that was needed, or the organization that would be needed, or gathering community involvement. But none of that mattered to God. What mattered is that he was available. We see this pattern throughout the Bible. When God appeared to Isaiah, his response was "Here I am! Send me" (Isaiah 6:8). When God called out to the prophet Samuel, his response was "Here I am!" (1 Samuel 3:4). Peter, James, and John were fishermen, but used them to spread the Gospel throughout the world. God may place a calling, a burden or desire, upon you, that you don't believe you are qualified for. That doesn't matter. God isn't looking at your abilities, but He does look at your availability. Are you available for whatever God calls you to do?

May 31

"And God was doing extraordinary miracles by the hands of Paul, so that even handkerchiefs or aprons that had touched his skin were carried away to the sick, and their diseases left them and the evil spirits came out of them."
Acts 19:11-12

During these two years that Paul was preaching in Ephesus, God performed "unusual miracles" through Paul. These miracles that God performed were unique, not things that usually happened, or just coincidentally happened. No! These were unique miracles, or acts of power, that God accomplished. The unusual miracle was that God used Paul's "facecloths or work aprons" to heal people. These facecloths were really sweatbands that Paul would wrap around his head while he was working and repairing tents. These were used to keep sweat out of Paul's eyes while working, or to wipe sweat off his brow.

Luke also tells us that God used Paul's work aprons. Now, don't think of a flimsy, lacey piece of fabric like June Cleaver would wear in the kitchen. That's not what Paul wore while working. This would have been something like a leather apron that Paul wore to protect him and his clothing while working.

These "facecloths or work aprons" were dirty, covered with sweat, and probably stinky. It's not that there was any magic power in the handkerchiefs or aprons, but God used them to heal people. Why? Because there was a belief back then, that persists today, that in order for healing to take place, all things had to be clean and "just so." The dominant color used for healing was white, as it still is today. It seems like God is rebuking those false beliefs. God used these sweaty, dirty cloths to heal people of all sorts of diseases. It was a germaphobe's worst nightmare. There was no need for the sick to go to a doctor or hospital. They just needed Paul's sweaty and dirty cloths. This healed coughs and cancer, arthritis and appendicitis, toothaches and tummy aches, measles and mumps, leprosy and lupus, ear infections and evil spirits. There was nothing that God couldn't heal.

That is something that we need to remember about this. It wasn't Paul that did these miracles, and neither was it his handkerchiefs or aprons. It was God that did these miracles. Paul and his work clothes were the channel that God used. I can imagine the first time that this happened it was an accident, but then people began to superstitiously take his handkerchiefs and aprons to be healed. The only power that was healing anyone was God. It's all about Him.

June 1

"When the people saw that Moses delayed to come down from the mountain, the people gathered themselves together to Aaron and said to him, 'Up, make us gods who shall go before us. As for this Moses, the man who brought us up out of the land of Egypt, we do not know what has become of him.'"

Exodus 32:1

The entire time that Moses was on top of the mountain with God, the people didn't know when he would be returning. One day turned into three, which turned into a week, and then another week. The people began to get impatient. They didn't understand that God had a good reason for keeping Moses there with Him, and instead of learning God's reason for this, they allowed their impatience to cause them to stumble. Impatience is often the cause of impulsive actions which are sinful. At this point Israel had not learned how to live by faith and to trust God. They were so accustomed to looking for Moses for direction, that when he wasn't physically with them, they were lost. This is an important reminder to us to make sure that we are following God alone, and not any person. Keep our eyes focused on God, follow Him, that way no matter which person God is using here on earth as His spokesman, we won't get lost because we are following God, and not man.

Sadly, this didn't happen. The people began to freak out because Moses had been gone so long. They went to Aaron and asked him to make them a god to follow since they didn't know what happened to Moses. This is really sad. The Israelites knew that God had led them out of Egypt and through the wilderness. But now they are willing to follow a man-made god just so they can have a god that they can see. They knew God was the One performing all the miracles through Moses, but they could see Moses. Since Moses is gone, they want to make a new god that they can see and follow. This is why the apostle Paul reminded us that we are to live our life "by faith, not by sight" (2 Corinthians 5:7). It does not matter who the person is that God is using here on earth. We don't follow any person. We only follow God. That is why we can trust an unknown future to a known God.

June 2

"Also it causes all, both small and great, both rich and poor, both free and slave, to be marked on the right hand or the forehead, so that no

one can buy or sell unless he has the mark, that is, the name of the beast or the number of its name."
Revelation 13:16-17

This verse is well known, and for many centuries baffled people about what this really meant. What kind of mark could a person receive that would make this possible? Well, over the past forty years, beginning with the invention of the bar code, this has continued to become more and more viable. With advances in technology, today anyone alive can see this being not only viable, but it is happening. It wasn't too long ago that the only way business was transacted was with cash. Then along came checks, which later became credit cards. That was later replaced with debit cards, and now more business is transacted electronically than any other way. Forgot your wallet? Don't worry; you can pay for your transaction by scanning your smart phone.

The trend of going cashless continues. In 2020, amid a worldwide pandemic, this continued to become more and more of a reality. Wal-Mart announced that they opened a test store where there are no checkers, every line will be self-checkout and only debit/credit cards will be used. The government even helped create a coin shortage, which caused businesses to accept cards only, no cash. What not long ago wasn't conceivable is now very real. Why is it so important to get rid of cash? That way every single transaction is recorded, and controllable. If a person is out of line, according to whomever is in charge, their card, or chip, can become invalid, and therefore that person is not able to make any purchases. It is all about control, and compliance. Those not in compliance lose the ability to make purchases and provide for themselves and their families.

Should this scare us? Not at all! Remember, God has informed us that this is going to happen. This is another indicator that we are living in the end times, and Jesus' Second Coming is approaching. So, instead of being scared, or trying to stop these things from happening, we are to "...straighten up and raise your heads, because your redemption is drawing near" (Luke 21:28).

June 3

"But the king said to Araunah, 'No, but I will buy it from you for a price. I will not offer burnt offerings to the Lord my God that cost me nothing.' So David bought the threshing floor and the oxen for fifty shekels of silver."
2 Samuel 24:24

It is very exciting to see the excitement and anticipation of children when their birthday arrives. The thought of the presents that they expect to receive for their birthday keeps them "bouncing off the walls." Their non-stop chatter over the things that they want is interesting to observe; even though the list can change from day to day, and even hour to hour. Can you imagine the horror they would get if you told them their gift was going to be something that you no longer wanted? Can you imagine getting a gift from someone and finding out that it was something they no longer used or wanted? Most people would be disappointed and even angry. After all, who wants to receive another person's leftovers?

How often, though, are we guilty of doing this same repulsive act towards God? We spend our entire paycheck on things that we think we need, and if there is anything "leftover" than we give some of that to God. Or we take some of the change in our pockets and place it in the offering plate at church. Too often we do not give to God first or give Him the best that we have. King David understood this concept very well. After he had disobeyed God and was suffering the consequences of his choice, God instructed him to build an altar and offer a sacrifice to God on a specific plot of land. This land would eventually become the temple in Jerusalem. When David arrived at this land and requested the land to offer a sacrifice to God, the owner of the land offered it to King David at no charge. David refused this very generous offer because he knew that God would not be pleased with a gift that cost him nothing. The value of the gift is shown in what it cost us; not necessarily monetarily but cost us personally. For the gift to be meaningful, and to be received, it had to have cost him something. So, David purchased this property from Araunah, made the sacrifice to God, and God was pleased with David's actions.

May we learn from David and not give leftovers or unwanted belongings to God. May we give Him the best that we have and what is valuable and important to us. May our gifts to Him come from our heart. After all, He is more than worthy.

June 4

"Even if I am to be poured out as a drink offering upon the sacrificial offering of your faith, I am glad and rejoice with you all."
Philippians 2:17

Not only is Jesus an example of a life lived in total obedience to God the Father, both outwardly and inwardly, but so is the apostle Paul. An aspect of obedience that many people struggle with is an unwillingness to give up control. We may have that mistaken belief that for my life to be good I have to be in control of my plans and dreams, and then work towards fulfilling those dreams.

If we are going to live a life of obedience, then we must trust every aspect of our life to God; that means we surrender control of *all* aspects of our life to God. We don't hold on to things and attempt to control them ourselves, but we give them to God and allow ourselves to be "poured out as a drink offering." The picture of a drink offering reminds us that in Old Testament times, when a person brought an animal to sacrifice to God, they would also bring wine, or oil, to pour over the sacrifice as an offering to God (see Numbers 15:4-10).

It is important for us to remember that Paul was in prison while he wrote this. The circumstances of his life gave him good reason to complain and murmur. He had been in prison for several years already, and he faced the possibility of being executed at any moment. Yet he isn't complaining. He is practicing what he preaches. Paul is saying that his life is the drink offering that is poured out over the sacrifice, which is the faith of the Philippian believers. Their faith is what is most important. He is willing to labor tirelessly for them because he chooses to place their well-being above his own.

The apostle Paul isn't asking anyone to pity him, but to be "glad and rejoice" with him. Pouring out our self to help others, to shine brightly for Jesus, isn't a burden, but something that we can rejoice in, and be glad in. This isn't just for ministers and missionaries to do, but something that every one of us can do. It can happen in our marriages, at our jobs, in school, in our neighborhoods. We can live a life of both outward and inward obedience to God, which will stand out to the world like a lit candle in a dark room. A life lived like that will attract others to Jesus, and God's will shall be accomplished in our lives and bring Him glory.

June 5

"God meant it for good..."
Genesis 50:20b

Waiting is a part of life for all of us. We wait in line at the store, and there are even times we wait just to get into the store. Traffic lights turn red, and we wait for it to turn green. We wait to find the right person to marry and then we wait for children to be born. After we have children, we will find that we spend lots of time waiting for them to reach developmental milestones, and later for them to return home. Waiting is a part of life, but it is a part that many of us struggle with. Why do so many of us struggle with waiting? Part of it is that we measure whether we are successful or not by what we are doing, and when we are waiting, we aren't doing anything. It is a struggle to be idle.

God understands that clearly, but He also uses our times of waiting for a purpose. Joseph understood this. His brothers are scared (and for good reason), so Joseph comforts them by reminding them the evil they did, God allowed it because He used it to accomplish good. That good that God intended was not immediately seen. Joseph waited a long time for that to happen. He waited in Potiphar's house for years. Most of us would have spent that time trying to run away. He spent years in prison. We would have tried to plan an escape. Waiting on God is difficult. It is much more enjoyable to skip to the final chapter where everyone lives happily ever after. But those chapters in between are very necessary.

While we live in those in between chapters we cry out to God asking Him why we are dealing with the difficulties we are experiencing. We want God to give us the answer, and He generally does not. This is what makes waiting difficult. We want an answer right now, but don't get the answer for long periods of time. This is the point where too many people decide they aren't willing to wait any longer and choose to walk away from God. God doesn't answer them the way they expect, which causes them to doubt that God is answering them, or if even God exists. God isn't a TV show. The situation will not always be solved within 23 or 42 minutes. There are times when the solution to a situation will take years. The author of Hebrews reminds us of this when he wrote, "Abraham, having patiently waited, obtained the promise" (Hebrews 6:15). While we are waiting on God, don't give up hope. Remember that He is in control, and He will take what you are experiencing and turn it to good for His purposes. God is in control. Trust Him!

June 6

"If anyone thinks he is religious and does not bridle his tongue but deceives his heart, this person's religion is worthless. Religion that is pure and undefiled before God the Father is this: to visit orphans and widows in their affliction, and to keep oneself unstained from the world."

James 1:26-27

The apostle James provides us a way to measure whether or not a person's walk is equal to their talk. It is simple for a person to tell others how religious they are, but are they really what they claim to be? There is a way to verify whether their words are true or not: do they practice what they preach? James tells us that actions speak louder than words. True religion is shown by a person's actions, not simply by hearing the Word. When James uses the word "religion," he is referring to an "outward practice, or service to a god." It is not used in a positive manner, because the speaker claims to be religious, but their actions show that they are not in a correct standing with God. When a person is truly walking with God, it will be seen through the way that they live.

Generally, when a person thinks about religion, their thoughts are directed towards temples, ceremonies, and maybe even special days. That is not a "pure and undefiled religion" is about. For a religion to be pure and undefiled, it will show God's Word being put into practice in a person's life, and seen by others through their speech, service, and separation from the world. That's what it's all about; doing the work of God and providing need to the less fortunate and those who cannot provide for or take care of themselves. This is why James refers to looking after "orphans and widows." To be a disciple of Jesus can be seen in practical ways. In ancient times there were not social programs to assist people in need as there is today. Widows and orphans were completely dependent upon the generosity of others to live. They weren't able to work and provide for themselves, so all they received is what was given to them. If they didn't have enough given to them, then their choices were to beg, sell themselves off as slaves, or starve to death. Not a single good option in the bunch. This is why it was so important for believers to provide for the well-being of those who couldn't provide for themselves. This is what Jesus did for us, and what He is looking for us to do for others. Show how God has changed you by helping out someone in need.

June 7

"And they returned to Joshua and said to him, 'Do not have all the people go up, but let about two or three thousand men go up and attack Ai. Do not make the whole people toil up there, for they are few.' So about three thousand men went up there from the people. And they fled before the men of Ai."
Joshua 7:3-4

The children of Israel are fresh off their victory over Jericho. They began their conquest of the Promised Land and achieved their first victory. They are showing wisdom in not taking time to celebrate their victory, but knowing their battles are far from over they begin to prepare for the next battle. Joshua shows his military wisdom in sending out spies to gather as much information as possible before they begin the battle.

The spies returned and were not impressed with the city of Ai. This is where the children of Israel began to make mistakes. The size of the enemy is not always indicative of how difficult the battle will be. Because Ai was smaller and less impressive than Jericho these men thought it would be an easier battle. They were thinking they could easily defeat this smaller city. What they failed to recall is that they hadn't won the battle of Jericho. The victory was God's. All the Israelites had done was be obedient to God, and He gave them the victory; they had not earned the victory.

We need to be careful that we don't fall into this same trap in our own lives. God supplies us with spiritual victories in our lives. You might have achieved a victory over a certain sin in your own life, such as pornography, gossiping, lying, greed, covetousness, pride, etc. Be careful that you don't begin to take credit for that victory and become confident in yourself. The victory came from the grace of God, and as soon as we stop looking to Him, we begin to set ourselves up for failure. Just because we have received a spiritual victory does not mean that we will automatically win the next battle. We need to remain in close contact and fellowship with God, through prayer and Bible study.

Prayer is the next area where the children of Israel and Joshua made a mistake. Nowhere in this passage do we read of anyone approaching God in prayer and seeking His wisdom. We will see that there was sin in the camp that had not been dealt with, but Joshua was unaware of it. If he, and the people, had been seeking God He would have revealed that to them. "If any of you lacks wisdom, let him ask God, who gives generously to all without reproach, and it will be given him" (James 1:5). God does, and will, answer us when we cry out to Him. God does not want to see us defeated, as Israel will soon experience. Cry out to God; seek Him and His wisdom in all things. There is no battle or issue in our life that is too small for us to bring to God. Neither is there any battle small enough that we can confidently win in our own strength. We need God's wisdom and strength to be successful in everything.

June 8

"But it seemed good to Silas to remain there."
Acts 15:34

Silas traveled from Jerusalem to Antioch in order to assist Paul and Barnabas. He had no plans to stay there, but after being there, the Holy Spirit showed him that this is where he needed to be. Silas looks around Antioch and knows that this is where God is calling him to be at this time. This is often how God works.

Silas has no idea what his future is going to look like. We are going to see him help Paul in bringing the gospel to entirely new areas. He is not aware of any of this at this time. He only knows that this is the place God is directing him to be. This is how it often works in our own lives too. We sense and understand that we are doing what God is calling us to do, but we have no idea where it is going to lead. And that is a good thing.

If someone had told me when I became a Christian that I would be where I am right now, I wouldn't have believed them, and probably would have even resisted becoming a Christian. Following and serving God requires faith, trust, and obedience. God takes us through trials and experiences in our life to prepare us for what He has in plan for us. I had no plans or intentions of ever becoming a pastor, or even of living in Idaho. But by living a life of trusting and following God, here I am having the privilege and honor of both those things.

The Army says that joining them is an adventure, but it's nothing compared to the Great Adventure of the Christian life. This is why we are called to live a life of faith. Yes, we do make plans, but we make them lightly, giving God the power and control to change them to fit His plans. That is why through the apostle Paul, God said, "Come now, you who say, 'Today or tomorrow we will go into such and such a town and spend a year there and trade and make a profit'— yet you do not know what tomorrow will bring. What is your life? For you are a mist that appears for a little time and then vanishes. Instead you ought to say, 'If the Lord wills, we will live and do this or that.'" (James 4:13-15). Trust God, His plans are so much greater than any plans we can ever make.

June 9

"For God is not unjust so as to overlook your work and the love that you have shown for his name in serving the saints, as you still do."

Hebrews 6:10

Many of us measure our success by what we have done, just as we would in business or at work. We are successful at work when we can measure our productivity. I assembled more widgets today than yesterday, I completed 90% of the things on my "to-do list," the filing is complete, etc. What we are in the world determines how productive we are. We must be careful not to take this mindset and apply it to our spiritual lives. This is the mistake that many cults make, and those bound by works and/or legalism find them in this same trap.

The author of Hebrews reminds us that nothing we do for God is forgotten, even if no other person on earth is aware of it. God may place on your heart to pray for someone, and when you do God will reward you for being obedient. No one may know that you prayed for that person, but God does. There are times when it feels like we are accomplishing absolutely nothing. No matter what it is you do, it doesn't seem to work out. Things around you do not seem to change, and there are no obvious results seen. You may feel like a failure in this world. You pray, but nothing seems to be answered. Don't give up. Continue to be obedient to God and do what He has called you to do.

God has you where you are right now for a reason. Even if you are infirm and not able to go out into the world, it is for a reason. God can use a secluded person confined to a bed inside a house. Remember, the apostle Paul was chained to guards while in prison, and God used him to witness to those guards and they began to surrender their lives to God. Do what God places on your heart; pray for others, witness to others, and continue to read and study His Word. Don't look for results to gauge whether you are being successful or not. A lighthouse continues to shine even though it has no idea how many ships it has saved from the rocky coast. It may not be aware of having ever saved a life, yet it continues to shine in the darkness. That is what God has called you and I to do also. Even when we are not aware of any results from our witnessing and praying, we need to continue to witness and pray. God will reward you for being faithful, and there will be results that you are not aware of.

June 9

"Then Moses answered, 'But behold, they will not believe me or listen to my voice, for they will say, "The LORD did not appear to you."'"
Exodus 4:1

It is very important that we both realize and understand that God does not get upset with us when we ask Him a question. When God first told Moses that He was sending Moses to Egypt to deliver the Israelites from their bondage, Moses responded with a question, "Who am I..." (Exodus 3:11). That was a logical question, especially in light of how monumental a task it is that he is being called to do. God never chastised Moses for asking the question; in fact, God answered the question for him by giving him a promise: "But I will be with you" (Exodus 3:12). So, asking a question is not a problem, but after God has given an answer, and you continue to ask the same question, then it becomes a problem. This is the third time Moses is questioning God, and the second time after God has answered his question and given him a promise. This is totally inappropriate. Moses asking this question again shows that he does not believe God. God has told Moses the people will listen to him, but he doesn't believe that is true; this is why Moses continues to question God.

It is important that we learn from Moses. God doesn't give promises flippantly, so when He does give a promise, it is something that we can be assured is going to happen. If we do not, then we deal with the issue of unbelief. God's Word has never failed to happen in the history of the world, so we can take God's Word and believe it. This is simple, but let's be real, it isn't always easy. Let's take Moses as an example, he is going to go back to Egypt, where he is a wanted outlaw, and tell the people that the God of Abraham, Isaac, and Jacob has spoken to him and called him to lead all of Israel out of slavery. Their natural question is going to be "how do you know it was God?" His answer is because he spoke to a burning bush in the middle of the desert. It would not be easy to convince others that what he is saying is true. But he does have God's assurance that the people will listen to him, no matter how outlandish this may seem to be. God promises they will believe him, so, for him to continue to question God shows us that Moses is struggling with belief. What Moses needs is faith; to trust God and His Word. "Now faith is the assurance of things hoped for, the conviction of things not seen" (Hebrews 11:1). The reason for this is because "without faith it is impossible to please Him" (Hebrews 11:6).

June 10

"By this we know love, that He laid down His life for us..."
1 John 3:16a

To understand what true love is, we need to look at, and carefully study, Jesus' sacrifice on the cross. When we look at the cross, we get an undiluted picture of love. If you ever doubt whether Jesus loves you, all you have to do is look at the cross to realize that He really does! It is too easy to question Jesus' love for us while we are in the midst of difficult times. We may question His love for us, but we have to ask ourselves why would He die on the cross for us if He didn't really love us? It was extremely painful to have those spikes driven through His hands and feet. Having a crown of thorns pushed into His skull wasn't comfortable at all. Jesus didn't experience warm fuzzies while He was being tortured and executed. Love really has very little to do with warm fuzzies, feelings, or emotions. Love is all about commitment, endurance, and even sacrifice.

The world will tell you that love is mushy, filled with emotions, warm fuzzy feelings, or a rush of hormones. Love is much more than a feeling or an emotion. You cannot control your feelings or emotions, but love can be controlled, because true love must be voluntary. When Jesus died on the cross, it wasn't the Romans that nailed Him there. Neither was it jealous Jewish leaders that orchestrated His murder, or the angry mob that cried out for Barabbas to be set free, or an indifferent governor named Pilate, or a high priest named Caiaphas. What held Jesus to the cross was love. He willingly submitted Himself to God's will and chose to lay down His life in order to pay the penalty for our sin because His love for you and I is so great. Jesus had the power and authority to call down ten thousand angels to come set Him free, but He chose not to. He chose to die on the cross. That is what love does. Love gives voluntarily.

True love is also unselfish. That is why we read that Jesus "laid down His life for us." Love is all about laying down, not picking up. It is about giving, not just receiving. Love begins when a person sees someone else's needs as being as important as his own needs. Love is willing to lay down not only its own life, but its rights, its comforts, its time, its attention, and its energy for another person.

We also see that true love is unconditional. Why did Jesus die on the cross for us? Were we deserving of this? Had we earned it? No! Romans 5:8 tells us that "God proves His own love for us in that while we were still sinners Christ died for us!" This means that even before you chose to surrender your life to Jesus, He already chose to die for you. While we were still enemies to Him, He chose to love us. This means that Jesus made the first move, because true love initiates. Love doesn't wait for the other person to act. Remember when you were in elementary school, and you slipped a note to the little boy or girl that you liked? Your note said "Do you love me? Check yes, no, or maybe." You were afraid to say you loved them until you knew whether they loved you, or not. True love is unconditional. It doesn't matter whether they love you or not, if you really love them. True love takes the initiative, even if there isn't any promise of love being returned to you.

June 11

"And you shall say to him, 'The LORD, the God of the Hebrews, sent me to you, saying, "Let my people go, that they may serve me in the wilderness." But so far, you have not obeyed. Thus says the LORD, "By this you shall know that I am the LORD: behold, with the staff that is in my hand I will strike the water that is in the Nile, and it shall turn into blood."'"
Exodus 7:16-17

Moses is to remind Pharaoh that he had already been asked to let the children of Israel go so they could worship God, but he refused to let this happen. So, now he is going to be a witness to the power of God; the very God that Pharaoh wondered about and asked why he should listen to a God that he doesn't know. This is the main problem here: Pharaoh doesn't recognize God, so God is going to show him exactly who God is. Pharaoh is going to recognize God, and he eventually will honor God too.

Moses tells Pharaoh that he is going to "strike the water that is in the Nile, and it shall turn into blood." Moses here is an instrument of God, which means that when he strikes the river, it is literally the hand of God that is punishing the Egyptians. Moses is the spokesperson for God, but it is God doing all the work.

This is the first plague of the first series of three plagues. This plague, along with the next two plagues (water to blood, frogs, & gnats), caused discomfort to the people of Egypt. The second series of three plagues was more severe (flies, livestock killed, and boils), and it caused destruction throughout Egypt. The final series of three plagues caused great amounts of destruction and dread (storm, locusts, and darkness). These three groups of three were followed by the tenth and final plague, which was the most severe and destructive: the death of all the first-born males throughout the land of Egypt. The moral of this event is the longer that a person takes to recognize and acknowledge God, or to hear Him and obey Him, the greater the pain and destruction they will receive and endure as a result of their choosing to reject God instead of surrendering to Him. I hope and pray that this would be clear to us: don't reject God's Word, listen to Him and obey Him. The choice is yours. What will you choose to do?

Jun 12

"...he is a double-minded man, unstable in all his ways."
James 1:8

James has been writing about the importance of our attitude when we face a trial or temptation in our life. When we realize that God has allowed it in our life for a reason and a purpose, we can face the trial or temptation with joy, instead of anger or frustration. One of the purposes God has in allowing trials and temptations into our life is so we will realize that we need God because we do not have the strength, resources, or the wisdom to handle them on our own. Therefore, we need to seek God and ask Him for wisdom to help us not only get through the trials or temptations, but to get through them victoriously. When we ask God for wisdom, we need to "ask in faith, with no doubting" (James 1:6). Faith is trusting God and knowing that He will hear us when we pray, and He will also answer that prayer. If we come to God in prayer and doubt that He will hear us or answer us we are like a wave: up one moment, and down the next. We don't want to live that way, because that is a sign of immaturity, according to the apostle Paul. "So that we may no longer be children, tossed to and fro by the waves and carried about by every wind of doctrine, by human cunning, by craftiness in deceitful schemes" (Ephesians 4:14).

God allows us to experience trials and temptations so that we will grow in our faith and become mature believers. An immature believer is unstable, double-minded, or indecisive. As a believer, it is important we make a commitment to stand with God, and not allow anything, or any experience, to move us away from Him. I am going to stand with God and His Word. If I fall in life, I will fall with God and His Word. I am not going to leave God or His Word, and I will not walk away from this position. This is the mindset that we need as believers. Don't do as so many do, which is give God a deadline to act. It is so easy to do, telling God we give Him until the end of this week (or whatever time frame we give Him), and if You don't act by then, then we have a backup plan that we will follow. Don't do that. Be like the apostle Paul. He had been warned not to go to Jerusalem because he would have to face trials there, including possible jail time. What was Paul's response? "But none of these things move me; nor do I count my life dear to myself, so that I may finish my race with joy, and the ministry which I received from the Lord Jesus, to testify to the gospel of the grace of God" (Acts 20:24 NKJV). Paul decided that he was going to live His life for God, no matter the outcome. If he did well, he did well with God. If he suffered, then he would suffer with God. Believer, are you willing to stand with God, no matter what? It is not easy, but does provide a life that is stable, and will not pass away.

June 13

"Then God said to Noah."
Genesis 8:15

Noah spent a little over one year on the ark with his wife, his 3 sons and their wives, plus all the animals. That is a long time to spend cooped up inside a small, confined space. Earlier in Genesis 8 Noah removed the cover from the ark, so he knew that the ground was now dry. Noah had also sent out a raven, which did not return to him, and a dove, which did return to him. A week later he sent out the dove again, and this time it returned with an olive branch in its beak. One week later Noah again sent out the dove, and this time it never returned. This let Noah know that the ground was getting dry. Noah remained on the ark 29 more days after the dove didn't return, so the ground was now dry, yet he remained on the ark.

Noah was waiting to hear from God. We have no record of God speaking to Noah while he was on the ark. There are times in our life when we cry out to God, but God does not immediately respond to us. He allows us to wait for an answer. That is what is happening to Noah. God instructed Noah when to enter the ark and Noah is wise enough to wait for God to instruct him to leave. Even though Noah is able to look out and see that the ground is dry, and the failure of the dove to return a month ago, he will not leave. This is because Noah is following the advice of Proverbs 3:5. "Trust in the LORD with all your heart, and do not lean on your own understanding." Noah trusts God for the right time to move and is not relying on, or trusting in, his own understanding. What a great example for us to follow.

So often we make moves in our life because it "makes sense" to us. Instead of moving forward immediately because it looks good, we need to spend time seeking God's direction. Often this will cause others to question you and your timing. But as Noah shows us here, God's timing is perfect, and it does not follow our own understanding. What a great man of faith to not move until he receives instruction from the Lord. Oh, how I pray that we would become great men and women of faith and seek God, and then wait for His instructions before we make a move. The world will not understand us; in fact, other people, including Christians, will not either. But there is no better place to be than in the middle of God's will. That is why Noah was content to remain inside a cooped-up space with his family and all these animals instead of out roaming the land. He knew he was inside the center of God's will in the ark, and he would not move until God spoke to Him.

June 14

"...and self-control with steadfastness..."
2 Peter 1:6b

Peter has mentioned that the believer needs to possess virtue (or courage), knowledge, and self-control. The next characteristic that Peter mentions we need to have is steadfastness. Some translations of the Bible use the word patience or endurance or perseverance instead of steadfastness. Each of these words speak of the same thing: a person that will not be moved or swerve away from their deliberate purpose and remain loyal to their faith, even when facing great trials or struggles. This is different than self-control because self-control deals with the handling of the pleasures of this life, while steadfastness has to do with the handling of pressures and/or problems in life. Sadly, a person that who easily relents and gives in to the pleasures of life often is not disciplined enough to handle the pressures and problems of life either, which leads to them "giving up" instead.

God doesn't want us to give up, but He does desire that we grow in our faith and knowledge in Him, maturing as a believer to grow and develop the discipline and strength to handle the pressures and problems that we face in this life. You may have even noticed that the longer we remain on this earth, the problems we face don't seem to get easier, but as the days go on the pressures and problems intensify. The apostle Paul was familiar with this too. After he had finished his third missionary journey he was on his way to Jerusalem and stopped in the city of Miletus and spent some time pouring into the elders and leaders of the church in Ephesus. He explained to them that he knew difficult times were waiting for him in Jerusalem. He didn't know exactly what was going to happen, but that it could include him being imprisoned. Even though he knew difficult and rough times were ahead of him, he didn't shrink back or stop going forward. Quite the opposite happened. Paul was very steadfast, and he continued to move forward, even knowing that it could lead to trouble for him. He said, "I do not account my life of any value nor as precious to myself, if only I may finish my course and the ministry that I received from the Lord Jesus, to testify to the gospel of the grace of God" (Acts 20:24). He knew what God had called him to do, and nothing, not even the threat of physical harm to himself, was going to move him away from God's calling. That, my friend, is steadfastness. This is what God desires from each of us too. To be willing to choose to continue to follow and serve God, no matter what we face here on earth.

June 15

"If you really fulfill the royal law according to the Scripture, 'You shall love your neighbor as yourself,' you are doing well."
James 2:8

There are many different laws in the world today. In fact, many believe that there are too many laws. There are so many laws that those in charge of keeping the law often don't even know all the laws that they are to enforce. In Jewish society there was one law that all people were aware of and tried to keep in their personal lives: the Mosaic Law. James now writes about another law, the "Royal Law." Which law is this? "Love you neighbor as yourself." Why does James refer to this law as the Royal Law? That is a good question, and there are a few reasons.

First, this is the Royal Law because the law was given by the King. Jesus shared this with the disciples in John 13:34, but even before that, God had given this command in the Law. It is found in Leviticus 19:18, which says, "You shall not take vengeance or bear a grudge against the sons of your own people, but you shall love your neighbor as yourself: I am the LORD." We are to show love towards our neighbors. Love is what should be flowing out of our lives because

"because God's love has been poured into our hearts through the Holy Spirit who has been given to us" (Romans 5:5). In addition, as a true believer, we have been "taught by God to love one another" (1 Thessalonians 4:9).

Secondly, loving others is a Royal Law because it "rules" over all other laws. Romans 13:10 reminds us that "love is the fulfilling of the law." This is why when Jesus was asked what the most important law is, He answered, "'Hear, O Israel: The Lord our God, the Lord is one. And you shall love the Lord your God with all your heart and with all your soul and with all your mind and with all your strength.' The second is this: 'You shall love your neighbor as yourself.' There is no other commandment greater than these" (Mark 12:29-31). Think of how many thousands of laws that could be erased from the books if we would just love our neighbors. There are so many unnecessary laws that would not be needed if we simply loved all other people.

The final reason why loving others is called the Royal Law is because when we obey this law and love others, it causes us to be royalty. A person who is filled with hatred is a slave to their hatred, but love sets us free from selfishness and hatred and allows us to love others and reign like a king. It is love that enables us to obey God's Word, and to treat others as the Bible teaches us to.

June 16

"But Jacob did not send Benjamin, Joseph's brother, with his brothers, for he feared that harm might happen to him."'
Genesis 42:4

You may have heard people say some of the following quotes: in fact, you may have even said them yourself. "If it wasn't for bad luck, I wouldn't have any luck at all." "I can't catch a break; everything goes against me." "Murphy's Law strikes again." "The whole world is against me, that's why I can't ever get ahead." All too often we may feel this way because things don't go the way we expect them to go or want them to go. If a couple things go differently than we want, we may find ourselves beginning to feel like we can't do anything right because everything is working against us.

That is exactly how Jacob is feeling. His dearly loved wife, Rachel, has passed away. His favorite son, Joseph, has disappeared and Jacob was told and shown evidence that he had been killed. Jacob still has eleven sons at home, but only one of them truly matters to him; that is Benjamin, the son of Rachel and the true blood-brother of Joseph. At this time there is a very severe famine which causes Jacob and his family to not have enough food to eat. They know that there is food available in Egypt, but Jacob refuses to allow Benjamin to go there with his brothers because he is sure that some calamity will come upon Benjamin, just as has already happened to Rachel and Joseph.

Jacob has allowed life to turn him into a bitter, pessimistic, and cynical man. Instead of looking at the future and seeing great possibilities, he only sees problems and disasters. Why is that? He has lost his faith and trust in God. The author of Hebrews reminds us what faith is: "faith is the assurance of things hoped for, the conviction of things not seen" (Hebrews 11:1). Faith means that we trust God even when things look bleak, and even when things have not been working out how we expected them to. To have faith and trust in God means that our focus isn't only on what we can see, and what has happened in the past. This is why the apostle Paul reminded us that "we walk by faith, not by sight" (2 Corinthians 5:7).

May we learn a lesson from Jacob. Don't become cynical when things haven't worked out the way you expected. That simply means your expectations were wrong. Don't allow past failures to dictate and direct your future. Remember that God is in control. Trust Him. Have faith in Him.

June 17

"Then Hezekiah said to Isaiah, 'The word of the LORD that you have spoken is good.' For he thought, 'Why not, if there will be peace and security in my days?'"
2 Kings 20:19

Hezekiah was king of Judah, and he was a good king. He loved the Lord and served God throughout this life. He became very sick. In fact, he was deathly sick, and he cried out to God to save him. God spoke through the prophet Isaiah and his life was extended 15 years. During those 15 additional years Hezekiah welcomed and entertained some dignitaries from a small, unknown, far-away nation; Babylon. Hezekiah showed these dignitaries from Babylon everything in his kingdom, including all the treasures in God's temple. After all, this was a small, unknown nation; so, he did not see any harm in this. Isaiah came to the palace as they were leaving and pressed Hezekiah as to who they were and what he had shown them. He finally relented and admitted he had shown them everything the kingdom had. Isaiah responded with a word from God, "Hear the word of the LORD: Behold, the days are coming, when all that is in your house, and that which your fathers have stored up till this day, shall be carried to Babylon. Nothing shall be left, says the LORD. And some of your own sons, who will come from you, whom you will father, shall be taken away, and they shall be eunuchs in the palace of the king of Babylon" (2 Kings 20:16b-18).

God had just pronounced judgment on Judah and the descendants of Hezekiah through the prophet Isaiah, and Hezekiah's response is that God's Word is good because it won't happen in his lifetime. Wow! Talk about a selfish attitude. He is saying that he is alright with any bad things happening, as long as it happens after he is dead. This is a wrong and selfish attitude. Maybe it bothers us so much because we sometimes find the same attitude in ourselves? The

Bible says this shouldn't be the attitude of Christians; we are to be others-centered. "Do nothing from selfish ambition or conceit, but in humility count others more significant than yourselves. Let each of you look not only to his own interests, but also to the interests of others" (Philippians 2:3-4). This is especially true as a parent. Hezekiah was just told that he would be leaving death and destruction for his children, and he was ok with it. As parents we are to leave better things for our children, and grandchildren. "A good man leaves an inheritance to his children's children, but the sinner's wealth is laid up for the righteous" (Proverbs 13:22). We need to examine our heart constantly, and make sure our children, and grandchildren, are prepared and equipped for the future.

June 18

"You shall have no other gods before Me."
Exodus 20:3

This is the first commandment. This first commandment flows very logically from the understanding of who God is and what He has done. God is the only god that can alter the course of history, therefore, He is also the only God that we serve. This commandment also set Israel apart from all the other ancient nations, who worshipped and followed numerous gods. The practice of following more than one god is known as polytheistic. "Poly" means "more than one," and "theism" is the study of deities, or gods. In contrast to the other nations, this first command directed Israel to be monotheistic, following one God only.

God shows how realistic He is; He acknowledges that there are other gods that are worshipped and followed in the world. These other gods that were worshipped in ancient times are still worshipped today, even though the names may have changed, the gods haven't. Let's look at some of these other gods:

1. Baal. The god of power. People looking for power and control over others are worshipping the god Baal.
2. Asheroth. The goddess of sexuality, sexuality, pleasure and reproduction. It is easy to see that this god is still worshipped by many today.
3. Mammon. The god of money and prosperity. In 1 Timothy 6:10 we are told that "the love of money is a root of all kinds of evils." Money itself is not evil, it is the love of money. This means that it isn't just those that are rich that worship Mammon today. In fact, lotteries would not be so popular except that many people with little money still worship Mammon.
4. Molloch. The god of practicality. Many people ignore their families in order to be practical and get ahead in life. Molloch is still worshipped today.

God says not to have any gods before Him. This does not mean that we can keep other gods in our life, as long as we keep the One true God first. No! The word "before" can also be translated as "against." This first commandment requires the believer to serve God exclusively, and no other gods in any way, shape, or form. God doesn't just want to be added to our life, He wants everything in our life to be given to Him. This is very different from other religions, where worship of other gods is acceptable, and often even encouraged. Why is God exclusive, when other gods are happy and content to allow their followers to worship other gods? Because all other gods work together as a team to lead people away from the One true God and to mislead people to hell. No other gods are allowed to, or able to, stand before the One true God. That is why "at the name of Jesus every knee should bow, in heaven and on earth and under the earth, and every tongue confess that Jesus Christ is Lord, to the glory of God the Father" (Philippians 2:10-11).

June 19

"For every kind of beast and bird, of reptile and sea creature, can be tamed and has been tamed by mankind, but no human being can tame the tongue. It is a restless evil, full of deadly poison."
James 3:7-8

Have you ever gone to the circus and seen the amazing things people have trained elephants to do? They jump rope, stand on two feet, move heavy objects that no person could even dream of doing. Why are they able to do these amazing feats? Because they have been trained. Not only elephants, but people have trained lions, tigers, bears, and other wild animals. These are animals that can easily tear a man to pieces, but they have been trained not only to not do that, but to perform spectacular things. Birds can be trained to talk, and even snakes can be trained by snake charmers. You can even see whales, seals, and walruses following commands and performing to entertain audiences. All kinds of animals can be trained; even animals you wouldn't necessarily dream of training.

Yet, there remains one animal that no person can train. That is the tongue. People have an incredible capacity to accomplish amazing feats. Have you ever heard of John Colter? He traveled on the Lewis & Clark expedition, but he didn't return because he loved the wild lands of the west. One day he was outside of present-day Bozeman, Montana when he was captured by Blackfeet Indians. They respected him and offered him a chance to outrun them to remain alive. John Colter was unarmed and naked, being chased by people intent on killing him, and armed with weapons. He was fast, evaded capture, and ended up running 150 miles to the nearest trading post to remain alive. Other people have even cut off parts of their body that were trapped, to stay alive. But even people that are able to perform these heroic feats to stay alive cannot tame their own tongue. Fire can be tamed. Animals can be tamed. We cannot tame our tongues. This does not mean the tongue cannot be tamed. We cannot do that, but God can! God is the only One that is mightier than our tongue. It is imperative that we surrender control of our tongue to God. To do this, we must first surrender our heart to Him, because "out of the abundance of the heart the mouth speaks" (Matthew 12:34).

June 20

"Since therefore Christ suffered in the flesh, arm yourselves with the same way of thinking, for whoever has suffered in the flesh has ceased from sin..."
1 Peter 4:1

Suffering is something that the average person tries to avoid in their life. This is because suffering is not pleasant, it is not comfortable, nor is it enjoyable. But there can be good results or purposes that come from it. It is what the apostle Paul wrote about in Romans 8:28, which reminds us that "for those who love God all things work together for good, for those who are called according to His purpose." Knowing that good can come from suffering may not make it an enjoyable experience, but it can help us gain from that difficult time. When we experience suffering, especially when it is due to our faith in Jesus, the result of the suffering will be that sin's grip is loosened in our life. As we go through a period of suffering, it helps us more clearly see what sin is and what it does in our life, and that sin becomes repulsive to us. No longer will you be able to so easily give in to sin anymore. When your life is touched by the ugliness of sin you realize how ugly and awful sin really is and that isn't something to glibly joke about, to wink at, or to chuckle at. Sin is ugly.

Peter writes that after we suffer in the flesh we will cease from sin. Now, don't misunderstand what he is saying. He is not saying that suffering itself causes us to stop sinning. There are numerous examples in history to show that this is true. Look at Pharaoh. He went through extreme suffering during the ten plagues, and it didn't stop him from sinning. In fact, it had the opposite effect on him, it hardened his heart, and the pain from his suffering made him bitter. So how does suffering cause us to cease from sin? It is suffering *plus* Jesus. The apostle Paul writes about this is Romans 6, which says that when we identify with Jesus in His suffering and death, we will achieve victory over sin. As we submit ourselves to Jesus, we will have the same attitude towards sin that Jesus did, which causes us to overcome our natural self and grow in our new life in Jesus. When we suffer with Jesus in our life, the desire for sin will lessen in our life and our desires and appetites for sin will change. To keep it all in context Peter reminds us that "whoever has suffered in the flesh has ceased from sin, so as to live for the rest of the time in the flesh no longer for human passions but for the will of God" (1 Peter 4:1b-2).

June 21

"Then Israel said to Joseph, 'Behold, I am about to die, but God will be with you and will bring you again to the land of your fathers.'"
Genesis 48:21

Bob Dylan sang "The times they are a-changin'." He was completely correct. He wrote that song to let the "older" generation know that things were going to be different. The current generation would do things differently, and it was going to frustrate the older generation, and they wouldn't understand it. That was true then, and it continues to be true every generation. The older generation often wonders what the younger generation will do. How will they make things work out? Jacob wants to make sure that Joseph doesn't get too comfortable with the "new" way of doing things here in Egypt, and that he will continue to follow the Lord. The future of Israel wasn't in Egypt, but back in the Promised Land. To ensure that they would leave Egypt and return to their homeland, Jacob leaves Joseph with a special promise from God, a promise that is designed to keep future generations following God and recalling their spiritual heritage that needs to be passed down to every future generation. Jacob didn't get frustrated with the younger generation, instead he prepared them for the future.

The promise that Jacob passed on to Joseph was one that had been given to him, and he had experienced it through his entire life. What he passed on wasn't just theoretical head knowledge, but truth that he had personally experienced. When Jacob was a young believer God told him "I am with you and will keep you wherever you go" (Genesis 28:15). God gave him the promise that He would always be with him. Then, a few years later, God said, "Return to the land of your fathers and to your kindred, and I will be with you" (Genesis 31:3). God again reassures him that God will always be with him. At this point in Jacob's life, this promise from God was the only thing he had to keep him going, because it seemed everything was going against him. Fortunately, this promise was all he needed. It carried him through his life. Jacob passes this promise to Joseph, assuring him that God will be with him just as God has been with him. The same is true for us today; God is always with us every single day of our lives.

June 22

"And the winepress was trodden outside the city, and blood flowed from the winepress, as high as a horse's bridle, for 1,600 stadia."
Revelation 14:20

The apostle John describes a scene that would have been unfathomable for him to imagine. There will be a battle that stretches for approximately 180 miles. During John's day this was not possible, but with today's modern warfare and weapons this is very realistic. It is not only imaginable, but we have seen battle scenes that have covered this distance, as it will again here in this final battle.

We are told that this battle will take place outside of the city, which is Jerusalem. The battle occurs outside the city because God is protecting His city, the city where He will establish His kingdom from. At the end of chapter 13 it looked like the Beast was going to be victorious and conquer the world, but now at the end of chapter 14 we see that God is victorious, not the Beast. God defeats the Beast and is able to protect the city where He establishes His kingdom from. God cannot be defeated. That is wonderful news.

John is describing the Battle of Armageddon, which will be described in greater detail in Revelation 16. The prophet Zechariah also prophesied this battle about 500 years before the birth of Jesus in Zechariah 14:1-4. This battle will take place approximately 60 miles north of Jerusalem near Mount Megiddo. The carnage in this battle is going to be horrific. John tells us that the blood will flow up to the bridles of a horse. It is possible that this describes an actual river of blood that high, or is could be describing that the blood splatter will reach that height. Either way, the destruction from this battle will be devastating.

For us today it is important for us to realize that even when it appears that Satan is winning, that God is still in control, and He will be victorious. Satan loves it when it appears that he is winning and it causes anxiety in believers, but his ultimate fate is destruction. Jesus is victorious. He cannot, and will not, be defeated. We can take that to the bank and rest in that truth. No matter how things may appear, Satan is defeated, and Jesus is the victor.

June 23

"And they offered great sacrifices that day and rejoiced, for God had made them rejoice with great joy; the women and children also rejoiced. And the joy of Jerusalem was heard far away."

Nehemiah 12:43

The world is continually filled with things that will depress you and bring you down. Shelves in stores are empty because of supply chain problems. Housing costs continue to rise, crime is getting out of hand, the media is in every aspect of life and glorifies things that cause depression and fear. Cases of child abuse, rape, pornography, marital infidelity, malpractice, drug abuse, political scandals, and crises in every imaginable area of life seem to be growing every year. Listen to the media daily and it's no wonder that the joy of life is sucked out of so many people. Living in the world that we do; many people question whether or not a person can even be filled with joy any longer. Is it possible? Yes! It is. Do you want to know the secret to joy? How can a person reach the goal of joy in their life?

The first thing to recognize is that the goal is not to have joy. If joy is your goal, you will never reach it, because joy is a by-product, not a goal. So, what is the secret to joy? It is living a life of fellowship with God. How do we have fellowship with God? Through prayer to God, worship of God, obedience to God and His Word, study of God and His Word, and service to God. In short, living a life that is dedicated to God. This type of life comes at a cost, a great cost to the person who chooses to live this way. Instead of living the life you choose and want, you live your life to please and honor God. It's no longer about what you want or desire, but what does God want and desire from you. The beauty of this is that no matter what is going on in your life, you can have joy because joy comes from within and is not determined by circumstances. The apostle Paul wrote the book of Philippians while he was in jail and the Emperor Nero was deciding whether to kill Paul or not. What is the theme of the book of Philippians? Is it the conundrum that Paul is in? No! It's all about joy. Do you desire to have joy in your life? If you do, then stop searching for joy and begin to live a life that pleases God. You won't find joy, but it will find you.

June 24

"Your lamb shall be without blemish, a male a year old. You may take it from the sheep or from the goats..."
Exodus 12:5

The lamb that each family chose and had to live with them for four days as part of their family had certain requirements that had to be met. There is a good reason for this; this lamb was to become a sacrifice to God. Therefore, the lamb could not be defective, it had to be "without blemish." This lamb had to be as close to perfect as it could be, because when we offer a sacrifice to God, we need to give our best, not second-hand junk or leftovers. We don't want to be like the man whose cow gave birth to twin calves. He was so excited that he went to the church and told the pastor that he was going to give one of the twin calves back to God in thanks for the blessing that he had received. As he looked at the two calves, he couldn't decide which calf to give to the Lord. After a week, one of the calves got sick and it died. The man went back to the pastor and stood there very sadly as he told the pastor that God's calf had died. All too often we are like that farmer in that we want to give back to God what is easy for us to give, that which isn't difficult or cost us too much.

Later when the law was written, God repeated what was already established here at Passover. Leviticus 22:21-22 says, "And when anyone offers a sacrifice of peace offerings to the Lord to fulfill a vow or as a freewill offering from the herd or from the flock, to be accepted it must be perfect; there shall be no blemish in it. Animals blind or disabled or mutilated or having a discharge or an itch or scabs you shall not offer to the Lord or give them to the Lord as a food offering on the altar." There is good reason for this. God is holy and perfectly righteous. Therefore, nothing less than a perfect sacrifice is able to satisfy His requirements. In fact, there is no sacrifice on earth that is able to meet God's requirements. This is why Jesus, the perfect Lamb (see 1 Peter 1:19-20) came to earth and died upon the cross. Only God was able to offer a sacrifice that was perfect and holy enough to meet His requirements. So, He did, because of His great love for you and for me.

June 25

"These are the two olive trees and the two lampstands that stand before the Lord of the earth."
Revelation 11:4

There is nothing worse than running out of an item. Whether you are cooking, baking, doing a chore around the house, or exercising, running out of what you need is frustrating. Wouldn't it be nice to have a never-ending supply of what you need? For example, sometimes people install a natural gas line in their backyard and hook their BBQ grill or smoker to it so that they don't have to take their propane tanks and continually get them refilled. There is always a steady supply of gas being pumped into their yard, and they never have to worry about whether they filled the propane tank. It also eliminates that feeling of dread when your grill won't ignite because you're ready to cook dinner, but you're also out of propane. The same thing applies to exercising. My wife and I enjoy riding our bikes together, but there always comes a point when we are so tired that we can't go any further. How wonderful it would be to never tire out.

While this is true in the physical world, it is also true in the spiritual world. These two witnesses that God sends to the earth during the Tribulation are the fulfillment of vision that was given to the Old Testament prophet Zechariah. In Zechariah 4:14 God prophesied about "two anointed ones who stand by the Lord of the whole earth." In Revelation 11:3 we saw that these two witnesses are filled with great power, and now we are told the source of that power. Zechariah was told that these two olive trees that stand next to God have a "pipe" that fills them with olive oil directly from the olive tree. "I see a solid gold lampstand there with a bowl on its top. It has seven lamps on it and seven channels for each of the lamps on its top. There are also two olive trees beside it, one on the right of the bowl and the other on its left" (Zechariah 4:2-3). Their lamp never burns out because the supply of oil never stops. This is what Jesus shared with His disciples, when He taught "I am the vine; you are the branches. The one who remains in Me and I in him produces much fruit, because you can do nothing without Me" (John 15:5). We need to remain connected to Jesus in order to receive a continual filling of the Holy Spirit, which will empower us to live our life for Jesus. Without the power of the Holy Spirit, we will not bear spiritual fruit. These two witnesses are a reminder to us of the important of being connected to Jesus to fill us with His power.

June 26

"Then the word of the LORD came to him [Elijah], 'Arise, go to Zarephath, which belongs to Sidon, and dwell there. Behold, I have commanded a widow there to feed you.'"
1 Kings 17:8-9

The only constant we have in life is change. So why is it that so many of us fight change? Elijah has been directed by God to leave Jerusalem and to live by the brook Cherith. After being there a while, the brook dried up and now God is directing Elijah to move again. God gives him a promise that He will take care of him as long as he obeys. How does Elijah respond? Elijah "arose and went to Zarephath" (1 Kings 17:10).

Change is something that we will continually deal with in our lives. We need to remember that change is not necessarily bad. We often think it is because it upsets our lives and what we are used to. The longer we live and the more things that we have, the more we become attached and have roots set down, which make it more difficult to accept change. When we deal with change, we learn to place our roots in God instead of things on earth. Moses learned to do this when he lived in constant flux for 80 years. This is why Moses said, "Lord, you have been our dwelling place in all generations" (Psalm 90:1). Moses learned that he could not find refuge in a home, or a tent, or any ministry. The only refuge he could find was in God.

God allows change to come into our life for the same reason. When we remain in one place too long, we become so comfortable that we will never move. We also can become so accustomed to the surroundings that we no longer look to God for guidance and direction. For these reasons God allows change to come into our life. The change could be physical, such as moving to a new state or city, but it can also be within our personal life. Change can occur in the ministries that we are involved in, the friendships that we have, or in other areas of our life. No matter where the change in our life is, it tends to take us into an area that we consider unsafe. At least it may appear to be unsafe to us, but that often is because it is with uncharted territory or moving us outside of our comfort zone.

It is good for us to be moved outside of our comfort zones because that stretches us, makes us stronger, and also forces us to rely on God for strength. When God calls us to change in our life, we are wise to boldly step forward to accept the change instead of whining and trying to hold on to that which we are familiar with and know. It takes faith to follow God, especially when change is involved. Take heart though, God has promised that He will never leave us nor forsake us. When we obediently follow God, we will not always know where He is leading us, but we can rest assured that He is leading us. So, when we don't know where the next step will lead us, and what change will be involved, we can step forward in confidence because God knows exactly where He is leading us. So, step out in faith, accept the change He brings, and confidently know that He will continue to provide for you, just as He did for Elijah.

June 27

"Blessed be the God and Father of our Lord Jesus Christ! According to His great mercy, He has caused us to be born again to a living hope through the resurrection of Jesus Christ from the dead..."
1 Peter 1:3

Dreams are a wonderful thing. I can remember as a child how I would spend hours in the backyard with my mitt, a baseball, and a net that I "pitched" the ball to. I was amazing. In fact, I could confidently say that I was the best pitcher around. There wasn't a hitter in the Major League's that could hit my pitches. It seemed like every day I was able to go out and throw a perfect game. As the best 10-year-old pitcher in the world, I was just waiting for the Los Angeles Dodgers to give me a call and sign me to a contract. After all, it was in their best interest to sign the best pitcher in the world. They never did call, and it took only a couple of Little League games, to realize that I wasn't the greatest pitcher in the world. Truth be told, I wasn't really all that good. My dream of being a major league pitcher died at an early age. Maybe being a major league pitcher wasn't your dream, but whatever your dreams were, time has a way of destroying those hopes. Over time our dreams begin to fade, until they had passed away and died.

Fortunately, not all dreams fade away and die. Jesus gives us a "living hope." A living hope is a hope that lives, one that will never fade away and die. We have this hope not simply because Jesus died on a cross, but because He rose from the dead. As His children, He graciously passes that on to us. This means that our hope is not here in this world. Our hope isn't just to be a major league pitcher (or anything else on earth), to be successful, to make millions of dollars, etc. Our hope is in Heaven. Every day that we live brings us a day closer to the reality of us joining Jesus in Heaven. That hope is what keeps us moving forward, even when surrounded by grief, frustration, difficulties, or even worldwide pandemics. All these things cause our hope in God to grow and become more and more beautiful. One day soon, we will join Jesus in Heaven for eternity. How wonderful and glorious that will be. We can be confident in this because it is a hope that doesn't fade.

June 28

"And the LORD God made for Adam and for his wife garments of skins and clothed them."
Genesis 3:21

Adam and Eve were still covered with the itchy and scratchy fig leaves that they had made. They made these clothes to cover their nakedness because there was an appropriate sense of shame with their nakedness. Today there are many places that are referred to as "clothing optional." These nudists talk about the beauty of the human body and how "free" and "natural" it is to openly display their body in front of all other people. They need to remember that God Himself took steps to provide clothing for Adam and Eve to cover their nakedness. God provided clothing for them because it is right to do so.

People like to joke about the "world's oldest profession" in hushed tones as they refer to prostitution; but here we see that the clothing business is really the world's oldest profession. Adam and Eve attempted to cover themselves with their own works, but it was not sufficient. God made clothes for them out of animal skin. Through this they realized that for their sin to be covered, it required the shedding of blood. This is also referred to as atonement, or a covering. Leviticus 17:11 puts it like this, "For the life of the flesh is in the blood, and I have given it for you on the altar to make atonement for your souls, for it is the blood that makes atonement by the life." God made it very clear that our sins cannot be covered, or atoned, unless an animal gives its blood on the altar.

Many people today attempt to cover their sin by their own works; by sewing together all their religious deeds. They teach Sunday School, go to church every Wednesday evening, attend a weekly Bible study, serve in a jail ministry, the parking lot ministry, go to every retreat offered, pass out Bible tracts, and help feed the homeless every Thanksgiving. Now, these are all great things to be involved in, but they are not able to save us; they cannot cover our sins. Our good works are like monopoly money. They are great for the game, but they are not legal tender and are no good to us anywhere except in the game. Our good works are not legal tender before God, but they do need to be seen in our life. God insisted on a sacrifice; a perfect lamb was to be offered and its bloodshed. Jesus is that perfect Lamb, and He shed His blood on a cross on Calvary. Just as Adam and Eve were clothed in a garment that was purchased with the life of another, we also are clothed with a garment of righteousness that was purchased with the life of another, Jesus Christ.

June 29

"And the twelve summoned the full number of the disciples and said, 'It is not right that we should give up preaching the word of God to serve tables.'"
Acts 6:2

The twelve disciples face a situation of division within the church, and they make a decision that is going to prevent the church from being further divided, and from splitting. The disciples recognized what their priorities were and were willing to give all other ministries to other people to run. What was the priority for the twelve disciples? It was to spend time in prayer and the study of God's Word in order to teach the church. The disciples didn't believe that they were too good to serve others, and they weren't opposed to serving tables and serving food to others, but there were other people that were capable of doing that too. The main priority of the disciples was to make sure that the church was well fed spiritually.

This is still true today. Sometimes churches have unrealistic expectations of the pastor. They expect him to preach powerful sermons on Sunday, but they also expect him to run around all week visiting everyone one and their cousin, take care of all the church facilities, and many other duties, leaving little to no time for the pastor to spend time praying and studying, much less his family, which is his first ministry. The twelve disciples wisely came to the conclusion that for the health of the church, they needed to hand off some ministries and duties to others so they could have the time to be in prayer and study of God's Word so that the church would be better fed spiritually. It is important for the pastor to have time to spend in prayer, study of God's Word, and to prepare their teaching.

Delegation is not an easy thing for most people to do. Even pastors can have a difficult time with it. But it is very important, even within the church. This is why it is so important for the body of believers to be ready and willing to be active participants in church. Every church member is capable of visiting and calling those who can't make it to church due to age, illness, vehicle problems, etc. Individual church members are also capable of running ministries, such as Bible studies, monthly men's or women's breakfast, home studies, feeding the poor, repairing vehicles for widow's and single mom's, etc. Don't get the mentality that that is the job of the pastor, because it's not. For the church body to be healthy, every part of the body needs to be involved, doing its part.

June 30

"Who has measured the waters in the hollow of his hand and marked

off the heavens with a span, enclosed the dust of the earth in a
measure and weighed the mountains in scales
and the hills in a balance?"
Isaiah 40:12

Each of us faces situations in our life that appear to be insurmountable, and most definitely overwhelming to us. We get overwhelmed when the situation is too large for us to grasp or comprehend. Since it is larger than we can understand, people too often transfer that same inability to God. Because we are overwhelmed with the situation, many people believe that God will be overwhelmed by the situation too. That's not true though.

It is so important for us to get an idea of how big God really is, and then we would have a better understanding of why the situations that overwhelm us don't overwhelm Him. The Pacific Ocean is one of seven oceans in the world. The Pacific Ocean, by itself, covers more than 30% of the earth's surface. It covers more than 60 million square miles, and averages 13,000 feet in depth. That is huge, but not to God. He holds the Pacific Ocean, and the other six oceans, in the hollow of His hand. We aren't even able to hold an entire cup of water in the hollow of our hand, but God holds the waters of all the oceans in His.

Scientists continue to argue over how large the universe really is. The truth is that no human really knows. The best estimate is that the universe is approximately 28-billion light years in diameter. How far is a light year? It is about 5.9 trillion miles. That is a number that most human minds cannot even comprehend. Yet, God holds the universe in the span of his hand. I have pretty large hands, yet the span of my hand won't even reach the long side of an 8½ x 11-inch piece of paper.

Our human mind cannot even begin to comprehend how big God really is. That means that any problem or situation that overwhelms us will not overwhelm God because it isn't a huge problem to Him. This is why we need to bring our problems to Him, and then allow Him to deal with it. The psalmist provides us with a good reminder; "Be still, and know that I *am* God" (Psalm 46:10 NKJV). What overwhelms us does not overwhelm God. We can trust Him and rely on Him. Don't fret or stress over things, but instead bring them to God. He's got it. In fact, He's got the whole world in His hands.

July 1

"For Christ did not send me to baptize but to preach the gospel, and not with words of eloquent wisdom, lest the cross of Christ be emptied of its power."
1 Corinthians 1:17

Every one of us has to take a stand so that others will know what is important to us. The apostle Paul reminds us that baptism is important, but not the most important thing. Paul was sent to Corinth by God for a specific purpose and reason, which was to preach the gospel. Why is the gospel more important than baptism? Because the gospel saves a person and baptism does not. This does not mean that baptism isn't important. After all Jesus gave His disciples instructions to baptize people. Jesus said, "Go therefore and make disciples of all nations, baptizing them in the name of the Father and of the Son and of the Holy Spirit" (Matthew 28:19). While baptism is important, it is not essential to salvation, which is why Paul's primary concern and effort was placed into preaching the gospel. Paul wanted to see people saved and their lives changed or transformed. Too often people place too much emphasis on baptism, desiring a certain pastor to baptize them, or being baptized in the Jordan River. There is nothing wrong with either of those things unless you would be disappointed to be baptized by someone else or in a different location. Our concern must be with the power of the gospel first.

If our focus is on baptism, who baptizes us, or the location of the baptism, we are in danger of stripping the gospel of its power. The gospel doesn't change. The gospel is that Jesus came to earth, died on the cross, was buried, and rose from the grave. Is sharing this life changing truth with others your primary concern? Don't allow other issues, like baptism, or current fads to become more important. You will burn out or become frustrated attempting to keep current with whatever is popular currently. Be like Paul, be singularly minded and focused, simply sharing the truth of the gospel. Keep focused on that simple message, not trying to impress people with the wisdom of your own words, or impressing people by being cool, hip, stylish, etc. The focus of all we do needs to be removed from ourselves and kept on Jesus. Only He has the power to change people's lives. As wonderful as baptism is, it cannot change a person's life; only Jesus can do that.

July 2

"For, speaking loud boasts of folly, they entice by sensual passions of the flesh those who are barely escaping from those who live in error."
2 Peter 2:18

Peter gives us great warnings about the dangers of false teachers. This is an important warning because there are so many people that don't know how to differentiate between a religious huckster and a true servant of Jesus. The average person gets drawn in by the religious huckster because the words they speak are impressive. Literally, the warning Peter gives here is that the false teacher uses "inflated words that say nothing." Their words are puffed up, there is no substance or value to them, but they sure do entice the ear of the hearer. The words that they speak appeal to the fleshly lust of the natural man, and this is why they can attract so many people to them. There is no power in their words, but it appeals to our flesh. Without a moving of the Holy Spirit, this is what people want. Jesus dealt with this Himself. When Jesus fed the 5000 men, plus women and children, with 2 fish and 5 loaves of bread people quickly gathered around Him and asked for more of this delicious bread that He fed them with. The people didn't want Jesus, they simply wanted to be fed and have their fleshly appetites filled (see John 6:47-66).

What Peter is warning us against is following what satisfies our flesh but has no value or meaning to it. He doesn't want us to get led astray by the eloquence of a speaker. We need to pay attention to the content, that is more important than the impressiveness of the delivery. This is how the apostle Paul handled his ministry. The apostle Paul said to the Corinthians, "And I, when I came to you, brothers, did not come proclaiming to you the testimony of God with lofty speech or wisdom. For I decided to know nothing among you except Jesus Christ and him crucified. And I was with you in weakness and in fear and much trembling, and my speech and my message were not in plausible words of wisdom, but in demonstration of the Spirit and of power, so that your faith might not rest in the wisdom of men but in the power of God" (2 Corinthians 2:1-5). Make sure the preacher you listen to doesn't just impress you with their words, but that their words express the power and glory of Jesus Christ. We need to hear the Gospel communicated to us so that we are not simply manipulated by an impressive orator.

July 3

"But the wisdom from above is first pure, then peaceable, gentle, open to reason, full of mercy and good fruits, impartial and sincere. And a harvest of righteousness is sown in peace by those who make peace."
James 3:17-18

The earth is filled with earthly wisdom, which we don't want to confuse with earthly knowledge. Earthly knowledge can be good, but earthly wisdom is not. You see, true wisdom comes from God, so any wisdom that does not have God as its source, is wisdom that is going to fail you. Earthly wisdom may appear to be successful for a time, but it will ultimately fail every single time. This is why God's wisdom is superior. Satan is the originator of earthly wisdom and all its fruit, but Godly wisdom also bears fruit. The fruit that earthly wisdom produces is envy, selfishness, bragging, lying, and a refusal to believe the truth; it is demonic and evil. This is the opposite of Godly wisdom, which is pure, peaceful, gentle, willing to yield, full of mercy, doesn't have favorites, and isn't hypocritical.

Jesus came to earth to teach us His wisdom. This is why the apostle Paul tells us that "in whom (Jesus) are hidden all the treasures of wisdom and knowledge" (Colossians 2:3). This means that no person can be filled with Godly wisdom until they have surrendered their life to Jesus. Jesus is wisdom. God has also given us the Bible so that we can learn wisdom from it. This is why the first fruit of God's wisdom is purity. God is holy, and His wisdom, therefore, is also holy, or pure. This speaks of having no pollution or defilement in it. God's wisdom leads us to a life of purity, and holiness. A life of purity will also lead to a life of peace. Man's wisdom causes competition, rivalry, and even war. This is the opposite of Godly wisdom. Peace is based upon holiness, so true peace can only come from God.

Fruit is produced by the life that a person lives. Contained within that fruit are seeds that will reproduce after its own kind. This is why God calls the believer to sow Godly fruit: purity, peace, gentleness, etc. As we sow these fruits of righteousness in our lives, God will reproduce even more righteousness into the lives of others. We are what we live, and what we live we sow, which will determine what we reap. What kind of fruit are you sowing in your life?

July 4

"There was a certain man of Zorah, of the tribe of the Danites, whose name was Manoah. And his wife was barren and had no children. And the angel of the Lord appeared to the woman and

said to her, 'Behold, you are barren and have not borne children, but you shall conceive and bear a son.'"
Judges 13:2-3

Announcements are always exciting to receive, whether the announcement is for a wedding, a birthday party, or the birth of a child. Announcements almost always bring exciting news. Since you were sent an announcement, you also share in the excitement of the event. In the book of Judges, the "Angel of the Lord" is a reference to the pre-incarnate Jesus, or Jesus before He came to earth in the form of a baby. He came to bring some good news to Manoah and his wife, who was barren. Throughout the Bible this is a common way that God operates. God loves to miraculously allow barren women to give birth to children. These women have waited for long periods of time, and not been able to have children. Now, when they do have a child, it is obvious that this child is a blessing from God. He has done something that was not able to happen naturally. At the birth of this child, God then received the praise and honor. God does this because that way there is absolutely no mistake that it is God directing and controlling these events. God is in control!

When God wants to do something spectacular in the world, He doesn't send an army, but He sends an angel. Oftentimes that angel will visit a couple and announce that they will have a baby. Babies are tender and fragile, not what you would expect to change the world. They are dependent upon others, and they can't protect themselves; God uses the weak things of the world to confound the mighty (see 1 Corinthians 1:26-28). God works this way because He is patient; He is not in a rush. He will wait for that baby to grow up, to mature, to complete God's plan and will. This is why every baby that is born is both precious and a gift from God. Every child that is born, no matter what the circumstances are, is born with potential. No child is an accident, and no child should be unwanted. Every child born is created in the image of its Maker, God.

It is sad that we live in a society that sees an unborn baby as a menace instead of a miracle, an inconvenience instead of an inheritance. May we help ensure that all children are welcomed and given the opportunities to grow and fulfill the potential that they are born with.

July 5

"For Christ is the end of the law for righteousness to everyone who believes."
Romans 10:4

When a popular television show ends there is lots of hoopla, media attention, and many sad viewers. People are sad that a show they've followed for years has ended. This ending can create a feeling of melancholy in a person. But endings do not have to be that way. There are other times that we are super excited about endings. I have nothing against either Doctors or Dentists, but I am always glad when an appointment with them is finished.

Endings can be a good thing, like with an expiration date. Ever tried to drink milk that had "ended?" If you haven't, I don't suggest trying it. Endings can be a very good thing. Paul is telling us that we can stop striving to keep the law to be righteous. First, on this side of Heaven we will never be righteous, and secondly, we will never be able to keep the entire law and become righteous. Despite that we can become righteous. How does that work?

When Jesus came and lived on the earth in the form of a man, He lived a perfect life. He never sinned once. So, when He died on the cross and later rose from the grave, He conquered and defeated both death and sin. In living a perfect and sinless life on earth as a man, Jesus fulfilled the law. Jesus extends His righteousness to all who confess with their mouth that Jesus is Lord and surrender their life to Him. We are righteous because of what Jesus did, and therefore we can stand in the presence of God Almighty. Without the grace of God, we would not be able to receive Jesus' righteousness.

The law has been fulfilled and completed in Jesus. Does this mean that we no longer need to worry about the law? After all, since Jesus fulfilled the law, we don't need to worry about it any longer and can just have faith in Him, right? No! The law is still valid and useful; after all, Jesus fulfilled it, He didn't demolish it. The law still shows us God's standards for a life that pleases Him, along with our continued need for a Savior. But the law is no longer the basis for our relationship with God. That is based upon faith and God's grace.

God is a holy God, and we allow Him to work in us, changing us from the inside out so that we can also live a holy life that brings glory and pleasure to Him.

July 6

"And he said, 'Who are you, Lord?' And He said, 'I am Jesus, whom you are persecuting.'"
Acts 9:5

Saul answers God with a question, "Who are You, Lord?" This is an important question that every one of us needs to ask. Who exactly is the Lord? Saul is going to spend the rest of his life getting to know the answer to this question. We also need to do the same. When we ask this question sincerely, God will answer it, as He does here for Saul.

God answers Saul very plainly, telling him that "I am Jesus, whom you are persecuting." Whoa! This had to crush Saul. He thought that he had been helping God and doing these great and wonderful things but, in reality he was persecuting the One he claimed to love. Instead of helping God, he was just persecuting the long-awaited and promised Messiah, the Son of God, the Son of David. This meant that Jesus of Nazareth was truly the Messiah, and he had been laying hands on the members of the Way, mistreating the children of God. This event changed Saul's outlook; his good works and legalistic self-righteous life was just filthy, dirty, soiled rags (see Isaiah 64:6 and Philippians 3:6-8).

God said to Saul that "It is hard for you to kick against the goads." What did He mean by that? A goad was a long stick that was sharp on one end or had a sharp piece of iron stuck into the end; it was used to control the direction and movement of cattle. To "kick against the goads" described a stubborn, obstinate attitude that refused to go the right way; it resulted in pain and injury only to the person who refused to be corrected. God is saying that Saul is an ox; he is stubborn, refusing to go the right way, but he is valuable to God the farmer. This is why God continues to "goad" Saul towards the right way. God is patiently waiting for Saul to submit to God's will and go the right way.

Thank You God for patiently waiting for us too. May we learn to submit to Your will quickly and not kick against the goads.

July 7

"Therefore I will judge you, O house of Israel, every one according to his ways, declares the Lord God. Repent and turn from all your transgressions, lest iniquity be your ruin."
Ezekiel 18:30

Every person has done something in their life that they aren't proud of. When that happens, most people will come up with an excuse as to why they did what they did. They will say something like, "The devil made me do it." Or, "I had no other choice." You might have even heard (or said), "Everyone's doing it, so it's no big deal." Each of these statements are an attempt at justifying doing what you know is wrong. That is why it is so very rare to hear someone say, "I was wrong, and I accept responsibility for my choices and actions."

When we make a mistake there is only one direction that we can point to; that is back to ourselves. Too often people try to point towards others, or even try to blame God for their choices. Those are both wrong; when we mess up we can blame no one other than our own self. If someone else was to blame, then the penalty for any wrongdoing would belong to them, but it belongs to us. That is what God was telling the prophet Ezekiel. God said, "I will judge each one of you according to his ways." In other words, we will receive either punishment or rewards for the choices that we make. But whatever we receive will be because of our actions, not someone else's.

Does this sound fair to you? When Ezekiel said these words to them, they responded by saying, "The way of the Lord is not just" (Ezekiel 18:25). Listen closely to God's response to them: "Is my way not just? Is it not your ways that are not just?" (Ezekiel 18:25). God told the Israelites that their way of thinking was wrong. God is not unfair. Even though it is not popular today, God does require individual personal responsibility. We must own up to the choices and actions that we make, whether good or bad. Don't try to blame anyone else for what you have done.

If you have made poor decisions in the past, the good news is that you can change. Listen to what else God said: "When a righteous person turns away from his righteousness and does injustice, he shall die for it; for the injustice that he has done he shall die. Again, when a wicked person turns away from the wickedness he has committed and does what is just and right, he shall save his life. Because he considered and turned away from all the transgressions that he had committed, he shall surely live; he shall not die" (Ezekiel 18:26-28).

July 8

"...for you know that the testing of your faith produces steadfastness."
James 1:3

There are very few people in the world who enjoy tests. You may remember what you felt like when you found out you had a test in school. Your heart rate would accelerate, you skin might get clammy, it felt like your brain stopped working as you suddenly forgot everything that you'd ever known. Tests have a way of producing anxiety and stress in a person. But there is a purpose for tests, and it isn't to create anxiety and stress. It isn't to create faith in a person either, as some people mistakenly believe. When we go through tests, or trials, in life, it does not produce faith in us. What it does is reveal what faith we do have, or don't have. This is a major reason why God allows us to experience trials in our life; it is so that we can see the level, or depth, of our faith.

Don't think that God allows us to have trials so He will see the level, or depth, of our faith. He already knows. The purpose is for us to realize the depth of our own faith. When we realize that we don't have the necessary resources to get us through the trial, the result should be that we are drawn closer to God because He has the inexhaustible and needed resources. As we draw closer to God, we will see a growth in our faith. Not only that, but as we go through our trials with joy, our faith will become evident to those around us. That is who God wants to see our faith. Our faith is a testament to God, and God uses that to draw others to Him. So, the trials we go through will not produce faith in us, what they do is show our faith to others. What is it then that does produce faith? It is God's Word! "So faith comes from hearing, and hearing through the word of Christ." (Romans 10:17). As we hear, trust, understand, and obey God's Word, we will find our faith growing stronger and stronger.

God allows us to go through trials so that others can be a witness to our faith in Him, but those trials also do produce something in us: patience. This is a characteristic that is very much needed in our relationship with God. In fact, this is a characteristic of God; He is patient with us. He is long-suffering with us. Sadly, we often tend to be very impatient with Him. If God doesn't immediately answer our prayer, then we begin to look for different ways to get the answer we're looking for. You may have found, as I have, that when we take matters into our own hands, we tend to make a mess of things. How much better it is for us to learn to be patient and wait for God.

July 9

"And when she came to the mountain to the man of God, she caught hold of his feet. And Gehazi came to push her away. But the man of God said, 'Leave her alone, for she is in bitter distress, and the LORD has hidden it from me and has not told me.'"
2 Kings 4:27

Elisha is a great example for us to follow. He was known as a great man of God; a person whom God used mightily to proclaim His Word to the nations of Israel and Judah. In fact, God used Elisha to perform many miracles in God's name throughout the area, both to Jews and Gentiles alike. His reputation was known to the nation's leaders, and to ordinary people in the land. Even though God used Elisha in a powerful and extraordinary way, Elisha was still a human being; and he knew that too.

The woman in this story is a Gentile, a Shunamite woman. She and her husband were prominent people in their village, and they saw God through Elisha so they built a room for him at their house so that he would have a place to stay whenever he was in the area. This woman was also barren, which was a disgrace in that society. God prophesied through Elisha that she would have a son one year later, which happened. When this son was older, he suddenly died, so the woman went and sought out Elisha. She told no one that her son had died, but Elisha was able to tell that she was distraught. He did not know the reason for her pain and anguish, but he knew that God did. Even though he was a mighty man of God, he knew he was limited as a human being and that God has no limitations. He knew as a human that every miracle he had performed, and every prophecy given by him was done through the power of God and not himself. What God had done through him had not gone to his head, and he remained humble and submitted to God.

How we need to remember that too. God will use us to accomplish His purposes, but the results come from God and not our doing. God will use you to speak, pray or prophesy His truth to others. Remember that it is God speaking through you, and not your great wisdom or intellect at work. Remain humble and give all the praise to God for the work that He has done and is doing. We have very limited power and knowledge, but God's power and knowledge are unlimited; and He desires to share His power with others through you and me. Praise God, because He does not need us, but chooses to use us.

July 10

"And when Paul had seen the vision, immediately we sought to go on into Macedonia, concluding that God had called us to preach the gospel to them."
Acts 16:10

"Turn off the TV! It's time to go to bed." "It's time to take a break from playing and go clean your room." These are things parents tell their children to do, and parents often find out that their children have a sudden case of deafness. They say they didn't hear these things, which is why they don't do them right away. As adults we often have the same problem. It may not be with our parents, but either with a spouse or with our bosses at work. We fight the same tendency to do our own thing as our children do.

Through a vision God told the apostle Paul that he was to go to the region of Macedonia and preach the Gospel there. Notice how quickly Paul and the others responded to his vision. They didn't ask for a vote from all team members to see if this was the "right" thing for them to do. Neither did he look at the polls to see if this was a popular decision to make. There were no tweets or FaceBook posts asking what others thought about this decision. No! Paul knew that God had a perfect plan, and he was an obedient servant of God's. As soon as the Holy Spirit told Paul where to go, he didn't hesitate one moment. He obeyed and went where he was told to go.

We can learn so much from Paul. When God speaks to us, we need to respond with obedience. It doesn't matter what others think, or even if they approve. Obey God! Most Americans spend too much time concerning themselves with what others think, or how we will be perceived or thought of by others. We need to be more concerned with how and what God thinks of us. He would rather us be obedient to Him than accepted and popular by the world. In fact, we can be assured that the world will hate us, not accept us. Jesus told us that very plainly in John 15:18-19. "If the world hates you, know that it has hated Me before it hated you. If you were of the world, the world would love you as its own; but because you are not of the world, but I chose you out of the world, therefore the world hates you." Take heart, while the world won't accept us, and will in fact hate us, God not only accepts and desires our obedience, He even rewards obedience to Him. The world's hatred is temporary, but God's reward is eternal.

July 11

"Then the people of Israel cried out to the LORD, and the LORD raised up for them a deliverer, Ehud, the son of Gera, the Benjaminite, a left-handed man. The people of Israel sent tribute by him to Eglon the king of Moab."

Judges 3:15

After eighteen years of bondage, the nation of Israel cried out to God. God heard them and gave them what they needed, a person to deliver them from bondage. God is merciful. He had every right to get rid of Israel because of their continued disobedience to Him, but instead He listened to their cries and gave them a deliverer. God gave them someone who would free them from the bondage they were currently in.

The deliverer that Jesus provided was Ehud. There was something different about Ehud; he was left-handed. Today this doesn't mean much to us, but back then this was a big deal. A person who was left-handed was considered handicapped, so they would be forced to become right-handed. This isn't just an ancient practice but was still practiced recently. My wife's grandma was born left-handed, but was forced to become right-handed in the 1930's and 1940's. The belief of left-handed being a handicap is still present in our modern language. The French word for left-handed is "gauche," which is also translated as crude, uncouth, or socially awkward. The Latin word for left-handed is translated as "sinister," which means "evil" or "wicked."

God took a person who was handicapped, a person who was viewed to be lacking, deficient, or inadequate, and used them to deliver Israel from bondage. God chose to use someone who wasn't perfect to deliver them. How encouraging. This is why God can use someone like you, or me. God chooses to use people who aren't perfect.

Growing up Ehud probably wondered why he was born the way he was. Why was he left-handed in a right-handed world? He didn't measure up to everyone else. What good can I do?" Have you ever felt that way? We all have at one time or another. We need to remember God doesn't make mistakes. God created us; He knit us together in our mother's womb just the way we are. He made us the way we are for a reason. Ehud was considered handicapped by the world, but not by God. God created him the way he was for a particular reason. God has done the same thing with you. God created you the way you are because God can, and will, use you. God will even use what you consider to be a weakness, or disability, just as He did with Ehud.

July 12

"For I have derived much joy and comfort from your love, my brother, because the hearts of the saints have been refreshed through you."
Philemon 1:7

I would love others to be able to say this about me: "We love to have Paul around because we are refreshed when he is with us." How wonderful is that. That is what Paul is saying about Philemon.

There are two kinds of people in the world.

1. Those which are enthusiastic and excited about life. They love life. They are optimistic. They are full of hope and faith, which causes them to see the bright side of things. When you spend time around this kind of person, your spiritual battery gets recharged. You want to be around this kind of person; you are blessed by them.
2. The other kind of person in the world is the opposite of the first kind. They are like spiritual leeches. They are spiritual scavengers; like parasites, they feed off of others. Instead of recharging your spiritual battery, they drain it. This kind of person is pessimistic, negative, and likes to complain. Their focus is on themselves and what you can do for them. If you're honest, you will admit that you don't like to spend lots of time around this person.

What kind of person are you? Are you a light? Or a leech?

Did you know that it is possible to make more friends in two months by being interested in others than you can in twenty years by trying to get others interested in you? I read about a man who changed one word in his vocabulary, and the result was he now had lots of friends. For many years, every time someone made a comment, this man would respond by saying, "Ah, bologna." He replaced "bologna" with "amazing." Now, when people tell him something, he says, "Ah, amazing," and now he has lots of friends.

"Lord, help us to be the kind of friends that encourage and refresh others."

July 13

"Then He said, 'Do not come near; take your sandals off your feet, for the place on which you are standing is holy ground.'"
Exodus 3:5

God give Moses two instructions:

1. "Do not come near." Moses is instructed to keep his distance from God, don't get too close. This is a reminder to us that we are not to get too "chummy" with God. God is not our next-door neighbor, like some genie in a bottle that is just waiting to grant us our requests. It is true that God is with us, but not one of us. God is so much greater than we can even imagine. That is why Isaiah the prophet reminds us that God Himself said, "My ways higher than your ways and My thoughts than your thoughts" (Isaiah 55:9). There is, and always will be, a distance between us and God because God is pure and holy, and we are not. No matter how good a person may be, we will never be able to reach God's level, because He is greater than we can ever be.
2. "Take your sandals off your feet." Taking your sandals off is a sign of respect and humility. Those who are poor or

> needy often have no shoes, and when compared to God we are both poor and needy. Servants often went barefoot, and we, as God's children, are called to be His servants. In many countries in the East, you take your shoes off before entering temples, churches, palaces, and even private homes. When I was in Vietnam, I quickly learned to wear shoes that were easy to take off, because this was the first thing you did upon entering a home or church.

Both of these instructions were given to Moses for the same reason: "the place where you stand is holy ground." God was present, and He is holy; therefore, this place was holy. As a sign of reverence and respect for God's holiness, Moses couldn't draw too close to God, and he took off his sandals in God's presence. Moses' sandals were covered with dirt and dust, which means they were polluted, or defiled. God is holy and undefiled, so Moses must remove this defilement in order to come into the presence of God. God says, "I am the LORD your God. Consecrate yourselves therefore, and be holy, for I am holy" (Leviticus 11:44). We will continue to get dirty and defiled from this sinful world that we live in, which is why Jesus said, "The one who has bathed (or saved) does not need to wash, except for his feet, but is completely clean" (John 13:10).

July 14

"...inquiring what person or time the Spirit of Christ in them was indicating when He predicted the sufferings of Christ and the subsequent glories."
1 Peter 1:11

Have you ever seen a picture where the artist has hidden pictures within the drawing? You know they are there, but you can't see them.

Then, after you find the hidden pictures, you see them all the time because now they are so obvious. This is how the Old Testament prophets would be now if they were able to look back at what they had written. Look at what the Old Testament prophets knew about the coming of the Messiah. They knew that he would be a descendant of King David, as prophesied by the prophet Jeremiah in Jeremiah 23:5. The prophet Micah told us that He would be born in the city of Bethlehem, in Micah 5:2. The prophet Zechariah even foretold that the Messiah would be humble as He rode into Jerusalem on the back of a donkey in Zechariah 9:9. King David wrote about how the Messiah would suffer for us in Psalm 22. The Holy Spirit inspired each of these men to write these prophesies about the Messiah, but even though each of them searched diligently to understand more about the Messiah, when He was coming, or Who He would exactly be, they were not able to find out. This information was hidden from their understanding.

We are now able to look back at their writings and see Jesus so clearly because He fulfilled each of these events perfectly and completely. His identity may have been hidden from those who wrote about them before they happened, but now that they have occurred, there is no doubt that Jesus is the One Who perfectly fulfilled every prophesy made about the coming Messiah in the Old Testament. How encouraging it is for us to know that every word written about the Messiah was perfectly and completely fulfilled by Jesus. This is a reminder to us that God is in complete control over every event, and that the Holy Spirit is God, knowing exactly what is going to happen. This is the same Holy Spirit that we have today. What does the Holy Spirit do today? "...He will convict the world concerning sin and righteousness and judgment: concerning sin, because they do not believe in Me; concerning righteousness, because I go to the Father, and you will see me no longer; concerning judgment, because the ruler of this world is judged" (John 16:8-11). Thank God that we have the Holy Spirit working in us today.

July 15

"For the priests bearing the ark stood in the midst of the Jordan until everything was finished that the LORD commanded Joshua to tell the people, according to all that Moses had commanded Joshua. The people passed over in haste."
Joshua 4:10

Why were the Israelites in a hurry? Didn't they understand that when you hurry it's much easier to make a mistake? When you hurry it's much easier to get ahead of God. That's why the Bible reminds us often that we need to wait for God. "Wait for the LORD; be strong, and let your heart take courage; wait for the LORD!" (Psalm 27:14). "Be still before the LORD and wait patiently for Him" (Psalm 37:7a). "Wait continually for your God" (Hosea 12:6b).

It is a good rule of thumb for us to wait on God, but that doesn't apply to every situation in life. Generally, when we hurry it is for one of two reasons.

1. We are afraid.
2. We are excited.

Were the Israelites afraid the waters would return suddenly and drown them as they were crossing the Jordan River into the Promised Land? After all, this did happen to the Egyptian army in the Red Sea. Were the people afraid? I don't believe so.

I believe the Israelites were so excited to be in the Promised Land that they hurried to the other side to receive God's promise. They were like children on Christmas morning. They couldn't contain their excitement, they couldn't sit still, and the excitement of this promise being fulfilled caused them to hurry. This is a good thing. They were witnessing the fulfillment of a promise God has made many years before. They were excited seeing God's faithfulness.

This excitement is contagious too. We need to have this excitement in our lives today. Too often I see people going to church, to Bible study, or talking about their personal devotions like it's a chore. We need to be excited about these areas of our life. Each of these areas is an opportunity for us to draw closer to God, learn more about Him and see Him work in our lives. This is exciting stuff. The creator of the universe is personally interested in you, wants to spend time with you, and desires to use you to share His love with others. Talk about exciting. Do you have that excitement in your life? Are you in a hurry to see God work and fulfill His promises today? I pray that we excitedly hurry to God.

July 16

"But when they had commanded them to leave the council, they conferred with one another, saying, 'What shall we do with these men? For that a notable sign has been performed through them is evident to all the inhabitants of Jerusalem, and we cannot deny it.'"
Acts 4:15-16

These religious rulers were in a bit of a pickle here. The simplest thing to do would be to deny that this had ever happened, but they couldn't do that, especially with the miraculously healed man standing right in front of them. So, they sent Peter, John, and the former lame man outside so they could have a private pow wow.

The fact that this man was standing in front of them meant they couldn't deny that he had been healed. Also, since he had been sitting outside the Beautiful Gate for such a long time, he was well known, which meant lots of people knew who he was, and they recognized the miracle that had happened. In Acts 4:22 Luke tells us this man was over 40 years old. Think about that for a minute. When Jesus was born, this man would have been around 7-8 years old. When Jesus was a 12-year-old boy, sitting in the temple discussing Scriptures with the religious teachers in Luke 2:46, this man would have been around 19-20 years old. Every one of these religious rulers knew this man because they had walked by him numerous times. Peter and John, along with the rest of the disciples, had done the same thing for years. This means that Jesus had also walked by him yet chose to not heal him. Why? The timing was not yet right. God waited for this exact moment because it was His right time. About 2000 men had come to a saving knowledge of Jesus the night before. That's amazing. But, as these religious rulers were drawn together to discuss this, there was a young man in their midst that God was preparing for great things: a religious leader named Saul, who would become better known as the apostle Paul. The timing was right for this healing, and God used two of His children to perform this miracle and draw many more to Him.

God can use events that we think are bad, and through them He will later bring out something wonderful, as He did with Saul. That is why that same Saul would later write, "We know that for those who love God all things work together for good, for those who are called according to His purpose" (Romans 8:28).

July 17

"You shall come to your grave in ripe old age, like a sheaf gathered up in its season."
Job 5:26

Getting old is not all fun, but it isn't all bad either. The aches and pains take longer to heal as we get older, but life also has a way of becoming much richer and fuller as we age too. It seems there are two types of old people; those who radiate joy and share what they have learned, or those who are bitter and complain over how life has treated them.

Recently I read an article about the salvaging of old ships and the quality of wood that was found on the ships. It was reported that the age of the wood did not determine the quality of the wood alone. Another important factor was the straining and twisting the ship encountered during storms, the chemical reaction produced from the bilgewater running over the wood, and the cargo carried, also affected the wood.

The author described how a fashionable furniture store on Broadway in New York City exhibited some boards and veneers that were cut from a beam off an eighty-year-old ship. The coloring and grain of these boards were beautiful and attracted lots of attention from their customers. In the same display were some mahogany beams that came from a ship that had sailed the seas sixty years ago. These beams were just as beautiful as the oak wood. What had made the mahogany wood so beautiful? The years of strain and pressure of sailing through storms on the seas had constricted the pores of the wood and deepened its colors. Those beams were purchased by a wealthy New York family, and the wood was used to create a cabinet that now sits on display in their home.

We also can be like those mahogany beams. As we go through life, we will encounter storms that will cause strains on our life. As we go through those storms we get soaked and covered by the waves that come crashing over us. We experience bilgewater being poured over us, as people pour their waste on us. We also have many types of cargo that we carry during our life. Burdens of family members, friends, and work are experienced by all. Those burdens can be heavy, such as dealing with problems, struggles and heartaches. But they also can be burdens of joy, such as family vacations, accomplishments of children, or just watching children and grandchildren grow up.

As we live our lives and age, we have a choice to make. Either we live a life just for ourselves, and selfishly allow the burdens and effects of life to allow us to become bitter and complaining; or we can sail through the rough seas of life, carry the burdens that are given to us, and help others as we live life. What kind of example are you becoming?

July 18

"What good is it, my brothers, if someone says he has faith but does not have works? Can his faith save him?"
James 2:14

The apostle James asks a very important question here. Can a person be saved by their faith if they have no works? He also answers this question in verse 20, saying "faith without works is dead" (NKJV). There are some who say that here James is contradicting the apostle Paul, who wrote "you are saved by grace through faith, and this is not from yourselves; it is God's gift—not from works, so that no one can boast" (Ephesians 2:8-9). Is there a contradiction here? Absolutely not. Listen to the apostle Paul's next words that he wrote: "For we are His creation, created in Christ Jesus for good works" (Ephesians 2:10). Paul is correct, we are not saved by works, but by faith. James here is simply clarifying the type of faith that a saved person has: a faith that works. You may have heard this saying: "faith alone saves, but the faith that saves is not alone - it has good works with it."

Faith and works belong together. When a person is saved, their salvation can be seen through the works and actions of their life. This means that their faith must be "living." A "dead" faith will not have works, but a living faith is seen by its works. This means that our faith can easily be seen by others through the actions of our life. This isn't limited to just "spiritual" things but can also be seen through our compassion for others with basic needs, such as food, shelter, and clothing. When coming across a person needing food, clothing, or shelter, and when a person has the means to do so, you will see their living faith in action by helping them get the things that they need. A living faith won't just "pray" that they will receive what they need but will help them get those things. In other words, a living faith won't substitute prayer for action. Prayer is important, but so is action. This is why the apostle John told us "If anyone has this world's goods and sees his brother in need but closes his eyes to his need—how can God's love reside in him? Little children, we must not love with word or speech, but with truth and action" (1 John 3:17-18). A living faith is one of action. Read Hebrews 11, sometimes referred to as the Hall of Faith, and you will read about people whose lives were defined by their actions. God spoke to them and told them to do something, and they obeyed. Faith is evidenced through actions.

July 19

"Then Midianite traders passed by. And they drew Joseph up and lifted him out of the pit, and sold him to the Ishmaelites for twenty shekels[c] of silver. They took Joseph to Egypt."
Genesis 37:28

Joseph had just been sold into slavery by the very people who should have loved and supported him. Instead, they were jealous and sent him an unexpected change in his life. God had spoken to him through dreams about how his family would bow down to him someday. Now, all that was lost. Imagine how he must have felt. He was shocked and scared as his brothers grabbed him and threw him into the empty well. The feeling of relief when he was pulled out of the well was quickly dashed when he realized he was being betrayed and sold as a slave. His life was over. All of this came out of left field and took him by surprise.

Life is often like that. Storms come out of left field and take us by surprise. As the storm hits it feels like our life is over. We wonder how we can survive. It often appears that we won't be able to make it through the day, much less the storm. But we do survive. And we continue to face the battle day after day. That is because storms do pass. Sometimes storms are very short, as a cloud covers the sun and plunges the world into a dark shadow, then very shortly the sun comes shining through again. Whew! That storm is over, and life can return to normal. Other storms last for longer periods of time. Joseph's storm lasted about 13 years. But God was with him the whole time; just as He is with us as we go through storms.

God allows us to go through storms, not because He doesn't like us, but to strengthen us and remind us that He is there with us. Jesus sent His disciples into a storm (Mark 4:35-41), but He was with them the whole time, and even told them beforehand that they were crossing over to the other side; they would make it. God does the same for us today. God also promised us that He "is faithful, and he will not let you be tempted beyond your ability, but with the temptation he will also provide the way of escape, that you may be able to endure it." (1 Corinthians 10:13). You may feel that your life is over because the storm you are in is just too much for you. God is allowing it in your life to draw you closer to Him so you will look to Him for your strength. He will bring you through this storm because He is in control. Then, one of these days, you can be like Joseph and say, "you meant evil against me, but God meant it for good" (Genesis 50:20b).

July 20

"And on her forehead was written a name of mystery: "Babylon the great, mother of prostitutes and of earth's abominations."
Revelation 17:5

Your name is a powerful tool. At birth most people are assigned a first name and a middle name, in addition to being given a last name by their parents. How powerful is your given name? Watch how quickly an unruly child settles down when they hear their parents calling them loudly by their first name, middle name, and last name. That loud and unruly child can become very docile and quiet in a matter of nanoseconds. When they hear all three of their names being used together, it gets their attention. Knowing a person's name gives you power too. Instead of just yelling out, "Hey you," when you call a person by their name it shows that there is recognition, they know who you are.

This prostitute here at the end of times also has a name, a name that is placed upon her forehead. She is called Babylon, the mother of prostitutes. It is important that we realize this is not the literal city of Babylon, but she is a representation of spiritual harlotry, or all spiritual systems that draw people away from God. It is all false religions that worship and follow Satan instead of God, the Creator of all things. Satan's world system of false religion did indeed begin in the city of Babylon (read Genesis 11:1-9), but it has spread across the entire world since then. Since this began in Babylon, Babylon is used to represent all false religions, just like the Bible also uses the idea of harlotry to represent idolatry, or false religion.

We could say that Charles Dickens' famous book, A Tale of Two Cities is taken from the Bible. Read the Bible from Genesis to Revelation and you will see two cities mentioned continually. These two cities are Jerusalem (God's holy city) and Babylon (the source of false religion). Every person is following one of these two cities. You are either seeking after God or you are seeking after false religion. Which city are you following? God has given us a great promise. "You will seek Me and find Me, when you seek Me with all your heart" (Jeremiah 29:13). Seek after God with every ounce of your being, and you will find Him.

July 21

"You are the Lord, the God Who chose Abram and brought him out of Ur of the Chaldeans and gave him the name Abraham."
Nehemiah 9:7

The playground during elementary school was either the greatest time of school, or the worst, depending on whether you were very athletically inclined or not. Those that were athletically inclined would be chosen quickly and then excelled at whatever game was being played, while those that were not very athletic were standing there in a line waiting to be chosen by a team, knowing that neither team really wanted them, but one of them would be "stuck" with them. That is a terrible feeling. Because when you are chosen it tells you that you are wanted, but when you are the last one in line and the next team has to take you tells you that they didn't want you but have to take you. Being wanted and chosen makes a huge difference.

Abram was a man chosen by God. God chose him, not because he was better than others, but simply because God chose him. But it's not just Abram, but also you, and me. God chose us to be His children. That means that He wants us. Not because of how great we are or what greatness we bring to His "team." God chooses us because He loves us. That is also true for the other believers in your church. Look around at those sitting next to you and around you in church. God chose them, just like He chose you. You may be wondering why God chose the person next to you. After all, they are a bit strange, and don't really fit in very well. Looking at them you may wonder what God sees in them. That's ok. Others look at you and wonder the same thing. That's also true for me and every other believer. After looking around you begin to get the idea that God is the one getting the raw end of the deal. He chose us, and He didn't get the best end of that deal. That's true, but remember, He didn't choose us because of what we had to offer. He chose us because of what He had to offer. It's what He has to give to us. What does God give to us? He gives us His love, His power, His Spirit, and the greatest gift of all: eternal life. "If you confess with your mouth that Jesus is Lord and believe in your heart that God raised him from the dead, you will be saved. For with the heart one believes and is justified, and with the mouth one confesses and is saved" (Romans 10:9-10).

July 22

"And when they came to him, he said to them: 'You yourselves know how I lived among you the whole time from the first day that I set foot in Asia..."
Acts 20:18

Paul begins his message by reminding the elders of the church in Ephesus of how he had lived his life in their midst. He gives his life as an example for them of how to live. He is not saying that he is the example to follow instead of Jesus, but he is an example of how to follow Jesus. Paul is not lifting himself up as an example of a "religious celebrity" for others to follow and worship. Instead, Paul is saying that his life has been spent humbly following and serving Jesus, and he desires others to do the same.

This is also a reminder to us that we are an example to others of how a Christian is to live. It doesn't matter how long you've been a Christian, whether it is just a few weeks or a few decades, you are an example. It doesn't mean that any of us are perfect, but it does mean that we are to be striving and trying to live like Jesus did. What kind of example are you? If you aren't as good of an example as you would like to be, what needs to change?

Too often we hear of people who say the reason they're not a Christian is because of some jerk who claimed to be a Christian, and now they want nothing to do with Jesus at all. Here is an example of that. You may have heard of Mahatma Ghandi, the non-violent Hindu civil leader in India. He came to London to study in 1888. He had read and studied much about Christianity, and he was considering becoming a Christian. One Sunday he decided to attend a local church so he could talk with the minister. Upon arriving at the church, the usher refused to seat him, and instead told Ghandi to go worship with his "own kind." He left the church and said, "If Christians have a caste system, I might as well remain a Hindu." The poor example of this usher turned Ghandi away from following Jesus. How sad that is. Paul is reminding the Ephesian elders that he lived his life in such a way that he was an example that led people to Jesus. In fact, Paul had the same mind as Jesus Christ. "Let this mind be in you which was also in Christ Jesus...He humbled Himself" (Philippians 2:5, 8 NKJV).

July 23

"So the Lord God caused a deep sleep to fall upon the man, and while he slept took one of his ribs and closed up its place with flesh."
Genesis 2:21

Genesis is full of firsts, and here is the first surgery ever performed in the history of the world. God was even concerned with Adam's well-being and used anesthetic, putting him out for the surgery. We all have heard that God took one of Adam's ribs to create Eve. I grew up being told that and believed that men had one less rib than women because of this event. That is a myth, it is not true. Men and women have an equal number of ribs. The Hebrew word that is translated rib is *tsela*, and this is the only time it is translated rib. This word is in the Bible 35 times, and 20 of those times it is simply means "side." We do not know exactly what God took from Adam's side, and it really isn't important either. The advances we have made in science and cloning have shown that every single cell in our bodies contains the entire genetic blueprint for our body. All God needed to take from Adam was some cell's and then change their genetic blueprint to create a new person.

It is important that whatever God used to create Eve from did come from the side of Adam. The Biblical scholar Matthew Henry commented on this by saying, "The woman was taken from Adam's side – not from his head to rule over him – not from his feet to be trampled on – but from his side to be equal with him, from under his arm to be protected, and from close to his heart to be loved." What a beautiful description of how a husband should view his wife. This is the foundation for the marriage, or union, between one man and one woman. God did not create Eve in the same manner as Adam; by taking a lump of clay, forming it into a woman and then breathing into her. Man was already a living being, and God made woman from him. This is important because it proves that there is only one beginning to the human race, through Adam. If God had created Eve just like Adam there would be two different human races, but there isn't. We all come from Adam.

God caused Adam to fall into a deep, almost death-like, sleep. Then from out of his side God brought forth a bride. This is also a picture for us of what would happen many centuries later. The final Adam was hanging on a tree when a Roman soldier stuck a spear into His side, causing the birthing fluids and water to pour out. From this we see another bride being brought forth, that of the church. From Jesus' side, the final Adam, comes His bride, the church, you and me. Like the good husband that He is, Jesus keeps His bride close to His side and loves her and protects her. Praise God.

July 24

Blessed be the God and Father of our Lord Jesus Christ, the Father of mercies and God of all comfort, who comforts us in all our tribulation, that we may be able to comfort those who are in any trouble, with the comfort with which we ourselves are comforted by God.

2 Corinthians 1:3-4

Most people would choose to not have to deal with problems, trials or periods of darkness in their lives. When we go through times like these it is very difficult, and painful. But, as with all things that God does, there is a reason and a purpose. God uses these times in our life.

Since God is a God of love, why would He allow us to go through times of difficulty? One is that He is the "God of all comfort." When we are in the midst of difficult times we have a choice to make. Either we are drawn closer to God, or we turn away from Him. When we are drawn closer to Him we will experience the comfort that He can provide. Even in the midst of the most trying circumstances, God is there providing us with a peace that passes all understanding (see Philippians 4:7).

Secondly, God allows us to experience times of difficulty in order for us to be a witness and light to others. People are watching you, especially non-believers. They watch how you are through times of difficulty, and God can use that to soften their hearts and draw them to Him. Your response to circumstances can be a witness to non-believers, and God can use your response as a tool to bring them to salvation.

Thirdly, God allows us to go through difficult trials so we can minister better to others. When we experience someone else who is struggling with a situation, we sympathize with them. But, when we have dealt with the same thing, we are able to empathize with them because we understand what they are going through. We can "feel their pain" (see Romans 12:15), and also offer them encouragement, prepare them for things that will happen, help prepare them for what is ahead, and share with them how God met you and led you through your time of trial.

God loves you so much, and He desires to use you to bring glory to Him as you share with others. This is why He allows us to experience difficult times. No matter what difficult times you are in, know that God can, and will, use it for His glory and to draw you closer to Him so that He can comfort you. Keep looking to God and keep your focus on Him and not whatever trial you are facing.

July 25

"At that time I will search Jerusalem with lamps, and I will punish the men who are complacent, those who say in their hearts, 'The Lord will not do good, nor will He do ill.'"
Zephaniah 1:12

Many people enjoy coffee. There are many ways that people prepare their coffee to drink. Some like it as an espresso, cafe latte, cappuccino, venti latte half decaf with skim milk, filled with cream and sugar, iced, and some even like it as just plain black coffee. Other people enjoy tea, whether it is iced tea, sweet tea, sun tea, earl grey tea, etc. But whether you like coffee or tea, it boils down to drinking them one of two ways: hot or cold.

You won't find coffee or tea being advertised or sold as either tepid tea or room temperature coffee. Why? They don't taste good that way. Drinking either beverage at room temperature leaves an awful taste in your mouth, so the drink is either warmed up or cooled down. God agrees with that. He also likes things hot or cold, not lukewarm. In fact, God warns, "because you are lukewarm, and neither hot nor cold, I will spit you out of my mouth" (Revelation 3:16). This doesn't just apply to how you prefer to drink your coffee or tea; it applies to your spiritual life also.

Through the prophet Zephaniah, God is warning the nation of Judah that they will be judged because spiritually they have become lukewarm. They are going through the rituals of serving Him, but it is an empty ritual. They are not on fire for God, their desire is not to live for Him and please Him through their lifestyle, heart attitude, and the choices they make. In fact, the way they were living was no different than the rest of the world, and in some areas it was even worse. Sadly, the same thing can often be said about the church and Christian people today.

The church is called to be a witness to the world. Too often either there is no difference between the church and the world, or the difference is so little that it cannot be seen. This happens when people have become lukewarm. To avoid becoming lukewarm we need to make sure that we have a "burning desire" to live for, and to please God. This "burning desire" will be kindled into a burning fire as we spend time getting to know God and growing our relationship with Him through studying the Bible, prayer, and fellowship with fellow believers. When we are growing closer and closer to God, we will have a desire to share His Word, and what He is teaching us, with others. People will be able to look at you and notice that you are not the same as the world. Those that are lukewarm are happy and content sitting on their couch doing nothing, while those who are "hot" for God will be investing in the lives of others.

May we be so full of the Holy Spirit that when we are stung by a mosquito it will fly away singing "there is power in the blood."

July 26

"As they ministered to the Lord and fasted, the Holy Spirit said, 'Now separate to Me Barnabas and Saul for the work to which I have called them.'" NKJV
Acts 13:2

The elders, and leaders, of the church in Antioch spent time "ministering to the Lord." The word used for ministered speaks of being in service to God. Ministering, worshipping, working, are all parts of serving God. This is why Luke tells us they "ministered to the Lord." They weren't ministering for the Lord, but to the Lord. What they were doing wasn't to receive praise from people, but to please God. They were serving Him. This is the first job of every Christian. Everything we do in our lives isn't done so we can be praised by others, but for us to serve God.

Part of their service to God was fasting. What is fasting? It is refraining from something, or certain things, for a period of time in order to control the flesh. While abstaining from whatever is chosen, you spend that time in prayer to God. For example, you may decide to fast from eating for a period of time (one day, one meal per day for a week, a certain item of food, etc.), and instead of eating you spend that time praying to God. This is what the leaders of the church at Antioch were doing.

While they were fasting, the Holy Spirit spoke to them, calling them to separate Barnabas and Saul for a work they were called to. God had a specific job for Barnabas and Saul to do. The apostle Paul would later write, "For we are His workmanship, created in Christ Jesus for good works, which God prepared beforehand, that we should walk in them" (Ephesians 2:10). This is further confirmation of what God had already said about Saul. When Saul was converted, he spent three days blind in Damascus, and during that time God told Ananias that Saul "is a chosen instrument of Mine to carry My name before the Gentiles and kings and the children of Israel. For I will show him how much he must suffer for the sake of My name." (Acts 9:15-16). This is a serious call for a serious ministry. It isn't for the fainthearted or weak, as we will see.

Just as God had a special calling for Barnabas and Saul, He also does for each of us. It may not be to go as a missionary to a foreign land, but that doesn't mean His calling for you is any less valid or important. Every one of us has a calling to "minister to the Lord" right where we are at this very moment. At your job, at school, in your community, and even at home.

July 27

"They read from the book, from the Law of God, clearly, and they gave the sense, so that the people understood the reading."
Nehemiah 8:8

Communication breakdown happens when there is a lack of communication or a failure to properly exchange and/or understand what is trying to be communicated. There are multiple reasons why this can happen, but one of the most common reasons is due to the receiver of the message perceiving the message differently than the sender intended. The receiver hears the message through their ears instead of the sender's ears, and they have a different understanding of the message. This happened here in Nehemiah because the people were hearing Hebrew Scripture through Babylonian ears. The people were born and raised in Babylon, that was their knowledge, experience, and understanding. They had not been raised in a Hebrew culture, like their grandparents, so they did not understand what was being read. This happens today in churches all too often. Instead of hearing with Babylonian ears though, we hear with worldly ears because we are too immersed in the world's culture and way of thinking, which causes us to not clearly, or properly, hear and understand God's Word.

To help clear up any communication breakdowns, Ezra had thirteen additional priests dispersed throughout the crowd of people to help explain what God's Word meant. They explained what they were hearing and how it applied to them. They did not offer their opinions, but simply helped people understand God's Word. A proper understanding of God's Word is the key to all spiritual growth. Notice also that Ezra read through the Law. He didn't only read from the sections that he knew, liked, or enjoyed. He read it all. This is so important. Too often churches don't teach the entire Bible any longer. Most American churches like to teach the New Testament on Sundays, except maybe for Revelation because that's too difficult to understand. The Old Testament isn't taught, except for a few stories in Sunday School. This has led to much of our church population being Biblically illiterate. It is imperative that churches teach the entire Bible, every single book from Genesis to Revelation need to be taught, known, and understood by the congregation. This is vital to our spiritual health and well-being. "My people are destroyed for lack of knowledge" (Hosea 6:4a). God's Word is powerful, and there is rich information for us to learn from in every single book in the Bible. "For as the rain and the snow come down from heaven and do not return there but water the earth, making it bring forth and sprout, giving seed to the sower and bread to the eater, so shall my word be that goes out from my mouth; it shall not return to me empty, but it shall accomplish that which I purpose, and shall succeed in the thing for which I sent it" (Isaiah 55:10-11).

July 28

"And he said with a loud voice, 'Fear God and give Him glory, because the hour of His judgment has come, and worship Him who made heaven and earth, the sea and the springs of water.'"
Revelation 14:7

Many people wonder what it is that they are supposed to do with their life. What does God want me to do? Am I in God's will for my life? Some even question whether or not God has a plan, or will, for their life. The short answer for that is, He does! People during the Tribulation will be asking the same thing, and God sends an angel to give them, and us, the answer to those questions.

During the Tribulation, most of all people on earth will pledge their allegiance and support to the Antichrist. In fact, not only support, but they will also worship him. Their worship of him will be worship of Satan, which is what he has desired since the beginning of time. While this is going on, this angel will come and call all people on earth, sinners and saved alike, to "Fear God and give Him glory." The word fear does not mean to be afraid of, but to reverence. The angel is letting all people know that they need to stop giving their reverence and respect to the Antichrist, and to give it to God instead. Worship God. This raises the question, how does one worship God? Worship of God is seen in the life of a person when they surrender their will to God. This is done when a person admits that they are a sinner, and in need of a Savior, Who is Jesus, God's Son; the One Who died on a cross to pay the penalty of our sin.

One day every created thing will bow down in submission and surrender to Jesus. The apostle Paul reminds us "at the name of Jesus every knee should bow, in heaven and on earth and under the earth, and every tongue confess that Jesus Christ is Lord, to the glory of God the Father" (Philippians 2:10-11). Just as the people during the Tribulation will have a choice whether or not they willingly bow down and worship Jesus, we also have that same choice to make today. Jesus said the most important question every person will have to answer is, "who do you say that I am?" (Mark 8:29). How you answer that question will determine your future. There are 2 choices. Either Jesus is the God, as He said, or He is wrong and is not God. Which will you choose? Surrender to God and willingly serve Him today or reject Him and be forced to worship Him one day. To choose to worship Him willingly is so much better.

July 29

"...But his brothers could not answer him, for they were dismayed at his presence. So Joseph said to his brothers, 'Come near to me, please.' And they came near."
Genesis 45:3b-4a

When you have wronged a person, and you know that you did, and that wrong is exposed to others, it is embarrassing. As your wrong is exposed you want to hide so no one can see you. Imagine how Joseph's brothers felt at this moment. Joseph has kept his identity hidden from his brothers as he only spoke to them through an interpreter; they had no idea this Egyptian ruler was their brother. As far as they knew he only spoke Egyptian because they had never heard him speak Hebrew. And they had good reason to be afraid, or "terrified," of Joseph. After all, this Egyptian ruler had graciously received them, fed them, provided them with food and provisions for their return to Canaan, and after they left, they were found to have not only their money for the grain in their bags of grain, but Joseph's personal cup was also found in Benjamin's bag. It appeared that they had taken advantage of Joseph's kindness to them and instead of being grateful, they responded by stealing from him. They are in a tight spot. It does not take much to imagine how terrified these eleven sons of Jacob are. No wonder they were terrified when Joseph suddenly spoke to them in Hebrew. Suddenly they understood that when they were privately discussing their past sins, this Egyptian ruler understood everything they said. He heard them admit their sin of selling Joseph into slavery.

Joseph is the only one here who is aware of what is going on. He holds all the cards and can do anything he wants to with his brothers. In fact, his brothers are completely at his mercy. It is a good thing that mercy is exactly what Joseph was extending to his brothers. Joseph chose to forgive his brothers, not because they were afraid of him, but because God had forgiven him. Jesus told us that those who are forgiven much gladly forgive others since we have been forgiven much (see Luke 7:47). This is what Joseph understands, and so he readily forgives his brothers. This is an example for you and me to follow. Jesus has forgiven us much. If we appreciate what He has done for us, we will also forgive others. Not because they deserve it, but because we also have been forgiven, even though we don't deserve it. That is what mercy is all about. God has been merciful to us. May we do the same and be merciful to others.

July 30

"For what credit is it if, when you sin and are beaten for it, you endure? But if when you do good and suffer for it you endure, this is a gracious thing in the sight of God."

1 Peter 2:20

Persecution and suffering are a part of life. Not a fun part of life, but they do exist, and will continue to exist, because we live in a fallen world, a world filled with sin. When we do wrong and reap the consequences of our actions, there should be no surprise when for that suffering. Do something stupid and you should expect to suffer for what you did. That is true for both the believer and the nonbeliever. It is sad to see when a believer does something stupid, suffers for it, but then complains that they are being "persecuted." No, you're not; you did something stupid and are dealing with the consequences of your actions. Make no mistake about it, God will not give anyone brownie points for suffering when it is due to their behavior. If you act like a jerk, expect to suffer for acting that way. That should be common sense, but it does seem that not everyone understands that. But there are instances where a person does suffer, or is persecuted, even though they haven't done anything wrong.

Jesus experienced this Himself while He lived here on earth. Remember, He never sinned, yet He suffered and was mistreated by others even though He did no wrong. God does see that, and He does reward those who patiently endure through being unjustly persecuted for not doing anything wrong. In fact, as a believer we should expect that to happen since we live in a world that is opposed to us living for Christ. Jesus said we should expect this to happen. "Behold, I am sending you out as sheep in the midst of wolves, so be wise as serpents and innocent as doves. Beware of men, for they will deliver you over to courts and flog you in their synagogues, and you will be dragged before governors and kings for my sake, to bear witness before them and the Gentiles. When they deliver you over, do not be anxious how you are to speak or what you are to say, for what you are to say will be given to you in that hour" (Matthew 10:16-19). God is aware when we suffer mistreatment in His name and He will equip us with everything we need to endure through those times to glorify Him, and He will reward those who do experience unjust mistreatment. Continue to draw close to Him, trust Him, and seek Him in all that you do.

July 31

"Then he said to me, 'This is the word of
the Lord to Zerubbabel: Not by might, nor by power, but by My
Spirit, says the Lord of hosts.'"
Zechariah 4:6

Have you ever been in a situation where you feel completely overwhelmed? You look at the amount of work that needs to be done, and then you look at the amount of time you have, or energy, or resources, and you realize that what needs to be done is not going to be finished. What needs to be done is much greater than what you have to get it done with. This will often result in causing a person to feel depressed; or to give up, believing there is no reason to continue to go on. If you can relate to this, you are in good company; you are not alone.

Israel had been living in captivity in Babylon for the past seventy years. They were allowed to return to their homes in Jerusalem and found their city destroyed. The walls that surrounded and protected the city, and their temple, lay on the ground in a huge pile of rubble. The people desired to rebuild the temple so they could worship the Lord, but the rubble was so great that the people became depressed and stopped building the temple. This is when God spoke to the prophet Zechariah and gave these encouraging words. "'Not by might, nor by power, but by My Spirit, says the Lord of hosts." God reminds the people that He will give them the strength needed to accomplish the work He has given them to do. God knows that the people have neither the strength nor the might to accomplish this task, but He will accomplish the work through them.

God doesn't want us to rely on our own strength or abilities either. God works through us to do His will. This means that the responsibility to get the work done is on God, not us. It is His work. God calls us to be faithful and to keep our eyes and focus on Him, not on the work to be done. When we do this, we can finish what God calls us to do because it is the Holy Spirit getting the work done. God does not want us to rely on our abilities, our giftings, our personalities or charisma, etc. Neither are we to rely on our resources, our bank accounts, our marketing skills, etc. We are to rely on the Holy Spirit. Keep our eyes focused on Jesus and continue to serve Him. He will get the work done. Don't keep looking at the work to be done because the amount of work, and the current condition of its rubble, is enough to get us down and sidetracked. Keep looking to God and allow Him to accomplish His work.

August 1

"Come now, you who say, 'Today or tomorrow we will go into such and such a town and spend a year there and trade and make a profit'— yet you do not know what tomorrow will bring. What is your life? For you are a mist that appears for a little time and then vanishes."

James 4:13-14

In the business world people are often asked to have a 5-year plan and a 10-year plan. This is for a person to know where they plan to be at those times, so they take the necessary steps to accomplish those goals. That is a good thing to do. Jesus calls us to be prepared and to plan for the future. But He also calls us to have a loose grip on our plans, but to stick close to Him so when those plans change, we can continue to follow Him. He is who we are to follow, not our plans.

Too often we hold tightly to the plans we make, whether it be for the long run, or even for the day. When our plans get changed it is easy to get upset, and even to resist the changes, attempting to follow the plans we have made. When we do that, we will miss opportunities God brings our way. We need to hold loosely to our plans and be sensitive to the leading of the Holy Spirit in our lives.

Most of us do not give much thought to the gift we have been given, the gift of today. We take the day for granted and go on with our lives and the plans we make each day. We fail to grasp the wonder that our internal organs are doing what they were created to do. Our heart continues to beat, our lungs force oxygen through our bodies, our kidneys and liver and intestines are doing their job. We drive 65 miles per hour in a little box on a narrow road with other people travelling at the same speed in the opposite direction right next to us. All it takes is a slight turn of the wrist and our life on earth could be over. If any of our organs ceased to function properly our life could end instantly. I do not say this to be morbid, but because it is reality. God gives us each day as a gift, but do we treasure the day that way? Our life is precious, and what we do each do is of value. Not one of us is promised tomorrow, so it is vital that we make the most of each day and be sensitive to God's leading to change our schedule in order to accommodate His schedule. God desires to use each of His children as a witness to others, and to be a blessing to others. But if we get so caught up in our plans, we will miss His. Treasure each day that God gives us and use it to His glory.

August 2

"And they were all filled with the Holy Spirit and began to speak in other tongues as the Spirit gave them utterance."
Acts 2:4

The rushing wind and flames of fire were just symbols of the real gift, which was being "filled with the Holy Spirit." Today we don't long for or desire to hear a mighty rushing wind, or see flames of fire on anyone's head, because this was a one-time phenomenon. But, being filled with the Holy Spirit remains available to every single believer today. What did these believers do in order to receive the gift of the Holy Spirit? They were obedient to Jesus' words, they believed Jesus' promise to them, they were unified, and they received God's gift by faith. When believer's do these things, they still will be "filled with the Holy Spirit."

Why did the believers need to be "filled with the Holy Spirit?" They needed the power of the Holy Spirit to fulfill Jesus' command to them, which was to be witnesses of Jesus to the world (see Acts 1:8). This couldn't be done on their own power, so God filled them with the Holy Spirit to enable them to fulfill His commands.

Nowhere in the Bible are we commanded to be baptized by the Spirit, because that is a work that God performs when a person submits themselves to God. But the Bible does command us to be "filled with the Holy Spirit" (see Ephesians 5:18). Each one of us needs to be filled with the Holy Spirit because we need His power to help us effectively serve God. Since we can be filled with the Holy Spirit, does that also mean that we can be emptied of the Holy Spirit? The answer is yes! Being filled with the Spirit can be a temporary thing, depending upon the individual believer. One moment we are filled with the Holy Spirit, but then through acts of disobedience, we can lose that filling. Once we repent of our wrongdoing, then we can again be filled with the Holy Spirit.

The reason we need and want to be filled with the Holy Spirit is so that we can be changed into the image of God. When we are filled with the Holy Spirit, we allow Him to change our temperament and to make us more like Jesus in thought, word, and deed. This allows us to be a witness to the world around us of the power of God, and the change that He has performed in our life. The filling of the Holy Spirit is always available to us and is available for every single believer. There is no believer that is an exception to this. This means that there is no excuse as to why every single believer in the world shouldn't be filled with the Holy Spirit.

August 3

"The woman conceived and bore a son, and when she saw that he was a fine child, she hid him three months.."
Exodus 2:2

The Bible tells us that Moses' parents did this on faith, but what was the catalyst that caused them to hide him? The NKJV & HCSB translates it that Moses "was a beautiful child." Other translations say that Moses was "goodly" (KJV), "special" (NLT), "fine" (NIV & ESV), "exceptionally well-formed" (Berkeley). The problem with all these translations is that they don't provide us with an acceptable reason why Moses' parents would do this and defy an order from the Pharaoh. Of course, he was beautiful, good, special, and well-formed. What parent doesn't think this of their child? I find it difficult to believe that his parents looked at Moses and were impressed with his rare beauty, much too beautiful to feed to the crocodiles in the Nile River. If that was the case, only the ugly babies would have been drowned in the river, and I don't know many parents who believe that their baby is ugly, which means no baby boys would have been drowned. This would mean that every parent would be defying the Pharaoh's order, and there is no record that this ever happened.

The text in Exodus 2:2 can literally be translated as "she saw that he was good." The Hebrew word that is rendered "good" is often used by Moses in the Torah, and it is used to describe something very pleasant that has been given by God. During the creation, at the end of each day God declared that what He had created "was good." This means that Moses' parents hid him simply because he was a child, a gift from God that was good. This was true for Moses, and it is true for every single baby that is born; they are a gift from God. Psalm 127:3 tells us that "children are a heritage...a reward." King David reminds us that God "formed my inward parts; You knitted me together in my mother's womb. I praise You, for I am fearfully and wonderfully made" (Psalm 139:13-14). Every single child is divinely created, and therefore "good." It is sad to see how far removed much of today's society is from the faith and understanding of newborn babies that Moses' parents had. Those that support abortion tells us that children are not good, they are a burden, inconvenient, and a nuisance, so they need to be killed. That is simply not true. That viewpoint simply refuses to see babies the way that God sees them, as good and made in the image of God. The "sophisticated" ways that abortionists kill babies today is no more humane that throwing them into the Nile to be eaten by crocodiles. We need to pray for the safety of the unborn and do everything we can within our powers and abilities to save and help babies.

August 4

"I, Jesus, have sent my angel to testify to you about these things for the churches. I am the root and the descendant of David, the bright morning star."
Revelation 22:16

Authenticity is a huge concern for people in the 21st Century. The reason for this is because there are so many fakes, so many forgeries. Creating knock offs that look like the real thing is a huge business and causes people to do extra homework to verify that what they have is the "real deal." Reading through the book of Revelation causes many people to believe that what they are reading is so fantastic that it can't be true. Much of this book reads like a science fiction movie, or a fairy tale. But Jesus inserts a statement here verifying that what you have read is completely true and accurate. Jesus Himself sent an angel to John the apostle to tell him these things. What Jesus does here is verify that everything in the book of Revelation is true. There is nothing fake in this book.

Jesus sent this angel to tell John these things so that the church will know what is coming, and what will happen. Knowledge of the future is not a private event, known only by the elite and powerful. No! It is written here so that it will be common knowledge for all believers. God isn't trying to hide anything from His children but is giving us a both a warning about what will happen and an encouragement to draw near to Him and be ready for His return. In other words, Jesus is giving His children all the tools they need to live a life here on earth that prepares us for Him and His return, and a life that will also bring glory and honor to Him.

Then Jesus says something interesting. He says He is "the root and the descendant of David." Jesus says that David comes from Him but that He also comes from David. How can that be true? It is, because when Jesus came to earth as little baby born in Bethlehem, He was a descendant of King David through both Mary and Joseph (see Luke 3:23-38 and Matthew 1:1-17). But, as Christ Jesus has always existed (see John 1:1), way before David did. Jesus spoke the world into existence, which makes Him the root that David, and all created things, came from.

August 5

"Do you not know that in a race all the runners run, but only one receives the prize? So run that you may obtain it."
1 Corinthians 9:24

I am not a runner. Running a race does not interest me, but the apostle Paul related our life to a race, and each of us is running in the race of life. At the end of the race, we will receive a prize for how we ran the race. This is what Paul was saying to the church in Corinth. To enter this race all one has to do is admit that they are a sinner and that they need Jesus as their Savior. There are no other requirements for entrance.

This is so much different than other races. When I was in High

School, I ran on the track team for two years. I participated in the long jump and the triple jump. One year our team was invited to attend an invitational track meet in Pasadena, CA. We were all very excited to go to this meet. Finally, the day arrived, and we went to the meet. When we got there we were told that each participant had to meet or exceed certain requirements to participate. When I saw the minimum distance for the triple jump, I was very nervous. The minimum jump was a little farther than I had ever jumped. They allowed me to participate still, so I jogged down to the end of the runway. As I sprinted down the runway, I hit the mark and jumped the best jump in my life. I cannot tell you how embarrassing it is to do your best and still end your jump on the runway; I missed the sand pit by a couple of inches. The judges disqualified me, and I was not able to participate in the rest of that meet. I was not able to meet the minimum requirement to get in.

Praise God He doesn't follow those same requirements. There is no entrance exam to make sure you are good enough to qualify for Heaven. If there was, we would all be in trouble, because only Jesus has been able to meet the requirements. I am so glad that He paid the price I could not pay, and He loves me so much that He wants me to come into Heaven with Him. He does not look at me and see my inadequacies. He looks at me and sees that my sins are paid for and covered by the blood of Jesus. Jesus doesn't look at what abilities I have, or how good I am at doing something. What He looks at is to see if I have humbled myself before Him and that I am available for Him to use. God will use those who are available, not those with abilities.

The race that we are running is open to all runners. There are no minimum requirements. So how do we win the race to receive the prize? The winner is the person who finishes the race. Run the race to finish. This requires perseverance. There will be many times the race becomes difficult, and you will want to quit. DON'T. Do not give up but continue to run.

Another beautiful thing about this race of life is that you don't have to finish within a certain amount of time. Mile runners are shooting to break the 4-minute mark. But the race of life is an endurance run. God is not looking for you to break a certain time mark, but to finish the race. Keep your eye on the finish line because that is where the prize is. The finish line will keep you on course and give you motivation to finish the race. Keep your eyes on Jesus, seek Him, follow Him and DO NOT give up. Keep running and you will receive the prize of eternal life, along with a reward of a crown. Don't give up now, no matter how difficult the race is, keep running. The finish line is getting closer and closer. Keep running. You will win!

August 6

"In Judah it was said, 'The strength of those who bear the burdens is failing...'"
Nehemiah 4:10a

Goals are an integral part of life. It has truly been noted that nobody plans to fail, but many fail to plan. Part of planning is setting goals. Many people enjoy setting goals and then working to accomplish those goals. This past year I began a new hobby and set some goals that I wanted to accomplish. My new hobby is riding a road bike, and the goal I set was to complete a century ride, or ride 100 miles on my bike in one day. To meet that goal, I didn't just go out and ride 100 miles the day I picked up my bike. No way! My behind would have been way too sore to accomplish that goal at that time. What I did was keep setting goals to ride further and further distances and ride multiple times per week. The first month I couldn't ride my bike 20 miles, but after a while I met that goal, then as I kept riding 3 to 4 times per week, I saw my riding distances continue to increase. By the end of the summer, I not only completed a century ride, but did 5 of them, and four of them in four consecutive days. But let me tell you when the hardest part was; it was when I was halfway done. I was tired, wore out, had a sore behind, and not sure I could complete the goals I had set.

This is what Nehemiah and the people of Jerusalem are experiencing. The walls are halfway done, and their enemies are harassing them, making fun of them, pointing out their weaknesses, and the people are tired, wore out, and not sure they can finish building the walls. They needed to hear what the apostle Paul would later write, "And let us not grow weary of doing good, for in due season we will reap, if we do not give up" (Galatians 6:9). What they were doing was difficult, but it was also important. Remember, the wall is what gave the city protection, but now that the wall was halfway built, their work became more difficult. Instead of bending over the pout the mortar and set the stones, now they had to reach over their heads. Hour after hour of doing this was physically taxing. The people needed to be reminded of the importance of what they were doing, and to be reminded of the vision of why they were doing this. The same is true for us. Why do we do the things we do? Especially when we are tired and wore out. Remember what Jesus did for us to give us the vision to continue to do what He has called us to do, which is to love others and lead them to Jesus. Don't grow tired of doing that. May we "be steadfast, immovable, always abounding in the work of the Lord, knowing that in the Lord your labor is not in vain" (1 Corinthians 15:58).

August 7

"After this I saw another angel coming down from heaven, having great authority, and the earth was made bright with his glory."
Revelation 18:1

Throughout the book of Revelation, the apostle John has been sharing the visions that God is giving him of what will happen in the future. Each time he has used the phrase "after this," he shares a fresh and new vision. The vision from Revelation 17, the destruction of the world's false religious system, is over and now a new vision is given to John. This vision overlaps the previous vision as they both relate to the rule of Antichrist's world empire, but the world's false religious system has already been destroyed, and this new vision now focuses on the world's commercial system. The world and its system is made up of three different components: religion, government, and commerce. Antichrist will rule over all three of these areas, until he ends up destroying them.

In this new vision the apostle John sees another angel coming down to him from Heaven. This angel is just like the angel that came to him in the previous vision where the world's false religious system was destroyed (see Revelation 17:1). It is not the exact same angel, but they are both alike. Since this angel comes out of Heaven down to earth, it is interesting to note that he "glows" after coming out of the presence of God in Heaven. His glowing is so obvious that it is seen by the entire world.

These angels that are dispatched from Heaven come down to earth with great authority. The angel in Revelation 17 was given the authority to destroy the world's false religious system. This is why the image given to the world's system was of a harlot, or prostitute; she was used, abused, and then thrown away. Antichrist used her for his purposes and advancement, and when she was no longer needed, she was destroyed and discarded. This angel that comes from Heaven has the same authority and power as the last angel did. God is systematically destroying Antichrist and the world's system that he is using for his glory and power. Evil will have its time. It will appear that it is winning and in control, but that appearance will be short lived. Remember, God is in control, and He will ultimately destroy Satan and his followers. This is why God has given us this preview of the future. Not to scare us with what will happen, but to assure us that He is in control, and everything is going according to His plan.

August 8

"When they had preached the gospel to that city and had made many disciples, they returned to Lystra and to Iconium and to Antioch, strengthening the souls of the disciples, encouraging them to continue in the faith, and saying that through many tribulations we must enter the kingdom of God.'"
Acts 14:21-22

Paul and Barnabas had been rejected in Antioch, run out of Iconium, and stoned to death in Lystra. But, in Derbe, Paul preached the exact same message he taught in the other three cities, and here people responded to his teaching and accepted Jesus as their Lord and Savior, surrendering their heart and life to Him. Paul's dogged determination paid off.

Notice what Paul's goal was: they "made many disciples." Paul wasn't interested in the size of the crowds he was preaching to, or how many people he could get to come forward to an altar call. His goal was people becoming disciples, or followers, of Jesus. It's not just about learning Bible verses, even though that is very good to do, it's about laying down your life and following Jesus. It's all about there being less of you and more of Him. It's not about having every problem in your life solved, but it's about taking up your cross and following Him daily.

When Paul and Barnabas were finished in Derbe they returned to the last three cities they had visited: Lystra, Iconium, and Antioch. It would have been a shorter and quicker trip for them to go straight south and return to Antioch in Syria. But they didn't do this. Why? Because there were still new believers in each of those cities, and Paul and Barnabas cared for them. So they returned in order to strengthen their faith and to encourage them to "continue in the faith." Walking with God is not an easy thing to do, especially year after year and trial after trial. Paul knew they were going to face trials and persecutions, so he did all that he could do to prepare them to be able to withstand those trials, and to remain standing.

It's not easy to persevere through the Christian life, but Jesus gave us a promise to help us endure. Jesus said, "In the world you will have tribulation. But take heart; I have overcome the world" (John 16:33). Jesus has overcome and defeated the world, sin, and death for us. That is why it is so important for us to keep "looking to Jesus, the founder and perfecter of our faith" (Hebrews 12:2a).

August 9

"Since all these things are thus to be dissolved, what sort of people ought you to be in lives of holiness and godliness."
2 Peter 3:11

Peter has informed us that one day the entire world is going to melt. If that's the case, how then should we live our lives here on earth today? The fact that this world isn't going to last forever should cause us not to worship it, or to place our trust in it. Yet this seems to be exactly what most people do. What do you live for, or work for? Generally, it is for material things here on this earth: houses, cars, vacations, insurance, investments, etc. Why are these things that we strive after? Especially since they are going to melt. How then should we live?

Peter reminds us of the future of this world, not to scare us, but to remind us that we are simply pilgrims passing through to our eternal home. Our destination is a much better world, one that is not corrupted, and one that will last for all eternity. If we are just passing through, then we shouldn't be too attached to things here, and this sort of lifestyle will set us apart from the rest of the world. Our lives need to be characterized by holiness and godliness. Peter wrote "He who called you is holy, you also be holy in all your conduct" (1 Peter 1:15). Peter didn't make this up, he was quoting what God told the Israelites after their exodus from Egypt. God said, "You shall be holy, for I the LORD your God am holy" (Leviticus 19:2). God calls us to live a life separate from the world, set apart for Him.

Recently I read a story about a rabbi in the city of Jerusalem. He lived in a small apartment in the city, and the only furniture in his house was a chair, desk, and a bed. A visitor came to his apartment and was shocked at the emptiness of the apartment. They asked the rabbi where his furniture was. He responded by asking the visitor where their furniture was. They responded by saying their furniture was at home, they didn't bring it with them because they were traveling. The rabbi smiled at them and responded, "So am I." This is Peter's reminder to us. We are traveling through this world, keep your eyes and your focus on Jesus.

August 10

"'You know that Abner the son of Ner came to deceive you and to know your going out and your coming in, and to know all that you are doing.' When Joab came out from David's presence, he sent messengers after Abner, and they brought him back from the cistern of Sirah. But David did not know about it."
2 Samuel 3:25-26

Fear. Just the thought of it scares many people. Every one of us has things that we are afraid of. Fear often brings in one of two results: immobilization or lack of clarity. Many people clam up when facing fears and end up being able to do nothing. Others will act on what they think they see, but the fear does not allow them to see the situation clearly. Acting upon false information does not produce good results.

This is what happens in this Scripture. The kingdom of Israel has been divided since King Saul died. David has been ruling over Judah, and the rest of Israel has been following Saul's son Ishbosheth, who was led by general Abner. Abner realizes he was wrong in his actions and is now working to unite all Israel under the leadership of David. He has been communicating with David and just met with David to work out the final details. Joab is the general of David's army and he returns to David just after Abner has left. Joab is very upset and even though he wasn't present in the meeting, he tells David that Abner is deceiving him and attempting to destroy David. How does Joab know this? He doesn't. He is acting out of fear.

Joab is afraid that Abner is deceiving King David on behalf of Ishbosheth and he acts on that belief. Joab is also afraid that he could lose his position as general to Abner. Abner and Joab are in equal positions of authority, and Abner is a decorated veteran of war. In fact, earlier Abner had also killed Joab's brother in battle. All these details are clouding the judgment of Joab, and he is acting upon this information instead of trusting and following his leader. King David is aware of all these things, but he also personally met with Abner and had additional communication with him, so David knows the true situation.

Joab acts upon his fears and what he thinks is true. This leads him to send messengers to call Abner back for a supposed meeting with David. When Abner returns, Joab meets with Abner, brings him outside the city gate and then murders him. Joab is convinced that he is helping protect David and his kingdom. In reality, his actions are bringing shame to David and not realizing God's plans for him. Joab was running in front of his leader and not following the wishes and directions of his boss, King David.

How often do we do the same thing. When we act upon our fears and fail to seek out God for wisdom, our choices and actions bring disgrace upon God instead of honoring Him. While that is not our intention, it can be the result. We can think that we know exactly what is going on and act upon that, which is not always correct. We need to trust in God and follow His lead. Trust is not easy. It can be very difficult to wait for God because our flesh wants to jump in and either receive an immediate answer or fix what we perceive is a problem right away. But that is not always how God operates, and neither is that His plan. So, we will act upon our fears and move out to do what we think is right without trusting God. When we do this, we will get the same disastrous results that Joab did. Our failure to trust God can bring shame to God, additional problems in our life, and place unneeded strain upon relationships.

Joab's actions resulted in the death of the person who was able to bring a peaceful unification of Israel. It created problems for Judah, Israel, and the person Joab was trying to help, King David. Instead of trusting his boss, Joab acted upon his fears, and it led to disastrous results. May we turn to God for wisdom when faced with our fears and trust Him. It will not be easy, but it will be worth it.

August 11

"Now therefore, if you will indeed obey My voice and keep My covenant, you shall be My treasured possession among all peoples, for all the earth is Mine..."
Exodus 19:5

God is giving Israel a promise, but there is a prerequisite that is required. What is it? Obedience. God is telling Israel that He requires them to obey what He is going to share with them. Obedience is the key. It isn't enough to know what God's Word says. What is important is doing God's Word. That why they prophet Samuel said, "to obey is better than sacrifice" (1 Samuel 15:22).

The promise that God gives to Moses to tell the Israelites is that if they will obey His Word and keep His covenant, then they will be "a special treasure" to God. Now, the whole world belongs to God, as Psalm 24:1 reminds us. "The earth is the LORD's and the fullness thereof, the world and those who dwell therein." Out of all the nations in the world, God has chosen Israel to be His treasured possession, as God said in Deuteronomy 14:2, which says, "you are a people holy to the LORD your God, and the LORD has chosen you to be a people for His treasured possession, out of all the peoples who are on the face of the earth." Since God chose the Israelites to be His special people, does that mean that they are better than the other nations? No! God reminded the Israelites that He chose them, not based upon their goodness or anything that they did to deserve it, but simply because of His grace. "For you are a people holy to the Lord your God. The Lord your God has chosen you to be a people for His treasured possession, out of all the peoples who are on the face of the earth. It was not because you were more in number than any other people that the Lord set His love on you and chose you, for you were the fewest of all peoples, but it is because the Lord loves you and is keeping the oath that He swore to your fathers, that the Lord has brought you out with a mighty hand and redeemed you from the house of slavery, from the hand of Pharaoh king of Egypt" (Deuteronomy 7:6-8).

God chose the Israelites to be His special people, and then He set them apart so that they would be a blessing not only to Himself, but to the entire world. The Israelites belonged to God; they were a special treasure to Him. That is not unique to Israel, but it is also the same for every believer. The apostle Paul wrote that he wanted all believers to know how much they meant to God. He wrote, "having the eyes of your hearts enlightened, that you may know what is the hope to which He has called you, what are the riches of His glorious inheritance in the saints..." (Ephesians 1:18). Do you know and realize how valuable you are to God?

August 12

"And they sing the song of Moses, the servant of God, and the song of the Lamb, saying, 'Great and amazing are Your deeds, O Lord God the Almighty! Just and true are Your ways, O King of the nations! Who will not fear, O Lord, and glorify Your name? For You alone

are holy. All nations will come and worship You, for Your righteous acts have been revealed.'"
Revelation 15:3-4

Singing is a huge part of the history of the church, and it will continue to be even into the future. The government may attempt to crack down on the church and even make it illegal to sing in church, but that won't stop the true church from singing songs to God. As the apostle John gives us a glimpse into Heaven, we see this multitude of victorious martyrs singing a song of praise to God. John gives us two different names for this song: the song of Moses and the song of the Lamb. It is one song that has two titles. These two titles give us a perfect union between the law and love: or between the Old Covenant and the New Covenant. God used Moses to deliver the Israelites from bondage, and afterwards they sang a song of praise about their deliverance. The Lamb has delivered these martyrs from their sin through His death on the cross, and they also respond by singing a song of praise to God.

Notice the words to this song. There is a word, or a variation of it, that is repeated throughout the song. That is the word You, or Your. This is a reference to God. The entire focus of the song is on God, not those that have been delivered. God delivered the people, and they respond with praise to the One Who delivered them. He is worthy of praise, no one else.

There are four things that God is praised for in this song. Obviously, this list is not complete, but highlights a few things that God is praised for. He is to be praised for His works, "Great and amazing are Your deeds." We also praise God for His ways, "just and true are Your ways." The third thing God is praised for is His worthiness, "who will not fear, O Lord, and glorify Your name?" The fourth thing God is praised for in this song is His worship, "all nations will come and worship You." While we may not know the tune to this song, today we can sing songs of praise to God for these things.

August 13

"Now before this, Eliashib the priest, who was appointed over the chambers of the house of our God, and who was related to Tobiah, prepared for Tobiah a large chamber where they had previously put the grain offering, the frankincense, the vessels, and the tithes of grain, wine, and oil, which were given by commandment to the Levites, singers, and gatekeepers, and the contributions for the priests."
Nehemiah 13:4-5

God had instructed the Israelites to never allow an Ammonite to enter the Temple because these people refused to help, or even be hospitable, the Israelites when they entered the Promised Land. Instead of being hospitable to the Israelites, the Ammonites hired a person to pronounce a curse upon the Israelites to drive them back out of the land. As long as Nehemiah remained in Jerusalem the people of Israel followed God, but as soon as he returned to Babylon they began to walk away from God. This became obvious when Eliashib the priest emptied out a room in the Temple that was to be used by the priests for God's work, and he turned it into a room for Tobiah the Ammonite to live in. Tobiah wasn't even supposed to be in the Temple, much less living there.

Sitting here today it is easy to come down hard on Eliashib for these actions he took. How dare he disobey God's Word and desecrate the Temple by not only allowing Tobiah to enter it but changing it from God's plan to housing an enemy of God in it. Before we come down on Eliashib we need to look at our own lives. Is there a Tobiah that has wormed his way into our life? Have we given a throne that belongs to God and allowed anyone or anything else to sit on that throne? We, as believers, as the Temple of God (see 1 Corinthians 6:19-20). Have we allowed any enemy of God to set up house within us? Does the enemy have any furniture within our hearts that needs to be removed? Is it possible that the Holy Spirit has so little room in our hearts because we are allowing so many other things to reside in and take over our own heart? May we follow the example of King David and give God permission to "Search me, O God, and know my heart! Try me and know my thoughts! And see if there be any grievous way in me and lead me in the way everlasting!" (Psalm 139:23-24).

August 14

"Let it be known to you therefore, brothers, that through this man forgiveness of sins is proclaimed to you, and by him everyone who believes is freed from everything from which you could not be freed by the law of Moses."
Acts 13:38-39

Paul now gets to the "heart" of his message and shares what the Gospel is all about. There is only one way for a person to have their sins forgiven. You can't receive forgiveness by following a set of rules and regulations; you can't be "good enough" either. The only way a person can have their sins forgiven is through Jesus. Receiving forgiveness has absolutely nothing to do with us. This is why later Paul would write, "For by grace you have been saved through faith. And this is not your own doing; it is the gift of God, not a result of works, so that no one may boast" (Ephesians 2:8-9). It is sad to see so many people refuse to accept God's grace and instead try to find ways to receive salvation through their own actions. It can't be done. Salvation cannot be earned; it is given by grace.

This is why Paul then goes on to state that God's grace justifies us "from everything from which you could not be freed by the law of Moses." The law is not able to justify a guilty person. What is this justification? Justification is the act where God declares the believing sinner to righteous in Jesus Christ. Some have helped simplify this explaining justification as "just as if I'd never sinned." It speaks of how God sees us as we stand before Him. He sees no sin in us because a believer's sin is covered by Jesus' shed blood. Our sin has been removed.

Our sin is only able to be removed by God's grace. The law is not able to remove our sin. It can cover it, but not remove it. The law can corner a person, convict a person, condemn a person, but it cannot cancel a person's sin. What the law does is examine a person's behavior, it looks at their works, judges them, and finds them lacking. There is only one way a person can be justified: through the death of Jesus on the cross, and His resurrection from the grave. When we accept the work He did for us as our substitute, then our transaction to justification is complete. We are then able to stand before God and be accepted by Him because when God now looks at us He sees the beauty of Jesus and not our sins. Jesus did for us what the law is not able to do. Thank You Jesus!

August 15

"So Moses made a bronze serpent and set it on a pole. And if a serpent bit anyone, he would look at the bronze serpent and live."
Numbers 21:9

Was there some sort of magical power in the bronze snake? No! What it did require was faith. It required faith to believe what Moses told them to do. Think about it, you could "logically" conclude that the bronze snake didn't have any magical powers. Therefore, there would be no need to look at it. Instead, what you needed was anti-venom for the snake bite. That is logical, but that refusal to look at the snake would also bring about their death. Meanwhile, the believer would acknowledge that they didn't understand how looking at a bronze snake would save them, but they're going to do it because God said to. They would look at the snake in faith, and after looking at the snake they would still be alive.

The serpent on the pole was representative of Jesus on the cross. How do I know this? Because Jesus said so. It's found in John 3:14-15. "And as Moses lifted up the serpent in the wilderness, so must the Son of Man be lifted up, that whoever believes in Him may have eternal life." Jesus said that He would be lifted up just as Moses lifted up this bronze serpent. When Jesus said this, He was saying that anyone that looked to Him would not perish but would receive eternal life.

How can Jesus be represented by a serpent? Throughout the Bible serpents are used as a picture of evil (see Genesis 3:1-5 & Revelation 12:9). That is true, but also the Bible speaks of bronze as representing judgment because bronze passes through the "fires" of judgment. This is why the altar in the Tabernacle was made of bronze, because this is where sins were "judged." So, the bronze serpent is not speaking of evil, but of evil that has been judged. This bronze serpent is a picture of evil that has been judged and dealt with.

You see, when we were born, we were born with a sin nature because we have all been bitten by the serpent. We are dying from this bite, as the apostle Paul said, "For the wages of sin is death" (Romans 6:23). For this reason, God has judged sin on the cross. "For our sake He made Him to be sin who knew no sin..." (2 Corinthians 5:21). Jesus took our sins, placed them on His back, and paid the penalty for them. Jesus dealt with our sin on the cross. This is the moment when God judged both sin and Satan. They were destroyed at this moment. This means, for us to be healed from the venom of sin, we need to look in faith to the place where sin was judged – which is the cross. Faith in Jesus is the only way for us to be saved from the venom (or poison) of sin.

In order to be saved, the people had to look to this bronze serpent that was lifted up. You could look and be saved, or don't look and die. It was that simple. It is still that simple today. Either you are looking to Jesus as your Savior because you recognize that you are a sinner, or you aren't. If you're not looking to Jesus, it doesn't matter how many times you go to church, how many times you've been baptized, whether you give money to church, or even if you do good works. If you're not looking to Jesus, then you have chosen to die. Without looking to Jesus, you are going to hell. In order to receive eternal life, you must look to Jesus. It is that simple.

August 16

"Resist him, firm in your faith, knowing that the same kinds of suffering are being experienced by your brotherhood throughout the world."
1 Peter 5:9

Challenges are something that we all experience on a regular basis. These are the backbone of game shows. Many people thrive on challenges and are always looking for new challenges in their life. In our spiritual life we also are faced with a daily challenge, which is to not be defeated by our enemy, Satan. Peter gives us a key to successfully completing the challenge to no become defeated by Satan. How do we do that? We do it by resisting him. Our English word resist is a combination of two Greek words, the English translations are *stand* and *against*. We resist the devil by standing against him. Think of a soldier and how they "stand" at attention. They are not sitting down and relaxing, but they are in an upright position, prepared for battle, with every sense being awakened and ready for battle. The believer needs to be ready and prepared in Jesus so that they can stand against the devil and his lies, his threats, and his temptations.

In order for a person to be able to resist they must first be standing. This is why the apostle Paul reminds us that God gave us spiritual armor so "that you may be able to stand against the schemes of the devil" (Ephesians 6:11b). A person that is not standing will not be able to resist the devil. It is important for us to remember that we resist the devil, not in our own strength, but with our faith in God. We are only able to resist the devil through the power of the Holy Spirit and with the armor that God gives to His children in faith. Peter is writing these words because he knew that he could not resist the devil on his own. He had tried that previously and failed spectacularly on the night that Jesus was arrested. He fell asleep in the Garden, attacked Malchus, the high priest's servant, and denied Jesus three times. Jesus warned Peter earlier that evening that he would fail Jesus, but instead of listening to Jesus he instead argued with him. His own pride led to his downfall instead of his relying on the power of the Holy Spirit to lead him to being able to resist the devil. The same thing is true for each of us in our own daily life. Use the weapons God has given us, which is the Bible and prayer. These will help us resist the devil by standing against him.

August 17

"Then I said to them, 'You see the trouble we are in, how Jerusalem lies in ruins with its gates burned. Come, let us build the wall of Jerusalem, that we may no longer suffer derision.' And I told them of the hand of my God that had been upon me for good, and also of the words that the king had spoken to me."
Nehemiah 2:17-18a

One of the most difficult aspects of life is dealing with people. They don't always see things the same way you do, and they can be unpredictable in how they act and respond to things. While people can be frustrating, they also can bring more joy than anything else on earth. This is because God has created us to be part of communities, to belong to groups of people, not to be isolated and alone. Now, there are tools and ways to deal with others that will either help us or hurt us in being part of a community and joined together to others. We can learn lots from Nehemiah in how he dealt with others. For instance, even though he came to the people in Jerusalem as a representative of the king, with the power, blessing, and resources of the king, he didn't simply expect the people to obey him because of his position. Instead of lording his authority over the people, he was one of them.

Nehemiah understood the importance of community. He was a fellow Jew, not just an employee and representative of the king. So, when he began to share the vision that God had given him for rebuilding the city of Jerusalem, he didn't begin by blaming them for their failure to rebuild the walls themselves. Placing blame and criticism upon people first will kill all motivation for those people to listen to you and help you. This is why Nehemiah showed them that he was one of them. He was encouraging them to be part of the solution so they would be motivated to help fulfill God's plans and purposes for Jerusalem. This is why he didn't offer them bribes or rewards to build the walls, but that they would help simply help because of their shared love of God and vision for their city. Nehemiah was wise to realize he couldn't accomplish this task on his own. He needed the help of others. This is true for the majority of God's works; they are not done alone but require the help of others. God placed this burden, or vision, upon Nehemiah. He spent four months praying over it and planning, three months traveling, and three days inspecting the city and its walls before he shared this vision with others. He continually waited for God's timing and allowed God to lead him as he brought others together to both share and fulfill God's vision.

August 18

"And while they were gazing into Heaven as He went, behold, two men stood by them in white robes, and said, 'Men of Galilee, why do you stand looking into Heaven? This Jesus, who was taken up from

you into heaven, will come in the same way as you saw Him go into Heaven.'"
Acts 1:10-11

As Jesus ascends to Heaven, the attention of the disciples was riveted towards the sky. They were gazing at Jesus as He returned to Heaven. What had begun in a cradle, now ended in a cloud. God had come down to earth in the form of a man, and now He returned to Heaven.

The disciples are so intent in gazing after Jesus that they miss the appearance of these two men that stood by them. These two men brought the disciples out of their confusion, and kept them from gazing into the clouds, when they had duties that needed to be done here on earth. They are angels, and they break the disciples' focus and direct them to be obedient to what Jesus called them to do, which is remain in Jerusalem until they're baptized with the Holy Spirit, and to be witnesses of Him to the world.

Part of what these two angels were doing was removing the disciples' eyes off the physical, the things they could see, and to get their eyes onto the invisible. They completely relied upon Jesus during His entire ministry on earth, and now it was time for them to venture out on their own to do what Jesus called them to do. It is the same for us today. We can easily become dependent upon another person, and the thought of them not being right there alongside us can be very frightening. This is why it is imperative that we keep our focus and trust solely on Jesus. He is where all our trust must remain, not on anyone or anything that we can see.

These two angels also provided the disciples with encouragement. They said, "This Jesus, who was taken up from you into heaven, will come in the same way as you saw Him go into Heaven." This same Jesus would return. It wouldn't be a different Jesus, but the exact same Jesus they had just spent the past three years with would one day return back to earth the same way He had just left earth. This meant the first coming of Jesus was complete. The Old Testament prophecies of Jesus, the Messiah, coming to earth had all been fulfilled to the letter. Not every prophecy was fulfilled though. There were some prophecies given about His Second Coming, and we can rest assured that every one of them will be fulfilled to the letter, just like they were at His first coming. Isn't that great news? Jesus is coming again!

August 19

"And the LORD said, 'Do you do well to be angry?'"
Jonah 4:4

Jonah had just demanded God fulfill his own wishes and demands by killing him (see Jonah 4:3). Notice how God responds to Jonah. He doesn't "blast" him, or even respond with a lecture (which he did deserve). No! God responds very tenderly, and with a simple question. By His response God shows that Jonah was correct in his description and understanding of God: He is "gracious and merciful...slow to anger and abounding in steadfast love" (Jonah 4:2). If God was anything else, He would have judged Jonah on the spot, most likely with death.

Jonah had absolutely no right to be angry that the residents of Nineveh had received the same grace, mercy, and compassion that he himself had received. Only God had the right to be angry with the Ninevites over their sins, and He chose to forgive them. The same question needs to be asked of ourselves. Who do we think we are to hold on to anger at others that God has forgiven? Why do we think we can play God and taking their punishment into our own hands? When we keep negative attitudes towards others, speak harsh words against them, or have actions that are not helpful, then we are being like Jonah and running ahead of God to hand out the justice that we believe is needed instead of allowing God to deal with the issue correctly. When God asks us, "are you right to be angry?", there is only one correct response, "No Lord, vengeance belongs to You, not me!" (see Deuteronomy 32:35).

God also likes to ask questions, because the answer to those questions reveals the heart of the person being asked. Look at some of the questions that God has asked: Where are you? Who told you that you were naked? What is this you have done? (Genesis 3) Where is your brother Abel? What have you done? (Genesis 4) Why did you despise the word of the LORD by doing what is evil in his eyes? (2 Samuel 12) Whom shall I send? Who will go for us? (Isaiah 6) Who do you say that I am? (Matthew 16) What do you want Me to do for you? (Matthew 20) Are you betraying the Son of Man with a kiss? (Luke 22) Saul, Saul, why are you persecuting Me? (Acts 9)

Answer God's questions honestly. God asks these questions for a reason: to help us see His truth accurately and honestly, drawing us closer to Him.

August 20

"To them God chose to make known how great among the Gentiles are the riches of the glory of this mystery, which is Christ in you, the hope of glory."
Colossians 1:27

Hope is defined as "a confident desire in something that is going to happen." It is much more than just wishful thinking because there is a confidence and expectation in what will come. Hope is powerful, and able to help us get through times of difficulty, because there is reason and motivation to keep moving forward. The question we all must ask is, "What is your hope?"

For most people in the United States their hope is related to the economy. Their hope is in their income and the things that can be purchased by it; or investments and the assurance they can bring in times of distress; or insurance and the promise of protection. In short, hope is generally associated with a life of comfort, ease, and protection. This is what we often call "The American Dream." The American Dream says that "life should be better and richer and fuller for everyone, with opportunity for each according to ability or achievement." Even the church in America has taken over this concept. In fact, the church has even adopted this thought and re-invented the gospel to fit the American Dream. Many sermons are preached saying Christians should be prosperous and financially well off, with each person having multiple vehicles, houses, exotic vacations, and various play toys. While this sounds wonderful and enticing, it is also un-Biblical. Pastors, churches, and individuals need to replace the American Dream with Biblical truth.

The truth is found in the gospels (Matthew, Mark, Luke and John). In these books of the Bible, we see how Jesus lived here on earth. According to the American Dream, and many churches and pastors, Jesus would be defined as a failure because "Foxes have holes, and birds of the air have nests, but the Son of Man has nowhere to lay His head" (Matthew 8:20). Read through the gospels and it quickly becomes apparent that Jesus' focus was not on material things, but on people and relationships. That should also be the focus for His disciples. Owning multiple vehicles, houses, and going on exotic vacations is not wrong, but that is not the focus Christians need to have; it is not our hope. People and relationships need to be our focus because Jesus Christ is our hope. He has called us to be like Him, and that was His focus. Jesus said He always did what pleases God the Father (see John 8:29). As Christians our goal is to be the same, to please God the Father. Investing ourselves into others and sharing the good news of Jesus with them pleases God. Sharing that true hope with others will change this world.

August 21

"O Lord, you are my God; I will exalt you; I will praise your name,

for you have done wonderful things, plans formed of old, faithful and sure."
Isaiah 25:1

We are to praise God because He is God. We also praise God because He has done wonderful things. We praise God because He is faithful and true. But what are we to do when things aren't going well? How are we to respond when we are in the midst of trying and difficult circumstances? Where is God during times of trouble?

The answer, of course, is that God is right there with us. God has promised that He will never leave us nor forsake us (see Hebrews 13:5). While we are experiencing difficult times, we can still praise God. Why is that? Because God is still faithful and true.

When we experience times of trouble, we smack a hand on our forehead and begin to fret and worry because Plan A is not working out. We then begin to scramble to figure out Plan B, and sometimes even Plan C. While we are doing that, it is comforting to know that God is not doing the same thing. There has never been a time when God has smacked His forehead with the palm of His hand because His Plan A didn't work out, and He doesn't know what to do next. God's plans do not always make sense to us, but they do to Him. "For My thoughts are not your thoughts, neither are your ways My ways, declares the Lord. For as the heavens are higher than the earth, so are My ways higher than your ways and My thoughts than your thoughts" (Isaiah 55:8-9).

To help us understand this, let's look at Joseph in the Old Testament. He was the 11th of 12 sons, and 10 of his brothers couldn't stand him. They ridiculed him and made fun of him. They hated him so much that they even sold him as a slave and told their dad he had been killed by a wild animal. While in Egypt as a slave, Joseph was falsely accused of a crime and then spent the next few years in prison. Do we find him crying and complaining to God about this? No. Joseph understood that God works in strange ways, and even when things are difficult (and sometimes even unpleasant), it is something that God has allowed into your life for a reason. God is still in control, and He will work it out for good (see Romans 8:28). And God did, making Joseph second in command of the most powerful nation on earth, at that time.

Even when people purposefully do mean and/or evil things to you, God is able to use that for His good. Again, Joseph is a perfect example of this. He was betrayed by his brothers, lied to, and even sold as a slave out of jealousy. Was Joseph angry over this? Did Joseph seek revenge on his brothers? No! Again, he understood that God was still in control the whole time. His brothers were afraid of him when they eventually met up again, but Joseph did not have revenge on his mind. He said, "you meant evil against me, but God meant it for good" (Gen 50:20). God has not changed, so when we are experiencing troubling times, remember that God is allowing it in order to accomplish His purposes in your life; and He is still in control.

August 22

"Behold, I am coming like a thief! Blessed is the one who stays awake, keeping his garments on, that he may not go about naked and be seen exposed!"
Revelation 16:15

It is a terrible feeling to come home and find that it has been burglarized. When this happens, the homeowner feels not only vandalized, but as a victim their sense of security is shattered. They feel violated, scared, and there is an unease now even within their own house, which should be their sanctuary. There is no way to know when this will happen. A thief does not publish their itinerary so that the homeowner is not able to provide additional security to their home. Jesus is saying that He is going to return to earth one day, just like a thief; without warning and when most do not expect it to happen. This means that His return to happen at any moment. Be prepared for the unexpected. So, how should we respond to this?

Our response to Jesus' return is to always be ready. Jesus taught this while He was here on earth when He taught about the ten virgins, or bridesmaids, in Matthew 25:1-13. Five of these young ladies were prepared for the arrival of the groom, and they were immediately taken into the wedding reception with the groom, while the five unprepared bridesmaids were left outside and not allowed into the reception because they were not prepared. Now here in Revelation, John does not describe bridesmaids, but he gives us the imagery of a soldier. John has been describing a battle, the ultimate battle between good and evil. In battle it is important that the soldiers involved are ready and prepared. If a soldier is asleep without their armor and weapons, that soldier will be ineffective and not prepared. It will be as if they are naked, which will cause them shame. They will be shamed because others will see that they were unprepared for the battle that they were supposed to be fighting in. This is true for us today. We are in a battle, a spiritual battle. Every day we need to put on the armor of God (see Ephesians 6:13-18) so that we are prepared for the battles we will face, and to be ready and prepared for the return of Jesus, which could happen at any moment. Lack of preparation will bring shame. Avoid that shame by being prepared.

August 23

"Now therefore, please let your servant remain instead of the boy as a servant to my lord, and let the boy go back with his brothers."
Genesis 44:33

When we are dealt with personal confrontation, we can respond to it in one of two ways: face it or flee from it. Judah chose to deal with Joseph's confrontation head on. He didn't run away from it but showed through his response how much he had changed over the past twenty years, when he and his brothers sold off Joseph as a slave. Now, when he is dealt with the same opportunity with Joseph's "little" brother Benjamin, Judah makes sure that history doesn't repeat itself. The last fifteen verses show very passionately how far Judah is willing to go to ensure that this doesn't happen again. Judah is so committed to Benjamin safely returning to his father that Judah makes the decision to offer himself as a sacrifice to ensure Benjamin's safety. Wow! He is so committed to Benjamin's safety that he is willing to remain in Egypt as a slave in order to Benjamin to return safely to Canaan and their father. Judah loves his brother so much that is willing to substitute himself in Benjamin's place so that he doesn't have to suffer his punishment.

What a wonderful picture of Jesus Judah is for us. He is willing to take the place of another and suffer the punishment that is due them. There is one big difference though between Judah and Jesus. While it is commendable that Judah was *willing* to do this, Jesus actually *DID* this for us. Jesus willingly substituted Himself on the cross and died for our sins. He did this so that He could bring "many sons to glory" (Hebrews 2:10). Jesus didn't have to do this, but He did so because of His great love for us. Jesus is perfect. He never committed a single sin, so there was no reason for Him to be on the cross. But, as He hung on that cross, our sins were placed upon Him, and He paid the penalty of our sins. The penalty of our sins has been covered; it is covered with the blood of Jesus. It is Jesus' blood that cleanses us and makes us "white as snow" (Isaiah 1:18). This is why, Jesus, the Lion of the tribe of Judah, said, "I am the way, and the truth, and the life. No one comes to the Father except through Me" (John 14:6). Thank You Jesus for paying the penalty of our sin and showing us through Your actions how much You really do love us.

August 24

"He waited seven days, the time appointed by Samuel. But Samuel

did not come to Gilgal, and the people were scattering from him. So Saul said, 'Bring the burnt offering here to me, and the peace offerings.' And he offered the burnt offering."
1 Samuel 13:8-9

Saul has been king of Israel for a few years at this time, and he finds himself surrounded by the Philistine army. Samuel told him to wait for him, and he would offer sacrifices to God before they went into battle. The Philistine army is much larger than the Israelite army, and the Israelite soldiers are afraid. They begin to hide in caves, and some of them even begin to desert Saul and go AWOL. Samuel said he would be here in seven days, and it is now the seventh day; and Samuel has not been seen. What is Saul to do?

Saul needs to be obedient to what God said to do, which is to wait for Samuel. But that is difficult to do. Saul knows his soldiers are scared, and if they aren't hiding already, then they are beginning to desert. He expects Samuel to be here already, and he knows something needs to be done before he has no army left. So, being the leader, Saul goes ahead and offers the sacrifices to God himself. The problem with this is that he is not a priest, and only the priest is to offer sacrifices to God. He is disobeying God. He is not willing to wait. Waiting is very difficult. People have expectations, and waiting is not one of them. It is so much easier to act like Saul and step in and do what is expected by others in order to please them. But, in doing so, God is then displeased. Because of Saul's decision and actions, his descendants were not allowed to be king of Israel. "And Samuel said to Saul, 'You have done foolishly. You have not kept the command of the Lord your God, with which he commanded you. For then the Lord would have established your kingdom over Israel forever. But now your kingdom shall not continue. The Lord has sought out a man after his own heart, and the Lord has commanded him to be prince over His people, because you have not kept what the Lord commanded you.'" (1 Samuel 13:13-14).

Did you catch that? Because Saul refused to wait, he was rejected by God. God desired a person after His own heart, which is a person who will wait for God and not do his (or her) own thing. David was this person, and he became the next king, and his descendants ruled after him. This happened because he was willing to wait for God, and His timing. David waited at least seven years after being anointed king before he became king. What did he do during those years? He defeated Goliath, shepherded sheep, served King Saul, led the army, and destroyed the enemy, and then had King Saul attempt to kill him and chase him throughout the desert. Yet, David continued to wait; even when he had opportunity to kill Saul and become king, he refused to do so. David was a man after God's own heart because he waited for God's timing, he trusted God, and he sought God's will instead of his own.

Waiting is not easy, but it is well worth it. Whatever God has revealed to you will happen, be willing to wait for His time. Do not give in to your own expectations, or the expectations of others. Seek to wait for God and please Him alone.

August 25

"And when they could not find them, they dragged Jason and some of the brothers before the city authorities, shouting, 'These men who have turned the world upside down have come here also…'"
Acts 17:6

When the mob arrived at Jason's house, they didn't find Paul or Silas, so they settled for Jason, and dragged him out of his house and to the city's rulers. They accused them of one crime: "turned the world upside down."

What a great compliment this was. Considering that Thessalonica was only the second city in the continent of Europe to be reached, this was a bit of an exaggeration, but it shows the power of the Gospel. When Paul went someplace, things happened. Souls were saved, sides were taken, lines were drawn, and feelings were stirred. Paul didn't quietly sneak into town, drop off a few gospel tracts, preach to a small group and receive a nice honorarium, and then quietly leave town in the middle of the night. No! When Paul was in town, everyone knew about it.

By complaining that they had "turned the world upside down," they were really saying that Paul and Silas had radically impacted the town, and it would never be the same again. What a great compliment. It is so sad that towns aren't saying this about Christians today. We need to be doing the same thing.

Jesus came to earth in order to turn it upside down, because the world does things backwards. The world system is like a triangle, with masses of insignificant people on the bottom, and the rich, powerful, and elite at the top of the triangle. It is a struggle to reach the top and become the greatest. Jesus taught the opposite of this. Jesus said, "Truly, I say to you, whoever does not receive the kingdom of God like a child shall not enter it" (Mark 10:15). You see, to be truly great we must be innocent like a child, not powerful and influential like a ruler. In fact, Jesus also said, "whoever would be great among you must be your servant, and whoever would be first among you must be slave[e] of all. For even the Son of Man came not to be served but to serve, and to give His life as a ransom for many" (Mark 10:43-45). The kingdom of God is truly opposite from the world. True greatness is not seen in how many people are serving you, but in how many people you are serving. The Gospel really does "turn the world upside down."

August 26

"Animals blind or disabled or mutilated or having a discharge or an itch or scabs you shall not offer to the Lord or give them to the Lord as a food offering on the altar."
Leviticus 22:22

Can you imagine going to a restaurant and ordering your favorite meal. When the meal arrives you cannot believe what you find. Your food was prepared with old, moldy and rotten food. Instead of serving you a nutritious meal, you receive garbage. To make matters worse, you still receive a bill for the food, and then you are expected to pay for the entire meal. If you are like most people, you would be insulted by this. How would any business expect you to pay full price for a meal that wasn't satisfactory? At the very least, if you were served a meal like this, you should expect to receive it for free, if not receive a free meal at a later date for such a disgusting meal being served to you.

As shocking and upsetting as receiving a meal like that is to us, many people present "gifts" to the Lord like that. We would not readily and happily accept a meal that is not satisfactory, and God does not readily and happily accept offerings to Him that are not satisfactory either. God is our Creator and Lord; He deserves nothing but the best that we have. This Old Testament law was put into effect to ensure that the Israelites would not attempt to offer any sacrifice to God that was not satisfactory. Today, we need to follow this idea too. We do not need to bring animal sacrifices any longer because Jesus died on the cross for our sins as the perfect, and complete, sacrifice. Instead, the things that we do "offer" to God need to fit the requirements of what is offered to Him.

Notice that what is offered to God cannot be "blind or disabled or mutilated or having a discharge or an itch or scabs." This means that what is offered needs to be healthy and the best you have. In keeping with the theme of meat, what is offered needs to be "prime choice." God deserves to be given the best, not what is otherwise rejected, left-over, or not needed any longer. When we no longer have any use for an item, is that when we feel it is ok to "give to God" by donating it to church or a missionary group? God is not pleased with that any more than He would be with an injured animal in Old Testament times. When we give to the Lord like that it does not show that God is worthy. He is worthy and deserves nothing but the best that we have.

God did pay the price for our sins so that we can be saved, that is the best news we can ever receive. Do we really want to show our thankfulness to Him for doing that by giving Him what should be discarded? Give to the Lord because He is worthy and give to Him what is good because of what He has done for us. Give with a thankful heart.

"The point is this: whoever sows sparingly will also reap sparingly, and whoever sows bountifully will also reap bountifully. Each one must give as he has decided in his heart, not reluctantly or under compulsion, for God loves a cheerful giver" (2 Corinthians 9:6-7).

August 27

"For while we were still weak, at the right time Christ died for the ungodly. For one will scarcely die for a righteous person—though perhaps for a good person one would dare even to die— but God shows his love for us in that while we were still sinners, Christ died for us."

Romans 5:6-8

E-Bay is a fun website to go to, and it can be very addictive. It is an on-line auction, and most auctions last for one week. You go on the site, search for an item you are interested in, and find out what the lowest bid accepted is. If you are willing to pay more than what is offered, you enter your bid. Most people are attempting to get a "good deal" on items, so they bid as low as possible, barely going above the current bid. As the auction is coming to an end you will often find the bid increasing quickly, as people attempt to be the last bidder and thereby "winning" the auction. If there are multiple people interested in the same item, the price can drastically change at the end.

God does not participate in E-Bay. That does not mean that E-Bay is evil, but that is not how God operates. God does purchase things for Himself. He also has others competing against Him for everything He purchases. Unlike me, God is not cheap. He is not trying to get the lowest price possible when He makes a purchase. Instead, God is the opposite. God states the highest possible price at the beginning. God sets the bar so high that no one else can match His offer.

God did this back in the Garden of Eden right after Adam and Eve sinned. He stated then that He would send His Son Jesus to die on the cross and pay the price for sin. There was no greater price that could be paid. God would willingly allow Jesus, Who never committed a single sin, to die a cruel and painful death on a cross in order for our sins to be paid for. God did this because sin brings death, which is separation from God. God is holy and cannot be in the presence of sin, which is unholy. This is why He paid the highest price possible. By Jesus dying on the cross, and raising from the grave, the price of sin has been paid, and the power of death has been broken. Jesus lived as a man, enduring the same temptations that we do; yet He did not sin. Because of this, He is now the bridge between sinful people and a holy God. The price has been paid so that we can enter the presence of God and live with Him forever. Praise God that He loves us so much that He would give all He has so we can spend eternity with Him.

August 28

"When the Man saw that He did not prevail against Jacob, He touched his hip socket, and Jacob's hip was put out of joint as he wrestled with Him. Then He said, "Let Me go, for the day has broken." But Jacob said, "I will not let You go unless you bless me."'
Genesis 32:25-26

As the wrestling match went on and on, it appeared to be an even match; there was no apparent winner. But it was only even in appearance because God could have won at any moment. God is giving

Jacob the chance to "give up" and to completely surrender to God, but he won't do that. God desires to prevail over him and is bringing Jacob to the end of himself so he has nothing left and the only thing he can depend on is God. Jacob is a stubborn man and refuses to surrender, so God helps force his hand. To help Jacob realize his dependence upon God, God touched him and dislocated his hip. If you've ever dislocated a finger, you know how painful this must have been.

This is a devastating injury for a wrestler. It would be like breaking the arm of a pitcher, the leg of a running back, or the shooting hand of a basketball player. Jacob was now helpless and no longer able to force an offensive battle; all he could do was hold on defensively. Even though Jacob has lost, he continues to desperately hold on, so God tells him to just let go. This is such an important place for us to come to. When we finally realize there is no way we will win, and we are just "spinning our wheels" by resisting, and all we need to do is let go. There is no need, or benefit, in continuing to hold on. We need to admit that God is greater than us and that we are not able to conquer Him.

Even though Jacob refuses to let go, this is not a picture of a strong man twisting the arm of God. This is a picture of a broken man who is pleading with God. Jacob pleads with God for His blessing. He finally admits that he is dependent upon God and needs God's help, not his own craftiness.

Jacob believed that the enemy he was afraid of was Esau, but he now realizes he was his own enemy; his fleshly nature needed to be conquered by God. This is a great point for each of us to arrive at too. We need to "wrestle" with God until we get to the point where He breaks us, even if it means He has to cripple us. That way we are dependent upon Him, and there is more of Him than us in ourselves.

August 29

"As obedient children, do not be conformed to the passions of your former ignorance..."
1 Peter 1:14

As a parent one of the greatest things that we can teach our children is the importance of being obedient. The wisdom and experience that a parent has earned helps them to understand things their child does not get. When the child listens to their parents they can avoid mistakes and problems. While this is true here for us on earth it is also true spiritually. God our Father also knows what is best for us and when we are obedient to Him, we can avoid pain, suffering, and mistakes in our own life too. As God spoke through the prophet Samuel to King Saul and told him that "to obey is better than sacrifice" (1 Samuel 15:22). Peter is telling us the same thing here. As a believer, it should be our goal to be an obedient child to our Father, God. When we are obedient to God, that means that we won't be ruled by, or slaves to, the passions, or lusts, that control our natural being.

Peter tells us to not "be conformed to the passions of your former ignorance." The apostle Paul told us the same thing when he told us to not be "not be conformed to this world" (Romans 12:2). I find it to be very interesting that that a major goal of many people in the world is to be free and different from those around them, yet they end up imitating each other and being alike. God calls us to be obedient to Hm instead of being just like the world. Why is obedience so important to God? Because obedience to God is a sign of our salvation (see Romans 1:5). The flip side of that is disobedience is a sign that a person is following their natural lusts and desires, not following God. As a child of God, we are to follow Him and not our sinful desires which is an act of disobedience. "And you were dead in the trespasses and sins in which you once walked, following the course of this world, following the prince of the power of the air, the spirit that is now at work in the sons of disobedience— among whom we all once lived in the passions of our flesh, carrying out the desires of the body and the mind, and were by nature children of wrath, like the rest of mankind" (Ephesians 2:1-3). Obedience is a sure sign that a person has been born again. As a child of God, we are to live a life of obedience to Him and not live the same way that we did before becoming a child of God.

August 30

"Then Adonijah the son of Haggith came to Bathsheba the mother of Solomon. And she said, 'Do you come peacefully?' He said, 'Peacefully.' Then he said, 'I have something to say to you.' She said, 'Speak.' He said, 'You know that the kingdom was mine, and that all Israel fully expected me to reign. However, the kingdom has turned about and become my brother's, for it was his from the Lord. And now I have one request to make of you; do not refuse me.' She said to him, 'Speak.' And he said, 'Please ask King Solomon—he will not refuse you—to give me Abishag the Shunammite as my wife.'"

1 Kings 2:13-17

Adonijah was one of King David's sons, and here he is attempting to get what was previously denied to him. Adonijah was not pleased with the way his father David was performing his duties as king, and he knew that David was close to death, so he allied himself with many leaders in King David's administration and pronounced himself as king (see 1 Kings 1:5-10). He had the backing of many leaders, so it looked like a peaceful coup was about to take place. Adonijah did have the support of many people in Israel, but he is exaggerating when he says, "all Israel fully expected me to reign." It was something that he wanted, but not all people supported. Also, God had spoken through David previously and announced that his son Solomon would be the next king. Even though Adonijah had sacrificed animals and held his own ceremony pronouncing himself as king, David held the true coronation making Solomon king, and the whole nation of Israel accepted Solomon as their king (see 1 Kings 1:38-40).

Even though God had spoken and Adonijah was told he was not to be king, he continues to attempt to get what he wants, even after God told him NO. He is very deceptive in going to Bathsheba, the mother of Solomon, and attempting to receive permission to marry one of the "wives" of King David. He knew that "marrying" a wife of the former king would solidify him as the king of Israel and he would be getting what he wanted, even though God had said no. Too often we do the same thing as Adonijah. We don't like the answer God gives us, or we still want what is not best for us, so in our selfishness we attempt to circumvent God and fulfill our fleshly desires anyway. I have seen too many people do this and force their will over God's will. The results of doing this always lead to pain and misery. It did for Adonijah; in fact, it led to his death (see 1 Kings 2:22-25).

When we make the same mistake of putting our desires ahead of God's will, does it lead to our death too? The answer is yes! It may not lead to physical death, as it did for Adonijah; but it does cause spiritual death. When we force our will over God's will, we are ignoring God and putting to death our spiritual self while feeding our flesh. When we feed our flesh, there is no room for the Spirit to live in us, so we are truly dying too. We need to learn from Adonijah and humbly accept God's answers, allowing our fleshly desires to die so that He can grow in us. We need to be more like John the Baptist and say, "He must increase, but I must decrease" (John 3:30).

August 31

"Each one must give as he has decided in his heart, not reluctantly or under compulsion, for God loves a cheerful giver."

2 Corinthians 9:7

There are some people that believe the church is overly concerned with giving. And, when you mention the word giving, most people immediately think of money. It is true that money is something that we can give, and people do give money to the church, but money isn't the only thing we can give. I would even go so far as to say that money isn't the most important thing that we can give. You may wonder what is more important to give than money? Your time. Your talents. When we give of ourselves, including our money, we show how valuable the person or thing is that we are giving to. If they weren't of great value, then we wouldn't be giving of our time, talent, or treasures (money). So, when we give to others, we practice the exercise of selflessness. Giving is a way to combat selfishness, and that is a very good thing.

In addition to giving, it is very important how we give. The apostle Paul reminds us that "God loves a cheerful giver." The word for cheerful is the Greek word *"hilaros."* It is from this word that we get our English word hilarious. In other words, God loves a hilarious giver. When you give, whether it is of your time, treasure, or talents, make sure that you can give with a smile on your face, not grudgingly.

It has been said that there are three different types of givers in the world, and every single person is one of those three types. One type of giver is a flint. In order to get the flint to give anything you have to hammer on it, and then all you get is chips and sparks. The next type of giver is a sponge. In order to get the sponge to give anything you must apply lots of pressure while continually squeezing it. The third type of giver is a honeycomb. The honeycomb is continually giving naturally, as it overflows with its own sweetness. Which type of giver are you?

September 1

"Thus says the Lord of hosts: These people say the time has not yet come to rebuild the house of the Lord."
Haggai 1:2

God begins His message through Haggai by saying "these people." Not His people, but these people. The word "these" is a word of distance. It's like if I came home and my beautiful wife met me at the door and welcomed me home with these words, "Do you know what your child did today?" When I hear that it is MY child, I know it's not going to be good news. When she says, "Do you know what our child did today?" then I know it is something good. We aren't going to hear good news about the children of Israel right now.

Why wasn't the Temple completed? Because these people said, "The time has not come for the house of the Lord to be rebuilt." The people weren't saying that the Temple shouldn't be built, but they were making excuses as to why they hadn't done it yet. They were waiting for a time when they would have no opposition to their work, or problems to deal with while building the Temple. They attempted to make their excuse sound spiritual by saying it's not God's time for them to do this yet. In reality, they were justifying their disobedience by placing the blame on God, when it really belonged on them.

We see in the book of Ezra that when they did begin to rebuild the Temple, there was much opposition to their rebuilding of the Temple. Instead of persevering through this, they interpreted this as a sign from God that they weren't supposed to rebuild right now. They were saying, "All this difficulty we're experiencing must be a sign from God that this is the wrong time to build the Temple. Let's wait until we receive no opposition to this work."

They should have known that because they were doing the work of God that they would be opposed by the world. That is what will always happen. When we are doing a work of the Lord, we can be sure that we will receive opposition. That doesn't mean we are to give up, but that we continue to persevere and work through the opposition in obedience to what God has called us to do. Instead of persevering, these people rationalized away their responsibility to obey God.

Lord, help us persevere through difficult times, remaining obedient to You and not rationalizing away what You have called us to do.

September 2

"But He gives more grace. Therefore it says, 'God opposes the proud but gives grace to the humble.'"
James 4:6

The world is filled with pride. Groups and organizations plan marches and events to show the world how proud they are of themselves, their ideologies, and their beliefs. What is it that people are so proud of? It is their sin. The root of pride is rejection of Jesus. This began with Satan. Satan is a created angel, created to worship God and to do God's will. But, instead of worshipping God, Satan desired for others to worship him. Satan said, "I will ascend to heaven; above the stars of God I will set my throne on high; I will sit on the mount of assembly in the far reaches of the north; I will ascend above the heights of the clouds; I will make myself like the Most High" (Isaiah 14:13-14). Satan has a "I" problem. Everything he stated was about himself, and how he wanted to be worshipped as god, instead of God being worshipped. This is what led to his downfall. This is why the root of all pride is rebellion against God.

This is also why God hates pride. God is not able to extend His grace to those that are proud because grace and pride are eternal enemies. Pride says that the person should be blessed because of how great and wonderful they are, or at least their accomplishments are;

whether these accomplishments are real or imagined. Grace, on the other hand, chooses to not deal with us on the basis of us, whether good or bad, but instead deals with us on the basis of Who God is. The proud will not receive God's grace, but He instead chooses to give His grace to those that are humble. Notice, the humble do not receive God's grace because they have earned it by being humble. God's grace cannot be earned; if it could, it would no longer be grace. Being humble puts a person in position to freely receive God's grace.

The world is in a war, or conflict, against God. This is why our flesh fights against the Holy Spirit, and why Satan opposes Jesus, and God. Pride is one of Satan's greatest, and effective, tools. Resist the devil, and his attempts to inflate pride in your life. Become humble and allow God's grace to flow into your life.

September 3

"Now there arose a great outcry of the people and of their wives against their Jewish brothers."
Nehemiah 5:1

The residents of ancient Jerusalem willingly came together for a common goal: to rebuild the walls of their city for protection. As they worked towards this common goal the people were united. They were encouraged that God was with them and had sent Nehemiah to help organize them to rebuild the wall. There was opposition from enemies, which caused the people to risk their lives as they worked together in rebuilding the walls. As the walls reached their halfway point there arose another attempt from Satan to stop the work. He failed to stop the work with taunts and attacks from enemies, so he now went with a different tactic. Since the people were unified, that is where he attacked them. There was now inner turmoil within the residents of Jerusalem, and this caused them to choose which side they would be on. Satan knows that one of the most effective ways to stop a work of God is to create dissension amongst God's people. Dissension causes mistrust, struggles, and discouragement among people who had been previously united.

God hates division among His children. In fact, the wise King Solomon wrote "There are six things that the LORD hates, seven that are an abomination to him: haughty eyes, a lying tongue, and hands that shed innocent blood, a heart that devises wicked plans, feet that make haste to run to evil, a false witness who breathes out lies, and one who sows discord among brothers" (Proverbs 6:16-19). A person that created discord, or division, is an abomination to God. The body of Christ, or the Church, was created as one body, a body that is unified. The apostle Paul reminds us that "the body is one and has many members, and all the members of the body, though many, are one body, so it is with Christ. For in one Spirit we were all baptized into one body—Jews or Greeks, slaves or free..." (1 Corinthians 12:12-13a). It is so important that as believers we don't allow our enemy, Satan, to break the unity of the church by creating schisms and divisions. We need to remain unified in Whom we serve, along with our goals and purposes, or Mission Statements. What is our goal as believers? That we love others. Jesus said, "By this all people will know that you are my disciples, if you have love for one another" (John 13:35). Jesus also reminds us that love needs to be the goal of our lives when He said, "You shall love the Lord your God with all your heart and with all your soul and with all your mind. This is the great and first commandment. And a second is like it: You shall love your neighbor as yourself. On these two commandments depend all the Law and the Prophets" (Matthew 22:37-40).

September 4

"And the beast was given a mouth uttering haughty and blasphemous words, and it was allowed to exercise authority for forty-two months. It opened its mouth to utter blasphemies against God,

blaspheming his name and his dwelling, that is, those who dwell in heaven."
Revelation 13:5-6

When the antichrist appears on the world scene there will be an order of things that will follow him. The first is that people will be filled with wonder over him. Following that will be worship, as people will worship him, which brings Satan nothing but delight. The next thing that the antichrist will bring is words. The world will be filled with his words. Antichrist will be a worldwide sensation. He will be on every imaginable news program, talk show, late-night show, etc. The words he speaks will be broadcast throughout the entire world. No matter where you are, you will be surrounded by this person. In fact, the only thing that will be larger than the words he speaks will be his ego. Since he will seem to be unsurpassed in the world, he will become a very arrogant person. It is very possible that he will be the most arrogant person in the history of the world.

There will also be a theme to the words that he speaks which are continually broadcast throughout the world. That theme is blasphemy. Remember, antichrist is nothing more than the mouthpiece of Satan, the dragon. He is a tool of Satan, or a human embodiment of Satan. Therefore, everything he does will be exactly what Satan would do. This is why the words he speaks will be blasphemous. The inhabitants of the world will have become so hardened in their hearts that they will speak to us his blasphemous words, which will encourage even more blasphemous words to be spoken. It will be a vicious downward cycle. Every word that is spoken out of his mouth will be against God and everything that God stands for.

This is a bleak scene. But there is hope, even in the midst of this. There is one word used twice in verse 5, and that is the word "given." It is important that we remember antichrist is a tool. He has no power of his own. The mouth with which he speaks blasphemies is given to him. The authority that he has for 42 months is given to him. This means that he has limits placed on him. Who controls those limits? It is God. God gives him the ability and power that he uses, but God also limits it. As bleak as things appear, God is still in control, and He will bring it to an end in His time. That is comforting. Praise God that He is in control!

September 5

"Two things I ask of you; deny them not to me before I die: Remove far from me falsehood and lying; give me neither poverty nor riches; feed me with the food that is needful for me, lest I be full and deny You and say, 'Who is the LORD?' or lest I be poor and steal and profane the name of my God."
Proverbs 30:7-9

Most people have a bucket list, whether it is written down on paper or just kept in their head. A bucket list is a list of things they want to accomplish before "kicking the bucket." The things placed on this list can be varied; from riding in a hot air balloon, or snorkeling in the Bahamas, to seeing my children serving and following God. No matter what is on our list, whether for fun and pleasure or truly life changing, it shows what we are truly interested in.

King Solomon wrote that he had two things he wanted to see before he died. In this short prayer he wrote, he is asking God to protect him from temptation, much like we see in the Lord's Prayer in Matthew 6:9-13. Both prayers also ask for basic needs to be met, and for God's honor to be upheld.

The first thing Solomon asked for was protection from God over his mouth. He desired to speak the truth and not to deceive anyone. There is much danger that can come from what we say, but when a guard is set over our mouth and discretion is used, much good can also come from our words. Jesus tells us, "...out of the abundance of the heart the mouth speaks" (Matthew 12:34b). Whatever we allow into our heart, through our eyes, will be what comes out in our speech. Therefore, it is imperative that we place a guard on our eyes and mind in order to filter and protect what we allow into our heart. When we speak evil or deceitful words to others, it is a reflection of what is in our heart. There are steps we can take to minimize this from happening, but as Solomon said, we need the strength of God to make this reality in our life.

The second thing Solomon asked for was to have his daily supplies met. Even though he was the richest man in the world, he understood the power and control money has in our life. Because of this, Solomon did not ask for riches, but for his needs to be met. When our needs are not met a person will be tempted to steal in order to provide their needs, such as clothing, food or shelter. This profanes the name of God, because He said He will provide for His children (see Luke 12:22-34). But the opposite is also true. When a person has more than they need they can begin to trust in and rely on their belongings instead of God. Since they have provided everything they need, they no longer look to God for help or direction. This also profanes God, since they no longer rely on Him, and we are truly nothing without Him.

The apostle Paul echoed these words to his young protégé Timothy. "For we brought nothing into the world, and we cannot take anything out of the world. But if we have food and clothing, with these we will be content" (1 Timothy 6:7-8). God is faithful, and He will provide all our needs. He does not always give us our wants though, because what we want could easily draw us away from Him. We need to keep following Jesus and learn to be content with what we have been given.

September 6

"Likewise, husbands, live with your wives in an understanding way..."
1 Peter 3:7a

The apostle Peter writes for seven verses about the relationship between husbands and wives. He spends the first six verses addressing the wife, and only one verse addressing the husband. Over the years there has been much conjecture over why. There is a good reason for this. Think of it like going to a pet store and buying a pet fish. While in the store you don't just buy a fish, you also purchase a tank, fish food, chemicals to stabilize the water so your fish will live, plants and other things to go in the tank, and you would also purchase a book that provides you with instructions on how to take care of your fish. The fish, on the other hand, simply goes home with you without any instructions at all. Why? He doesn't need the instructions; the instructions go to the smarter person. See how that applies to Peter's writing to married couples? Ha ha ha. Women receive more instructions because living with men is difficult. Men only get one verse because Peter keeps it simple to help men understand.

Peter gives three simple instructions to men. The first instruction is that they are to "live with your wives in an understanding way." This means that husband and wife do much more than just live in the same house. The man is supposed to live with his wife. This means there is unity and communication between husband and wife. The apostle Paul wrote about this too. He wrote, "husbands should love their wives as their own bodies. He who loves his wife loves himself" (Ephesians 5:28). Not only does he love his wife, but he understands her. How does this happen? Just like he did in school, he has to study. In fact, the husband should be working towards earning his doctorate in his wife. He needs to know everything there is to know about her. He does this because his wife is his best friend. He knows the things that she loves, what she enjoys, what she needs, what her dreams are, her favorite color, her favorite dinner, etc. After learning everything there is to know about his wife, the husband then needs to take that information and apply it to their life. Date her; take her out to her favorite restaurant, just the two of you. Spend time with her and continue to "date" her, whether you've been married for one year or fifty years. When a husband does this, he will be blessed with a close personal and intimate relationship with his best friend. This is how God designed marriage to be.

September 7

"When Joseph saw that his father laid his right hand on the head of Ephraim, it displeased him, and he took his father's hand to move it from Ephraim's head to Manasseh's head."
Genesis 48:17

Mistakes happen. Things don't always go the way that we plan, or expect, them to go. When this occurs, we often get frustrated, sometimes even upset, and then do what we can to reverse or correct the mistake. This is what Joseph attempts to do. His dad, Jacob, has brought Joseph's two sons before him, as he is ready to die, and is going to bless them. Joseph stands his sons before Jacob, placing the older son by Jacob's right hand and the younger son by his left hand because this was the custom of the day. The older son was expected to be blessed, and the right hand was the symbol of strength, which would go to the oldest son. Joseph had everything put in place as he thought it should be. But then he saw that his dad crossed his hands so that the right hand was on the younger son. Oy vey! He must have thought that his poor dad was losing it. He didn't even know which of his boys was which one and had gotten them mixed up. Time to take things into his own hands, literally, and correct the mistake his dad had made.

There is only one problem with this. Jacob hadn't made a mistake. He knew exactly what he was doing. The birthright normally did go to the oldest son, but not always. Plus, God doesn't follow societal expectations or customs. We need to remember that God is sovereign. This means that He doesn't make mistakes. This is the fifth time in the book of Genesis that the blessing wasn't given to the first-born son. God chose Abel over Cain, Isaac over Ishmael, Jacob over Esau, Joseph over Reuben, and now Ephraim over Manasseh. Jacob should also understand this as he chose Rachel over Leah, the younger over the older. There may have been no earthly reason for this to happen, and there doesn't appear to be, but there is a divine reason for it. God does not make mistakes in what He does. We may not see it or even understand it, but we can rest assured that there is a good reason for it. We need to make sure that we are trusting God and not trying to "fix" what we perceive to be mistakes.

September 8

"...we ought to lay down our lives for the brothers."
1 John 3:16b

Since Jesus laid down His life for us, we also show how great our love for Him is by laying down our life for others. This shows us that a Christian's love is always tied to the cross, because that is where love starts.

Jesus has demonstrated how great His love is for us, we are to do the same for others. Remember, the demonstration of love involves sacrifice. The apostle Paul reminded us of this when he wrote, "Do nothing from selfish ambition or conceit, but in humility count others more significant than yourselves. Let each of you look not only to his own interests, but also to the interests of others" (Philippians 2:3-4). I love you because Jesus first loved me. The more of Jesus' love that I receive, the more love that I'll have to give to others. That's how love operates.

When you think of a shadow, you think of darkness because a shadow is created when light is blocked out. There is one exception to that rule, the shadow of the cross illuminates. The shadow of the cross is where Jesus was sacrificed, and from that point the light of His sacrifice pours in. The light of Jesus' sacrifice on the cross helps us to see issues of life clearly. I can clearly see the depth of corruption within myself, and why Jesus had to suffer such an awful punishment. But the light of the cross also shows me the richness of value that I have also received. Since such a heavy price was paid for my sin, it shows me that I am truly loved and desired by God. Why else would He pay so much for me?

Jesus was willing to suffer so much for me on the cross, why wouldn't I be willing to sacrifice some for others? I can cook a meal and bring it to a family that is in need. I can sacrifice some spending money to share that money with a person who has lost their job. I can also make the sacrifice of being willing to spend some time with the student who is not popular, and no one seems to care about. Love will show them that they are loved and cared for. You see, love thinks about others.

September 9

"Then Joseph fell on his father's face and wept over him and kissed him."
Genesis 50:1

Joseph experienced many things in his life, and many of them were difficult. His brothers hated him so much that they considered killing him but chose to just sell him as a slave instead. He was falsely accused of rape and spent time in prison. These events forced him to deal with abandonment, isolation, false accusations; things that many people deal with today. In addition to these things, he also had to deal with the death of his dad. Having a parent die is a difficult thing. No matter whether they are old or young when they die, it is difficult to deal with the death of a parent. Even those who have belief in an afterlife and know they will be reunited someday still struggle when a parent dies. This is called grief, bereavement, and sorrow. It is to be expected.

It is unhealthy for a person to attempt to suppress what is natural. King Solomon was one the wisest people to ever live, and he reminds us that there is a time to die, to weep, and to mourn (see Ecclesiastes 3:2, 4). Even God expects us to cry and mourn when a loved one dies, that's why He gave us the ability to shed tears. Shedding tears is a normal part of mourning. "Weeping may tarry for the night, but joy comes with the morning" (Psalm 30:5). There is a time, or a season, to mourn. So, don't try to hide it, to suppress it, or to keep it from happening. Any attempt to not mourn is not natural, and it's not healthy. When a loved one dies, mourn.

There is a season to mourn, but that season also comes to an end. For the believer, we know that there is an afterlife. This is why we do "not grieve as others do who have no hope" (1 Thessalonians 4:13). We have hope for the future. As believers we know that we will be reunited in Heaven one day with other believers. What a glorious day that will be. But we also know that our great enemy, death, will one day be defeated too. Jesus died on a cross and was buried in a grave. But that's not the end of the story. On the third day He rose from the grave, alive! Death has been defeated, and one day soon we will be in Heaven, in God's presence where "He will wipe away every tear from their eyes, and death shall be no more, neither shall there be mourning, nor crying, nor pain anymore, for the former things have passed away" (Revelation 21:4).

September 10

"And do not grieve the Holy Spirit of God, by whom you were sealed for the day of redemption. Let all bitterness and wrath and anger and clamor and slander be put away from you, along with all malice. Be kind to one another, tenderhearted, forgiving one another, as God in Christ forgave you."
Ephesians 4:30-32

Watching the news is enough to cause the average person to become both bitter and angry. Look around and you see all sorts of wicked behavior, injustices being done to people, and people that are being abused, taken advantage of, or being hurt. When we are the person that any of these happen to, it is easy to become bitter. That is a natural reaction; but it is not what God desires us to do.

God is very direct by saying that when we allow bitterness to come over us, it grieves the Holy Spirit. The word "grieve" means "to offend, or to cause sorrow." When we dwell and focus on what was done to us, or the evil around us, it causes us to become bitter, and the Holy Spirit is deeply saddened by this. This doesn't mean that we just ignore it and it will go away. These things are difficult to deal with, but as Christians we need to keep our focus on something other than the injustice done. What needs to be our focus? God!

When we change our focus from injustices done to God, our perspective will change. This is not easy to do; I won't lie to you and say that it is. What it requires is faith and trust. When we trust God and place our faith in Him, we remember what He has done for us, and the fact that He is in control of what is going on, which allows us to respond to a bad situation with something other than bitterness and anger. Then we can respond with kindness and compassion, forgiving the person who wronged us, just like Jesus has already forgiven us. How freeing this is? This means that we are not bound and confined by bitterness and anger. We have been set free and are now able to live the way God has created us to be: like Jesus.

Is this even possible? Yes it is! Read the book of Genesis and you will see how Joseph was hated and mistreated by his brothers. They beat him, sold him as a slave, and he ended up spending years in prison in a foreign land. He had good reasons to be bitter and angry. But he wasn't! He trusted God, and God used those times of hatred and envy to accomplish His plans. Joseph even told his brothers "You meant evil against me, but God meant it for good..." (Genesis 50:20). Don't hold on to grudges. Let them go. Trust God and allow His love to flow through you to forgive and bless others.

September 11

"And they stood up in their place and read from the Book of the Law of the Lord their God for a quarter of the day; for another quarter of it they made confession and worshiped the Lord their God."
Nehemiah 9:3

The Israelites just finished celebrating the Feast of Tabernacles for the first time in many years, and two days later they come back together in the Temple for a service. This is amazing because it isn't the Sabbath, and it isn't even Christmas or Easter. You know, the only two times many people go to church. The people gathered in the Temple simply because they wanted more of God in their lives. They had a desire to hear God's Word, to learn more about Him, and to worship Him. What a great reason to gather with fellow believers. Not because it's required or expected, but simply because that is what they desire. This is proof of the work that God was doing in the hearts of the Israelites, both nationally but also individually. What a service this was. They spent six hours reading God's Word, and then six more hours confessing their sins and worshipping God.

The act of confessing sin is so important. This doesn't mean that we have to sit in a booth with a wall dividing us from the person to whom we confess our sins to. We confess our sins to God. What does it mean to confess our sin to God? Confession is really an acknowledgment of sin. It means that we agree with God about the sin in our life, the sin that we have committed. When we confess our sin, it means that we agree with God that what we did, or thought, was wrong, it is sin. The reason we do this is because it shows that our heart is broken over our sin. This is important because a seed cannot be planted unless the ground is first broken. Our heart is the soil that God plants in, which means it must be broken for God's Word to establish root in us. In order for God's Word to be established in us, our heart must first be broken. Once it is, then God's Word can be established in our hearts so that through the work of the Holy Spirit godly fruit can be produced in our lives. Godly fruit will not be produced in the life of a person whose heart is hard, unwilling to be broken. What fruit will be produced in a person with a broken heart? "The fruit of the Spirit is love, joy, peace, patience, kindness, goodness, faithfulness, gentleness, self-control; against such things there is no law..." (Galatians 5:22-23)

September 12

"Servants, be subject to your masters with all respect, not only to the good and gentle but also to the unjust."
1 Peter 2:18

When the apostle Peter wrote this letter, many of the people in the churches he wrote to were household slaves, or servants. Slavery is a touchy subject, both back then and today too. There is no time in Scripture where slavery is encouraged, but it is mentioned since it was an accepted part of society at the time it was written. This is why Peter encourages his readers to submit to their masters. He did not say to submit to their master if the master was kind, generous, and treated them well. That would be easy to do, and most likely was already happening. Even if the master was unjust and mistreated their servant, or slave, Peter is still telling them to submit. Submission is what is expected from the believer, and it isn't dependent upon the behavior of the master. Submission is a choice made by the slave.

This is still applicable to us today. Instead of us being servants, or slaves, we are employees, and everything Peter says applies to employees today. As a Christian employee, we need to be submissive to our boss and employer, no matter whether they deserve it or not. It is sad to see that in our culture today, even in the church, many people have the belief that they only need to submit to their employer if they "deserve" it. That's false. As believers we are to submit whether our employer treats us well or if they mistreat us. There is a good reason why God instructs us to do this. It isn't because He's trying to toughen us up or to take advantage of us. As we learn to submit to others simply because of their position of authority, we also begin to learn to submit to God because of His supreme authority. Sometimes God asks us to do something that is uncomfortable, unpleasant, or that we simply don't want to do. Because we don't want to do it, does that mean it's ok for us to disobey God? Of course not! We are to submit to Him. The same thing is true for us at work. We are to submit simply because of their authority, not because they deserve it or not. The more we learn to submit to those in authority over us, the more we will submit to God, the One with supreme authority over all.

September 13

"So God created man in His own image, in the image of God He
created him; male
and female He created them."
Genesis 1:27

Here is the simple fact of man's creation. God created man out of nothing. God does not give us inside details on this creation, just that He is the Creator and we are created in His image, or likeness. God also created both male and female. This does not mean that Adam was an androgynous being, meaning being both male and female. In chapter 2 we will see more details on the creation of man and woman, but here in chapter 1 God is making the general statement that He created both man and woman. There is a real difference between men and women because God created us that way. Today we see the world attempting to minimize the differences between men and women, claiming that we are all the same. That is a lie; if we were the result of mindless evolution that could be true, but we are not. God created man and woman to be different, it was not an accident. Not only are there physical differences, but there are also emotional differences too. Let me give an example. Recently one of our daughters complained about a bug bite on her lip. I was home with her, and it didn't look bad. I told her she was ok, to keep doing her work and she would be fine. Later my wife came home and was told about the same bug bite. Her reaction was different, as she immediately hugged her, and gave her medicine to help her feel better. There are innate created differences between men and women.

Now, before we go any further let's make sure we understand that we are talking about the general rule of people. There will always be an exception to every rule. In general men are physically stronger than women. In general women have natural instincts towards caring and nurturing, being thoughtful and considerate; most men do not. There has also been lots of discussion on which gender is superior. I will tell you right now which gender is superior. Men are absolutely superior to women at being men, while women are absolutely superior over men at being women. When a man tries to be a woman, or a woman tries to be a man, you end up with something that is inferior. God created us differently, and instead of trying to erase those differences they need to be accepted and celebrated.

September 14

"...and brotherly affection with love..."
2 Peter 1:7b

Peter now lists the seventh characteristics for the believer. Following virtue (or courage), knowledge, self-control, steadfastness, godliness, and brotherly affection (or kindness), comes love. The other six characteristics are complete with love. In fact, even if you possess the first six characteristics, you miss out completely if you don't have love. The apostle Paul reminds us of that when he wrote, "If I speak in the tongues of men and of angels, but have not love, I am a noisy gong or a clanging cymbal. And if I have prophetic powers, and understand all mysteries and all knowledge, and if I have all faith, so as to remove mountains, but have not love, I am nothing. If I give away all I have, and if I deliver up my body to be burned, but have not love, I gain nothing" (1 Corinthians 13:1-3). You can be filled with courage, knowledge, self-control, remain steady, live a godly life, and be kind towards others, but if you don't have love, it doesn't mean a thing. Love not only needs to be our reason for doing things, it needs to pour out of our beings because it is the essence of our being.

How important is it that we are filled with love? Jesus said, "A new commandment I give to you, that you love one another: just as I have loved you, you also are to love one another. By this all people will know that you are my disciples, if you have love for one another" (John 13:34-35). In other words, if we are a disciple, or a follower, of Jesus, then we are to be known by our love for others. Sadly, all too often Christians are only known for the things they oppose, or the works they have done for others. While those may not necessarily be bad things, we, as believers, need to be more known for the love we have for others. Don't get me wrong, standing up for the right thing is good, and doing good works to help others is noble, but if they aren't done with love, then they are of no value. God wants His children to be known for their love. At the church I attend we put it this way, we are to love up (God), love in (the church), love out (the world around us), and we to love now. Love is to be the purpose of our life. "The aim of our charge is love that issues from a pure heart and a good conscience and a sincere faith" (1 Timothy 1:5).

September 15

"And after the earthquake a fire, but the LORD was not in the fire.
And after the fire the sound of a low whisper."
1 Kings 19:12

Elijah faithfully and obediently served God. God used Elijah to defeat King Ahab and Queen Jezebel of Israel and their 850 false prophets who worshipped false gods. This was a very spectacular event. After Elijah defeated and killed these 850 false prophets, Queen Jezebel was very upset and said she was going to kill Elijah. Of course, after killing 850 false prophets, Elijah had no reason at all to be concerned. But he was not only concerned, he was scared to death. He ran away to hide in the wilderness. While Elijah was there, God appeared to him and spoke to him. God spoke to Elijah to bring him comfort.

When God doesn't speak to us through mighty miracles or miraculous signs, it isn't because we're not living a holy enough life. That is just how God chooses to operate. Here was Elijah faithfully and obediently serving God. Yet when God came to speak to him it wasn't through spectacular means like mighty gusts of wind, an earthquake, or a fire. God came and spoke to Elijah the same way He speaks to us, through a soft whisper, or a quiet, still voice. You see, if God shouted to us or used some miraculous way to get our attention there would be no way for us to miss it. This is why God chooses to use a soft whisper. He wants to make sure that we are listening to Him. That we are "in tune" with Him. He wants us to be seeking Him, not to forcibly stop us.

Spend time with God; get to know Him and His voice. He desires to have a personal and intimate relationship with each one of us. As we do, we will find that we know Him better, and become familiar with His leading and guiding us. When He whispers to us, we will hear Him and respond accordingly since we are "in tune" with Him. That is the best place to be in the world. To get there we need to make sure that our hearing is both protected and working well. We must have a good relationship with God to hear Him when He comes and whispers to us. Good hearing is important. Not only will we hear God's instructions for our life, but it will also keep us in good spiritual balance so that we don't stumble.

September 16

"And Jacob said to Pharaoh, 'The days of the years of my sojourning are 130 years. Few and evil have been the days of the years of my life, and they have not attained to the days of the years of the life of my fathers in the days of their sojourning.'"
Genesis 47:9

There are places where you know that you belong. When you are there, you can relax and get comfortable because you belong there. That isn't always the case though. Sometimes you will find yourself in a place where you know you don't belong, or where you know that you won't be there long. It may be a nice place, but you're just passing through on your way somewhere else. Other times it is a place that isn't the greatest, but you make do with it since you know you won't be there long. This is what Jacob is telling Pharaoh. He is a pilgrim. He is moving on. He is on a journey in a place where he is just passing through. Yes, life has been difficult, far from easy, but since he's just passing through and heading to a much better place, it's ok. This is the same attitude that Christians need to have about living on earth. Yes, it is difficult and far from easy, but it's ok. We're just passing through. We won't be here forever because we have a much better place that we're going.

This unique approach to life isn't just a "pie in the sky" or "Pollyanna"-like attitude. The Bible tells us others have lived this same way and commends them for it. Abraham and many others "acknowledged that they were strangers and exiles on the earth" (Hebrews 11:13). If earth isn't their real home, where is their real home? "But as it is, they desire a better country, that is, a heavenly one. Therefore God is not ashamed to be called their God, for he has prepared for them a city" (Hebrews 11:16). The apostle Peter also encouraged those on earth to live with this same attitude. "Beloved, I urge you as sojourners and exiles to abstain from the passions of the flesh, which wage war against your soul. Keep your conduct among the Gentiles honorable, so that when they speak against you as evildoers, they may see your good deeds and glorify God on the day of visitation" (1 Peter 2:11-12). As pilgrims we know that we are here only for a little while. This means that even though we will endure persecution and difficult times, it will only be for a short time, at least in view of eternity (it may seem like a long time while we are here). So, don't give up hope. Don't give in and become just like the world we are in. Know that we are heading to a much better place, so we can hold on loosely to the things of this earth as we reach out for our real home in Heaven.

September 17

"...but as He Who called you is holy, you also be holy in all your conduct..."
1 Peter 1:15

Peter writes to believers who are living in foreign lands. He has a challenge and an encouragement for them. Where they are living their goal isn't to fit in and be like everyone around them, but instead, they are to be holy. We need to ask ourselves a question here, what does it mean to be holy? Holiness does not mean moral purity, but instead speaks about the idea of being separate, or apart. Peter is reminding us that as children of God we are to be separate from the world because God has set us apart from the world for a specific use. This should sound familiar to all of us because we have certain items in our houses that we keep just for specific uses. For example, we have certain pots in our house that we use to cook food in. Those pots are then cleaned in the dishwasher in the kitchen. There is also a washing machine that we use to wash our clothes. But we also have a shower, or bathtub, that we use to wash our bodies in. Close to the shower, or bathtub, is a toilet that we use to get rid of our bodies' waste. Each of these items have a very specific use. You wouldn't think of washing your dishes in the shower, nor would you wash your clothes in the dishwasher. Neither would you cook your food on the toilet. The reason why is because each of these items are kept in your house for a specific purpose; they are set apart.

Peter reminds us that we are also set apart. Unlike the world, we are called to be set apart from sin. There is a reason for this. We are called to be separate from sin so that we are holy, just like God Himself is holy. This phrase Peter borrows from the book of Leviticus where it is often repeated; the word holy is used 94 times in Leviticus. God is separate from His creation. He is not like us humans. This is why it is important that we realize that God's love for us isn't like the love we have for others because His love is a HOLY love. This also means that His justice is different than our justice because His justice is a HOLY justice, and so on with each of His attributes. You see holiness is not something that we possess but it is something that possesses us. We need to remember that a holy person is not an odd person. A holy person simply is a different person than the world around them. As a holy person we are called to live a lifestyle that is different from the unbelievers around us. This means that we are not to be conformed to the world around us. Don't be odd but do be different.

September 18

"But the midwives feared God and did not do as the king of Egypt commanded them, but let the male children live."
Exodus 1:17

These midwives were in a tough spot. They had been commanded by Pharaoh to kill every male child as he was born. They knew this was wrong, but it was what the law told them they had to do. What were they to do? Well, they "feared" God. This doesn't mean that they were afraid of God, but that they had so much respect for God, that they would willingly choose to disobey a law of the land in order to be obedient to God. What we are talking about here is civil disobedience. These midwives chose to disobey a law because it was evil and contradicted God and His Word.

This may be the first time we read of civil disobedience in the Bible, but it was not the last time, and there will continue to be instances when civil disobedience is the right thing to do until Jesus returns. In fact, theologian Francis Shaeffer said that if Christians never practice civil disobedience, then the government is the object of their worship. The laws of man will at some point contradict God's laws and His Word, causing believers to have to make a choice, and a stand.

It is true that the Bible teaches that as believers we are to submit and obey to the governments of the land where we live, such as Romans 13:1-5. This does not mean, though, that we place the government in place of God. As believers, obeying God and His Word is our first priority. When the laws of this land violate, or contradict, God's law, then the choice for us should be pretty simple: obey God. This requires faith because when we choose to obey God instead of the laws of this land, we will have to deal with the consequences of that choice. Shadrach, Meshach, and Abednego dealt with this in Babylon when the law told them they had to bow down and worship an idol. They refused, but they were thrown into a burning furnace because of their decision (see Daniel 3). The apostles dealt with this in Acts 5, when they were commanded to not talk about God anymore. Peter responded by saying, "We must obey God rather than men" (Acts 5:29). They did end up paying the penalty for their decision too.

So, as believers, when do we disobey the law of the land and participate in civil disobedience? Before this is done, we should spend much time in prayer and study of the Scriptures to make sure we are correct in doing so. But, whenever the law of the land causes us to be in disobedience to God, then the choice for us should be very clear: God first!

September 19

"Of Issachar, men who had understanding of the times, to know what Israel ought to do, 200 chiefs and all their kinsmen under their command."
1 Chronicles 12:32

In this section of Scripture, we are told the numbers of people who began to follow David, and how his army grew in both numbers and might. King Saul had recently been killed in battle, and David was serving as King of Judah, but not over all Israel. More and more Israelites were following David and preparing to crown him as king over all Israel. Read through 1 Chronicles 12:23-40 and you get the picture of a nation preparing to crown a new king. The tribe of Issachar is the only tribe who is said to have understood the times. This indicates that they knew God's Word and promise that David would be king and were able to discern that the time was right.

Oh, how we need to be like the tribe of Issachar. We need to understand the times that we live in. Jesus spoke much about the Last Days when He walked on this earth and told us what to look for and expect. "For as were the days of Noah, so will be the coming of the Son of Man. For in those days before the flood they were eating and drinking, marrying and giving in marriage, until the day when Noah entered the ark, and they were unaware until the flood came and swept them all away, so will be the coming of the Son of Man" (Matthew 24:37-39). Jesus said the people in Noah's day were more concerned with satisfying their fleshly desires than they were about spiritual matters; this was because they had rejected following God in order to satisfy their flesh. The days before Jesus comes again will be the same way.

We also have seen the nation of Israel restored after almost 2000 years of not existing. This has never happened before in the history of the world. Why has this happened? Because God said it would. We also see the world becoming more and more of a unified one-system economic market every day. The technology is also available for every person to receive a "mark" in order to participate in this unified economic system. This is reality. Everything Jesus said would happen before He raptures His church home is in place. Following the Rapture will be seven years of tribulation, and then the Second Coming of Jesus Christ. This is the hope of every Christian. This hope will change the way we live our lives, and to have compassion on those who are lost to share this hope with them. Jesus will call His church home soon. Are you ready? Do you understand the times?

"For the Lord Himself will descend from heaven with a cry of command, with the voice of an archangel, and with the sound of the trumpet of God. And the dead in Christ will rise first. Then we who are alive, who are left, will be caught up together with them in the clouds to meet the Lord in the air, and so we will always be with the Lord" (1 Thessalonians 4:16-17).

September 20

"To each and all of them he gave a change of clothes, but to Benjamin he gave three hundred shekels of silver and five changes of clothes."
Genesis 45:22

Partiality occurs on a regular basis, even though it is damaging. The dictionary defines partiality as "unfair bias in favor of one thing or person compared with another." This occurs because there are distinctions between people. Some people are good athletes, some aren't. Some people are blessed with great intelligence, others struggle with it. There are distinctions between people in all areas of life, art, business, finance, education, popularity, etc. Joseph was aware of this because it affected his family. Joseph's dad Jacob wasn't the favored son by his parents, Esau was. Jacob favored his wife Rachel over Leah. He favored Joseph over his older brothers. This resulted in the ten older brothers hating Joseph and being jealous of him. This is the damage that partiality creates. While distinctions and partiality are a part of life, we are wise to avoid them and accept people for who they are, not what we want them to be.

Joseph shows partiality in giving his brother Benjamin four more changes of clothes than the other brothers, plus 300 pieces of silver. This could have been justified because Benjamin was the only brother that wasn't involved in taking Joseph's robe and selling him into slavery. But there is no justification here. Joseph simply chooses to bless each of his brothers. Previously they had taken his clothes, so he chooses to respond by blessing them with new clothes. Instead of focusing on what they had done to him, Joseph chose to turn their bad choice into a blessing for them. How much better would our world be if we chose to respond this way too? How would things be different if when someone mistreated you that instead of getting even you chose to bless them back?

We see great maturity from the older brothers because there is no mention of jealousy over Benjamin receiving more than them. Why is that? Instead of focusing on competition between each other, they were thankful for what they received. They didn't compare their offerings to the others and become jealous that someone received more than they did. This is another great lesson we can apply to our lives. Learn to be thankful for the things we have instead of being jealous over what others have.

September 21

"Then Elisha prayed and said, 'O Lord, please open his eyes that he may see.' So the Lord opened the eyes of the young man, and he saw,

and behold, the mountain was full of horses and chariots of fire all around Elisha."
2 Kings 6:17

Discouragement, despair and hopelessness are tools the devil uses to keep Christians from being effective for God. These emotions are caused by choices we make. Some argue that they come about because of the conditions or situations a person is in, but that is not true. No matter what situation you find yourself in, you choose how you will respond to it.

What is it that allows us to be brought to the point of discouragement or despair? It depends on how we see things. Elisha and his servant were in the same situation. Both were inside the same house that was surrounded by the same army of Arameans. The servant looked outside and saw they were surrounded and responded with fear. He wondered out loud what they should do (see 2 Kings 6:15). Elisha also saw they were surrounded by these soldiers who were there to capture him. But he did not panic in fear because he saw beyond the soldiers, and he saw the spiritual resources that God provided to take care of him. Elisha knew that he was in a spiritual battle.

Like Elisha, we are in a spiritual battle. We fight against the forces of the devil. If we keep our eyes on the trials, physical battles, and problems that we are facing, we will not be victorious. The smallest trial we face here on earth can crush us and bring us to misery and despair, if we allow it to. To avoid that from happening, we need to keep our focus on Jesus, and pray like Elisha did. We need to pray that our eyes are open so that we see the battles and problems we face for what they really are, spiritual battles. The neighbor, co-worker, student, friend, child, or spouse that you are having problems with is not the problem. It is a spiritual battle, and to be victorious we need to see things as God does, and to see the spiritual weapons that He has supplied us with to fight the battle. Failure to use spiritual weapons will lead to frustration and defeat. According to Ephesians

6:17-18 God has given us two main weapons to use: the Bible and prayer. Prayer is what Elisha used here, and God was faithful to answer his prayer and opened the eyes of his servant so that he saw the truth and reality of the situation. What was the result, the servant was no longer fearful because he saw that God had the situation under control.

The servant had a choice to make; how was he going to view the situation? He could look at what he was able to see, which led to despair, or he could look to God and overcome the situation. He made the correct choice.

September 22

"And when the dragon saw that he had been thrown down to the earth, he pursued the woman who had given birth to the male child."
Revelation 12:13

In 2020 one of the hot topics is the subject of racism. There are large movements and huge protests loudly shouting for racism to end, as it should. There is no place for racism in our world. All people, no matter the color of your skin, are created "in the image of God" (Genesis 1:27) and therefore are all equal. The color of your skin does not make you better than, or less than, any other human. This is true for the color of our skin, but it is also true for each person's culture, or ancestry. Sadly, amidst all the calls for ending racism, some racism continues. Chief among them is anti-Semitism. Anti-Semitism is described as "hostility to, prejudice against, or discrimination against Jewish people. There is a reason why groups opposed to racism are still racist themselves if they are anti-Semitic. The root cause of this is Satanic.

The dragon is Satan, and when he was kicked out of Heaven when he opposed God and desired to be seen and worshipped as a god, he has done everything he can to thwart and hinder the work of

God. This is why we see his opposition to "the woman who gave birth to the male child." The male child is a reference to Jesus. Who gave birth to Him? Mary, and she was a Jewish girl. This is why Satan is anti-Semitic. He hates the Jews, because the Jewish people are God's chosen people, and through them salvation came to the world. Jesus was born a Jew, and through Him salvation has come to all people. Read through history and see how anti-Semitic Satan is and the many different times he has attempted to destroy Jews and continues to do so today.

John tells us that he "persecuted" the Jewish people. The Greek word that is translated persecuted means "to pursue, to chase, or to hunt." It is done consciously and with dogged effort. Satan does not give up, and he will continue to pursue them. The tool he uses will change with the times, but it will not stop until Jesus returns. We are getting close to the day when Jesus will return, and until that day arrives, we will continue to see racism in the world because Satan will continue his anti-Semitic attacks in an effort to stop the work of Jesus. He will not succeed, but he will continue to try.

September 23

"And do not be grieved, for the joy of the Lord is your strength."
Nehemiah 8:10b

There are many people who are in search of strength. You can find them in gyms on a daily basis as they pump iron over and over again trying to gain strength. There is a limit to how much muscle mass or strength a person can gain. A limit will be reached. But there is a way to gain unending strength. A strength that has no limit. How do you get this strength? We find the answer here in the book of Nehemiah. "The joy of the Lord is your strength."

How can a person acquire the joy of the Lord? Here are a few facts about it. First, it isn't found by being in the right place. In fact, the joy of the Lord is independent of your circumstances. In Acts 16 Paul and Silas were falsely arrested, beaten, and imprisoned. In spite of these dire circumstances, they were locked in the innermost part of the jail singing songs of praise. Why? Because even though their situation was not good, they were filled with the joy of the Lord. Secondly, the joy of the Lord is found in obedience. The world may consider you a failure by their standards and expectations, but if you are doing what God has called you to do, even if failing in the world's eyes, you can be filled with the joy of the Lord. Joy doesn't come with worldly success. Jesus was considered a failure by worldly standards. He was rejected and sentenced to death on a cross. But He wasn't a failure. How did Jesus look at the cross? The author of Hebrews tells us that "for the joy that was set before him endured the cross, despising the shame, and is seated at the right hand of the throne of God" (Hebrews 12:2).

So, how does a person get the "joy of the LORD?" The joy of the Lord is received by a person keeping their eyes and focus on Jesus. Not looking to the world for validation or success, but in looking at Jesus and living a life that pleases Him. When we keep our eyes on Jesus, He will be our focus and desire. The second desire is for others, while pleasing self is third. That is why joy is spelled j, then o, then y. J is for Jesus, o is for others, y is for you. That is the order that we are to focus on. Jesus first, others second, and yourself last.

September 24

"And immediately he proclaimed Jesus in the synagogues, saying, 'He is the Son of God.'"

Acts 9:20

After Saul had been converted and surrendered his life to Jesus, he had one thing that he wanted to do: share this Good News with others. Saul had been trained as a rabbi by Gamaliel, so he took advantage of the synagogue custom where any Jewish man was allowed to speak on the Scriptures at a synagogue meeting. The word was out; people knew that Saul was in town to arrest and hassle those people that believed in Jesus. He was a well-trained rabbi; any of the synagogues in Damascus would have welcomed him in with open arms.

As Saul walked to the front of the synagogue, a hush would have descended upon the room. Every eye in the building would have been focused on and directed towards Saul. The room would be filled with anticipation; what would he have to say? Saul went over to the attendant and asked for a particular scroll, and once it was handed to him, he read a section of Scripture. As he finished reading, the scroll would be handed back to the attendant and put away. Now, Saul was ready to speak. The crowd breathlessly waited to hear him denounce this cult because of its heresy in following Jesus the Nazarene. They wanted to hear how he was going to put an end to this cult and hunt down every single follower of Jesus.

But, when Saul opened his mouth, he began to preach to them that Jesus the Nazarene was the Messiah, the Son of God. He clearly taught them the truth about Jesus. Instead of destroying the Christians in Damascus, Saul went to the people he was trying to "protect" and preaches to them all about Jesus. Saul's life had been so completely changed by Jesus that he wanted to make sure that everyone else knew about Jesus and could be changed just as he was.

May we be filled with the same desire as Saul. May our hearts burn within us, prompting us to share the Good News about Jesus with our friends, neighbors, and co-workers. Jesus is the Messiah. Who have you shared that with lately?

September 25

"At that time the LORD said to Joshua, 'Make flint knives for yourself, and circumcise the sons of Israel again the second time.'"

Joshua 5:2

The Israelites had just crossed into the Promised Land, which was filled with their enemies, who wanted to kill the Israelites. This command from God does not make sense, humanly speaking. God was asking them to do a procedure that would incapacitate every male in the nation. This was not something like a sprained ankle; take 2 aspirins and call me in the morning. Every male would be down and out of action for the next few days. What if one of those nations attacked Israel? They would be like sitting ducks, with no one to defend them. The nation would be destroyed.

By being obedient, the nation of Israel would be placing themselves in a vulnerable position. They would have no level of protection themselves; they would be completely dependent upon God. If God failed to protect them and defend them, they would be destroyed.

That is the reason God commanded them to circumcise all the males in Israel at this time. God desires their obedience but, more importantly, He also desires them to be dependent upon Him. This brought them to the area of their heart. Would they have the faith and trust to follow God in a seemingly impossible situation? When you are in a situation that seems impossible, where does your heart lead you? Too often it begins to question what is happening. Our heart is filled with questions of anxiety and fear. What if the enemy comes and attacks us this afternoon? What if they come tomorrow morning? Joshua and the Israelites had to fight off these thoughts of fear from their position of vulnerability to be obedient to God. Joshua and the Israelites were obedient, and we see that God did protect them the whole time it took for the men to heal and be able to get back on their feet and fight to protect the nation.

God calls us to be vulnerable too. When we face a seemingly impossible situation God calls us to "cut off the flesh" and allow Him to protect us. We need to be vulnerable and admit our weakness; we cannot take care of the situations we are in. We are weak and not able to protect or defend ourselves; we need God's help. This is where God desires us. Honestly admitting our need for Him. When we do, God will faithfully show Himself to protect and defend us. "But He (God) said to me, 'My grace is sufficient for you, for My power is made perfect in weakness.' Therefore I will boast all the more gladly of my weaknesses, so that the power of Christ may rest upon me" (2 Corinthians 12:9).

September 26

"Be patient, therefore, brothers, until the coming of the Lord. See how the farmer waits for the precious fruit of the earth, being patient about it, until it receives the early and the late rains."
James 5:7

Patience is something that most people simply don't have time for. Whether we have time for it or not, it is something that the believer needs to implement in their life. There is a good reason for this too; because judgment is coming, so believers need to patiently endure until Jesus' return (see James 5:1-6). James doesn't just tell us to be patient, but he also gives us an example that we can follow, the farmer. When a farmer plants his crops, he doesn't expect the crop to appear the very next day, and when it doesn't immediately appear, neither does he give up. What the farmer does is continue to work hard while he patiently waits for his crop to appear. He does not stand around doing nothing while he waits for the crops; he is constantly working while he waits for the crops to appear. This is why James tells believers to patiently wait for the Lord. He doesn't tell believers to clothe themselves with a white robe and then climb a tall hill and wait for Jesus to return. No! He is telling us to patiently wait for Jesus' return, but to continue working while we wait.

In Bible times the farmer did not irrigate their crops; they waited for the early rain and the late rain. The farmer would plow their fields in the fall and wait for the early rains to soften to soil. Then in springtime they would again be waiting for the late rain to help the crops mature before harvest time. This takes a great amount of faith because the farmer has absolutely no control over the weather. Too much rain will cause a crop to rot, while not enough rain will dry out and ruin the crop. So, while the farmer waited for the seasons, he continued to work while exercising his faith. This is exactly what James is reminding us that we need to do as believers. We experience spiritual "seasons" in our life, times when we are being plowed to prepare us for a crop, and other times when much fruit is being harvested in our life. Then, there are other times when we are simply waiting and trusting in God to bring either the early or late rains in our life. No matter where we are in our spiritual seasons, we need to be patiently and diligently doing the work that God has called us to do, such as reading and studying His Word, and sharing that Good News with others.

September 27

"The heart is deceitful above all things, and desperately sick; who can understand it? 'I the LORD search the heart and test the mind, to give every man according to his ways,
according to the fruit of his deeds."
Jeremiah 17:9-10

There is a popular saying, "I am following my heart," that is often used as an excuse for the things we do and the choices that we make. There is a problem with this though. The prophet Jeremiah is letting us know that the heart cannot be trusted because it is deceitful. Deceitful means "fraudulent, crooked, or polluted." The picture is of something that will trip us up and steer us in the wrong direction. When we "follow our heart," we are heading for disaster. It is like walking down a lush tree lined path in the woods, not realizing that trees have covered the "Bridge Out" warning sign. We fail to realize the danger ahead.

The problem is that our heart is entirely selfish. The heart is completely consumed with satisfying our flesh. We can attempt to mask it and justify certain behaviors, but the root of our heart is to please self. Don't get down on yourself when you realize it, this is human nature. The natural motives, attitudes, desires, and perspectives in our heart mislead us from God's truth because their goal is to please self instead of God. What can be done to change that? Spend time drawing closer to God. This is done by reading and studying the Bible and spending time in prayer. As we draw closer to God and know Him better, He will work on and change our heart to become more like His. Those secret motives, attitudes, desires, and perspectives that mislead us are then able to be changed and replaced by God's love, grace, patience, and forgiveness.

God then examines, or tests, us to give us what we deserve. This testing will show us the true intent of our heart. The testing can be painful; both the test and what we find out. It may not be pleasant to go through, yet the result is worth it. We find the pollution that resides within us and can release it to God so that He can purge it from us. We are not able to change our hearts, only God can do that. Allow God the opportunity to look at your heart and show you what resides there. Do not follow your heart, but allow God to inspect your heart, to change it, and follow Him. "Search me, O God, and know my heart! Try me and know my thoughts! And see if there be any grievous way in me, and lead me in the way everlasting!" (Psalm 139:23-24).

September 28

"If you are insulted for the name of Christ, you are blessed, because the Spirit of glory and of God rests upon you."

1 Peter 4:14

In this world we can, and will be, insulted for many different things. Since the world loves to divide people into so many kinds of classifications, people from different groups will love to insult you because of the group or groups that you belong to. This is true for sports teams. People on the east coast love to insult followers of sports teams on the west coast, and vice versa. The same is true for styles of music. People that love one style of music have no qualms insulting people that don't love their same style of music. This also happens with food, cars, activities, etc.

Generally, the world is fairly accepting when a person says they belong to a religious denomination. Say you are a Baptist, or a Lutheran, or a Methodist, or go to Calvary Chapel, or are an agnostic, and the world is ok with that. But tell them that you are a Christian, a follower of Jesus Christ, and things can heat up very quickly. Once the name of Jesus is brought into the conversation people often lose their willingness to be accepting. Why is that? It is because there is power in the name of Jesus. Satan, the prince of this world, hates the name Jesus, and this is why people go crazy when His name is mentioned. The spiritual power and authority that we have in this world is in Jesus, which is why we will encounter opposition when we mention His name. Go ahead and pray in public, as long as you don't mention the name Jesus.

Since the world is so opposed to the name of Jesus, it is imperative that we, as believers, live our lives in such a way that we bring glory and honor to His name. Every single time that we are insulted or mistreated because of Jesus, we are given an opportunity to bring glory and honor to His name. Even when the world tells us not to say His name, we continue to speak His name because He is our authority, our power, our hope. It is not easy to suffer for the name of Jesus, but Peter also knew the reality of how suffering for the name of Jesus is also a blessing. Suffering for His name is proof that we are following Him. our suffering is because we identity with Jesus. He said that would happen to His followers. "If they persecuted Me, they will also persecute you. If they kept My word, they will also keep yours. But all these things they will do to you on account of My name, because they do not know Him who sent Me" (John 15:20b-21). It is painful to go through this suffering, but God can bring blessing out of suffering and persecution.

September 29

"...so that the land could not support both of them dwelling together; for their possessions were so great that they could not dwell together, and there was strife between the herdsmen of Abram's livestock and the herdsmen of Lot's livestock. At that time the Canaanites and the Perizzites were dwelling in the land."
Genesis 13:6-7

There are only so many sheep that can graze on an acre of land. With both Abram and Lot being rich, they soon found troubles arising from them staying in the same place. There would be enough land for them both if they would separate, like God told them to do long ago in both Ur and Haran. But Abram chose to disobey God and now he is suffering the consequences of his choice. But God's will is going to be done. It could have been done by Abram obeying, but since he did not obey, God is now providentially allowing an irritation between Abram and Lot to grow which will force the separation to occur. God's plan will always be accomplished; if not sooner, then later. If we fail to see the need for obedience, then God will create the need for it.

The biggest problem that occurred from this quarrelling and fighting between Abram and Lot was that it ruined their testimony to the people in the land. The people saw them come into the land, and they saw Abram build his altar to God and worship God. Now they witness them getting into fights over wealth and possessions. The Canaanites and Perizzites would not be interested in learning about God because they saw nothing different in them, and nothing that would attract them to God. They were seeing that there was no difference between these followers of God and themselves. Donald Grey Barnhouse put it well when he said, "Many people will never listen to what any believer says because of what some believers are." Ouch! That hurts.

It is both sad and amazing how many Christians fight, argue and bicker with each other, and even justify their actions. Actions like these tell the world that we are not different than they are, and there is no reason for them to change. Instead, we are called to "Be kind to one another, tenderhearted, forgiving one another, as God in Christ forgave you" (Ephesians 4:32). God did not say this is a suggestion for us, but He is telling us how we need to act towards others. Yes, God does know that this means it will not always be fair, and neither will it always be right. But we are not to use those as reasons to justify our actions to not be kind and compassionate towards others. Jesus said, "By this all people will know that you are My disciples, if you have love for one another" (John 13:35). We are to be known for love, not arguing, fighting, and bickering.

September 30

"Then I looked, and behold, on Mount Zion stood the Lamb, and with him 144,000 who had his name and his Father's name written on their foreheads."
Revelation 14:1

During the period of the Tribulation, the Antichrist and the False Prophet will have their sights set on destroying any, and all, followers of Jesus. Their goal will be to have everyone remaining on earth to worship them, what they say, and to follow them blindly, which the majority of those remaining on earth will gladly do. But there is always an exception to every rule. The exception here will be these 144,000 believers that the apostle John sees standing on Mount Zion with Jesus, the Lamb. These 144,000 followers were first introduced to us in Revelation 7, where we are told that they are all single Jewish men, 12,000 men from each of the 12 tribes of Israel. During the Tribulation they will be targeted by the Antichrist and the False Prophet. This means that they will be engaged in battle, the forces of the world will try to kill them, but they will fail. At the end of the Tribulation period, not even one of these men of God will be killed or lost. They will spend their time preaching the goodness and truth of the Gospel, that Jesus came into the world, died on the cross, was buried, and rose from the dead, just as Scripture says. He loves us and wants to see every single person surrender to Him so that they can be saved. Their message is not popular and will be rejected by most people that hear it. This doesn't stop them from peaching though.

John tells us one other thing about these 144,000 evangelists, God gives each of them a special mark. In Revelation 13:16-17 we read of the mark that the followers of Satan have placed on either their forehead of right hand, but the followers of God also have a mark placed on them. The mark that Satan's followers receive is to allow them to participate in the world's system, but the mark that God's followers have is placed on them by God to protect them. Did you know that if you are a believer in God, then you also are marked? God protects His children, and no harm can come to them that He does not allow. "My sheep hear My voice, and I know them, and they follow Me. I give them eternal life, and they will never perish, and no one will snatch them out of My hand" (John 10:27-28).

October 1

"...who says of Cyrus, 'He is my shepherd, and he shall fulfill all my purpose'; saying of Jerusalem, 'She shall be built,' and of the temple, 'Your foundation shall be laid.'""

Isaiah 44:28

The world loves to talk about random events and happenings. But there is no such thing as a random event. The dictionary defines random as "done, chosen, or occurring without a specific pattern, plan, or connection." Since God is in control of every circumstance in your life, nothing random ever happens. Every single event will fit into God's specific plans and purposes. We may have absolutely no idea how that will happen, but it will.

Isaiah wrote about Cyrus, and how God would use Him to accomplish His purposes. Doesn't sound like such a big deal, until you realize that this was written about 100 years before Cyrus was born. Can you imagine how confused and bewildered people were when Isaiah wrote this. Who is Cyrus? We've never heard of him. Isaiah must have a loose nut in his head; this makes absolutely no sense.

In addition to Cyrus not being born, Isaiah also prophesied that he would help to build Jerusalem and lay the foundation for the temple. This had to confuse Isaiah's readers, because they were both standing when this was written. But, 100 years later Jerusalem was in ruins, the temple had been destroyed, and Cyrus was the brand-new king of Babylon. Can you imagine the shock on his face as this was read to him? I would love to see that look (I will check out this DVD in Heaven).

To the people of Isaiah's day, his writing must have seemed very random. But they were prophetic. The Holy Spirit revealed this to him to show King Cyrus, and us, that God is in control of all events in history. He can control circumstances to fit His plan and purpose. He is still doing the same thing today. No matter what you are going through or experiencing, know that God is in control, and it is for a specific reason. We can receive much comfort in knowing this when we are going through times of difficulty. There is a reason and a purpose for it, and God will use it for good.

Just as God knew how He would use Cyrus before he was born, He also knows how He will use you. There is nothing random that will ever happen in your life. God has a plan; and a good one too.

October 2

"Know this, my beloved brothers: let every person be quick to hear, slow to speak, slow to anger; for the anger of man does not produce the righteousness of God."
James 1:19-20

Have you ever noticed that many people simply like to talk? Sometimes I wonder if people even know what it is that they are saying, or if they simply talk because they enjoy hearing the sound of their own voice. When I was younger one of my aunts used to describe people that talked too much as "having diarrhea of the mouth." This problem led to the sage advice, reminding us that we have two ears and only one mouth, so we should listen twice as much as we speak. This isn't a new saying because King Solomon said the same thing thousands of years ago. Solomon said, "When words are many, transgression is not lacking, but whoever restrains his lips is prudent" (Proverbs 10:19). This is exactly what James is saying here. James says that we "must be quick to hear, slow to speak, and slow to anger." It is not possible for us to listen to what others are saying when we are so busy talking. When we spend too much time talking, and not listening, what we also do is send the message that what we have to say is more important than what others have to say.

One way for a person to learn to be slow to anger is to learn to listen to others and talk less. When we listen more than we speak we are being others-centered, instead of self-centered. Much of our anger is caused by us being self-centered instead of others-centered. We get angry when things don't go the way we want them to or expect them to, or when our plans and schedule get interrupted. This anger comes from being self-focused. This is why James is telling us to listen more, speak less, and that will help us become angry less.

Why is it so important for us to be angry less? We want to be angry less because when we are angry we cannot produce the righteousness of God. The dictionary describes righteousness as "behavior that is morally justifiable or right." In Scripture, righteousness refers to relationships between two or more parties, especially referencing our personal relationship with God. We can stand before God as being righteous because of Jesus' death on the cross. God accepts us as being righteous because of what Jesus did for us. But, when we are angry, our righteous standing before God is not able to be seen by others. This is why it is so important for us to learn to control our anger. A good place to start is to listen more and speak less.

October 3

"What the cutting locust left, the swarming locust has eaten. What the swarming locust left, the hopping locust has eaten, and what the hopping locust left, the destroying locust has eaten."
Joel 1:4

The car that you drive has been equipped with warning lights on the dash. They are there for a reason; to let you know when trouble is coming. When you see a warning light you have a choice to make. Will I "listen" to the warning and get the problem fixed? Doing this will remove the warning light from your life. Or will I ignore it and hope it goes away? If that doesn't work, will I grab a hammer and smash the warning light so that it is no longer blinking in my life? While smashing the blinking warning light seems funny and a bit extreme, it isn't much different than what many people do in their own personal lives. God gives us warnings to get our attention and turn us away from trouble and back to Him. Too often people destroy the warning and continue living the way they have and pay absolutely no attention to the warning given them.

Joel is warning the nation of Israel that a swarm of locusts will come and destroy their crops because of their continued disobedience to God. The people had a choice to make. Would they heed the warning, change their lifestyles, and return to God, or would they ignore the warning and continue to live the way they wanted? The choice was theirs to make.

God continues to send warning lights to us today. It may come in the form of a traffic ticket, a health scare (like cancer), a broken relationship, a bad report card in at school or a bad performance review at work. God also sends us warnings through His Word. It may even come through the words and counsel from a trusted friend or family member. Do we pay attention to these "warnings," or do we ignore them and continue to live the way we have chosen? When we heed the warning light in our car and get it taken care of and corrected, we can continue to drive with no problems. The same is true in our own lives. When we heed God's warnings, come back to Him and make the necessary changes in our life, God promises blessings for us. "I will restore[d] to you the years that the swarming locust has eaten, the hopper, the destroyer, and the cutter..." (Joel 2:25). God promises that He will restore to us what has been destroyed in the past due to the poor choices we have made. God promises blessings to those who will heed the "warnings" that He sends to us. Pay attention to those warnings, and don't ignore them, but correct them.

October 4

"And they devoted themselves to the apostles' teaching and the fellowship, to the breaking of bread and the prayers."
Acts 2:42

In this passage Dr. Luke describes for us what the church really is. Far too often when we think of "the church," what we think of are the buildings. But the building is not the church; they are only structures where part of the church will meet. The church is a living and breathing organism; it is made up of all believers. The church cannot be confined to a building, or a time of meeting together. Another mistake many make is thinking the church is a group of people that meet on Sunday morning. That is not true. The church meets every hour of every day. Church happens as we live our lives. Church is not about going to a building to sing a few songs and listen to a man speak for about an hour or so, and then go home. Church is a group of people who have surrendered their lives to Jesus Christ as Savior of their lives, and how they interact with each other to change and influence the world around them.

Dr. Luke lists here four things that we as a church need to be doing in our lives. The first thing is being devoted to the apostles' teaching; other translations describe this as doctrine. What is doctrine? It is the principle basis of what we believe, which is God's Word. The apostle Paul wrote that he had faithfully taught all Scripture to the church at Ephesus (see Acts 20:27). Aquila and Priscilla practiced this when Apollos was incorrect in what he was teaching, so they took him aside and privately taught him what God's Word really said (see Acts 18:26). The Apostle Paul also wrote that the Bible is God's inspired Word and is the basis for our doctrine (see 2 Timothy 3:16a).

Secondly, the church is to be practicing fellowship. Every one of us needs to be in fellowship with other Christians. "Not neglecting to meet together, as is the habit of some, but encouraging one another, and all the more as you see the Day drawing near" (Hebrews 10:25). This is why the church does meet together, whether it be Sunday morning or a mid-week study. This also is why we need good Christian friends that we get together with, at each other's homes or just getting together with each other. The reason is for encouragement, especially as the time for Jesus' second return draws closer, which it does every day.

Thirdly, the church is to get together to break bread with each other. This happens when we share meals with each other, and often goes hand in hand with fellowshipping with each other. This is more than sharing meals though, it also refers to the body of believers getting together to celebrate communion with each other. "For I received from the Lord what I also delivered to you, that the Lord Jesus on the night when He was betrayed took bread, and when He had given thanks, He broke it, and said, 'This is my body, which is for you. Do this in remembrance of Me.' In the same way also He took the cup, after supper, saying, 'This cup is the new covenant in My blood. Do this, as often as you drink it, in remembrance of Me.' For as often as you eat this bread and drink the cup, you proclaim the Lord's death until He comes" (1 Corinthians 11:23-26).

Fourthly, we as a church are to be committed to prayer. Prayer is powerful; more powerful than most of us believe. 1 Thessalonians 5:17 reminds us to pray always, and James 5:16 reminds us how powerful prayer is. Prayer is not something to be done before a meal, but a regular and constant aspect of our lives.

We as believers are the church; active, alive and bringing light and hope to a dying culture around us that so desperately needs it.

October 5

"Benjamin is a ravenous wolf, in the morning devouring the prey and at evening dividing the spoil."
Genesis 49:27

As Jacob finishes prophesying over his sons, he comes to his final and youngest son, Benjamin. He accurately describes characteristics that his descendants will be known for: they will be violent warriors. Some translations don't just say he is a wolf, but a ravenous wolf; a wolf with an appetite that is not satisfied. At times this was a very good trait, but there was also a time when this trait almost wiped out the entire tribe of Benjamin.

During the time of the judges, it was reported that the people did whatever pleased them since there was not a single ruler or leader over the nation. This was clearly seen with the tribe of Benjamin in Judges 19-20. This took place in the city of Gibeah where the men of

Benjamin gang-raped a woman and killed her. Their sexual immorality was like a ravenous wolf. When the other tribes of Israel heard about this, they attacked Benjamin and at the end of the battle only 600 men in the tribe of Benjamin remained alive. Their violence and insatiable appetite almost destroyed the tribe.

Read through the Bible and you will find many valiant warriors and soldiers that came from the tribe of Benjamin. One of the greatest judges came from Benjamin; his name was Ehud (Judges 3:12-31). The men of Benjamin were some of the bravest warriors in the battle to defeat Sisera in Judges 5. The first king of Israel, Saul, was a Benjamite. During his career, his wolf-like attitude was seen in his successful campaigns on the battlefield, but also in his numerous attempts to kill his successor, David and his ruthless killing of everyone in the priestly city of Nob (1 Samuel 22:6-19). Other notable soldiers from Benjamin were Abner (2 Samuel 2:23), Sheba (2 Samuel 20:1-22), and Shimei (2 Samuel 16:5-14). Another well-known warrior came from the tribe of was the Pharisee known as Saul from Tarsus. Before he became known as Paul the apostle, his ravenous wolf-like behavior was seen in how he pursued and persecuted Christians. "And Saul approved of his execution. And there arose on that day a great persecution against the church in Jerusalem, and they were all scattered throughout the regions of Judea and Samaria... Saul was ravaging the church, and entering house after house, he dragged off men and women and committed them to prison" (Acts 8:1, 3). Once again, God spoke through Jacob and accurately prophesied how his descendants would be.

October 6

"... for I know that through your prayers and the help of the Spirit of Jesus Christ this will turn out for my deliverance..."
Philippians 1:19

Not knowing what is going to happen causes fear and anxiety in many people. Most people enjoy knowing what is going to happen; knowing the results of an action brings peace to most people. When a decision is made, and the consequences of that decision can bring more than one result can be very nerve wracking. This is what the apostle Paul is dealing with. He is in jail because of his faith in Jesus Christ, and for faithfully preaching Him to others. While he is in prison, some ministers in the church have tried to take advantage of his position by replacing him and his ministry. He is even aware that some ministers have been preaching with improper motives. Despite all the opposition he is facing, there are some believers, such as the Philippian church, which continue to faithfully support him and pray for him. Paul says this is a huge help, and he also knows that through these prayers and the Holy Spirit that he will be delivered.

Notice though, that while he is confident that he will be delivered from his current predicament, he doesn't know how he will be delivered. There are multiple ways that he could be delivered. He could be released from prison, but he could also be executed. Very opposite results, but both would end up causing his deliverance. Paul is not concerned with how he will be delivered, but he receives comfort from the fact that he knows God will deliver him. He is similar to three young Hebrew men many years earlier. Hananiah, Mishael, and Azariah. You may know them better by the Chaldean names that they were given Shadrach, Meshach, and Abednego. When told that they had to bow down and worship an idol, they said they wouldn't do it. They were threatened with death, and they boldly said "If this be so, our God whom we serve is able to deliver us from the burning fiery furnace, and He will deliver us out of your hand, O king. But if not, be it known to you, O king, that we will not serve your gods or worship the golden image that you have set up" (Daniel 3:17-18). Paul had the same faith. God would deliver him, just as He did Shadrach, Meshach, and Abednego. It didn't matter if it was through release from prison or death. Either way, God would deliver him. Trust in God, and that He will do what is right and best, is the best way to release anxiety.

October 7

"I warn everyone who hears the words of the prophecy of this book: if anyone adds to them, God will add to him the plagues described in this book..."
Revelation 22:18

Warnings are found everywhere in society. They are included on packaging on just about everything you buy. Some warnings make you wonder what happened before that this had to be written. For example, clothing labels that say, "remove child before washing." Another one that seems weird is on a hair dryer box, and it says, "Do not use while sleeping." Or, when you purchase a hot cup of coffee and there's a warning label on the cup of coffee telling you the contents may be hot. I sure hope so, that's why I bought a cup of hot coffee.

Not all warnings are funny though. Sometimes they are serious, and it is important that they are followed. The warning that Jesus gives here through the apostle John is that type of warning. The warning that Jesus gives us is to not mess with, change, or add to His Word. When the apostle John finished writing the book of Revelation at the end of the first century, God was finished writing the Bible. God spoke through various men, and the Holy Spirit led and instructed these men on what to write. The love letter that God wrote us was complete with the book of Revelation. This means that anyone who says that God appeared to them and gave them a "new revelation" is nothing more than a fraud and a false prophet.

There have been different people throughout the centuries that have claimed God spoke to them and gave them "new" words to write that their followers have accepted and followed as "scripture."

Mohammed, Joseph Smith, and Mary Baker Eddy are just a few examples. God is saying here through the apostle John that they will face divine vengeance for their lies and falsely attributing their writings to God. Folks, this is serious business. God is serious when He tells us not to mess with His words. This applies to not only the book of Revelation, but the entire Bible. The write of Proverbs was aware of this when he wrote, "Every word of God proves true; He is a shield to those who take refuge in Him. Do not add to His words, lest He rebuke you and you be found a liar" (Proverbs 30:5-6).

October 8

"The next Sabbath almost the whole city gathered to hear the word of the Lord. But when the Jews saw the crowds, they were filled with jealousy and began to contradict what was spoken by Paul, reviling him..."
Acts 13:44-45

The week following Paul's teaching in the local synagogue there was an excited buzz that spread around the city. What Paul had taught them was completely new to them; something they had never heard. His message was talked about by everyone in town that week. In fact, we could say Paul's message was the "talk of the town." So, the next Saturday, or Sabbath, almost the entire town showed up at the synagogue to hear what Paul was going to teach them this week.

When the Jews saw this large crowd that showed up to hear Paul, they were so excited about how many people were here to hear God's truth being taught. No! They weren't happy at all. In fact, Luke tells us that they were filled with envy and jealousy. They had never attracted this large of a crowd before. They were jealous over this large crowd because they had a desire to be popular more than being concerned with serving God. Not everyone will ever be popular and draw large crowds. But everyone can serve and please God. This is what Paul and Barnabas were doing, and it caused the Jews to be jealous.

So, instead of learning from Paul and Barnabas' example, this group of Jews became combative. Instead of Paul teaching the Gospel message, he found himself in the middle of a heated debate. Every time he shared truth from God's Word, someone would stand up and contradict what he said. People stood up and began to bad-mouth Paul and Barnabas; blasphemous lies were suddenly told about them. It was like there was a smear campaign happening in the middle of a weekly worship service in the synagogue.

What was the cause of this? Envy. Envy is very dangerous. It was envy that caused the Jewish religious leaders to hand Jesus over to Pilate. It was envy that caused the Jewish people in Jerusalem to turn against the preaching of the apostles in Acts 5:17. Now we see envy causing these Jewish men to refuse to accept the truth of God's Word and turn against Paul and Barnabas with such great anger and hostility. Remain humble and don't allow any room in yourself for envy.

October 9

"You shall march around the city, all the men of war going around the city once. Thus shall you do for six days. Seven priests shall bear seven trumpets of rams' horns before the ark. On the seventh day you shall march around the city seven times, and the priests shall blow the trumpets. And when they make a long blast with the ram's horn, when you hear the sound of the trumpet, then all the people shall shout with a great shout, and the wall of the city will fall down flat, and the people shall go up, everyone straight before him."
Joshua 6:3-5

Israel has wandered around the desert for forty years and has just seen the promise fulfilled regarding their entering the Promised Land. Can you imagine the relief and excitement to see God's promise to them being fulfilled, and they got to experience it. This was something they would be telling their children and grandchildren about the rest of their lives. What an exciting time to be alive.

How quickly that changed when the first city they came to in the Promised Land is Jericho. It was a walled city; completely fortified and seemingly impossible to defeat. How quickly their excitement changed to frustration, disappointment, depression and even feelings of defeat. Why did God bring them all this way to be stopped? He didn't!

In Joshua 5:13-15 God comes and speaks to Joshua, the leader of Israel. God visits with Joshua to give him the game plan, or instructions, for victory. God did not lead them all this way to be defeated. God cared for them so much that He personally came and delivered the plans they needed for victory. God came to give them assurance of their victory so they would not live in defeat or depression.

Joshua 6 gives us God's instructions to Israel; march around the city once a day for six days and seven times on the seventh day. This is a very strange military strategy. In fact, it doesn't even appear to make any sense. I'm sure God meant to show them the latest and most current Canaanite methods of scaling walls or finding breaches in a walled city to allow Israelite soldiers to penetrate the city and after cunning fighting to defeat the people of Jericho. That is how the world would operate. But God does not operate on the worldly system.

The plan God gave Joshua was guaranteed victory, all Joshua and all of Israel had to do was obey. That is how God operates. He gives us directions on what to do and we need to be obedient to Him. God's plans do not follow our way of thinking always, which is where faith comes in. Just like Joshua we need faith to follow God's Word. "And without faith it is impossible to please Him, for whoever would draw near to God must believe that He exists and that He rewards those who seek Him" (Hebrews 11:6). Seek God, spend time with Him daily and He will lead you and give you the instructions you need for victory.

You might find yourself in a place today that doesn't make sense to you, and possibly is contrary to worldly thought. Relax, it's alright. Remember, God doesn't follow the system or ways of the world. The race is not won by the swift, the battle doesn't belong to the strong and we will not win the battle by our strength. We must remember that the battle belongs to the Lord, and in Him we will be victorious. "Not by might, nor by power, but by My Spirit, says the LORD of hosts" (Zechariah 4:6). Follow God in faith, seek Him diligently and trust Him. When we find obstacles looming in front of us, do not live in fear, depression or feel defeated. Seek God, find counsel in His Word and allow Him to lead you. God is faithful and when we follow His ways, we are victorious.

October 10

"...do not be anxious about anything, but in everything by prayer and supplication with thanksgiving let your requests be made known to God."
Philippians 4:6

Paul says we're not to "worry about anything." Notice, this isn't a suggestion; it's a command. Worry means "to strangle," or "to pull in different directions." Paul is saying that there is absolutely nothing in this world that should strangle us or pull us in different directions. Why? Because we have help with all problems.

Whatever problem we have or face, we have help. We can bring that problem to God through prayer. What can we bring to God? Everything! This means that there is nothing to small, and neither is there anything too big for God. He wants to hear about it; and He wants to hear it from us, from our mouth. He wants to hear about the "little things" that you deal with on a daily basis, along with the really "big things" that can alter and change your life. Bring them all to God.

If there is a situation in your life that is strangling you (like struggling to find toilet paper or groceries), Paul isn't saying just pray and then "Don't worry, be happy." No! We don't ignore our problems or concerns, just smile and act like they're not there. Prayer is doing something. It is active. It is getting involved. Prayer is not our last resort; nothing else has worked so I guess I should pray to God. No! Prayer is our front-line defense. Pray immediately and pray always. Prayer is our first option.

Pray and "let your requests be made known to God." Yes, it is true that God already knows our requests, but He wants to hear them from you. God will wait to answer the requests until He hears it from you, so let Him know.

So, am I saying that every time we pray about our problems to God that He is going to fix them, so we don't have to worry about or deal with that problem or situation again? No! Then what is the value of praying? Because prayer may not always change the situation and make it better, but prayer will always change us and make us better.

October 11

"Then Moses made Israel set out from the Red Sea, and they went into the wilderness of Shur. They went three days in the wilderness and found no water."
Exodus 15:22

Moses was a man called by God and appointed by God to be the leader of the nation of Israel. But, when Moses led the people, he didn't just go where he thought best. Remember, there was the pillar of cloud that he followed. The Israelites were human just like you and me. They wanted to have a physical person to follow, to see, to listen to, and to follow. So, God used Moses to accomplish these things. Moses was the tool, or instrument, that God used to bring the

Israelites out of bondage in Egypt, through the Red Sea, and now on their journey to the Promised Land.

They didn't follow the typical path of traveling through a major trade route. Instead of that, Moses led them out into the wilderness, away from the major trade routes. This led to some difficulties for the Israelites. After three days of walking through the wilderness they couldn't find any water. This is the desert, so this can become a problem. Now, don't think that this means they had no water at all. They had water, but by not finding any more water in the desert, the amount of water they had was limited, and they weren't able to replenish their supplies. One day in the wilderness without additional water would be tolerable. Two days would be difficult, but doable. Now, after three days, they would be running out of water for themselves and their animals. The people would be getting a bit antsy about finding more water. Why would God allow this to happen?

God allowed this to happen because he was testing His people. God knew the condition of their hearts, but the Israelites didn't know their own hearts. People often think that they know the condition of their hearts, and I am sure this described the Israelites, but it is always worse than we think. That is why God reminds us that "heart is deceitful above all things, and desperately sick; who can understand it?" (Jeremiah 17:9). So, God allowed their hearts to be tested in order for them to grow. The Israelites wanted the same things that most people want today: an easy life. Instead of an easy life, we need to be praying that God would make us stronger men and women. Instead of praying for challenges that are equal to our abilities, we should be praying for abilities that will match, or exceed, our challenges.

October 12

"He who plants and he who waters are one, and each will receive his wages according to his labor."

Paul Verhoeven

1 Corinthians 3:8

There is no reason for competition between fellow workers. We are all on the same team and need to be working towards the same goal. As believers we are partners together in building the kingdom of God. In 1 Corinthians 12:12-27 Paul describes the church and how it is made up of many different parts. Each part is different than the other, but none can survive on their own. Each part is dependent upon each other to sustain life and to be productive in living and work. To be effective, we need to work together. If not, we end up fighting each other and working towards different goals, and a body is not created to go in more than one direction at a time. When that happens there is pain involved because the body is being pulled in directions it was not meant to. That pain will equal dissatisfaction and unhappiness within the body. Alan Redpath describes the results of disunity in the body. He said, "There is always grace given to us for any service which we undertake in His will, and I somehow think that the reason for so much unhappiness in Christian work is that many Christians spend much of their time envying the gifts of other people and the sphere of service allotted to them instead of happily serving the Lord in the task to which they themselves are called." We need to work together in the work we are called to.

Also notice, we are not all called to do the same work. The end of the verse tells us "each will receive his wages according to his labor." We all have a particular job that God has called us to, and we need to make sure that we do that job. When we do God will reward us for being obedient to His calling on our life. We are not all called to water, or all to plant seeds. Nothing would be accomplished if we all did the same thing. Instead, we need to do what God is calling us to do, and when we do, we will receive rewards for being faithful. Our rewards are based according to our labor, not upon accomplishments. Too often we try to mimic the world and see how many notches we can put on our belt to keep track of our successes. While these are gratifying to see, they are not what God is basing His rewards on.

God wants us to be faithful to His calling. Remember God is not looking for those with abilities, but those who are available. He wants people available to work for Him. The labor spoken of here refers to toil, or difficult work. It can be associated with pain and difficulty. It is not an easy life.

Lord, may we remain faithful and obedient to You and everything that You have called us to do.

October 13

"And Pharaoh said to Joseph, 'I have had a dream, and there is no one who can interpret it. I have heard it said of you that when you hear a dream you can interpret it.'"
Genesis 41:15

If you are like most people, you like to be recognized for the things that you do. Each person has something that they are good at, and recognition for that gift or ability is reassuring. In fact, many people place lots of effort and energy into making sure that they are recognized for their gifts and abilities. This has given rise to the many programs out there that are designed to make a person instantly famous. Why do people want this? They crave the recognition and rewards that come when others recognize their gifts. It is the very rare individual that is content to practice their gifts in anonymity.

In the Old Testament, Joseph shows us that he is one of those rare individuals, and a great example for us to learn from. Joseph had just spent the past few years being hidden in jail, but while there he continued to serve God by using his gifts and abilities to bring glory and honor to God. Very few people saw Joseph exercising his gifts or even knew about him. This didn't stop him from exercising his gifts. What gifts did he have? God had given him the ability to understand and interpret dreams. Every dream that had been told to Joseph, God had given him the meaning behind that dream, and they had all come true. Two people had witnessed this before, Pharaoh's chief butler and his chief baker. The chief baker was dead, but the chief butler was back serving in Pharaoh's court for the past two years. Pharaoh quickly sent for Joseph hoping that he would be able to interpret his dream, because no one else had.

Joseph is finally released from prison, brought before Pharaoh, and Pharaoh gives high praises to Joseph for his gifts and abilities. Most people would crave this praise and attention, and even begin to gloat a little. Joseph isn't most people. Instead of gloating, he deflects the praise away from himself and directs it back to God. Joseph is in a very unique position here, he has the power to negotiate with Pharaoh for anything he desires, but he refuses to do that. He has a unique ability, one that is in high demand, but Joseph doesn't take advantage of that. No! Instead, he makes sure that God is praised and glorified instead. What a humble man. We can learn much from him. Instead of making sure that we are praised by others or have the chance to negotiate the best deals for ourselves, we also need to make sure that God is glorified and receives all the praise and glory.

October 14

"And the man in whom was the evil spirit leaped on them, mastered all of them and overpowered them, so that they fled out of that house naked and wounded."
Acts 19:16

The seven sons of Sceva had no relationship with Jesus, which means they didn't have the power of the Holy Spirit. That means they had no power over the evil spirit, so the man that was possessed began to whup on these seven men. The whupping was so severe that the seven men ran out of the house to get away from the beating, and they ran away naked and wounded.

Why is this incident included in Scripture? Is it because it gives us a pretty funny scenario to look at? No! It is a reminder to us that we don't take the reality of spiritual warfare lightly. Don't attempt to get involved in spiritual battle with your own strengths and abilities. You will receive the same results as the seven sons of Sceva did.

It is also a reminder for us to be ourselves. All too often people witness a person that God is using and begin to model themselves after that person. They begin to imitate that person, talking like them, using the same "phrases" they use, etc. Don't do that. Be yourself. If you want to be used in ministry like that other person is being used, then seek the Lord. Spend time with God. Allow the Holy Spirit to fill you and to overflow through your life. God desires to use you, not you imitating someone else. You have unique and special gifts and abilities that God can, and desires to, use. Surrender yourself to God and He will use you.

What the seven sons of Sceva did was wrong, but we do need to commend them for being willing to confront evil in the name of Jesus. They didn't just stand by and watch a person be destroyed by evil; they got involved and attempted to heal the person. They also didn't "whitewash" the problem by calling it something else. They were willing to confront evil and get involved. How many of us are willing to do that? Christians need to be willing to step out of their comfort zones so they can help those around them that are imprisoned by evil and remain in bondage and slavery to evil. They need Jesus, because only He can heal them and to set them free.

October 15

"This Book of the Law shall not depart from your mouth, but you shall meditate in it day and night, that you may observe to do according to all that is written in it. For then you will make your way prosperous, and then you will have good success."
Joshua 1:8

In this verse God gives us His key to living a successful life. Unlike the world, this does not mean that we will be in positions of power or have lots of money. Those are worldly definitions, but not God's. God's definition is centered around His Word, the Bible.

God says that His Word needs to be what comes out of our mouth, and also what we spend our time thinking about. This means we are to meditate, dwell on, or ponder on what we are daily reading in the Bible. The Hebrew word for meditate is the same word used to describe a cow chewing its cud. A cow chews its food for a while, lets it rest and then brings it up and chews on it some more. This is done over and over again until all the nutrients are chewed out of the food. This is the same process we are to use with the Bible. We are not to just read the Bible and forget what we read. "All Scripture is given by inspiration of God, and is profitable for doctrine, for reproof, for correction, for instruction in righteousness, that the man of God may be complete, thoroughly equipped for every good work" (2 Timothy 3:16-17). In other words, the Bible has answers for everything we will face in life. It will show us what's right, what's not right, how to get right, and how to stay right. The Bible contains everything we need for a successful life.

The next key to a successful life is to obey God's Word. We need to be doers of the Word, not just filled with head knowledge of what the Bible says. God's Word is simple, but it is not easy. All too often we give up and stop doing what God has called us to do because it becomes difficult or is not what we expected it to be. Unfortunately, God has never promised us an easy life. There will be difficulties and trials in our life. God allows these times in our life to draw us closer to Him, and to refine us. When we go through difficult times God can change us and make us more like Him. Times of difficulty will remove our fleshly nature from us and replace it with God's character. Difficult times are not fun, but they are necessary for growth and refinement. As we grow in the Lord and look back at our life, we see how God used tough times to grow us. No matter how small or difficult the task is that God has called you to, respond faithfully and with bravery; be the best you can.

Where has God called you to be today? It might not be as glamorous as you have desired or imagined, but it is where God has called you to be. There is a reason and purpose for it, even though you might not be able to see it right now. Don't get down because your calling is ordinary or not glamorous but continue to obediently follow God. Wherever you find yourself right now, God will use it to prepare you for the high and holy work that He has created you for. Before we can ascend to greatness we have to descend. There will be suffering before we can reign. God's will is fulfilled in us in the ordinary as much as it is in extraordinary events. Continue to follow God, trust Him and obey Him. He will be with you through difficult times, and He will bring success to those who do not give up and quit. "Trust in the LORD with all your heart and lean not on your own understanding; in all your ways acknowledge Him, and He shall direct your paths" (Proverbs 3:5-6).

October 16

"This calls for a mind with wisdom: the seven heads are seven mountains on which the woman is seated; they are also seven kings, five of whom have fallen, one is, the other has not yet come, and when he does come he must remain only a little while."
Revelation 17:9-10

The angel here is encouraging the apostle John, and his readers, that those with wisdom will listen carefully to what is shared. This introduction reminds us that what follows is a difficult and complex section of this vision. Often after this section is read this section is often associated with Rome and the Papacy. The reason for this is because Rome is well known as the city on seven hills, and the angel here refers to the seven heads being seven mountains. This has led many to claim that the antichrist's false religion is built upon the Roman Catholic Church. There is a problem with this teaching, the original word says mountains, not hills. It is more accurate to see these seven mountains representing seven different kings, or rulers, as verse 10 clearly states. This in no way absolves the Roman Catholic Church of being a part of antichrist's false religious system, as I am sure it will be involved, but this false religious system is larger than Roman Catholicism.

We are told that five of the kings have fallen, one is, and one I yet to come; when he does come, he will be here for only a short period of time. What does this mean? When the apostle John wrote this, five different world empires had already fallen: Egypt, Assyria, Babylon, Medo-Persia, and Greece. One world kingdom was still ruling, which obviously was Rome. The kingdom that is yet to come is antichrist's final world kingdom. When the antichrist does rule it will be for only a short period of time. The antichrist's kingdom will not last long, but it will rule for a short period of time. In Revelation 17:11 we are reminded of the purpose of his kingdom, which will lead to destruction. God has told us what is going to happen later in history, so when it does happen exactly as He said it will, we can be assured that God is in control. He knows exactly what is going to happen. For God, the future is as clear as history.

October 17

"...his sons, and his sons' sons with him, his daughters, and his sons' daughters. All his offspring he brought with him into Egypt.'"
Genesis 46:7

Here in Genesis 46:7 we are given some great information: all the people that Jacob brought with him from the Promised Land to Egypt. These are the people that God used to create the nation of Israel. Notice that Jacob brought his sons, his daughters, his grandsons, and his granddaughters. He brought everyone in his family. No one was left behind. Each of these people were brought with him because God used them to accomplish His purposes and plans. It is simple to understand why God used Joseph. Every once in a while, a person comes along who is very special, and Joseph was special indeed. But God also used Jacob and Judah, and every other person in this family. Go back and read through the book of Genesis and you will see that these men made some serious mistakes. In other words, they are just like you and me. Despite them not being perfect, God used them. God still uses imperfect people. People like you and me. We don't want to focus on the sad and sordid details of our failures but find comfort in the realization that God will use you, no matter what is in your past.

There is a second truth contained in this verse about families. No one was left behind. Some people may think they are the "black sheep" of a family, but they are still part of that family. Jacob brought every single member of his family with him on this journey to Egypt. Here he shows the heart of God in his actions. God desires to see entire families saved. God rejoices when an individual surrenders their heart to Him, but His desire is for entire families to be saved. The apostle Paul shared this with the Philippian jailer when he said, "Believe in the Lord Jesus, and you will be saved, you and your household" (Acts 16:31). Now, when a person is saved it does not mean that every other member in their family is automatically saved. But it does mean that if that person is obedient to God that they can know God is going to work in the lives of their family members. I personally expect that I will one day see my children in Heaven with me, sitting in the presence of God for all eternity. Should He tarry and I receive grandchildren someday, I have the confidence that they too will join me in Heaven. This is the heart of God; to see families saved and serving Him.

October 18

"Therefore, preparing your minds for action, and being sober-minded..."
1 Peter 1:13a

Peter has been informing his readers how the Holy Spirit inspired the prophets of the Old Testament to prophecy about the Messiah so that His coming and His ministry wouldn't be a surprise to people. Even though the coming and works of the Messiah had been prophesied, people weren't prepared and missed His coming. Just as God prophesied about the coming of the Messiah, He has also prophesied much about the Second Coming of the Messiah, which is why Peter gives us some words of warning. Peter tells us that we need to have our minds prepared for action. What does this mean? Some translations of the Bible translate this as being "sober." A more common phrase today would be to "roll up your sleeves." Peter is calling us to be calm, steady, to be in control. This is especially true when it comes to the subject of Jesus' return. Some people wholly give themselves over to study of prophecy and end times events, neglecting the rest of Scripture. There needs to be a balance. We need to have controlled and disciplined study of God's Word, not just focusing on one aspect. What happens if we have an undisciplined study of God's Word? We lose our spiritual balance and won't be prepared for attacks and battles with the enemy. A little later on Peter is going to remind us of the importance of remaining sober, in control, because our "adversary the devil prowls around like a roaring lion, seeking someone to devour" (1 Peter 5:8).

How do we live soberly, or in control? The key to this is being disciplined, not living out of control or by feelings. We must guard our minds and watch what we allow our minds to focus on and dwell on. Every one of us has bad thoughts that enter our minds. That's going to happen, but we don't have to focus on or dwell on those thoughts. Turn them over to Jesus and allow Him to remove them from our minds. Change what it is that we focus on. Instead of focusing on the problems surrounding us in this world, center your thoughts on what Jesus has done for you, and the fact that He is going to come back for you, His child, and bring you to Heaven to the home He has prepared for you (see John 14:1-3). When our minds are focused on Jesus, many of the worldly thoughts to weigh us down will be removed and will stop hindering our spiritual growth and progress. It is important for us to remember that we are in a spiritual battle. Soldiers, when they are on duty, don't sit around daydreaming or worrying about things somewhere else. No! They are focused on what is going on around them. They are like how the Israelites were instructed to eat Passover. In haste, and ready to move out in a moment's notice (see Exodus 12:11). This is how we, as believers, are called to live today. Ready, prepared, and disciplined.

October 19

"And Ezra opened the book in the sight of all the people, for he was above all the people, and as he opened it all the people stood."
Nehemiah 8:5

One of the most often given reasons for not going to church is that the church services are too long. It takes up too much of a person's time, so they are no longer willing to go to church. This was not the case here in Nehemiah, as this church service lasted for around 6 hours (see Nehemiah 8:3). Even though this service lasted for six hours, there were no people nodding off and falling asleep or complaining that the service was going to long (now there would be a long line at the restaurant for lunch), nor did they complain that they would miss their afternoon tee time or miss the kickoff because church went too long. Instead of doing any of these typical reactions we see here in

America in the 21st century, these people instead stood when Ezra read the Word, and remained standing the entire six hours.

What made it so these people were willing, and able, to remain standing in one service for six hours listening to Ezra read God's Word? It is because they had a hunger for God's Word. This is the beginning of every spiritual revival that has ever happened. A hunger for God's Word. Ezra wasn't a captivating speaker that had his listeners hanging on his every word, and neither was he up there sharing his opinions to his followers. What Ezra spoke was simply God's Word, and this is what the people hungered for. They knew that it was through God's Word that they would get to know God. The prophet Jeremiah wrote this to them before they became captives in Babylon. Through Jeremiah God told the people "You will seek Me and find Me, when you seek Me with all your heart. I will be found by you, declares the LORD, and I will restore your fortunes and gather you from all the nations and all the places where I have driven you, declares the LORD, and I will bring you back to the place from which I sent you into exile" (Jeremiah 29:13-14). God was faithful to keep His Word, and now the people have a hunger to seek God so they will know Him. This is still true today. Seek God and He will be found. Have a hunger for His Word.

October 20

"And let steadfastness have its full effect, that you may be perfect and complete, lacking in nothing."
James 1:4

There is a saying that is popular today: "I may grow old, but I refuse to grow up." The sentiment behind this saying is that that person really doesn't want to adult today; they would rather go back to a time when they had fewer responsibilities. We all understand that. We've all been there. Life is difficult, and growing older requires us to constantly change and deal with things we didn't have to deal with before. It's understandable that we would like to go back to when things were simpler and easier. But that's part of growing up and becoming mature. The problem is when people do get older, they fail to mature. It's one thing for a four-year old to act like a four-year old, but when a forty-year-old acts the same way, it's not pretty.

If you asked people what their goal is for their life, what would they like to see their life be like, many people would respond that they would like to have a life without any pain. That wounds wonderful, doesn't it? But it's not real, and it will never happen. Also, that's not God's goal for our lives. It's not that God wants to see us dealing with pain, but those struggles that cause us pain, also cause us to grow and mature. You see, that is God's goal for you and me, that we grow to become mature and complete. That is why God allows us to deal with trials and troubles. They are opportunities for us to grow.

This is why it is so important for us to learn patience. Immature people are always impatient, but mature people learn how to be patient. I will admit that it isn't easy to remain patient while going through a difficult time. But the apostle Paul made a great promise to those who are patient during those times. "And we desire each one of you to show the same earnestness to have the full assurance of hope until the end, [12] so that you may not be sluggish, but imitators of those who through faith and patience inherit the promises" (Hebrews 6:11-12). Patience during trials and times of difficulty will cause us to become mature and complete. The Bible provides us with plenty of examples of those that didn't patiently wait for God, and the troubles that it brought them. God promised Abraham a son, but after twelve years he got tired of waiting. So, he took another wife and had a son with her (see Genesis 16). Today we still deal with the disastrous results of this. Moses was another one who failed to be patient with God. After God told Moses that he would be used to deliver Israel from Egypt, he acted the first time he saw an injustice being done to an Israelite. He murdered an Egyptian soldier, and this led him to spend the next forty years on the backside of the desert (see Exodus

2:11ff). As we learn to patiently wait for God during the trials we face, we will find ourselves growing spiritually mature, becoming more and more complete.

October 21

"But Noah found favor in the eyes of the LORD."
Genesis 6:8

The word "favor" is most often translated as grace. This is the first mention of grace in the Bible. The Hebrew word is "chen" (khane), and it means favor or grace. What exactly is grace? Grace is receiving what we don't deserve, and it is essential to help us live our everyday lives; so how do we receive grace? James 4:6 tells us, "But He gives more grace. Therefore it says, 'God opposes the proud but gives grace to the humble.'" This is a repeat of what God said through King David in Psalm 138. God gives grace to men and women who are humble, not full of themselves. When we believe that we can accomplish great things through our own intellect and abilities, we are fooling ourselves, because we cannot. We are reminded of this in Zechariah 4:6 when God said, "Not by might, nor by power, but by my Spirit, says the LORD of hosts." We need to realize that, apart from God dwelling in us, there is nothing good in any of us. Because we have nothing good in us, we cannot produce anything good. Only God can produce good, and by His grace He willingly shares with us.

It is important for us to realize that while we can receive grace, we cannot earn it. Grace is not a reward for living a righteous life. "By faith Noah, being warned by God concerning events as yet unseen, in reverent fear constructed an ark for the saving of his household. By this he condemned the world and became an heir of the righteousness that comes by faith" (Hebrews 11:7). God gave grace to Noah because Noah exhibited faith. As Warren Wiersbe put it so well, *"To understand God's truth but not act upon it is not biblical faith; it's only intellectual assent to religious truth. To be emotionally aroused without comprehending God's message isn't faith, because true faith is based on an understanding of the truth (Matthew 13:18-23). To have the mind enlightened and the heart stirred but not act in obedience to the message is not faith, for 'faith without works is dead' (James 2:14-26). The mind, heart, and will are all involved in true biblical faith. Everybody who has ever been saved from sin has been saved by 'grace, through faith.'* " No one has ever been saved through their own efforts, whether it be sacrifices offered, keeping the Law, or by doing great works. Salvation is a gift from God, and this means that it can either be rejected or received by faith. Noah received God's grace by faith, and this is why He found grace in the eyes of God. We also find God's grace when we live a life of faith.

October 22

"Then Samson went down with his father and mother to Timnah, and they came to the vineyards of Timnah. And behold, a young lion came toward him roaring. Then the Spirit of the LORD rushed upon him, and although he had nothing in his hand, he tore the lion in pieces as one tears a young goat. But he did not tell his father or his mother what he had done."
Judges 14:5-6

Samson was dedicated to God as a Nazarite (see Judges 13:4-5). A Nazarite was to avoid anything to do with grapes (including grape juice, wine, alcohol, etc.), touching anything that was dead, and cutting their hair (see Numbers 6:1-21). Since he was to have nothing to do with grapes, why was he traveling through a vineyard? Samson was placing himself in a compromising position. He had too much confidence in himself, and allowed himself to be where he shouldn't have been. He was on the edge of compromise.

While he was in the vineyard he was attacked by a lion, and

God's strength was upon him, and he killed the lion and tore it apart like it was nothing. He knew he shouldn't have been there, which is why he refused to tell his parents what had happened. Have you ever experienced that before? You know what you did was wrong, so you purposefully avoided telling anyone else what you did. When you find yourself in a situation like that, it's best to leave it altogether. Samson should have done that, but he didn't. Learn from his mistakes, don't copy them.

A few weeks later Samson returns to Timnah, and he again goes through the vineyards. It is possible that he is proud of himself for walking amid temptation and not giving in to it. As he is walking through the vineyard, he comes across the carcass of the lion he had killed. Bees had made a hive in the lion carcass, so Samson reaches in and grabs a handful of honey. In doing this he violated his Nazarite vow to never touch anything dead.

Samson was able to kill the lion with his bare hands because the Spirit of the Lord was upon him. Even though he was filled with God's Spirit, he still violated his vow to God. He exercised the free will that God gives us. Having God's Spirit upon you doesn't make you a godlier person, but it does give you the resources to be godlier. People can be wonderfully gifted by the Holy Spirit and yet remain spiritually immature, as Samson shows himself to be. May we learn from Samson and use our free will to be obedient to God.

October 23

"If anyone is to be taken captive, to captivity he goes; if anyone is to be slain with the sword, with the sword must he be slain. Here is a call for the endurance and faith of the saints."

Revelation 13:10

You may have heard the old saying "you reap what you sow." There is a good reason for this saying. It's true! This has been true since the beginning of time, and it will continue until the end of time. It will even remain true during the time of tribulation. Those who come alongside the beast and work to help him accomplish his diabolical plans will have to answer for their work. They will reap what they have sown. By supporting the beast, they will receive punishment for their part in helping him. God has prophesied this, but that doesn't mean people are forced to participate. Each person is given free will. Those helping made a choice, and they are therefore responsible for their choice and will answer for it and receive the fruits of their labor. Those working with the beast will force and lead others into captivity, but they will also become captives themselves. This is why Jesus said, "whatever you wish that others would do to you, do also to them, for this is the Law and the Prophets" (Matthew 7:12).

God prophesied the book of Revelation to the apostle John so that we can be prepared for what is coming. There is another great promise in this for us: these things will pass. These things won't last forever. There will be troubles. There will be persecution. There will be an antichrist. But these things will only be allowed to go on so long. They all will end. Our focus and attention is not to be on these things that won't last. Don't be looking for the antichrist or look to decipher the mark of the beast. God has given us these prophecies to help us understand that life is short, but Heaven is long. We will experience suffering and persecution here on earth. This is why Jesus came to provide us with an example of how to endure during it. Jesus, "When He was reviled, He did not revile in return; when He suffered, He did not threaten, but continued entrusting Himself to Him who judges justly" (1 Peter 2:23). Keep your eyes on Jesus and "be steadfast, immovable, always abounding in the work of the Lord, knowing that in the Lord your labor is not in vain" (1 Corinthians 15:58).

October 24

"Even when they had made for themselves a golden calf and said, 'This is your God who brought you up out of Egypt,' and had committed great blasphemies, You in Your great mercies did not forsake them in the wilderness. The pillar of cloud to lead them in the way did not depart from them by day, nor the pillar of fire by night to light for them the way by which they should go."
Nehemiah 9:18-19

Ask the average person on the street about God and you will often hear that God is an angry God. He is mad at those of us on earth for the way that we live and behave. You had better be good, otherwise He will be angry and come back filled with rage. People often describe God as an angry parent, so you had better be good so that He doesn't come down here and spank us. Are there times when God is angry and displeased with the actions and choices of His people? Yes. Does He punish people for doing wrong? Yes. Does God stomp around angrily, throwing a fit and responding in rage because of what His children are doing? No! Many people do not have a Biblical knowledge or understanding of God. Sadly, it's not just the average person on the street with this misunderstanding, but even many people inside churches that have this misunderstanding. Churches standing outside events telling homosexuals that God hates them, and AIDS is punishment for their sin and other examples like this are incorrect portrayals of God.

Does God punish sin? Yes. But God is not angrily stomping around in a fit of rage looking for the closest person so that He can thrash them. The Israelites rejected God and made an idol for them to worship. Was God angry? Yes! Did He punish them? Yes, three thousand people died that day (see Exodus 32:28). But, after this God still guided them and provided for them. God responded to their unfaithfulness by remaining faithful to them. Why? "If we are faithless, He remains faithful—for He cannot deny Himself" (2 Timothy 2:13). God's nature and character is that He is a God of love, grace and mercy, redemption, loving-kindness, and long-suffering. Does God judge and punish? Of course, He does, but that is not His first response. This is the Biblical concept of God that so many people do not understand, but it is so important for us to know.

October 25

"And Paul said, 'I did not know, brothers, that he was the high priest....'"
Acts 23:5a

The people standing around Paul were shocked that he would respond the way he did to the high priest. Paul says that he wasn't aware it was the high priest that he was talking to. Could it be true that Paul didn't know he was addressing the high priest? Yes! There could be a number of explanations for this:

1. Maybe Ananias wasn't wearing his high priest attire, so Paul didn't recognize him as high priest.
2. Ananias could have been out of Paul's line of sight, so Paul didn't know exactly who he was speaking to.
3. Paul had been gone from Jerusalem and the Sanhedrin for a number of years now so it is possible Paul didn't realize Ananias was now the high priest.
4. It is believed that Paul had very poor eyesight, so it is possible he wasn't able to clearly see who he was speaking to.
5. It is possible that Paul was speaking sarcastically, saying that he didn't realize a high priest could act the way he did.

There are some that believe Paul was excused for responding the way that he did since he was unaware of who he was speaking to. But ignorance is no excuse. You see, all the time we come across people that we really don't know as well as we think we do. Don't make the mistake of believing it is ok to "lash out" at someone because of what you think they are, or because of what you don't know about them. That's the whole point of this. We need to be very careful about how we treat others because we don't really know who we are addressing. This is perfectly addressed in a story I read about a German elementary school teacher. Every morning this schoolteacher bowed before the second- and third- grade students that entered his classroom. When asked why he did this, he said, "I don't know which of these students might one day be a king or a chancellor. I want to respect them now because I don't know what they'll become." The reason this story is known is because it was told by one of his more famous students — a man named Albert Einstein.

May we treat others with respect as an example of Jesus to others, not just because they have earned it or deserve it.

October 26

"And when He had said these things, as they were looking on, He was lifted up, and a cloud took Him out of their sight."
Acts 1:9

Jesus had just finished giving final instructions to His disciples, and then Luke 24:50 tells us that Jesus blessed the disciples. As He was doing this Jesus slowly began to rise up towards Heaven as He was surrounded by a cloud. Wow! What a sight this must have been. His resurrection was a miracle, and this was just as much of a miracle, but completely different.

When Jesus resurrected from the grave, it was done in secret. There were no witnesses waiting outside the tomb waiting for Jesus to come back to life. But Jesus' ascension to Heaven was a public event. This was not done in private, but there were witnesses that saw this happen. This difference is very important.

You see, Jesus could have simply "vanished" from sight and returned to Heaven without anyone knowing where He had gone. He chose not to "exit" this way because He wanted the disciples to know that He had gone. If He simply "vanished," they wouldn't know if He was just gone for a while, or if He was going to return shortly. Jesus made sure that the disciples witnessed His return to Heaven so that they knew without a doubt that He had returned to Heaven and would not be "reappearing" any moment; as He had done the past forty days.

In John 16:7 Jesus said to the disciples, "Nevertheless, I tell you the truth: it is to your advantage that I go away, for if I do not go away, the Helper will not come to you. But if I go, I will send Him to you." He had just promised them that the Holy Spirit would be given to them shortly, so now it was time for Him to return to Heaven so that the Holy Spirit could be given to them. The disciples now knew that it was time for Jesus' promise to be fulfilled.

In addition to this, it was also important for Jesus to return to Heaven so that Jesus is now able to be our Advocate before God the Father. Jesus, our great High Priest, intercedes as our Mediator between us and God the Father (see Hebrews 7:25). As our Advocate, He is able to forgive us of our sins. The apostle John wrote about this, when he said, "If we confess our sins, He is faithful and just to forgive us our sins and to cleanse us from all unrighteousness. If we say we have not sinned, we make Him a liar, and His word is not in us. If we confess our sins, He is faithful and just to forgive us our sins and to cleanse us from all unrighteousness. If we say we have not sinned, we make Him a liar, and His word is not in us." (1 John 1:9-2:1). Jesus continues to sit at the right hand of God the Father until it's time for Him to return to earth in His Second Coming.

October 27

"For who has despised the day of small things?" NKJV
Zechariah 4:10a

It is so easy for us to look at what other people are doing, or how God is using someone else and compare ourselves to them. Often when we do that it leads to discouragement, which is one of Satan's most effective tools. In our lives most of what we do can be categorized as "small" things. The things we are involved with in our lives do not appear to us to be "big" things. Martin Lloyd-Jones reminds us that "the small things are, nevertheless, the things of God. Some of God's things are very small, but they are God's; and if you do away with the small things in the world the big things will soon collapse."

God calls every one of us to do certain things and works for Him. He does not necessarily call us to do the same thing someone else is doing. What we are doing may seem small to us, but it is very important. If the seemingly small things are not done, what we perceive to be big things will not be able to be done. The Bible, and history, is full of seemingly small things that God used to accomplish great things. When God began the plan to free Israel from bondage in Egypt, it began with the tears of a baby (see Exodus 2). God used the sling of a small shepherd boy to kill a giant (see 1 Samuel 17). When God fed 5000 men plus women and children, He used some fish and bread from a little boy (see John 6). God is glorified through small things, and He uses them to accomplish great things.

Faithfulness in small things is required before God will use people to do greater things. Not everyone can be a King David. But, before David became king, he was a shepherd boy. During that time David was faithful in sitting on the hill watching and protecting the sheep entrusted to him. He had to go through those boring and monotonous times before God used him to defeat a giant. David was used greatly by God because he proved himself to be faithful no matter what task he was given, great or small.

Do not despise what you think are small things that God is asking you to do. Wait for Him, serve Him, and He will greatly use you, even in small things. Do not become discouraged by comparing yourself to someone else, just be faithful to God.

October 28

"Therefore do not be ashamed of the testimony about our Lord, nor of me His prisoner, but share in suffering for the gospel by the power of God."
2 Timothy 1:8

Because of the power, love, and discipline that God give us, we are not to be ashamed or embarrassed of Him or His servants. Jesus calls us to be like a child, a slave, and to be last instead of first. Some would be ashamed of this, but we shouldn't be. Some were afraid to be associated with Paul. After all he was on death row and an enemy of the state. If you were known as an associate of his, you would be guilty by association and could also come under the scrutiny of the government, and potentially receive the same sentence he was awaiting. 1 Peter 4:16 says, "Yet if anyone suffers as a Christian, let him not be ashamed, but let him glorify God in that name." Jesus promised us in John 15:20 that we would suffer; it is a promise we don't like to be reminded of.

So how do we suffer for the gospel? Romans 12:15, "Rejoice with those who rejoice, weep with those who weep." We cannot do this on our own; but God, Who is always with us, will give us the strength and power to accomplish this task. He does not always remove us from the difficulty, but He will see us through it; just as He is with Paul here.

This reminds me of an event that happened during the Boxer

Rebellion in China in 1899-1900. Extreme nationalist Chinese fomented a campaign of terror against officials of foreign governments, Christian missionaries, and even Chinese Christians. After they surrounded a certain mission station, they sealed all the exits except one. They placed a cross in the dirt in front of the opened gate and told the missionaries and students that anyone who walked out and trampled the cross would be spared. According to reports, the first seven students who departed trampled the cross and were sent on their way. The eighth student, a young girl, approached the cross, knelt down, prayed for strength, carefully walked around the cross, and was immediately shot to death. The remaining students, strengthened by that girl's courageous example, also walked around the cross to their deaths.

October 29

"I call heaven and earth to witness against you today, that I have set before you life and death, blessing and curse. Therefore choose life, that you and your offspring may live, loving the LORD your God, obeying His voice and holding fast to Him, for He is your life..."
Deuteronomy 30:19-20a

Moses was making his farewell speech to the nation of Israel just before they finally entered in and possessed the Promised Land to live in. He reminded them that they were given a choice to make, the same choice that every one of us must make today also. God is so gracious, it isn't a multiple-choice test, but simply one of two choices for us to make. We choose either life or death, blessings, or curses. Which choice will you make?

It is obvious that Moses wants the Israelites to choose life, and he even tells them how they do that, and the benefits of doing so. They choose life by loving God and remaining faithful to Him. Today we are not under the Old Covenant, like the Israelites were, but under an even greater covenant, the New Covenant. A greater covenant comes with both greater blessings, but also greater responsibilities. Before we choose whether we will love God or not, we have another question we must answer. Will we trust Jesus for our standing before God? Jesus stated that the question of trusting Him will determine our eternal standing. Jesus asked the disciples this question, and He is still asking it today, "who do you say that I AM?" (Matthew 16:15).

When we come to the point where we realize and admit that Jesus is God and that His death on the cross paid for our sins so that we have a right standing before God, then we can love Him. So, how do we show that we trust and love God? We follow Jesus' words, and we cling to Him, or remain in Him. "Abide in Me, and I in you. As the branch cannot bear fruit by itself, unless it abides in the vine, neither can you, unless you abide in Me. I am the vine; you are the branches. Whoever abides in Me and I in him, he it is that bears much fruit, for apart from Me you can do nothing" (John 15:4-5). In other words, Jesus isn't just a part of our life, He is our life. We realize that everything we do is because of Him, and for Him. Choose life by living wholly and completely for Jesus.

October 30

"For Christ also suffered once for sins, the righteous for the unrighteous, that He might bring us to God, being put to death in the flesh but made alive in the Spirit..."
1 Peter 3:18

People often ask why the Old Testament practice of animal sacrifice is no longer practiced. The reason for this is because the animal was sacrificed as a reminder of the sins of the people being paid for by the shedding of blood. This is no longer necessary because Jesus died on the cross and paid the penalty for our sin. Animals were continually sacrificed because they were not perfect and couldn't pay for the penalty of sin, therefore sacrifices were made continually. But Jesus is the perfect Lamb of God, He is perfect, and His blood was able to pay the penalty for our sins, so a sacrifice is no longer needed since the perfect sacrifice has been made. Since the debt is paid, no more payments are required. Us trying to pay for our sin through suffering is like sending in a payment for a bill that has already been paid. Since the debt has already been paid, Jesus is not looking for us to suffer, but there is something He is looking for. "Has the LORD as great delight in burnt offerings and sacrifices, as in obeying the voice of the LORD? Behold, to obey is better than sacrifice, and to listen than the fat of rams" (1 Samuel 15:22).

It is interesting to note that Peter here tells us that the Holy Spirit raised Jesus from the dead. When Jesus died on the cross, He died in His physical body, and now Peter tells us the Holy Spirit brought Jesus back to life. The apostle Paul that God the Father raised Jesus from the dead. "We were buried therefore with Him by baptism into death, in order that, just as Christ was raised from the dead by the glory of the Father, we too might walk in newness of life" (Romans 6:4). The apostle John says that Jesus Himself raised Himself from the dead (see John 2:18-22). Which was it? Was it God the Father, Jesus, or the Holy Spirit that raised Jesus from the dead? The answer is YES! Here were see a picture of the Trinity at work. God the Father, Jesus, and the Holy Spirit are One, they work together in unity. Jesus' resurrection from the dead was a work of the Triune God.

October 31

"I am able to do all things through Him who strengthens me."
Philippians 4:13

Sadly, this verse is often taken out of context and is often used to give people a super-Christian, or triumphant, mentality. This verse is not saying that God will help us do "anything" that we desire. I would like to play center in the NBA, but that's not going to happen. No matter how much I try to "psych" myself up and remind myself that "I can do all things through Christ Who strengthens me," I have to face reality; I am too short and too old to play in the NBA. So, if this isn't saying that we are able to achieve anything we want to with God's help, then what does this verse mean?

We need to remember to keep this in context. When it is taken out of context is when it gets misused. The context that Paul is talking about is being content. You see, it is not humanly possible to be content when things are not going well, or how we expect things to be. When we are down and out, in poverty, and/or a bad situation, it is only through God's strength that we are able to be content at that time. This isn't a theoretical practice for Paul, because he is currently chained to a Roman guard 24-hours a day as he awaits trial to see if he will be executed or allowed to remain alive. Paul is practicing what he is preaching.

We must keep this promise connected to John 15:5, where Jesus says, "I am the vine; you are the branches. The one who remains in Me and I in him produces much fruit, because you can do nothing without Me." Jesus is the vine and we are the branches. We can do nothing without Jesus. The purpose of the branch is to bear fruit; if it doesn't bear fruit it gets chopped off and burned. The branch is not able to bear fruit through its own self-effort; it is only able to bear fruit when it is attached to the vine. We can only bear fruit in our lives, and be content in less than stellar situations, when we are attached to Jesus.

The branch draws its life from the vine; it has hidden resources. That is how God designed nature to operate. Great trees are strong because they have sent their roots deep down into the earth where they draw water and minerals. The most important part of the tree is what you can't see; it's roots. It is the same for the Christian. In order for us to stand against the pressures of this world, we must draw upon the deep resources of God. The apostle Paul depended upon the power of God in his life, and that is what allowed him to be content at all times. We also need to draw deeply on God's power if we want to be content at all times. It is possible, because of Jesus.

November 1

"Then the king said to me, 'What are you requesting?' So I prayed to the God of Heaven."
Nehemiah 2:4

King Solomon is known as the wisest man to ever live. One of the thousands of proverbs that he wrote says, "The king's heart is a stream of water in the hand of the LORD; He turns it wherever He will" (Proverbs 21:1). This is one of the reasons why Nehemiah persevered and continued to pray over the past four months; God was preparing the heart of the king. Over these four months while Nehemiah was praying, he continued to serve the king through his job as cupbearer. Now when the time was right, God allowed his emotions to show enough that the king noticed something was bothering Nehemiah. As a cupbearer this was not good. Why was Nehemiah down? Was it something he drank? Had he uncovered a plot to kill the king? Being sad in the presence of the king could be a literal death sentence for Nehemiah. But it wasn't because God was answering his prayers and had things prepared, including the heart of the king.

God uses this time of waiting. It is not wasted. During this time Nehemiah had his purpose and intent refined, and he found that he was strengthened by God. This prophet Isaiah reminds us about this when he wrote, "He gives power to the faint, and to him who has no might He increases strength. Even youths shall faint and be weary, and young men shall fall exhausted; but they who wait for the LORD shall renew their strength; they shall mount up with wings like eagles; they shall run and not be weary; they shall walk and not faint" (Isaiah 40:29-31)

The King asked Nehemiah what he needed to help restore Jerusalem. Finally, after four months of praying the time was here. What was Nehemiah's first response? Did he immediately begin to spout out a list of things that he would need? No! His response shows us how close his relationship with God was, and how he depended upon God. He immediately prayed to God for wisdom on what to say and how to answer this question. Now think about that. Do you think he stopped, closed his eyes, folded his hands, and took a few minutes to pray? Absolutely not! I believe this is probably the shortest prayer in the Bible. In fact, it was probably a one-word prayer: HELP! This is important for us to remember. Prayer is simply talking to God. There are times for us to spend long times in prayer using many words. But that isn't always necessary. God hears His children, even when they offer up one-word prayers. Cry out to God. Live life with a complete devotion to God and lean upon Him for all things, just like Nehemiah did.

November 2

"The Lord said to him, 'What is that in your hand?' He said, 'A staff.'
Exodus 4:2

God gives Moses a sign to show that he is the one God is calling to lead Israel out of their slavery, and it also provides us with a principle of how God uses ordinary people to fulfill and accomplish His plans. God asks Moses what is in his hand? In other words, God takes whatever you currently do, what you have been trained in, and uses that to accomplish His purposes. Moses was a shepherd, so his hand held a rod, or a staff. This had been in his hands for the past forty years, which means that his years tending sheep in the desert hadn't been a waste of time. God didn't use the royal scepter that was in Moses' hands when he was a prince in Egypt, but He will use a simple shepherd's staff.

Moses isn't the only person that God has used what was in their hand in order to fulfill God's plans and purposes. Moses had a staff in his hand, and God used it. Shamgar had an ox goad in his hand (see Judges 3:31), and God used it in his hands to kill six hundred men and bring Israel to freedom. Samson held the jawbone of a donkey in his hand, and God used it to have Samson kill one thousand Philistines (see Judges 15:15). David had a sling in his hand, and God used it to defeat Goliath and help Israel route the Philistines who ruled over Israel (see 1 Samuel 17:49). A young boy had five little loaves of bread and 2 dried fish in his hands, and God used those to feed five thousand men, plus all the women and children that were there (see John 6:9).

How can you be used by God? Take a look at what is in your hand? God created you with certain talents, gifts, and abilities, plus you have been trained throughout your life to develop certain skills in the workplace. With what is in your hand right now God can use it in order to bless others, serve others, and to accomplish God's will and purpose. This is true no matter what is in your hand. It could be a computer, a horse bridle, a wrench, a hammer, a blood pressure cuff, a welder, a telephone, etc. God can use what is in your hand for His glory.

November 3

"And another angel, a third, followed them, saying with a loud voice, 'If anyone worships the beast and its image and receives a mark on his forehead or on his hand, he also will drink the wine of God's wrath, poured full strength into the cup of his anger.'"
Revelation 14:9-10a

Parents have the responsibility to teach their children that for every choice that is made there is a consequence. The consequences will not always match the choice that is made, but generally it will. When you make a good choice there will generally be a good consequence that follows, and when a bad choice is made you can expect a bad consequence to follow. That is seen here with these angels as they come to earth. The first angel came preaching the gospel of Jesus, which most people on earth rejected. The consequence of this choice was the second angel, who announces coming judgment to the earth. This also has a consequence, and we see this third angel coming to earth with the promised judgment, or wrath of God. This is a logical sequence of actions.

Since most people on earth have rejected the gospel, they will offer their worship to the beast. Included in this worship will be receiving the mark of the beast either on their forehead or the back of their right hand. Receiving this mark will not happen as an accident, but it will be a conscious choice that each person makes, knowing and realizing that by doing this they are showing their worship and allegiance to the beast. Many that make this choice may not realize the seriousness of it, but they will know what they are doing. It may seem like nothing more than an innocent civic pledge that will allow them to continue to live and be a part of society, but the consequences of this choice will bring dire results.

Every single person who accepts this mark of the beast will deal with the consequences of their choice, which is to "drink the wine of God's wrath." God's wrath will be poured out upon them in full strength, and here is the scariest part about this, it will last for all eternity. The saddest thing about this is that it is completely avoidable. No one is forced, or even destined, to receive God's wrath. God does not want that "any should perish, but that all should reach repentance" (2 Peter 3:9).

November 4

"When Ahab saw Elijah, Ahab said to him, 'Is it you, you troubler of Israel?' And he answered, 'I have not troubled Israel, but you have, and your father's house, because you have abandoned the commandments of the LORD and followed the Baals.'"
1 Kings 18:17-18

The reaction of Ahab to Elijah is a common occurrence today. Instead of accepting responsibility for the choices we make, instead we place the blame on others. Ahab made the decision to worship Baal and to ignore God, setting up places of worship for Baal and other false gods, and encouraged the people of Israel to forsake God and follow false gods. God, in His grace, sent Elijah to Ahab to announce the results of these poor choices, which was no rain upon the ground for 3½ years. Ahab then found it much easier to blame Elijah for the troubles Israel was in instead of looking for the true cause of the problems, which was himself and the choices he had made.

The United States government made a conscious choice in the 60's to kick God out of schools and have ever since worked diligently to keep God out of every public place. Our government continues to legislate laws that violate and contradict God's Word and legalize unrighteous behaviors. Then, when problems arise in society, the blame is placed on those so-called narrow-minded and intolerant religious fanatics. The government and media say we resist "scientific" advances, especially involving evolution. But the truth is that we are not the source of the problems. Our nation as a whole and especially our government and media, have rejected God and attempted to remove Him from all aspects of public life, which is the cause of the problems.

We also need to be careful in our own individual lives. When we experience difficult times in our life, do not be quick to blame God, our spouse, children, boss at work, co-workers, neighbors, or claim that we are just suffering persecution for being a Christian. The first thing we need to do is to examine our own life and make sure this is not a result of sin in our own life. Examining ourselves can be a very painful endeavor. "Search me, O God, and know my heart! Try me and know my thoughts! And see if there be any grievous way in me, and lead me in the way everlasting!" (Psalm 139:23-24). As Christians God has called us to be set apart, or different than the rest of society. Part of that is not blaming others for our problems. We need to accept responsibility for the choices we have made.

November 5

"And there arose a sharp disagreement, so that they separated from each other. Barnabas took Mark with him and sailed away to Cyprus."
Acts 15:39

Both Paul and Barnabas were correct in their choices about whether to bring John Mark along with them or not, but each of them was also wrong. Their disagreement is so sharp that they both decide to move on, to separate from the other. Here is a perfect example for us that God uses flawed people. Neither Paul nor Barnabas is perfect. Neither of them is willing to concede or work together. They remain firm in their convictions, and it drives them apart. This is why Pastor Chuck Smith used to say, "Blessed are the flexible, for they are not easily broken." We don't want to become so rigid in our ways of doing things that we refuse to work with others unless they do everything the way we want it done. Neither man was willing to concede one point to the other; they both contributed to this break-up.

Working with other people can be very messy. Relationships are that way. We all will have problems with someone else at one time or another. It is important for us to remember what Jesus said about how to deal with relational problems: "if you are offering your gift at the altar and there remember that your brother has something against you, leave your gift there before the altar and go. First be reconciled to your brother, and then come and offer your gift" (Matthew 5:23-24). Conflicts with others must be resolved for us to correctly and effectively worship and serve God. Failure to resolve a conflict will hamper our relationship and service to God. It's not necessarily about who's right and who's wrong. It's about restoring a relationship. After all, Christianity is all about relationships, especially ours with Jesus.

After this division Paul and Barnabas each started their own missionary teams and went in different directions. This has caused many people to say that God used this division to double the missionary work. It is true that God used it despite their division, but that's only because God can turn evil into good. Just because God brings good out of something evil, that doesn't make the evil right. Both Paul and Barnabas were still accountable to God for their actions, including their refusal to work together. Let us learn from their mistakes and do everything we can within our powers to restore our relationship with others.

November 6

"I also persevered in the work on this wall, and we acquired no land, and all my servants were gathered there for the work."
Nehemiah 5:16

Being a leader requires a person to a different set of standards. Nehemiah has confronted the nobles and officials of Jerusalem for taking advantage of their fellow Jews that were in dire straits. These leaders and officials loaned money at high interest rates so the people could purchase food and pay their taxes. In contrast to them Nehemiah was purchasing food for people and helping to pay their taxes with his own money. As a government official he could have received a food allowance, but he refused to do so. The reason he lived the way he did was because he was a leader, and through his life he was setting the tone for how people needed to live their lives. Nehemiah refused to follow the crowd and do what previous people in his position had done. There is a problem with following the crowd, crowds change. What the crowd wants one day will change in a few days. Think back to when Jesus rode into Jerusalem on the back of a donkey, the people cried out that He was their Messiah, but a few days later that same crowd was crying for Him to be crucified. Instead of following the crowd, Nehemiah built his life on God's Word, which doesn't change.

Nehemiah understood the importance as a leader of living his life above reproach. By living this way, he never gave the devil, or the enemy, an opportunity to find fault with him. For example, when Nehemiah arrived in Jerusalem there were very few people living inside the city because it was not a desirable place to live. Since this was not a desirable place to be, the land could be purchased for a very low price. Nehemiah also knew the God had led him there to lead the effort in rebuilding the wall around the city. When this was finished many people would move back into the city and the value of the land would greatly increase as people moved back into the city. With this "insider information" Nehemiah could have made lots of money by purchasing land when he first got there and then reselling that same land after the wall was rebuilt. He didn't do this because as a leader, his concern was for the welfare and safety of the people of Jerusalem, not to grow his bank account at their expense. A leader looks out for the well-being of their people and not just what will benefit themselves.

November 7

"A little leaven leavens the whole lump."
Galatians 5:9

Not many people bake bread any longer, so the picture of leaven is often not understood. Leaven is a substance, like yeast, that produces gases in the dough causing it to rise. You only need a small amount of yeast to cause a whole batch of dough to rise. A little bit goes a long way.

Often times leaven is likened in the Bible to sin. Sin works on the same principle as leaven. You don't need much of it to affect a whole lot. It is amazing to see how much damage can be caused by a small amount of sin. Many of us know this to be true, but we foolishly think that we also can be the one exception to the rule. If you are like me you know things in your life that are sin, but refuse to get rid of them. Sin is like leaven, because if it is allowed to remain it will infect everything that it touches. The only way to stop this is to remove it completely. "Do you not know that a little leaven leavens the whole lump? Cleanse out the old leaven that you may be a new lump" (1 Corinthians 5:6b-7a).

The apostle Paul is saying that we must remove sin from our life completely. There are those websites that you look at when no one else is around. That is sin. Stop it; get that out of your life because it will affect your whole life. Those trashy romance novels, TV shows and movies filled with sexual innuendos and immorality, books filled with foul language, friends that draw you away from the Lord. These are all sins that if not taken care of properly will affect and damage our whole life. This is not easy, but it is necessary. Sometimes it will really hurt. It can cause friendships to end. But it is better to lose a relationship that draws you away from the Lord than to allow sin to remain in your life. I have had to counsel people to do this in their life. Too often I have seen young people hang out and spend all their time with people who continually bring out the worst in them and encourage them to participate in sin. No matter how much you like that person, you are better off not hanging out with them. Remove that leaven from your life before it affects your whole life; cut it out completely.

I heard a story once about a dad who was being badgered by his children to go see a movie that he wouldn't allow them to go to. He pointed out that there was foul language, sexual innuendos and it promoted lifestyles that weren't pleasing to God. In desperation the children said, "But dad, it's only a little foul language and sexual immorality. It's not that bad; it won't hurt anyone." The father persisted and did not let the children go, and they remained mad at him. Later that night the dad brought out a tray of brownies from the kitchen. He told his kids he loved them very much and decided to bake these brownies for them to show them his love. Before they were able to bite into them, he gave them a warning, "while making these brownies I went into the backyard a grabbed a little dog poo and put it into the batter. But don't worry; it's just a little bit so it won't hurt anyone." Immediately the children dropped the brownies without taking a bite. He got his point across. Even though it's just a little bit it ruins the whole bunch. Sin is just like that little bit of dog poo. It takes something perfectly good and ruins it.

Don't allow that sin to remain in your life. No matter how painful it may be, remove it completely from your life. Be brutal, cut it out. You will be better off for it, and you will also be able to draw closer to God. Sin hinders our relationship to God and keeps us from getting close to Him. Be like the blind beggar, take the sin in your life and throw it away so that nothing will keep you from God. "And Jesus stopped and said, 'Call him.' And they called the blind man, saying to him, 'Take heart. Get up; He is calling you.' And throwing off his cloak, he sprang up and came to Jesus" (Mark 10:49-50). No matter how small or insignificant it may seem, if it is sin get rid of it. Throw it away so that it will not be able to trip you up or slow you down in getting to Jesus.

November 8

"And Jacob their father said to them, 'You have bereaved me of my

children: Joseph is no more, and Simeon is no more, and now you would take Benjamin. All this has come against me.'"
Genesis 42:36

Have you ever felt like the entire world is against you? You might feel like you should change your name to Murphy, because it seems that if it can go wrong, it will go wrong? You may look back at a time like that in your life, and now you can smile and laugh about it. But, when you are in the midst of a very difficult time, it is no laughing matter. There are times when it does feel like you are fighting against the entire world. That's where Jacob is currently.

Part of the reason that Jacob is feeling this is way is because God has to refer to him by his old name, Jacob. Back in Genesis 32:28 God changed his name to Israel, which means "governed by God." God refers to him as Jacob, because at this moment he is not being governed by God; he is being governed by his own mind, will, intellect, etc. Since Jacob is trying to solve, figure, and understand his trials and difficulties in life, it appears to him that the entire world is against him, nothing is working out.

The things that Jacob is seeing appear to be bleak, but that's because he has taken his eyes and focus off of God. The truth of the matter is that every single thing that is happening is for his good, not his harm. The apostle Paul reminds us of this when he wrote, "we know that for those who love God all things work together for good" (Romans 8:28). God is using these events and trials in his life to prepare him for wonderful things, such as reuniting him with Joseph, whom he believed to be dead, and deliverance from a terrible famine. Jacob can't see this now, but God is well aware of what He is doing. It comes down to faith.

This is why it is so important that we learn from Jacob and stop acting like him. Instead, we need to be like Israel, to be "governed by God." We need to remember that "faith is the assurance of things hoped for, the conviction of things not seen" (Hebrews 11:1). There will be times in our life that we cannot see what God is doing, or how

He is preparing us for future events, but we need to trust Him and continue to follow Him.

November 9

"Consider Him who endured from sinners such hostility against Himself, so that you may not grow weary or fainthearted."
Hebrews 12:3

Life can be very difficult at times, and the devil has one tool that he likes to employ when things are tough. It is a tool that he uses often and will not give up. What tool is that? It is discouragement. Discouragement stops a person from doing things, and steals their motivation and optimism. It can be completely demobilizing. Look around at society and you will see many discouraged people, those who have "lost heart." Discouragement can come from disappointment in relationships, sibling rivalry, out of control children, the checkbook balance, the stack of bills, losing a home, not finding a job, the political culture of our nation, etc. There is no lack of things that can lead to discouragement. So, what can be done to overcome this?

The author of Hebrews reminds us that we can overcome discouragement. In order to do that though our mind needs to be focused on Jesus. That's what "consider" means; to reflect and to think carefully about. When we are facing difficulties in our lives we need to reflect on Jesus and what He went through when He lived on this earth. Hebrews 12:2a says we are to be "looking to Jesus" because that is where our focus needs to be. When our eyes are on Him, they are no longer on us, our situation, or the problems we may be dealing with. Focusing on our situations brings us a microscopic view of things, because we only see what is happening to us right at that moment. That is why we need to take a step back and move our focus to Jesus. When we do it will help us see the "big picture." Read through the gospels and see what Jesus endured while He lived here on earth. He was mistreated, despised, hated, and literally had groups of people who spent their time scheming and planning on ways to discredit Him, embarrass Him, and finally to kill Him. In spite of all this He did not quit or lose heart. Instead, He "endured the cross, despising the shame, and is seated at the right hand of the throne of God" (Hebrews 12:2b).

No matter what you are going through currently, there is still hope. Do not give up or quit. Look to Jesus; He will help you. "For we do not have a high priest who is unable to sympathize with our weaknesses, but One who in every respect has been tempted as we are, yet without sin" (Hebrews 4:15). Whatever you are dealing with, Jesus has dealt with it too. He understands where you are and is there to walk alongside you through times of trial and difficulty. Hope is still there. Look to Jesus because that is where our hope resides.

November 10

"And the Lord spoke to the fish, and it vomited Jonah out upon the dry land."
Jonah 2:10

We need to remember that God is in control of these events. Jonah repents of his sin, surrenders to God, and God forgives him. Then God speaks to the fish, gives it a command, and the fish immediately responds with obedience. What a great example for us. Creation responds to God's Word with obedience. What was God's command to the fish? Vomit Jonah onto dry land. The Hebrew word for "vomit" means "to throw up." How humiliating! Jonah is a prophet of God, and this fish throws him up on the shore. We're not told where Jonah was vomited onto dry land. I like to believe that it was in Joppa, where he disobeyed God and tried to run away. That would be poetic.

Jonah was delivered from the belly of the fish after three days and three nights. This was a foreshadowing of Jesus' own resurrection from the dead. How do I know that? Because Jesus said so Himself. We read that in Matthew 12:40 when Jesus said, "For just as Jonah was three days and three nights in the belly of the great fish, so will the Son of Man be three days and three nights in the heart of the earth." There are some people who have a problem with this phrase. Since Jesus rose from the grave on Sunday morning, does this mean He was crucified on Thursday and not Friday, in order to have three days in the grave? In about 100 A.D. Rabbi Eleazar ben Azariah said, "A day and a night make a whole day, and a portion of a whole day is reckoned as a whole day." This means that Jesus didn't have to be in the ground for 72 hours, but He was for a portion of three days and three nights. This should be easy for us to understand. We say, "we spent the whole day at <insert a favorite place to go>." Does that mean we were there for an entire 24-hour period? No! It typically means we arrived there early in the morning and got home late at night. It is the same thing here.

Jonah was a sign of what Jesus would later do and experience. Jonah surrendered his life to God through faith. In the belly of the fish Jonah willingly laid down his life and surrendered himself to God's will so that others might live and not have to experience God's wrath. After he did this, death did not hold him, but he was released alive and free. This is a picture of what Jesus did for us. Jesus willingly laid down His own life and experienced God's wrath on the cross, so that we wouldn't have to, and that we can escape the penalty of death, and live forever. Praise God!

November 11

"So put away all malice and all deceit and hypocrisy and envy and all slander."

1 Peter 2:1

Garbage is big business. The entire global market for garbage disposal for the year 2022 is expected to be around $1.6 billion. That is huge! But over the next six years it is expected to grow to just over $2 billion. Why is this market so large and growing? Because people have lots of things that they need to get rid of. We all have trash things that are no longer useful to us, or simply things that are not good for us that need to be removed from our households. While that is true of our households, it is also true for our lives. Each one of us has things in our life that we need to get rid of. It could be a habit, a practice, or a character trait. Peter lists five habits that we all would be wise to throw away and remove from our lives.

The first habit Peter mentions is malice, which is the intention or desire to do evil. The second habit he mentions is deceit, which is using devious words or actions to get what you want. A literal meaning is simply not being honest with people. If you practice either malice or deceit in your life, you will try to hide it, which is the next habit, hypocrisy (pretending to be something you're not). As bad as those three habits are, Peter continues. The fourth habit he lists is envy, which is a longing for something that someone else has, such as possessions or qualities. The fifth and final habit Peter lists is slander, which is speaking evil of another person. There is a reason why Peter tells us to get rid of these habits from our life. If we allow these habits, attitudes, or actions to be in our life, then we will lose our spiritual appetite, no longer having a desire for God's Word. Think of it like this: if you eat a bunch of junk food before a nice fancy meal, your appetite will be ruined by all the junk food that you ate. By not filling up on junk food you will keep an appetite for good food. Spiritually speaking, that is God's Word. Removing malice, deceit, hypocrisy, envy, and slander from your life will help you keep an appetite and desire for God's Word.

November 12

"As soon as I heard these words I sat down and wept and mourned for days, and I continued fasting and praying before the God of Heaven."
Nehemiah 1:4

Nehemiah had a burden, or concern, for the city and the people of Jerusalem, even though he had never been there. His brother lived there and came back to Nehemiah and shares the current condition of the city; it lay in ruins and its city gates were burned down. These are terrible words that were shared with him. Notice his response. As soon as he heard these words he began to weep. He was heartbroken over the condition of Jerusalem and its people. There was no coercion from his brother. He didn't apply any pressure or even play to his emotions to bring out this response. His response came from a need. No one was telling him what he should feel. This wasn't even a popular media driven movement for the people of Israel. Nehemiah's weeping was simply because he cared for the city and its people, and when he heard their condition, it broke his heart. He had a God given compassion for them.

What was the next thing Nehemiah did after weeping and mourning? Like most people today he became angry, began pointing his finger at others and looked for the culprit who caused this. Isn't that a typical response? When something is wrong in the world, the world's first response is to find someone to lay all the blame upon. This doesn't fix or solve the problem, but it does pacify people's emotions and makes them feel better. By his actions, Nehemiah shows that he was more concerned with the condition of the city and its people than he was in casting blame. This is why he responded by praying to God and fasting. He brought his concern to the One who could do something about it. Instead of being directed by his emotions he responded with faith. When we allow our emotions to drive us, they will either dominate us or destroy us. When we respond with faith, we will maintain greater control over ourselves. Nehemiah knew that God was not only in control, but that He was able to change the conditions that had broken his heart. When you come upon a situation in your life that breaks your heart, make sure that you keep your emotions in check and not allow them to drive and control your life. Instead, respond in faith, bring the matter to God, and see how He will lead you to respond.

November 13

"For since, in the wisdom of God, the world did not know God through wisdom, it pleased God through the folly of what we preach to save those who believe."
1 Corinthians 1:21

It is interesting to look back at how people in the 50's and 60's thought that life would be like today. The prevailing thought was that since wisdom was increasing so rapidly life would become so much better. Not only would we have flying cars and live in space, but the problems that they dealt with then (such as racism, hunger, hatred) would be eradicated in the future. Obviously, this has not happened. It would even be fair to say that many of the problems the world dealt with back then are not only gone, but they are worse today. Why is that? Could it be that because the world depends upon its own wisdom its problems have only increased. Here in the United States our government and country said in the early 60's that we no longer wanted God in our schools or government. What has happened since then? We have relied only upon the wisdom of man and racism, hatred, hunger, crime, misunderstanding, wars, and conflicts all remain, and have even grown to become more regular and commonplace. Why can the world not solve their own problems?

The world will never be able to solve their own problems because they cannot understand the source of their problems. While the world is really good at placing blame on individuals, or even groups of people, for all problems, they fail to discover the source of all their problems, which is sin. Disobedience to God is what causes the problems of the world to continue. This is why those that the world considers to be the smartest generally don't know God. The reason for this is because God cannot be known though human wisdom. Often the smarter a person sees themselves as, the less knowledge they have of God because they don't see or realize their need for God due to their worldly wisdom. Their human "wisdom" causes them to reject God and oppose Him, but in the end, it proves how foolish they really are. What the world considers to be foolish is what will bring a person to know God. The world considers the cross to be foolish, but it is only through the message of the cross that we can know Jesus. Don't be misled by the "wisdom" of the world, but humbly acknowledge that Jesus died on the cross to pay the penalty for your sin. This is the source of true wisdom.

November 14

"Now Moses was keeping the flock of his father-in-law, Jethro, the priest of Midian."
Exodus 3:1a

Moses has spent the past forty years tending to the flock of his father-in-law, Jethro. After forty years of doing this, he is still taking care of the same flock. That's a lot of days and nights spent in the desert, busily working and taking care of these sheep. Notice, God is going to appear to Moses when he is busily working. God doesn't wait until he's finished or taking a break. No! God comes to him while he is working. This is how God often makes Himself known to us, while we are working. God appeared to Gideon while he was threshing wheat (Judges 6), to Samuel when he was busy serving in the temple (1 Samuel 3), while David was out in the field taking care of his father's sheep (1 Samuel 17:20), to Elijah while he was out plowing the fields (1 Kings 19:19-21), to four of the disciples while they were busy cleaning their fishing nets (Mark 1:16-20), and to Matthew while he was in his office collecting taxes (Matthew 9:9). God calls us, as believers, to be busy doing His work while we wait for His appearing. Through the Bible God has absolutely nothing good to say about laziness or being a slacker. "I passed by the field of a sluggard, by the vineyard of a man lacking sense, and behold, it was all overgrown with thorns; the ground was covered with nettles, and its stone wall was broken down. Then I saw and considered it; I looked and received instruction. A little sleep, a little slumber, a little folding of the hands to rest, and poverty will come upon you like a robber, and want like an armed man" (Proverbs 24:30-34). How about 2 Thessalonians 3:10-12, which says, "For even when we were with you, we would give you this command: If anyone is not willing to work, let him not eat. For we hear that some among you walk in idleness, not busy at work, but busybodies. Now such persons we command and encourage in the Lord Jesus Christ to do their work quietly and to earn their own living." For we hear that there are some among you who walk irresponsibly, not working at all, but interfering with the work of others. Now we command and exhort such people by the Lord Jesus Christ that quietly working, they may eat their own food."

Moses understood this clearly, as he spent forty years working until God appeared to him. He had no idea today was going to be the day; he simply went about his work as he did every other day. The day appeared to be just like every other workday, but this day was going to be special. In fact, it was going to completely alter his life. This is a great reminder to us that as we faithfully serve God by doing the jobs that He has called us to, we don't know when or how He is going to use our "ordinary" work in a spectacular way. The life of a believer can be used by God in an unpredictable and unexpected way, at any time. The day can look like just another ordinary day, but there is an invisible hand behind us calmly directing all things to accomplish His goals and purposes. Isn't that exciting?

November 15

"The nations raged, but your wrath came, and the time for the dead to be judged, and for rewarding your servants, the prophets and saints, and those who fear your name, both small and great, and for destroying the destroyers of the earth."
Revelation 11:18

During the Tribulation there will still be consequences to your actions. This means that people will receive what is due them for the choices they make while on earth. Their choices will either bring them punishment or reward. The punishment for the world is that it will be destroyed. This is a just punishment; God does not do this without good reason. You see, the world is angry with God. It isn't simply an emotional fit of anger, but it is a deep-seated resentment against Him. As the world is receiving judgment for its sin, the world refuses to repent, and instead grows in its anger and resentment against God. The world joins together in its anger and resentment against God, which will lead to the final battle in Armageddon.

Punishment is one possible consequence, but so are rewards. Those who have surrendered their heart to God will be rewarded. These 24 elders in Heaven refer to these as God's "servants, prophets...saints." Servants and prophets would encompass people in the entire span of history, like Noah and Abraham through the two witnesses of God who were just killed. But there is another group that is rewarded: saints. Who is a saint? Simply put, there are two kinds of people on earth. Either you're a saint, or you ain't. Every person that puts their faith and trust in Jesus by surrendering their life to Him is a saint. Some churches call people a saint after they have confirmed that they lived their life serving God, or there was a confirmed miracle done in their life. Those aren't Biblical definitions of a saint. Those definitions are based on that person's life, which is wrong. A person is a saint not because of what they have done, but due to their position, which is "in Christ." God rewards His children, all those who are His. No matter their position in life, their ethnicity, their nationality, their earthly wealth. Those things don't matter. A saint will be rewarded, not for what they have done, but because they belong to Jesus.

November 16

"Then the man said, 'This at last is bone of my bones and flesh of my flesh; she shall be called Woman, because she was taken out of Man.'"
Genesis 2:23

I love Adam's response when he first sees Eve, "At last." In this we see a mixture of relief, ecstasy, and joyful surprise. Can you imagine? This is every guy's dream. He falls asleep, and when he wakes up, there is the most beautiful woman he has ever seen standing before him, and she is naked. And God just gave them the command to "be fruitful and multiply." Wow! This is what he has been waiting for.

He recognizes that she is like him, which none of the animals were. He also recognizes that there are differences between them. She complements him and makes him whole. He has been given the authority and responsibility of being the head of the household, but they are equal. She is subject to him, but that does not make her less than equal. In speaking of equality Elisabeth Elliot said, "In what sense is red equal to blue? They are equal only in the sense that both are colors in the spectrum. Apart from that they are different. In what sense is hot equal to cold? They are both temperatures, but beyond this it is almost meaningless to talk about equality." The same applies to man and woman. They have been created completely different from each other, but they are both humans. Society is trying to erase the differences and completely misunderstands the idea of equality, but this is how God created them.

Adam again exercises the authority given to him by naming her Woman. This shows God had given him the authority and dominion of having the privilege to name her. He calls her Woman. This is not as effective in English as it is in Hebrew. In fact, some have claimed this is a compound word, saying she was man's woe because she tempted him to join her in eating the fruit and sinning. That is not true, because he named her before sin ever occurred. In Hebrew the word for man is *ish*, and woman is *ishah*. In the first marriage we see the woman taking the name of man. Adam recognized the differences between himself and all the animals, which is why he did not give his name to any animal. He did recognize that the woman was like him, yet different, and he gave his name to her. This is a very beautiful and romantic action that he takes. In doing so he recognizes that they are equal and share the same name.

November 17

"And we know that for those who love God all things work together for good, for those who are called according to His purpose."
Romans 8:28

This verse is a well-known verse, and often quoted by Christians as an encouragement, as it should be. This verse talks about the doctrine of Providence. To help us understand what providence means, J.I. Packer summed it up well when he said, "the doctrine of Providence teaches Christians that they are never in the grip of blind forces (fortune, chance, luck, fate); all that happens to them is divinely planned, and each event comes as a new summons to trust, obey, and rejoice, knowing that all is for one's spiritual and eternal good."

Something good doesn't happen to us because of "our lucky

stars." When we run into someone unexpectedly, it isn't a coincidence. God is in control of these events and is directing them. Scripture confirms this for us. Hebrews 1:3 says, "[Christ] upholds the universe by the word of His power." Proverbs 16:4 reminds us, "The Lord has made everything for its purpose, even the wicked for the day of trouble."

This brings up the question of evil. If God is in charge of everything, then why is there evil in the world? Does this mean that God is the creator of evil? God is not the creator of evil; evil was birthed by sin. We must remember that evil and sinful acts are under the divine authority of God. He allows them to happen because they ultimately lead to His divine purpose and plan (see Genesis 45:8). God has complete power and authority over sin and will use it for His good (see Genesis 50:20). We also need to remember that God does not cause sin; we are responsible for the sin in our lives. "Let no one say when he is tempted, 'I am being tempted by God,' for God cannot be tempted with evil, and He Himself tempts no one. But each person is tempted when he is lured and enticed by his own desire. Then desire when it has conceived gives birth to sin, and sin when it is fully grown brings forth death. (James 1:13-15)"

Evil happens because of the sinful nature of man. The choices we make lead to sin and evil. God does not cause evil, because He is holy. But, since God is bigger than sin and evil, they are forced to cooperate with Him. God does not cause sin or evil, but He has complete control over them and causes them to work together to accomplish His desires and goals in our life. God does not like sin or evil in our lives, but He is able to use the mistakes we make and cause them to work out for His plans. We can trust God, because He is in control of all things, and able to make everything work together for good. What a great God we serve!

November 18

"The scepter will not depart from Judah, nor a lawgiver from between his feet, until Shiloh comes; and to Him shall be the obedience of all the people." (NKJV)
Genesis 49:10

Jacob prophesies that Judah is the tribe that will rule over and lead the nation of Israel. It took 640 years for this prophecy to be fulfilled, but it happened exactly as Jacob said it would. When David became the second king of Israel, his descendants ruled over the nation of Israel for close to a thousand years. The second part of this prophecy took almost 1600 years to be fulfilled, but it was also fulfilled exactly as prophesied. Judah retained the right to rule, or govern, herself until the year of 6 or 7 A.D. For a nation to be said to have the right to rule, it is generally believed that that nation can enforce capital punishment as it deems necessary. Israel had this "right" taken away by the Romans, and when that happened the Rabbis and other spiritual leaders of Israel considered this to be a tragedy because they claimed that Scripture had not been fulfilled. You see, they did not believe that Shiloh had come to the earth. Shiloh is a Hebrew word that means "he whose right it is." Who has the right to rule? Messiah! When the Roman government took the right of capital punishment away from the Israeli government, the leaders of Israel did not see Messiah in Israel, which caused them to believe that the Hebrew Scriptures had failed.

They were incorrect because there was a young lad growing up in Nazareth. The Messiah was in Israel, but the spiritual leaders of Israel failed to recognize Him when He arrived. If Jesus is not the Messiah, then God's Word has failed. In 70 A.D. Israel's scepter was taken and there was no longer a lawgiver in the nation. This means that the Messiah, or Shiloh, had to come to earth before 70 A.D. Later the prophet Isaiah would repeat the words of Jacob, linking

Messiah to Shiloh. "For to us a child is born, to us a son is given; and the government shall be upon His shoulder, and His name shall be called Wonderful Counselor, Mighty God, Everlasting Father, Prince of Peace. Of the increase of His government and of peace there will be no end, on the throne of David and over His kingdom, to establish it and to uphold it with justice and with righteousness from this time forth and forevermore. The zeal of the Lord of hosts will do this" (Isaiah 9:6-7).

November 19

"But on that day I will set apart the land of Goshen, where my people dwell, so that no swarms of flies shall be there, that you may know that I am the Lord in the midst of the earth. Thus I will put a division[f] between my people and your people. Tomorrow this sign shall happen."
Exodus 8:22-23

The first three plagues affected everybody within the borders of Egypt, both Egyptians and Israelites. But now, here with the fourth plague, God makes a distinction between His people and His enemies. This plague is going to affect the Egyptians, but the Israelites will not have to deal with this plague at all. So, we could really say that the land of Goshen, where the Israelites lived, was the very first "no-fly" zone in the world. Why would God make this distinction? Flies were very common in Egypt, but God is showing that He is in complete control of these events by both creating such large swarms of flies, swarms so large that they had never been seen in such great numbers before, and by the fact that God is also able to control where these flies go and where they don't go. It was like there was some sort of invisible wall around the land of Goshen that the flies couldn't fly through, so Goshen had no flies at all, while Egypt was completely infested with flies. That is amazing, and shows how powerful God is, and that all creation listens and obeys Him.

God makes a distinction, or difference, between His people and His enemies. The word "difference" in verse 23 can also be translated as division. There was a division between the Israelites and the Egyptians, just as there remains a division today between believer and unbeliever. The nation of Israel belonged to God because they were His chosen people. Pharaoh refused to accept this difference. Today, believers are divided from unbelievers. Believers are "set apart" from the world because they belong to God instead of the world. This means that there is a distinction between us and the world. We should have different lifestyles, desires, attitudes, etc., because our goal in life should be to follow God, be more like Jesus, and to bring glory and honor to Jesus through our life. Our goal isn't simply to accumulate the most money, power, or toys; it is to bring honor and glory to Jesus. That in itself will cause us to be divided from and different than the world.

November 20

"...you yourselves like living stones are being built up as a spiritual house..."
1 Peter 2:5a

Every believer is a living stone that God uses to build a house for Himself. It is interesting that we are called stones and not bricks or boards. There is a good reason for this. When bricks and boards are manufactured, they are made to exact specifications. When you go to your local home improvement store and purchase bricks to build something, you expect every brick you purchase to be the same size and shape so that they will fit together exactly how you expect them to. The same is true for any wood that you purchase. That is not how stones are. Stones are individual; they come in all different sizes and shapes. This is why God compares His children, believers, to stones; because we are all individual, we are all different. This makes it more difficult to take stones and work them together into a building, but that is exactly what God does. To make stones fit together they must be chiseled, or ground, to make them fit together with other stones. That is what is happening to us here on earth.

When King Solomon constructed the Temple, the stones were cut, chiseled, hammered on, and chipped to make the stones fit together away from the Temple Mount. All this work was done in a quarry away from the mount "so that neither hammer nor axe nor any tool of iron was heard in the house while it was being built" (1 Kings 6:7). This is what we are going through here on earth. Earth is the quarry where we, living stones, are being chiseled, hammered on, cut, and ground so that we will fit together in Heaven to create a beautiful living Temple to God. In Heaven we will all fit together perfectly without the noisy sounds of construction being heard in Heaven. That explains why some other believers grate on you and rub you the wrong way. But let's not forget that we are that way to others too. God allows us to come into situations where we rub others to wear off their rough edges, and others do the same thing to us. We, as living stones, are being shaped and formed into exactly the perfect shaped stone that God has created us to be. So don't get mad or upset by the believer who is grinding you down but realize that God is allowing that to happen to reshape you into exactly what God needs you to be. God is in control, and He is shaping each of us to be a part of His spiritual home for all eternity.

November 21

"Your heart was proud because of your beauty; you corrupted your wisdom for the sake of your splendor. I cast you to the ground; I exposed you before kings, to feast their eyes on you."
Ezekiel 28:17

Is has been said that pride is the only disease known to man that causes everyone to be sick, except the person who has it. Pride seems to be an epidemic in our world today, but it isn't anything new. It has been alive and well on earth ever since sin entered the world. Pride has been ruining lives, and even nations, for thousands of years. God warned the prophet Ezekiel about three steps that lead to pride.

The first step is conceit. The king of Tyre was conceited because he had a proud heart. "Your heart was proud because of your beauty." The king looked at what he had accomplished and his position in life, and his heart was filled with pride because of his success. There are many areas where pride can enter our heart. Our good looks, business success, intelligence, money, house, family, personal possessions and toys, position in the community or within a field of study. Each of these areas has the potential to allow pride to enter our life. We need to remember that all we have is a gift from God. Anything good we have in our life is because God has allowed it, and not because of how great we are.

The second step was corruption. "You corrupted your wisdom for the sake of your splendor." When we begin to believe that we deserve, or earned, whatever is the source of our pride, then our minds have been corrupted. This is what happened to the king of Tyre. He believed all the good press that was written about him. He believed that he was more beautiful than others, had accomplished more because of his superior intellect, etc. We need to be careful to not allow success to go to our head. We need to remain humble. If we don't, we'll reap the third step.

The third step is condemnation. "I cast you to the ground; I exposed you before kings, to feast their eyes on you." As our hearts and minds become filled with pride, it will lead to our downfall, or destruction. Solomon reminded us of this when he wrote, "Pride goes before destruction, and a haughty spirit before a fall" (Proverbs 16:18).

Let us learn from the king of Tyre and lean on God's strength to help us avoid pride in our lives. "One's pride will bring him low, but he who is lowly in spirit will obtain honor" (Proverbs 29:23).

November 22

"Then he sent his brothers away, and as they departed, he said to them, 'Do not quarrel on the way.'"
Genesis 45:24

It can be very frustrating when others know you too well. This is what Joseph's brothers are dealing with at this moment. They are in Egypt purchasing food for the second time. After they arrived, they were taken to the Egyptian ruler's home for a meal, which caused them great amounts of anxiety. During this meal they found out that this Egyptian ruler was their long-lost brother Joseph. He forgave them for the past injustices that they had done to him, and there was a beautiful reconciliation between them all. Now, it is time for the eleven brothers to return to Canaan to their father, and to bring the food back that their families so desperately need. Remember, they are in the middle of a famine. As the brothers are preparing to leave Joseph turns to them and says, "Do not quarrel on the way." He knows them too well, and he is aware of their natural behaviors.

There is also good reason for Joseph to believe that his brothers will argue on their way back to Canaan. On their first trip to Egypt, he had overheard one of their conversations, before he revealed his true identity, and they did not realize he understood every word they said. "'In truth we are guilty concerning our brother, in that we saw the distress of his soul, when he begged us and we did not listen. That is why this distress has come upon us.' And Reuben answered them, 'Did I not tell you not to sin against the boy? But you did not listen. So now there comes a reckoning for his blood.'" (Genesis 42:21-22). Even though Joseph has forgiven them, they still had a natural tendency to determine the amount of guilt that each of them still had for what they had previously done. They could argue over their guilt all they wanted to, but it wouldn't accomplish anything because they had already been forgiven. Therefore, Joseph reminds them beforehand to keep their focus on grace and not guilt. We also need to focus more on grace than guilt. We can be confident that "If we confess our sins, He is faithful and just to forgive us our sins and to cleanse us from all unrighteousness" (1 John 1:9).

November 23

"Then I sent to him, saying, 'No such things as you say have been done, for you are inventing them out of your own mind.' For they all wanted to frighten us, thinking, 'Their hands will drop from the work, and it will not be done.' But now, O God, strengthen my hands."
Nehemiah 6:8-9

Nehemiah is doing a work for God, and for doing this his enemies respond by publicly stating lies to slander him. They went to the day's public forum and posted rumors with the intent to publicly damage Nehemiah's reputation, and to stop God's work from being completed. This reads like a headline from today's news, doesn't it? Nehemiah had a choice to make. How was he going to respond to these false rumors? Would he go on the offensive and begin to attack his enemies to take the focus off himself? Would he begin a nasty public fight to defend himself and prove every accusation to be false? He did none of these things. He publicly responded and said what was written is a lie, then he returned to his work. He didn't retaliate or try to "set the record straight." He didn't even defend himself, just a simple statement that what was posted about him was a lie. Then he turned to God in prayer and admitted to God that he was worried. He asked God for strength to continue the work he was doing. What a great response.

Nehemiah responded with faith. Even though he had faith in God, he was still worried. That doesn't mean he didn't trust God. There are moments in our life when the situations we are in can physically overwhelm our faith. We trust God, yet we struggle to remain calm, and our palms are sweating. We spend time daily praying to God, but our heart is still racing. We trust God, but we still struggle to sleep at night. This doesn't mean something is wrong with you, but it means you are in a spiritual battle. There is a battle inside you between the flesh and the spirit. King David experienced this. Listen to how he described it. "For I hear the whispering of many — terror on every side! — as they scheme together against me, as they plot to take my life. But I trust in you, O Lord; I say, 'You are my God'" (Psalm 31:13-14). Trust in God will carry you through every attack the enemy attempts. It is not easy, but God is faithful. Trust Him, even when it's dark.

November 24

"...give thanks in all circumstances; for this is the will of God in Christ Jesus for you."
1 Thessalonians 5:18

As we approach the day our nation sets aside as Thanksgiving, we need to look a little closer at Thanksgiving. While our nation sets one day a year aside for this, as Christians, this needs to be our attitude every day: not just once a year. Many people are going through difficult times and do not feel like giving thanks right now. It may be true that your situation has changed into something awful right now, but remember, God has not changed! God is still the same good God that He has always been, and always will be. God does not change! "Jesus Christ is the same yesterday and today and forever" (Hebrews 13:8). Since God does not change, and only our circumstances change, we can still give thanks to God, even when we are in the midst of difficult times. It is really unnatural for a Christian to not be thankful. Christians are to be thankful always because "And we know that for those who love God all things work together for good..." (Romans 8:28a).

Notice also that the apostle Paul is reminding us to give thanks to God in everything, not for everything. The difference is two very small words, but they make a very large difference. We are not to be thankful for everything, because sin causes hurt, trials, pain and suffering in our lives. But, during those times we are still able to be thankful to God. God allows every believer to go through times of difficulty in their lives. They are times of refining and strengthening in the life of the believer, and they also are times of witness to the unbeliever. As the unbeliever watches Christians endure through difficult times, still being able to praise God and give thanks, they realize there is a strength and hope that is missing in their own life. We can praise God during difficult times because He is using us to help save others, because He doesn't want to see anyone perish (see 2 Peter 3:9).

Thanksgiving needs to be a hallmark of the Christian's life because of all that we have to be thankful for. We can thank God that He loves us so much that He was willing to have His Son die on a cross in order to pay for our sins so that we can live with Him forever. We thank God that His mercies are new every morning, His grace is enough, He is always with us, and He never leaves us. We can thank God that He knows us intimately (every detail of our life), and He still loves us despite our failures and shortcomings. We thank God that He has changed us into new creations and given us the Holy Spirit to work in our lives and change us to become more and more like Him. When He did this, He also changed our hearts of stone to a heart of flesh, soft and able for Him to change and mold. We thank God because He provides everything that we need, and not just what we want. God loves us and looks out for our best interests, even disciplining us when necessary. We have so much to be thankful to God for. Do not wait for one day in November to thank God, but make sure it is a part of your life to thank God every day. He is so worthy and deserving of our thanks and praise.

November 25

"Honor your father and your mother, that your days may be long in the land that the LORD your God is giving you."
Exodus 20:12

As we begin this second section of the Ten Commandments, the ones dealing with others, and the first horizontal relationship with God addresses is family. This keeps family right where it belongs, in the center. The family is also the foundation of all other relationships, which is another reason why it comes first. In order for society to do well, the family structure needs to be healthy. The family structure will not be healthy without children honoring their parents. When there is fighting and war between the generations, the family structure will be destroyed.

One thing to notice about this command is that it doesn't say we are to honor our parents until we are eighteen years old. Honor for parents continues no matter your age, even when you are a parent yourself. Honoring your parent doesn't mean that they continue to make every decision for you, like they did when you were a toddler. Honor has to do with respect. Even when you are old and out of their house, you show honor to your parents by discussing matters with them and listening to their advice, even if you don't follow it.

This is a very important command for everyone to follow. This isn't simply because it is part of the Ten Commandments, but it is also repeated in the New Testament. In Ephesians 6:1-3 the apostle Paul wrote, "Children, obey your parents in the Lord, for this is right. 'Honor your father and mother' (this is the first commandment with a promise), 'that it may go well with you and that you may live long in the land.'" We are to honor our parents simply because it is the right thing to do. Along with that, this command teaches the importance of having respect for those that are older than you, otherwise known as our elders. Sadly, too often the elderly are an outcast group of people that we end of joining reluctantly because it's better than the alternative. It is important that as believers we are being an example for others on how to treat our parents with honor and respect and doing the same for the elderly. How we treat the elderly today will be how we will be treated when we are the elderly because we reap what we sow.

November 26

"And the king of Israel said to Jehoshaphat, 'There is yet one man by whom we may inquire of the LORD, Micaiah the son of Imlah, but I hate him, for he never prophesies good concerning me, but evil.' And Jehoshaphat said, 'Let not the king say so.'"
1 Kings 22:8

Jehoshaphat was the king of Judah, and he was visiting with Ahab, the very wicked king of Israel. Ahab had been at war with the king of Aram off and on for many years, but no fighting for the past three years. These two kings were discussing whether Ahab should go back to war with Aram again since Aram had captured the city of Ramoth-gilead from Israel. Ahab wanted to go back to war, and he had surrounded himself with approximately 400 prophets, and they all said he should go to war. So, he asks Jehoshaphat to assist him in the war effort, and he readily agrees, and then as an afterthought asks what the Lord's will is. Ahab brings in his prophets and they all say they should go to war. This does not satisfy Jehoshaphat, and he asks if there are any prophets of God left. Ahab says there is, but he doesn't like him because he never prophecies anything good, only evil for me. Ahab makes the same mistake many people make.

The mistake Ahab makes is that he is being selfish and wants people to validate his choices. His 400 so-called prophets are just yes men for him, but not Micaiah. Micaiah speaks the truth and Ahab doesn't like the truth because it doesn't always fit his plans and desires. We need to be careful that we do not become like Ahab. The truth is not always pleasant to hear, but it is needed. We need to make sure that we are not surrounded by yes men, but by people who will tell us the truth even when we might not like it. Jesus said, "you will know the truth, and the truth will set you free" (John 8:32). The truth will set us free as long as we follow it and change our selfish attitudes and desires.

Too often people are so focused on getting what they want that they will not accept anything different, including the truth. The apostle Paul spoke about people like this. "For the time is coming when people will not endure sound teaching, but having itching ears they will accumulate for themselves teachers to suit their own passions and will turn away from listening to the truth and wander off into myths" (2 Timothy 4:3-4). Embrace people in your life who are willing to tell you the truth; even when you do not want to hear it. Listen to what they have to say and seek God out through prayer and reading His Word. God will reveal to you His truth when you diligently seek Him. "Call to me and I will answer you, and will tell you great and hidden things that you have not known" (Jeremiah 33:3).

November 27

"The seventh angel poured out his bowl into the air, and a loud voice came out of the temple, from the throne, saying, 'It is done!'"
Revelation 16:17

Finally. This is the exclamation that many make when they reach the end of a journey, or a project, or complete something that has taken a long time. The proverbial light at the end of the tunnel has finally been reached. You are now able to relax and exhale. When you have been in the middle of a difficult time, this is what you have been looking forward to. This describes many people today. People who are worn and weary from dealing with a pandemic for nine months. Every single person has dealt with some interruption, and many have been decimated, losing jobs, security, and even the lives of loved ones. This has been a difficult period, and many are looking forward to the day when it will be finished.

That is how the people on earth will be feeling when the seventh angel pours out his bowl of judgment upon the earth. As the seventh bowl is poured out God Himself will speak from Heaven and announce that this is the final judgement. Finally. It is over. God will announce that "it is done!" God's judgment upon the earth has been long and difficult. Seven seals followed by seven trumpets followed by seven bowls of judgment. Judgment is now finished. Next will be Jesus coming to set up His kingdom for His Millennial Kingdom, or Thousand Year Reign.

This isn't the first time God has cried out that His work is done. He said the same thing when He hung on the cross. After many hours of agonizing torture on the cross where Jesus took all the sins of mankind on His shoulders, Jesus cried out "It is finished!" The work was completed. Jesus had finished His goal and purpose of coming to earth. He had paid the penalty of sin. Death is now defeated. Because of what Jesus did we no longer have to live in fear of death. It has no power over us. Jesus is victorious. He gives that same victory to everyone who surrenders their life to Him. Have you done that? If not, then today is the day to surrender your heart to Jesus. Allow Him to be Lord and Savior of your life.

November 28

"God spoke to Moses and said to him, "I am the LORD. I appeared to Abraham, to Isaac, and to Jacob, as God Almighty, but by My name the LORD I did not make Myself known to them.'"

Exodus 6:2-3

After God reassures Moses about that He is going to deliver Israel from Egypt, He reminds Moses Who He is: He is Yahweh, or I AM. He is the covenant-making God, but He is also the covenant-keeping God. When God makes a promise, He always fulfills that promise. God gave a promise to Moses, which He will keep, just as He previously met with and gave promises to Moses' ancestors, Abraham, Isaac, and Jacob.

It is interesting that God tells Moses that He had met with Abraham, Isaac, and Jacob, but they didn't know Him by the name Yahweh, or I AM. Did God make a mistake here? The reason I say that is because in the book of Genesis the name Yahweh is used some 160 times. Abraham, Isaac, and Jacob did know Yahweh. That is true. They knew Yahweh, the covenant-making God. God made a covenant with all three of those men. But they did not know God, or Yahweh, as the fulfiller, or keeper, of that covenant, because none of them were alive when the covenant God made with them was fulfilled. Moses, and the other Israelites alive at that time, knew Yahweh as the covenant-making God, but now they were also going to see and experience Him as the covenant-keeping God as He fulfills the promises, or covenant, that He made. This means that Moses and the other Israelites alive at that time were able to know God more fully than Abraham, Isaac, of Jacob did.

Abraham, Isaac, and Jacob knew God as "God Almighty," or El Shaddai, as it is in Hebrew. This name speaks of the strength and power of God. This is an apt and descriptive name of God, but there is much more to God than simply El Shaddai. This is what the patriarchs knew of God, but Moses and the Israelites were allowed to know much more about God than just His strength and power. By seeing God keeping, or fulfilling, His covenant, they were allowed to see another aspect of God. They were able to know God much more personally, or intimately, than their predecessors did. God revealed more of Himself to them, in addition to His power. This is even more so for us today. We have God's completed Word, the Bible, and therefore we have much more knowledge and information about God than Moses or Abraham did. God wants us to know Him on an even more intimate and personal basis. He wants us to know Him as El Shaddai (God Almighty), but He also wants us to know Him personally, as our Abba Father. Do you know God that personally and intimately?

November 29

"On that day they read from the Book of Moses in the hearing of the people. And in it was found written that no Ammonite or Moabite should ever enter the assembly of God, for they did not meet the people of Israel with bread and water, but hired Balaam against them to curse them—yet our God turned the curse into a blessing."
Nehemiah 13:1-2

You may have heard the adage "while the cat's away the mice will play." That is what Nehemiah experienced with Israel. Before Nehemiah ever went to Israel, he told the king how long he would be gone. After the wall was rebuilt and the temple was dedicated, Nehemiah returned to Babylon and continued to serve King Artexerxes as his cupbearer. There is no record of how long he remained in Babylon, but he returned again to Jerusalem to see how things were going. In his absence it is amazing how quickly things went south. This is a credit to the strong spiritual leadership of Nehemiah, but also discredit to the people for their lack of discipline and desire to maintain a close relationship with God.

When the Israelites were entering into the Promised Land after their wilderness wanderings, the people of Ammon and Moab refused to provide any help to the Israelites. Instead, they hired a Balaam to curse the Israelites. God turned those cursings into blessings, but He also made it a law that no Ammonite or Moabite was to set foot into the Temple because of these acts. After Nehemiah returned to Babylon, and the Israelites had dedicated themselves to God, they wandered away from this commitment and disobeyed God's Word. This serves as a warning to us. No matter how spiritual a person you are, you must remain vigilant and on constant guard in your relationship with God. Even the wisest and most spiritual person is in danger of moving away from God and repeating the same mistakes made here by the Israelites. What must a person do to distance themselves from God? Nothing. Absolutely nothing. The child of God has an enemy that never stops working and trying to get the child of God to fall away from God. So, if the child of God does not remain vigilant in maintaining their close fellowship and relationship with God, then their enemy is there waiting to pounce upon them and draw them away from God. Pray to God for the desire and heart to seek after Him every day when you wake up. God has given us a promise. "You will seek me and find me, when you seek me with all your heart" (Jeremiah 29:13).

November 30

"He is lodging with one Simon, a tanner, whose house is by the sea."
Acts 10:6

God knew exactly where Peter was. I love this about God. God never forgets a name, never loses an address, never makes a mistake, and He never has to pause a moment to remember where we are or what we're doing. And He doesn't even have a smartphone to help Him! That should comfort us. After all, God keeps track of the whereabouts of a hundred billion stars in millions of galaxies. He knows the path, the history, and the destiny of every speck of dust in space. Not only that, but He knows every single thing about me; and you! No matter where we go, He knows exactly where to find us. Since He knows where we are, He also can send people across our paths and into our lives to help fulfill His plans and purposes. How exciting is that?

What plan or purpose is God preparing for here? The uniting of both Jews and Gentiles to Jesus. Until this time, Jews and Gentiles were separated, or divided, from each other. Most Jews believed that Gentiles were created to be the fuel that kept the fires in hell going. That wasn't God's plan. There was a wall that kept the Jews and Gentiles separated; it was time to remove that wall. What was that wall? The Law of Moses. The apostle Paul writes, "For He Himself is our peace, who has made us both one and has broken down in His flesh the dividing wall of hostility by abolishing the law of commandments expressed in ordinances, that He might create in Himself one new man in place of the two, so making peace, and might reconcile us both to God in one body through the cross, thereby killing the hostility. And He came and preached peace to you who were far off and peace to those who were near. For through Him we both have access in one Spirit to the Father." (Ephesians 2:14-18). It matters not whether you are of Jewish or Gentile descent. To be a child of God you must become a "new person." In the sight of God, there is no longer a difference between the two. What matters is, are you a child of God? Have you surrendered yourself to Him? Salvation has nothing to do with nationality or ethnicity! It has to do with the completed work of Jesus on the cross, and whether or not you belong to Him.

December 1

"And if it is evil in your eyes to serve the LORD, choose this day whom you will serve, whether the gods your fathers served in the region beyond the River, or the gods of the Amorites in whose land you dwell. But as for me and my house, we will serve the LORD."
Joshua 24:15

Paper or plastic? Cash or credit? Regular or decaf? Unleaded or Supreme? Small, medium, large, or super-size? Each of us is faced with numerous choices that we must make on a regular basis. Some decisions are irrelevant and have little impact on your life. Other decisions impact your life dramatically. The consequences of some choices determine the direction of your life or stay with you the rest of your life. What type of work you do, whom you marry, how you pay your bills or accumulate bills, the lifestyle you lead; these decisions have a lasting effect on your life. The most important choice you have is which God (or god) you are going to serve. Your choice is really a matter between life and death.

Every day you choose whether or not you are going to serve God. If you choose not to, then you must also choose who or what you will serve. A choice must be made; to remain undecided is to choose to not serve God. Joshua reminded the people that they could refuse God and choose to serve the same gods their fathers did before entering the Promised Land, or the same gods the people who lived in the Promised Land did. What gods were these? They were all false gods, man-made idols. There are still many gods like this today. If you choose to not serve God you can choose to serve money, sex, pleasure, power, fame, possessions, etc. You can also serve religion. There are many people whose lives revolve around their "church," trying to follow the rules that are established for their conduct, and to satisfy the people there.

You have to make a choice. You cannot serve God and anyone or anything else. Choose for yourself, this day, who you will serve. Jesus said, "No one can serve two masters, for either he will hate the one and love the other, or he will be devoted to the one and despise the other. You cannot serve God and money" (Matthew 6:24). Your allegiance must be made, choose one or the other. Jesus also said, "Whoever is not with Me is against Me, and whoever does not gather with Me scatters" (Matthew 12:30). You must make a choice. To remain undecided is to choose to serve someone or something other than God.

December 2

"One of its heads seemed to have a mortal wound, but its mortal wound was healed, and the whole earth marveled as they followed the beast."
Revelation 13:3

Have you ever wondered what it would be like if you knew what was going to happen in the future? How would that change your life if you were aware ahead of time what was going to happen? When it did happen, would that confirm to you the truth of what you knew? That is what the book of Revelation does for us. God has given us a preview of coming attractions, what is going to happen in the future. That way, when it does happen, exactly as the Bible says it will, our faith in God will be strengthened. We know that the Antichrist will rise to power. But we are also told that he will experience an assassination attempt on his life. This was also predicted by the Old Testament prophet Zechariah; "Woe to my worthless shepherd, who deserts the flock! May the sword strike his arm and his right eye!

Let his arm be wholly withered, his right eye utterly blinded!" (Zechariah 11:17). This attempt will either be successful, he will die, and God will allow him to be resurrected, or he will be close to death, and when secluded away it will appear that he did die, when in reality he did not. In other words, his "resurrection" will be a counterfeit.

What else would we expect from Satan. He continually attempts to counterfeit what God has done. Satan is a master at making cheap imitations. They are good enough to fool many people, but they are not the real thing. The apostle Paul reminds us that the work of the Antichrist "is by the activity of Satan with all power and false signs and wonders" (2 Thessalonians 2:9). This false "resurrection" of Antichrist will be just one of many "false miracles" that happen. This is the character of Satan. The prophet Isaiah reminds us of Satan's heart and desire, when he wrote: "How you are fallen from heaven, O Day Star, son of Dawn! How you are cut down to the ground, you who laid the nations low! You said in your heart, 'I will ascend to heaven; above the stars of God I will set my throne on high; I will sit on the mount of assembly in the far reaches of the north; I will ascend above the heights of the clouds; I will make myself like the Most High" (Isaiah 14:12-14). Satan's desire is to be like God. This is why he continually attempts to copy what God does. But he is not God. There is only one God. Don't be fooled by Satan's cheap imitations. Worship God only. He is the one true God.

December 3

"And when the time drew near that Israel must die, he called his son Joseph and said to him, 'If now I have found favor in your sight, put your hand under my thigh and promise to deal kindly and truly with me. Do not bury me in Egypt.'"
Genesis 47:29

At first glance it appears that Jacob is not grateful for how Joseph saved and preserved Jacob's family in Egypt. Joseph went to great lengths to ensure that his family was saved in during this famine, and now his dad is asking him to guarantee that he won't be buried in the land of Egypt. When this happens it can be frustrating, and even cause a person to stop wanting to help others. After all, why help them if they don't even appreciate the help that you are giving them. That is understandable, but fortunately, it is not what Jacob is guilty of here. Jacob is grateful to Joseph for helping to preserve his family by having them move to Egypt. They not only survived the famine, but they grew in many ways: numbers, property, and prosperity (see Genesis 47:27). While Jacob is grateful, he still wants to ensure that he will be buried back in the Promised Land, Canaan, and not Egypt.

The reason for this is because Jacob, or Israel, knew that Egypt was not his home, the Promised Land was. This is where he desired to be. He was grateful for Egypt, but he knew that was not where he, nor his family, belonged. God had promised this land to his grandfather Abraham and to his descendants (Isaac, Jacob, etc.). Jacob longed to be in the land that God had promised belonged to him. Others knew this too. When he had his funeral, and his body wasn't placed in the ground, this would be a witness to everyone in attendance, both Israelite and Egyptian. His refusal to be buried in Egypt sent a strong signal that he knew God's Word, God's promise, and that he believed in them to the point of placing his life upon God's Word. He is an example for you and me to follow. Should the Lord tarry, one day we will also die and have a funeral. Have you given any thought to the message that it will give to those in attendance? Will they see through your life and desires that you are a child of God? Are you "looking forward to the city that has foundations, whose designer and builder is God" (Hebrews 11:10)? This will be the final public testimony of your life. What will it say? While you are thinking of that, also give thought to the witness and testimony of your life right now. Do people know what you live for and stand for? Or do they only know what it is that you are opposed to. Let's make sure that our lives are a witness that brings glory and honor to God.

December 4

"For whoever keeps the whole law but fails in one point has become guilty of all of it."
James 2:10

There seems to be no end to stories about husbands who have selective hearing. Their wife, or children, call out to them and ask them to either do something for them or to help them, and they don't hear them and therefore, fail to respond. But, when you tell them food is ready, they immediately get up to go eat. They hear what they want to hear and ignore what they don't want to hear. Sadly, that does happen, by both men and women. Selective hearing can cause problems within relationships, but selective obedience can cause even worse problems spiritually.

Selective obedience is when a person picks and chooses which commands of God that they believe they must obey, and which commands it is ok for them to ignore. God's Word is not a smorgasbord, where you pick out the things you like and get rid of the ones that you don't like. You can't decide that God was correct about not murdering someone, so you choose to obey that, but you have a difficult neighbor, so you ignore the command to love your neighbor. It doesn't work that way. Just because you don't like a command of God doesn't mean that you can ignore it or disobey it.

So far in James 2 James has been talking about how we as believers treat other people, especially in the realm of showing bias or favoritism. You see, when we show respect to one person over another because they appear to have more wealth or we can benefit from them and their wealth or position, then we will also find ourselves sinning. You can take any of the Ten Commandments, found in Exodus 20, and you can break any, and all, of them by showing favoritism to one person over another because of either their social or financial position. When we respect a person because of their position in the world, then we are rejecting God's Word, and we will have to deal with the consequences of that choice. As James reminds us here, you don't have to break all of God's law to be considered a law breaker, you only have to break one part of it to be a law breaker. Every one of us has already done that. When you disobey one law, then you show that you can break all of them. By rebelling against God's Word, you already have. So, since we are all law breakers, what should we then do? Repent! Confess your sins to God and ask Him for forgiveness. "If we confess our sins, He is faithful and just to forgive us our sins and to cleanse us from all unrighteousness" (1 John 1:9).

December 5

"Two are better than one, because they have a good reward for their toil. For if they fall, one will lift up his fellow. But woe to him who is alone when he falls and has not another to lift him up!"
Ecclesiastes 4:9-10

Every one of us needs other people in our life. This is not about marriage, but about other people in your life as friends. For some, making friends comes easily; but for others, it is work. As with most work though, the reward is well worth the effort. Good friends are necessary in order to have a full and rich life. Close friends of the same gender are also a necessity. Every one of us needs people we can be honest with, and friends who are able to tell us the truth and not just agree with what we say. Friends help develop our character, and we also will reflect their character in our lives.

Too often you hear about a leader in some ministry (pastor, musician, teacher, etc.) who has lost their ministry due to poor choices they have made in their life. In almost every case, that person is lacking a close friend of the same gender who they are accountable to. Over the years people who have had to step down from ministry generally have some of the same characteristics, such as "a loose spirit with few boundaries; rationalizes and justifies behavior; detached, reclusive, insulated from people, makes decisions without consulting others, unwilling to admit mistakes and failures; intimidating, unapproachable, secretive." Being accountable to a close friend will help avoid these characteristics in our lives.

Being accountable to another person helps protect us. They become like a guardrail on a mountain road. They are there to help keep us on the road and from crashing over the side to your death, or at least major injury. Your accountability partner will also help you remain focused on priorities and goals in your life. When you begin to wander off the path and away from what should be your priority, your accountability friend will gently remind you where you should be and redirect you. Without a friend holding us accountable it is too easy to become withdrawn and isolated. This is what the devil wants. When you are isolated and away from others, he has an easier time distracting you and causing you to question God's truth. Satan knows that division and separation are tools to distance us from God and to bring us down, which is his ultimate goal. Help avoid this by asking a close, godly person of the same gender to help hold you accountable. It will not keep you from sin, but they will help you back up when you do fall, and help you fall less often.

December 6

"...not domineering over those in your charge, but being examples to the flock."
1 Peter 5:3

God put people here on earth to be in community, or fellowship, with each other. When people get together it does not take long for some people to rise up into positions of leadership. This happens at home, where you live, at work, and even in church. Peter is writing this section of his letter to address the church leadership, and he is warning them of the authority that a pastor can have. There is the potential for great power and authority for a pastor to have, and the how the pastor handles the authority given to them determines what the health and condition of their flock will be. Typically, one of two things will happen. A pastor receives that authority and becomes a lord, or ruler, over the congregation, or they understand their role as a shepherd, that the congregation belongs to God and is simply entrusted to them to watch over and take care of. The authority belongs to God, not to the pastor, or shepherd. A pastor is not called to be a dictator, but to be an example for the congregation to follow.

A true shepherd understands that you cannot drive sheep, they must be led. I once heard a pastor share that while they were in Israel, they watched a flock of sheep come running down the street while a man came behind them running after them. He was surprised to see a shepherd running after his sheep instead of leading them, so he asked their tour guide why the shepherd was chasing his sheep instead of leading them. The guide said shepherds always lead their sheep, they never chase them. That wasn't the shepherd, it was the butcher that was chasing them. Shepherds lead by example, not rule as a dictator. This is why it has wisely been said that church needs leaders who serve, and servants who lead.

This is what Peter wrote to pastors and elders of churches, but it also applies to our home lives and work lives. In our relationships with other people, we need to ask ourselves if we tend to be a dictator or if we lead by example. Are you chasing after people and trying to control their every move, or do you allow them to follow the example that you give them to follow?

December 7

"...and the people of Israel said to them, 'Would that we had died by the hand of the Lord in the land of Egypt, when we sat by the meat pots and ate bread to the full, for you have brought us out into this wilderness to kill this whole assembly with hunger.' Then the Lord said to Moses, 'Behold, I am about to rain bread from heaven for you, and the people shall go out and gather a day's portion every day, that I may test them, whether they will walk in my law or not."

Exodus 16:3-4

We can either say the children of Israel had a distorted view of the past, or they simply had a selective memory. Their stomachs were growling from hunger, and this caused them to only remember the good things of the past. They conveniently forgot about being slaves or baking bricks underneath the blazing hot summer sun. Instead of the reality of what happened, they remembered the fresh bread, BBQed chicken and smoked tri-tips. This is a typical human response because unbelief has a very short memory. It didn't take them long to forget that while they were in Egypt they cried out to God for deliverance. Now that they had received their freedom, it didn't take them long to be ready to put their necks back into the yoke of slavery. Why? They thought this would fill their growling stomachs.

God heard them, and He even spoke to Moses about the Israelites complaining. The people were complaining about God, so He said, "I'm going to send down fire and judgment upon you ungrateful people!" No! He said, "I am going to rain bread from heaven for you." The people didn't deserve this blessing. It was simply God showing His great love for them and giving them mercy. God was going to bless them in spite of their disobedience and lack of faith. This is the heart of God. The people were going to get the food they were asking for and desiring, but they didn't know that it also was a test. So far, the Israelites have shown that they have not listened to God, nor have they trusted Him. Will they now? God will bless the people with just enough bread every day; well, at least six days a week. The people are going to have to trust that the bread will be there every day and only take what they need for that day. They can't be greedy and gather a week's worth of food. They have to learn to daily trust God. That is a great lesson for us today.

December 8

"And all were amazed and perplexed, saying to one another, 'What does this mean?'"
Acts 2:12

What amazed all these Jews from around the world was that they heard these 120 believers speaking in their own native language.

What was it that these believers were saying? Were they preaching the Gospel? No! They were proclaiming "the mighty works of God" (Acts 2:11). The believers were simply praising God. They were worshipping God in languages that were unknown to them. Luke mentions 15 different geographical regions in Acts 2:9-11, and believers from all those areas heard different believers praising God in their own language. That's amazing!

This is what the purpose of speaking in tongues is: to praise God! I know that speaking in tongues is a very controversial subject. There are those that believe this gift was for a specific period of time and is no longer active. On the other side of the spectrum are those who believe that it is very active and the practice of speaking in tongues is a sign that you are a believer. I don't believe that either of those views is correct. The truth is in the middle of those two spectrums. Speaking in tongues is a current and active gift that is available to believers. But it is also a gift that is abused in certain groups or denominations today. The gift of tongues is not to build up the person speaking in tongues so that they are praised or feel superior to those that don't speak in tongues. The gift of speaking in tongues was to make them a supernatural witness to others. The purpose of speaking in tongues is to glorify God, not the person speaking in tongues. This is where so many misuse and abuse this gift today. 1 Corinthians 12 and 1 Corinthians 14 give more information about this gift. Today there are some that believe you must speak in tongues to "prove" that you are saved. This is not Biblical. The gift of speaking in tongues is not given to every believer.

In fact, the apostle Paul said "Now I want you all to speak in tongues, but even more to prophesy. The one who prophesies is greater than the one who speaks in tongues, unless someone interprets, so that the church may be built up" (1 Corinthians 14:5). So, what does it mean to prophesy? That is speaking God's Word, truth, verbally for others to hear. It is more important to speak God's Word in a language that people can understand than to speak in tongues. That's why the apostle Paul also said, "in church I would rather speak five words with my mind in order to instruct others, than ten thousand words in a tongue" (1 Corinthians 14:19). This is why the gift of speaking in tongues has a very important role to play in an individual's personal devotions to God, but a very small role to play when groups are gathered together. There is nothing wrong with speaking in tongues, but it must be done decently and in order so that God is praised and glorified. It is more important to clearly speak God's Word so that others may hear, understand it, and be saved.

Here on the day of Pentecost we see God reversing the judgment given at the Tower of Babel in Genesis 11:1-9. At Babel people were scattered across the earth, but at Pentecost people from around the world were gathered together in unity. At Babel the people were unable to understand what other people were saying, but at Pentecost people understood what others were saying as they praised God. You see, that is the difference between Babel and Pentecost. The events at Babel were designed to praise men; for mankind to become their own god. The events of Pentecost all occurred with one unified goal; to bring praise to God. The building of the Tower of Babel was an act of rebellion against God, but Pentecost was a submission of believers to the will of God, allowing the Holy Spirit to fill them, empower them, and help them fulfill the commands of God.

December 9

"...then Moses stood in the gate of the camp and said, 'Who is on the Lord's side? Come to me.' And all the sons of Levi gathered around him."
Exodus 32:26

There's an old country song that says, "You've got to stand for something, or you'll fall for anything." It talks about the need for standing up for what's right, even if you are standing all alone; it's better to be correct and alone than wrong and in the middle of a crowd. It is often not easy to take a stand, but it is very important and needs to be done.

Moses encountered the need for this when he came down from Mount Sinai, where God gave him the Ten Commandments. God sent Moses down because the people were sinning against God and committing all kinds of awful sins. God was ready to wipe them out, but Moses interceded on their behalf. When Moses got down off the mountain, he became very angry when he saw the number of people who had turned their backs on God and were committing these sins. That is when Moses cried out "Whoever is for the Lord, come to me." All of the Levites gathered around Moses.

The entire tribe of Levi was willing to take a stand for God, and what is right, while the rest of the nation wasn't. The Levites had separated themselves from the rest of the nation by doing what was right. Since they were willing to do what was right, especially in trying and difficult circumstances, God gave them a special blessing for being obedient to Him. They became the tribe that served as God's representatives to the people of Israel.

Don't misunderstand what happened here. The Levites were against the other eleven tribes, yet they didn't back down. They were willing to be different, to be called names (like goody-two-shoes, or holy rollers, etc.), to be looked down upon, and even mistreated for not participating with everyone else. It is still difficult to stand against others today. We face the same problems that the Levites did. It still is not easy, but it is still necessary. God still rewards His children when they take a stand for what is right. When we stand for God, He also helps us from falling for the lies of the world.

Lord, please give us the strength to stand against the world's system so that we can be a bright beacon for Your truth, shining for all the world around us to see.

December 10

"Concerning this salvation, the prophets who prophesied about the grace that was to be yours searched and inquired carefully..."
1 Peter 1:10

Peter is writing about the glories of our salvation, that Jesus died and rose again so that we can live with Him forever. This was not something new, but had been prophesied throughout the Old Testament, even though the writers of the Old Testament didn't clearly understand the events that they prophesied. They were writing under the inspiration and leading of the Holy Spirit. This began all the way back in the Garden of Eden when the first promise of the Messiah was given. God spoke to the serpent and said, "I will put enmity between you and the woman, and between your offspring and her offspring; He shall bruise your head, and you shall bruise His heel" (Genesis 3:15). Then throughout the Old Testament there are prophesies given showing the great things the Messiah will do, such as His triumphal entry on Palm Sunday. The prophet Isaiah was probably confused when he wrote about the great suffering that the Messiah would go through in Isaiah 53. Same thing with King David when he wrote Psalm 22.

While the Old Testament prophets clearly wrote about the Messiah, they did not yet clearly see how He would fulfill the prophesies the Holy Spirit was directing them to write. They didn't just blindly write the words down, but Peter, also inspired by the Holy Spirit, let us know that the prophets searched very diligently to try and understand what they were writing. What does it mean to search diligently? You may have a pet dog in your home or know someone who does. Watch how that dog sniffs around with their nose searching for smells. They don't just sniff the air once and move on. No! They put their nose down and walk all over, going round and round in circles until either they are satisfied, the smell is gone, or they have identified what the scent belongs to. It's intense. This is how the prophets searched to try and understand what they were writing. They were able to perfectly write about the future because they were being led by the Holy Spirit. This is the same Holy Spirit that we are led by today. Like the Old Testament prophets, we have things that we don't understand or see clearly. That's ok, that's also why God gave to us the Holy Spirit. Jesus said, "When the Spirit of truth comes, he will guide you into all the truth, for he will not speak on his own authority, but whatever he hears he will speak, and he will declare to you the things that are to come" (John 16:13). Do you have questions when you read the Bible? That's good. Pray to God and ask Him for wisdom and clarification. He has given you the Holy Spirit to help you understand and to give you more insight into Who Jesus is.

December 11

"And from among his brothers he took five men and presented them to Pharaoh."
Genesis 47:2

There are times in our life when we need representation. This can come in multiple forms. It could be someone that stands in our stead for some sort of negotiation, such as a labor dispute. Other times we need someone to represent us in a court case, a lawyer, whether it be for a criminal or a civil case. There are even times when meeting a person of importance, or possibly even self-importance, that a representative is needed to make the introduction. This is what Joseph is doing for his family. He is the representative between Pharaoh, the most powerful person in the world at that time, and his family. Notice that Joseph doesn't overwhelm Pharaoh by bringing all eleven of his brothers, plus his dad. Joseph is an astute judge of character, and he knows Pharaoh well, so he brings only five of his brothers with him. No doubt, these five are the brothers that would make the best impression, and appearance, upon Pharaoh.

In a worst-case scenario, at least four of these five brothers are ones that mistreated Joseph earlier, even selling him into slavery. Despite their past failures and shortcomings, Joseph willingly presented them to Pharaoh. He didn't bring up their past failures or shortcomings but presented them to Pharaoh as his family. They belong to him. What a wonderful picture of grace this is. In fact, this is exactly what Jesus does for us. Every one of us has done things wrong in our life. We have even mistreated Jesus, misrepresented Him to others, and many other wrongs that we have committed in our life. Even though we have failures and shortcomings in our life, Jesus lovingly presents us to God the Father and doesn't mention our failures and shortcomings. Jesus doesn't present us before God to share all the sordid details of our sin. No! He presents us to God as His family. His son or His daughter. Jesus is the One "who is able to keep you from stumbling and to present you blameless before the presence of His glory with great joy" (Jude 24). Praise the Lord that He does this for all those who surrender themselves to Him as their Lord and Savior.

December 12

"When Ananias heard these words, he fell down and breathed his last. And great fear came upon all who heard of it."
Acts 5:5

Now, don't get the crazy idea that Peter killed Ananias because he didn't. Peter didn't even announce a "death sentence" upon Ananias. He simply confronted Ananias about his sin, and then he dropped down dead. Peter was probably just as surprised as everyone else.

The reason Ananias died is because God killed him after judging him for his sin. Does this seem kind of harsh? Really what is surprising is that God delays His judgment in every other case! This wasn't harsh because Ananias simply received the results of his actions. He chose to live a compromising life, but he was exposed and received the consequences of his actions. All too often when a person chooses to live a compromising life, their greatest concern isn't about the sin they are committing, but about being found out by others; being exposed. Don't fall into the trap that Ananias and Sapphira did, believing there would always be time to repent, attempting to hide their sin from others. We don't know how much time we have, so it is always best to live an uncompromising life.

The result of Ananias' death is that "great fear came upon all who heard of it." That is understandable. As word of what happened to Ananias spread throughout the early church, and how the Holy Spirit acted with swift judgment, people undoubtedly began to examine their own motives. After all, the Holy Spirit did something that Jesus had never done; struck down a person as judgment. This was a warning for the entire church, and even for us today. God sent a very strong message to remind us of the importance of being holy, and the importance of the motives of our heart.

We can learn much from Ananias. We would be wise to inspect our own hearts, and motives. Are there any areas of dishonesty in our own lives? Do we give any appearance of being holy when we aren't? Do we sing songs of praise to God routinely, or from our heart? How about when we pray? Is it done without thinking, or do we really mean every word that we pray? We never want to hear God say about us, "this people draw near with their mouth and honor Me with their lips, while their hearts are far from Me, and their fear of Me is a commandment taught by men" (Isaiah 29:13).

December 13

"Who is wise and understanding among you? By his good conduct let him show his works in the meekness of wisdom."

Paul Verhoeven

James 3:13

James asks a very important question here, "who of you are wise?" Too often people confuse wisdom and knowledge, but they aren't the same. In fact, they are very different. There are many people who have their heads filled with knowledge, but do not possess wisdom. Knowledge is knowing things, facts, and information. This is a good thing to have. Wisdom, though, is the ability to use knowledge and apply it. Therefore, it is possible to have knowledge, yet be lacking in wisdom, or knowing how to apply or use the knowledge that you have. So, the big question is, how do we get wisdom? King Solomon tells us that "the Lord gives wisdom; from His mouth come knowledge and understanding" (Proverbs 2:6). He later tells us that "The beginning of wisdom is this: Get wisdom, and whatever you get, get insight" (Proverbs 4:7). Why is it so important to have wisdom? Because "wisdom is better than jewels, and all that you may desire cannot compare with her" (Proverbs 8:11). So, we can see how important it is to have wisdom, but how do we know if a person is wise or not?

Wisdom is seen through a person's actions. His is why James says we can see a person's wisdom by their "good conduct." You see, actions are much more powerful than words. So, we can see a person's wisdom through their life; the choices they make, the actions they do, and the words they speak. All of these add up to show whether or not a person has wisdom. There is another indicator of wisdom, and that is meekness. It is important that we don't confuse meekness with weakness. Meekness is not weakness, in fact, it is quite the opposite of that. The definition of meekness is "power under control." It describes a horse that has been broken so that the rider is able to control the horse and use its power to the rider's benefit. A person that is meek is a person that is under control, not out of control. A meek person does not selfishly assert themselves or seek glory for themselves. If a believer is meek, then instead of seeking glory for themselves, they make sure the glory is directed towards

God. In Galatians 5:23 we read that meekness is one of the fruits of the Spirit. This reminds us that meekness cannot be manufactured by a person, it is a gift from the Holy Spirit. Therefore, true wisdom is seen in the life of a believer through the choices they make, the actions they do, and their being meek, or not selfishly seeking the praise of man, but directing all praise back to God.

December 14

"Samuel said, 'What have you done?' And Saul said, 'When I saw that the people were scattering from me, and that you did not come within the days appointed, and that the Philistines had mustered at Michmash...'"
1 Samuel 13:11

King Saul is dealing with a troubling situation. We can learn much from how he responds to the trouble at hand. His individual circumstance may be different than what we may face, but each of us must also choose how we will respond when faced with a difficulty. Saul had been king less than 2 years at this time, and he is facing a battle with the Philistines. Saul's army consisted of 3,000 soldiers, while the Philistine army was "like the sand on the seashore in multitude" (1 Samuel 13:5). Before going into battle, Samuel the prophet told Saul to wait for him, and in seven days he would offer sacrifices before they engaged in battle. As Israel's army looked at the huge army they faced, many got scared and began to go AWOL. It was the seventh day, and Samuel hadn't showed up yet, so Saul disobeyed God by offering the sacrifices himself. Right after he finished, Samuel showed up, smelled the BBQ and asked Saul what he did (see 1 Samuel 13:11). Saul had a choice to make. How would he respond?

The best alternative for Saul would have been to repent for the wrong he had done. He could have apologized to Samuel for not waiting, and asked God to forgive him. But he didn't. Instead, he chose to blame everyone else, except for himself. Saul responded to Samuel by attempting to justify his disobedience. He offered the sacrifices because "the people were scattering from me." He blamed the troops for his disobedience. Saul even blamed Samuel: "you didn't come within the days appointed." And, if that wasn't enough, Saul even chose to blame his enemies: "the Philistines had mustered at Michmash." Saul failed to take responsibility for his actions, but instead chose to apply blame to everyone else. The only person he didn't blame was the person responsible for the choice: himself!

The choice that we will have to make when faced with trying times is whether or not we will obey God. If we choose to disobey, we can't go blaming others. You may feel that you would be able to make better choices in life, but your spouse keeps "dragging you down," your parents made mistakes raising you, or your boss at work mistreats you, etc. You can't blame others for the choices that you make; the responsibility for that lies on your own shoulders. Personal responsibility is not a popular topic today, but that doesn't mean it isn't right. You are responsible for the choices you make; no one else is. What are you going to choose to do? Will you choose to obey God? Or disobey Him? The choice is yours.

"By this we know that we love the children of God, when we love God and obey His commandments. For this is the love of God, that we keep His commandments" (1 John 5:2-3a).

December 15

"Likewise, husbands, live with your wives in an understanding way, showing honor to the woman as the weaker vessel, since they are heirs with you of the grace of life, so that your prayers may not be hindered."

1 Peter 3:7c

One area where most men are driven is to have success in whatever field of work they do. It doesn't matter if they are a pastor, truck driver, accountant, teacher, lawyer, or businessman. Men generally are driven to achieve success. Along with success comes accolades, contentment, and sometimes even great material wealth. These can be nice to receive, but none of these should be the greatest goal in a man's life, especially if he is married. The greatest thing a husband can do is recognize and realize that his wife is a joint-heir with him in Christ. This is still a radical concept to many today, just as it was when Peter wrote it. Peter just wrote that men are to treat their wives "as the weaker vessel" and his very next words are a reminder that she is equal to him. This is why we can confidently say that men and women are equal, even if the man tends to be physically stronger, his wife is in no way inferior to him. Husbands have great authority and responsibilities in marriage, but it is important that they remember their wife is equal to them in spiritual privilege and eternal importance.

There is a reason why it is so important for a husband to realize that his wife is equal to him. If he fails to do this, and is not considerate or respectful of his wife, he will suffer the consequences of that choice. What is the consequence? His prayers will be hindered, or not answered. The Bible teaches that we are to have a living relationship with God, but that relationship is dependent upon our relationships with those around us. If we are not in right relationship with those around us, it will cause us to not be in right relationship with God. This is equally true in marriage. If a husband mistreats his wife, using and even abusing her, then his relationship with God will not be right either. For him to get in right relationship with God, he needs to be in right relationship with his wife. When a man realizes that there is a "dryness" in his relationship with God, or that his prayers don't seem to be answered, it could be because his relationship with his wife is out of whack. God loves us so much that He doesn't want to see marriages not being in proper alignment.

December 16

"And Saul approved of his execution. And there arose on that day a great persecution against the church in Jerusalem, and they were all scattered throughout the regions of Judea and Samaria, except the apostles."
Acts 8:1

Dr. Luke lets us know that Saul approved of Stephen's murder. He didn't see it as murder though because he was blinded by religion. He wasn't content with just the murder of Stephen; he also began to persecute the church. Stephen was just the first. His death opened the floodgates of persecution for the rest of the church. Saul even admitted this later after he had been "born again." Paul wrote in Galatians 1:13 and Philippians 3:6 about how he had persecuted the church.

Historians tell us that approximately 2 years had passed since the time that Jesus rose from the grave. For the past 2 years the apostles have remained in Jerusalem preaching the Gospel and being used by God to perform miracles and that turned the city "upside down." But that wasn't what Jesus had commanded them to do. Jesus had told them to "be My witnesses in Jerusalem and in all Judea and Samaria, and to the end of the earth" (Acts 1:8).

God allowed this persecution against the church to occur in order to help the church to obey His command. Sometimes we need difficult times to help us move to where God has called us to be. It is too easy to become complacent and comfortable where we are, so God allows circumstances in our life that will move us. That is what is happening here. Saul believes that he is getting rid of the church, which Judaism viewed as a cult, but in reality, he is just a tool that God is using to accomplish His purposes and plans.

What this persecution against the church did accomplish was that "they were all scattered throughout the regions of Judea and

Samaria." The church began to move to these other regions, but all twelve apostles stayed in Jerusalem. As the church, we are called to move to where others are. We aren't to be static, staying in one place and waiting for them to come to us. No! We need to move to them. May we learn to do this on our own volition, not needing God to allow uncomfortable trials to cause us to move.

December 17

"But if anyone has the world's goods and sees his brother in need, yet closes his heart against him, how does God's love abide in him? Little children, let us not love in word or talk but in deed and in truth."

1 John 3:17-18

Real love has eyes. Selfishness has a mouth, as it likes to gobble everything up and eat. Envy has an ear, as it takes in the latest, juiciest gossip. Pride has a nose, as it walks around with it stuck up in the air. Love has eyes because it sees the needs around it; love looks. Jesus provided us the perfect example of this during His life here on earth. Zacchaeus was hidden in the sycamore tree; no one knew he was there, except Jesus. In John 9:1 there is a story about a man who was born blind. The people of that city walked by him numerous times every day, but they didn't notice him, and they didn't help him. When Jesus saw him, He healed him and gave him sight. Love has eyes and sees the needs of others, even when everyone else misses it.

How many people do we pass by on a regular basis where we have missed the need in their life? We get too busy, and our vision is focused inwardly to ourselves instead of focusing outwardly on others and their needs. How many people have we missed? How many people have we left up in a tree because our focus has been on self instead of others? It is love that opens our eyes so we can see the needs of others.

This is the reason why we need to live our lives with our eyes wide open. Love not only see's needs, it also feel's needs. This happens because love is tender, compassionate, and empathetic. This is why the apostle John wrote that he who "sees his brother in need, yet closes his heart against him, how does God's love abide in him?" We feel the needs of others because God's love doesn't allow our hearts to be closed to them. As long as God's love is within my heart, my heart will be open, and empathetic, to the needs of others. This doesn't mean that I will always be able to meet the needs of others. There will be times that we aren't able to meet someone else's needs, but our heart won't be hard towards them. We will have a heart of empathy for them instead of giving them the cold shoulder.

When I see a person in need, and I turn my back on them instead of caring for them, I will stop feeling for them. When I stop feeling, I will stop seeing. When I stop seeing others, my focus will only be directed towards self and caring for three people: me, myself, and I. I don't want to grow up and become a bitter, old man. I want to live life with open eyes; seeing others' needs and caring for them.

Real love isn't content to just talk about doing something to meet the needs of others, but it is willing to roll up its sleeves and meeting those needs. John here is saying we need to be like Nike: Just Do It! Don't spend all your time talking about what you could do, or what needs to be done, but be a person of action and do it. If I have the goods that will satisfy your need, then my loving response would be to give that to you. That's what love does. It doesn't hold back until something is done for you, if you have it, then you give it. Love's desire is to do something. Love is willing to give and help others; love doesn't hold back, but love meets needs. This means we don't just do what is convenient or comfortable. Every one of us has a daily schedule that we try to follow. We don't work our loved ones into that schedule, but we work our schedule around those we love.

December 18

"Therefore the Lord Himself will give you a sign. Behold, the virgin shall conceive and bear a son, and shall call His name Immanuel."
Isaiah 7:14

Social distance. That is a phrase that became very prevalent in the year 2020 and following. This is the practice of keeping distance between yourself and others in a public setting, making sure there is little to no contact between people. The reason behind this is to minimize the opportunities to transfer, or pass along, any illnesses, whether people know they carry them or not. What this has resulted in is people fearing contact with others. There have even been memes created saying that if Jesus were here on earth, He would socially distance from others. That is a lie!

How did Jesus live His life here on earth? We are given a clue to how He lived by the name that was given to Him: Immanuel. The name Immanuel means "God with us." Jesus came to earth to dwell among people, His creation. People are created to be social creatures. Yes, there are exceptions to the rule, where some individuals thrive on being alone, but that is rare. We have been created to be in contact with others. This is what Jesus did when He confined Himself in a human body and resided on earth. He was in contact with those around Him. He did not social distance Himself from people.

When a child is scared, what do they crave? The touch of their parent. In a storm or after a bad dream a child will seek out their parents desiring their touch to calm them and help them rest or go back to sleep. A tired parent may try to reassure their child by telling them that Jesus is there with them, so they can go back to sleep. This generally won't pacify a child because they desire human touch. This is an innate desire within people. God created us to desire touch. This is why a hug, a handshake, a hand placed on the shoulder, etc., can bring healing to people. This is what Jesus did. When a person was diagnosed as a leper, they became a social outcast. They had to announce their presence if they were around people and then watch everyone quickly move out of their way. The only people they had any contact with were fellow lepers. What did Jesus do to lepers? He touched them (see Matthew 8:3; Mark 1:41; Luke 5:13). Touch can bring healing.

Jesus touched the leper, not because it was needed for their physical healing. He could have healed them with a word, but Jesus touched them because He knew they needed a physical touch since they hadn't had one in a long time. Jesus touched them because Jesus was love wrapped in skin. Sharing touch with another is an act of love. This is why Jesus loved others by touching them. He did this to blind people, deaf people, those with fever, even those who weren't expected to be touched, like lepers and dead people. Of course, be wise about it when touching others. Make sure that you have washed and aren't sick. When touching others, we want to help them, and heal them, but not pass along illnesses or diseases. Don't be fearful of touching others because that is an act of love that is desperately needed by so many.

December 19

"When she opened it, she saw the child, and behold, the baby was crying. She took pity on him and said, 'This is one of the Hebrews' children.'"
Exodus 2:6

God again shows how He is in complete control of this situation. For Moses to have remained hidden for three months, he must have been a very quiet and content little baby. But now, as soon as the Pharaoh's daughter looks into the basket, he begins to cry. What a coincidence! No, it's God's providence. Pharaoh's daughter looks at this little baby and her natural, God-given maternal instincts kick in. She is immediately taken in by this baby, and she cannot imagine throwing it back into the river to kill it, as the law that her father made commanded to be done. She couldn't do it. Why? Because she was filled with compassion. Compassion is a deep-seated emotion towards someone else, and then it motivates a person to move in action to identify with the other person. Pharaoh's daughter identifies with and understands the deep sadness and hurt of this baby boy, and this causes her to make sure that this baby is not killed.

Isn't it wonderful to see how God uses a baby's tears to control the heart of a powerful princess. God uses Moses, who is as "weak as a baby" to fulfill His plan. Read through the Bible and you will see that God likes to use something that is weak in order to accomplish a mighty work. God did this with Isaac, Joseph, Gideon, Samuel, David, John the Baptist, Peter, and especially with Jesus. God can do this "For the foolishness of God is wiser than men, and the weakness of God is stronger than men. For consider your calling, brothers: not many of you were wise according to worldly standards, not many were powerful, not many were of noble birth. But God chose what is foolish in the world to shame the wise; God chose what is weak in the world to shame the strong; God chose what is low and despised in the world, even things that are not, to bring to nothing things that are, so that no human being[might boast in the presence of God" (1 Corinthians 1:25-29). God used a baby's tears as His first weapon in His war against Egypt. If God can use a baby's tears, He can also use you, and He will.

December 20

"Now when they saw the boldness of Peter and John, and perceived that they were uneducated, common men, they were astonished. And they recognized that they had been with Jesus."

Acts 4:13

The Jewish leaders were upset with Peter and John because they were preaching with great authority, and seeing lives changed. In short, they were getting results from their preaching that the religious leaders did not get. Why? What was the difference? After all, the religious leaders had received the best education that was available at that time, while Peter and John were uneducated common laborers. At this time in history the students who were allowed to continue their education were those who performed best in school. The fact that Peter and John did not continue school showed that they weren't the brightest and smartest kids in their age group. But they were the ones God was using to change lives. How was that possible?

The religious leaders wanted to know too, so they brought Peter and John in for questioning. After "grilling" Peter and John they came to the realization that they received their power and insight from spending so much time with Jesus. And they were right. That is where their power came from. Jesus promised them He would give them the gift of the Holy Spirit when He returned to Heaven, "And while staying with them He ordered them not to depart from Jerusalem, but to wait for the promise of the Father, which, He said, 'you heard from Me; for John baptized with water, but you will be baptized with the Holy Spirit not many days from now'" (Acts 1:4-5). The Holy Spirit in Peter and John is what gave them the boldness and power that both impressed the religious leaders and changed the lives of those who listened to them. This is the same Holy Spirit that God has given to those who believe in Him today too.

Each and every one of us who have accepted Jesus as their Lord and Savior also receives the Holy Spirit in their life and is able to speak the gospel with the same boldness and effectiveness. While education is a good thing, it is not required for sharing God's good news. Some people feel they cannot share with others if they do not have a college degree in Bible. That is not true! Share what you do know. Share what God has shown you through your study of the Bible. Share what God has done, and is doing, in your life. God will use your words to change the lives of others. God gives us the following promise about sharing His word, "...so shall My word be that goes out from My mouth; it shall not return to Me empty, but it shall accomplish that which I purpose, and shall succeed in the thing for which I sent it" (Isaiah 55:11).

December 21

"So he stayed there that night, and from what he had with him he took a present for his brother Esau..."
Genesis 32:13

George Mueller was a great man of faith, and when he was asked what the most important part of prayer was, he responded "the fifteen minutes after I have said 'Amen.'" Jacob had just finished praying a great prayer to God. Praising God for His blessings in Jacob's life, even though he didn't deserve them and wasn't worthy of them. But, as soon as he finished praying he began to plot and scheme how to come out ahead in this situation. Instead of trusting God and having faith in Him, Jacob resorts to his own intellect. He decides to put together a very expensive present in the hope of pacifying Esau.

In Genesis 32:14-15 we see that the gift Jacob prepares for Esau consists of 580 total animals; including goats, sheep, camels, cattle, and donkeys. Each type of animal was sent over together in a herd with a servant leading the group of animals. Each servant was instructed to make the same speech: These animals "belong to your servant Jacob. They are a gift sent to my lord Esau. And look, he is behind us." Jacob continues to grovel before Esau. Jacob follows the last group of animals, and his hope is that Esau will be overwhelmed by the magnitude of the gifts and his heart would be softened so Esau will forgive Jacob and they can be reconciled.

This gift Jacob prepares for Esau is a good example of the way we trust in our ability to do things and make things happen apart from trusting God. We like to sing the song:

All to Jesus, I surrender, all to Him I freely give;
I will ever love and trust Him, in His presence daily live.
I surrender all, I surrender all,
All to Thee, my blessed Savior, I surrender all.

But we, so often like Jacob, mean, "I surrender all the goats. If that isn't enough, I surrender all the sheep. If that isn't enough, I surrender all the camels . . ." But what Jacob would not do is surrender himself. God desires that we surrender ourselves to Him. The rest of our belongings will follow; what He truly desires is us.

December 22

"...then the Lord knows how to rescue the godly from trials, and to keep the unrighteous under punishment until the day of judgment, and especially those who indulge in the lust of defiling passion and despise authority. Bold and willful, they do not tremble as they blaspheme the glorious ones..."
2 Peter 2:9-10

As we look around at the culture and society around us it sometimes appears that evil is triumphing, and people are getting away with sin. It may appear that way, but we need to remember that appearances can be deceiving. God is in control, and He is aware of what is going on, and those living in and promoting sin will reap what they have sown. The apostle Peter here reminds us that not only does God know how to rescue His children from trials, but that He also knows how to administer judgment to those who refuse to obey Him. Even though there are times when it seems like people are getting away with sin, know that the day of their judgment is coming. This is nothing for us to gloat over, but it is a reminder to us that God is faithful. He does not turn a blind eye to disobedience.

Every person born after Adam and Eve has had to deal with the same issue, sin. We are all born with a sin nature, and that sin nature causes us all to be depraved, to have a natural inclination to refuse to submit to God, or any other authority. Society shouts at us that we are to look out for ourselves, look out for number one, which is yourself. Bookstores are filled with self-help books that encourage you to do anything and everything necessary to help you succeed, even if that success comes at the expense of, hurting, or even humiliating others. The world says you don't need to be concerned about anyone other than yourself. This had led to the rise of pride. We are encouraged to be filled with pride over who we are, no matter whether we are good, evil, helpful, selfish. It doesn't matter. Just be filled with pride about you!

Jesus shows us a different way. Jesus modeled it for us. We do well to follow Jesus' example and do "nothing from selfish ambition or conceit, but in humility count others more significant than yourselves. Let each of you look not only to his own interests, but also to the interests of others" (Philippians 2:3-4). That is how God desires us to live. Not filled with Pride, but "to do justice, and to love kindness, and to walk humbly with your God." (Micah 6:8).

December 23

"And David said, 'Is there still anyone left of the house of Saul, that I may show him kindness for Jonathan's sake?'"
2 Samuel 9:1

This is an amazing choice that David made. Saul treated David like an enemy, even attempting to kill him. Despite this, David made the choice to be kind to one of his relatives. It had nothing to do with the person deserving kindness, David made the choice to be kind, not even knowing who he was going to be kind to. How much better would our world be if we made that same choice? All too often we choose to treat others the way that they have treated us. Imagine how good things could be if we were more like David; making the choice to be kind to others, especially to those who don't deserve it?

David made this choice to extend kindness to someone because of Jonathan. This was King Saul's oldest son, the one who should have been heir to the throne. But, because of Saul's disobedience to God, the throne was removed from Saul's family and given to David. You would think that this would have made Jonathan and David mortal enemies, but the opposite was actually true. Jonathan and David loved each other very much and were best friends. Jonathan's reaction to David being anointed as the next king, instead of himself, proves that Jonathan really was the greatest king Israel never had.

It is important for us to understand the reason why David made the choice to show kindness to someone who hadn't earned it. It had nothing to do with emotion, or an attempt to "do good." No! David was doing this to honor a covenant, a promise that he had made with Jonathan years earlier. This happened in 1 Samuel 20 when King Saul was attempting to murder David. David hid himself to spare his life, and Jonathan helped him. Before David left, he and Jonathan made this covenant together (Jonathan speaking): "But should it please my father to do you harm, the Lord do so to Jonathan and more also if I do not disclose it to you and send you away, that you may go in safety. May the Lord be with you, as he has been with my father. If I am still alive, show me the steadfast love of the Lord, that I may not die; and do not cut off your steadfast love from my house forever, when the Lord cuts off every one of the enemies of David from the face of the earth" (1 Samuel 20:13-15). David has now been king for approximately 15 years, most of his enemies have been silenced, and now he is going to fulfill this covenant he had made years earlier.

May we learn to make this same choice that David made; the choice to extend kindness to others whether they deserve it or not.

December 24

"...to an inheritance that is imperishable, undefiled, and unfading, kept in Heaven for you..."
1 Peter 1:4

Peter has been talking about the hope that God gives to us, a hope that is unlike anything the world has to offer. All earthly hopes will fade or diminish over time, but the hope that God gives is a living hope, one that continues to grow and become brighter and more alive on a daily basis. Now Peter adds on to that hope by talking about the inheritance we will receive as a child of God. An inheritance is when we receive property, money, titles, privileges, entitlements, obligations, or debts from someone close to you after they die. Instead of trying to describe the inheritance that we receive as a child of God, Peter tells us what it is not.

The inheritance that we receive from God is so great that there are no earthly words that can adequately describe what it is like or worth. This is why Peter instead tells us what our inheritance is not. There are three things that he tells us our inheritance is not. Our inheritance is imperishable, undefiled, and unfading. Our inheritance is imperishable. Some translators use the word incorruptible in place of imperishable. They both carry the same meaning, it is something that will last forever, something that cannot be ruined. It is also undefiled. This means that our inheritance is pure, it cannot be stained or ruined in any way. Undefiled also means that our inheritance never grows old, but is instead eternal, lasting in a perfect state forever. The third trait that our inheritance is not is unfading. It will never fade or diminish over time.

Imagine the most glorious inheritance that you could receive on earth. There is no amount of money or property that you could receive that would even come close to the inheritance that God gives to us, His children. What is it that God gives to us as our inheritance? It is God

Himself. When God established the priesthood, He said, "You shall have no inheritance in their land, neither shall you have any portion among them. I am your portion and your inheritance among the people of Israel" (Numbers 18:20). King David understood that is true for us too, not just the priests, which is why he wrote, "The Lord is my chosen portion and my cup; you hold my lot. The lines have fallen for me in pleasant places; indeed, I have a beautiful inheritance" (Psalm 16:5-6). God Himself is our inheritance, which means that it is not something we have to wait to receive. God gives Himself to us right now, right where we are. Our inheritance begins here on earth and will continue throughout all eternity.

December 25

"'O death, where is your victory? O death, where is your sting?' The sting of death is sin, and the power of sin is the law."
1 Corinthians 15:55-56

This verse is a quote from Hosea 13:14, and it shows that death has lost its power and its sting. How? Because Jesus died and rose from the dead. Our future resurrection will be in triumph over death due to the victory that Jesus won.

Here is an illustration to help us see what Jesus has done for us. A little girl was having a picnic with her daddy. Deathly allergic to bee stings, she became terrified as a bumblebee buzzed overhead. Seeing the bee, her father caught it and held it in his hand for a few seconds before letting it go. As it buzzed around once more, the little girl cried, "Daddy, Daddy, why did you let the bee go." Rather than explain it, the father chose to simply open his hand to show his daughter the stinger embedded in his palm.

As Christians, the sting of death has been removed. Death is not the end of life; it is just the beginning. We are no longer under the Law and its penalty of death because Jesus has set us free! Death was

Jesus' final enemy, as it is for us. But death does not have the final word. Death has lost its sting and its victory. For us Christians, death is as frightening as a scorpion that has had its stinger removed; or a poisonous snake whose fangs have been removed. When Jesus rose from the grave, He de-fanged death.

There is power in Jesus' resurrection. Jesus rose from the dead and death was defeated because it could not hold Him down. 1 Corinthians 15:20 says, "But in fact Christ has been raised from the dead, the firstfruits of those who have fallen asleep." As the "first-fruits," Jesus is the prototype of what we will become. Christians will follow Jesus and be resurrected too.

Since we will be resurrected that means we are not subject to the penalty of the Law, which is death, because we have been set free. Sin, death, and the Law go together. The Law reveals sin, and "the wages of sin is death, but the free gift of God is eternal life in Christ Jesus our Lord" (Romans 6:23). Jesus bore our sins while on the cross, and He also bore the curse of the Law while on the cross. "Christ redeemed us from the curse of the law by becoming a curse for us—for it is written, 'Cursed is everyone who is hanged on a tree'" (Galatians 3:13). The power of sin has been broken. We now have no reason to fear death because it has no power over us any longer. Praise the Lord!

December 26

"In the fifth year of King Rehoboam, Shishak king of Egypt came up against Jerusalem. He took away the treasures of the house of the LORD and the treasures of the king's house. He took away everything. He also took away all the shields of gold that Solomon had made, and King Rehoboam made in their place shields of bronze, and committed them to the hands of the officers of the guard, who kept the door of the king's house. And as often as the king went into

the house of the LORD, the guard carried them and brought them back to the guardroom."
1 Kings 14:25-28

During the height of King Solomon's reign, Solomon displayed the riches of Israel for all to see. "King Solomon made 200 large shields of beaten gold; 600 shekels of gold went into each shield. And he made 300 shields of beaten gold; three minas of gold went into each shield. And the king put them in the House of the Forest of Lebanon" (1 Kings 10:16-17). These golden shields were stolen by the king of Egypt, and Rehoboam replaced them with bronze shields. No longer were they left out on display but stored and locked up in a secure room. They were only brought out for ceremonial purposes, and then locked up again. The shields of Solomon were of more value and left out all the time, while the shields of Rehoboam were of less value and locked up. What does this mean?

In the Bible the shield is used as a symbol of faith. "In all circumstances take up the shield of faith, with which you can extinguish all the flaming darts of the evil one" (Ephesians 6:16). Solomon had passed along a rich faith that was prominently displayed to his son. Rehoboam was a wicked man, who did much evil in the sight of the Lord. He allowed the world (Egypt) to come in and steal his faith. It was replaced with an inferior faith. But to keep up appearances to others, it was brought out at certain times, so it appeared the faith was still there.

We can be just like Rehoboam. When we allow sin into our life, it will steal the foundation of our faith away. That itself can be embarrassing, so we replace it with an inferior faith that looks good to others but has little to no value. We bring it out for appearances when we go to church. The rest of the time our faith is hidden out of sight back at home. Jesus wants our faith to be golden again. He came and died on the cross for you and me to show His great love for us. He does not want us to be embarrassed by Him. Jesus said, "So everyone who acknowledges Me before men, I also will acknowledge before my

Father who is in heaven, but whoever denies Me before men, I also will deny before my Father who is in heaven" (Matthew 10:32-33). Do not be ashamed of Jesus. Make sure your faith remains golden. Come to Him, draw close to Him, and He will restore you and keep your faith golden.

December 27

"...knowing that you were ransomed from the futile ways inherited from your forefathers..."
1 Peter 1:18

Peter has been writing to fellow believers and reminding them of how we as Christians have been called to live a holy life. There is a reason for this, it is because a high price has been paid for our lives. There is a theological word for this, which is the word redemption. To many people today this word doesn't mean a lot, but to the readers in Peter's day it was a loaded word. You see, when Peter wrote this letter there were approximately 60 million slaves in the Roman Empire. A slave dreamed of the day that they would be redeemed, which meant that someone either released them from their slavery or a price had been paid to release them from slavery, whether by themselves or someone else on their behalf. This was very important to the people Peter was writing to since many of them were slaves. But it is also important to us today because this is the reason Jesus died on the cross, to pay the penalty for our sin so that we can be set free and no longer a slave to sin.

What exactly did Jesus do for us? "For we ourselves were once foolish, disobedient, led astray, slaves to various passions and pleasures, passing our days in malice and envy, hated by others and hating one another. But when the goodness and loving kindness of God our Savior appeared, He saved us, not because of works done by us in righteousness, but according to His own mercy, by the washing of regeneration and renewal of the Holy Spirit, whom He poured out on us richly through Jesus Christ our Savior, so that being justified by His grace we might become heirs according to the hope of eternal life" (Titus 3:3-7). How do we know that this works? "Because "if the Son sets you free, you will be free indeed" (John 8:36). Peter reminds these believers that before becoming a Christian they led an aimless and empty life just like us. Jesus paid the penalty for our sin so that our life can now be filled with purpose. That purpose is to live a life that honors and pleases Jesus our Savior. Jesus does not want you to live a life that is empty and miserable. He wants you to live filled with freedom and purpose.

December 28

"But do not overlook this one fact, beloved, that with the Lord one day is as a thousand years, and a thousand years as one day."
2 Peter 3:8

A difficulty that most children have is waiting. Time seems to move at a snail's pace. The younger you are the more slowly it seems to move. As a child it seems that Christmas takes forever to get here. Now, as an older adult, it seems like Christmas happens right after Christmas ends, there is very little wait in between. Like many youngsters life crawled along slowly while waiting to turn sixteen in order to get a drivers' license. Time does not move slowly any longer. In fact, the older I get the faster that time seems to go by.

Peter is hinting at that thought in this verse. Here on earth, we are like young children, and time seems to move slowly and take forever. God, in Heaven, see time in a completely different manner. That's the point Peter makes. He is not giving us a rigid prophetic formula, that to God one thousand years is the same as one day. God created the earth in six days and rested on the seventh. That was around six thousand years ago, so He must be coming back soon because we will enter in the Millennium, the 1,000-year rest, soon. It is possible, but that's not the point of Peter. God sees time in a completely different way than we do. What seems to us as taking forever, is nothing more than a moment to God. People on earth see God as being slack, but to God it has been just a moment.

The reason for this is because God exists outside of time. He is not limited by, or confined within, time like we are. Read through the Bible and you will see that God is never in a hurry, but neither is He ever late. He always arrives right on time. God could have created the entire world in an instant, but He chose to do it in six days. He could have liberated Israel from Egypt in a moment, but he chose to do it over time, and then spend the next forty years growing and developing Moses and the people of Israel. Trust God. He is faithful to finish the work that He begins, in His time.

December 29

"According to the grace of God given to me, like a skilled master builder I laid a foundation, and someone else is building upon it. Let each one take care how he builds upon it."
1 Corinthians 3:10

One of the most famous buildings in the world is the Leaning Tower of Pisa. This tower is the bell tower of Pisa Cathedral, and it is known for its nearly four-degree lean. Why does this tower lean four-degrees? It is due to the tower having an unstable foundation. The purpose of a foundation is not only to hold up the building, but to stabilize the building against side-to-side movement and to be strong enough to be strong enough to withstand terrible weather conditions, such as storms, heavy rains, or harsh winds. Jesus taught about this in His Sermon on the Mount when He said "everyone who hears these words of Mine and does them will be like a wise man who build his house upon the rock. And the rain fell, and the floods came, and the winds blew and beat on that house, but it did not fall, because it had been founded on the rock" (Matthew 7:24-25). The Leaning Tower of Pisa was not built upon a rock foundation, and it now leans because of it. The apostle Paul writes to the Corinthian Church and reminds them of their foundation.

God used the apostle Paul to establish the church in Corinth, and Paul was very deliberate in the foundation that the church was built upon. The foundation of the church was not a set of principles to follow, it was built upon a Person, Jesus Christ. Jesus said, "on this rock I will build My church, and the gates of hell shall not prevail against it" (Matthew 16:18). Jesus said this is response to a declaration Peter had just made, which was, "You are the Christ, the Son of the living God" (Matthew 16:16). The foundation of the church is Jesus. The true church of Jesus is not to build upon the purpose of accomplishing something politically, or legislatively, a moral cause, or even to be socially responsible. It is Jesus, and Him crucified, buried, and rose from the grave. When Paul came to Corinth, he "decided to know nothing among you except Jesus Christ and Him crucified" (1 Corinthians 2:1). Every church that is built upon the foundation of Jesus, and Him alone, will withstand any rain, flood, or storm they experience.

December 30

"He went and lived by the brook Cherith that is east of the Jordan... And after a while the brook dried up, because there was no rain in the land."
1 Kings 17:5b, 7

Elijah confronted evil King Ahab and told him there would be no rain in the land for three years. God then directed Elijah to go to this little brook, and He miraculously provided food for Elijah during this drought. But eventually the brook dried up because of the lack of rain. No longer was this brook providing the needed nourishment for Elijah.

Now the brook Cherith became a form of disappointment for Elijah. He is faced with a failure, because no longer are his needs being met. Because of this the brook also became to him a form of humiliation. Here he has been trusting and following God, and now that has led to failure. You may have experienced this in your own life. It may have been a job or a relationship that failed, and you fell flat on your face. That can be humiliating. But that can also be exactly where God wants us to be. Wait a minute you say, God wants me to be humiliated? Possibly.

We become humiliated when our pride is crushed, broken, or defeated. That is where God wants us, because when our pride is removed, then God can work in us. Pride is a stumbling block that keeps God away. In order for God to operate in our lives and make us into the men or women of God that He desires, He must be allowed into our lives. For that to happen it is often necessary for things to be removed from us so that we are not distracted from seeing God. For Elijah, this meant the brook had to be removed. For us, we may need to have a job removed, or a relationship, a loss of money, health, friends, family, reputation, computers, internet, video games, etc. When these areas that have blocked God are removed from our lives, then we are able to realize that all we truly need is God. This is God's ultimate goal for us.

God will remove things from our life so that we are faced with a choice. Either we realize our need for God and draw closer to Him, or we become angry at Him and walk away from Him. When we have had all other things removed, then we will have a desire for God alone. When we have nothing else left, we will have our desire for God; and that is enough to sustain us. The psalmist Asaph said, "Whom have I in heaven but You? And there is nothing on earth that I desire besides You" (Psalm 73:25). God desires us to have this same desire in our own lives. He is willing to remove things from our life in order to get us to this point. So, when something is removed, don't get angry about it, but draw closer to God. Realize that He is everything that you need.

December 31

"He who testifies to these things says, 'Surely I am coming soon.'
Amen. Come, Lord Jesus!"
Revelation 22:20

Tag is a game that has been a favorite of people for many years. In this game people hide from the person who is "it." After the person who is "it" has counted to the previously agreed upon number, they loudly proclaim "Ready or not, here I come." This is the warning that they will be quickly looking for every person who is hiding. They aren't going to yell this and then go hide in the house and ignore the people that are hiding, unless of course this is the ploy of a frenzied and tired parent. This is the warning that Jesus gives through the apostle John. He tells us that He is going to return, and it will be suddenly, speedily, or without delay. When Jesus returns, it will not be a drawn-out affair. It will happen suddenly and quickly.

There are some who scoff at this since Jesus proclaimed this warning almost 2000 years ago. This is why Jesus didn't say it would be soon, but that it would happen suddenly. When Jesus told the disciples about His return He said, "concerning that day or that hour, no one knows, not even the angels in heaven, nor the Son, but only the Father. Be on guard, keep awake. For you do not know when the time will come" (Mark 13:32-33). We should be thankful that Jesus has delayed His return, because if it happened earlier, the chances are good that we wouldn't have been saved. As the apostle Peter reminds us, "The Lord is not slow to fulfill his promise as some count slowness, but is patient toward you, not wishing that any should perish, but that all should reach repentance" (2 Peter 3:9).

Jesus desires every person to be saved. This is why He is waiting to return, so that more people will be saved.

Throughout the book of Revelation, the emphasis is on being ready and prepared for Jesus' return. We need to always be ready for His return. Not only do we need to be ready, but as believers we also need to be looking forward to His return. The phrase "Come, Lord Jesus" is one Greek word. It is a word that the early church was familiar with and often used. It is the word "Maranatha." May that be the desire of our heart too. Come quickly Lord Jesus. Maranatha!

About the Author

Paul Verhoeven lives in Idaho Falls, ID with his wife Melanie. They have three adult children. Paul has been involved in Church ministries for over 30 years, including serving as a pastor at Packinghouse Church and Calvary Chapel Challis. Currently he serves in various ministries at Watersprings Church in Idaho Falls. In his spare time Paul enjoys spending time with his family, reading books, playing his guitar, and riding his bicycle. He is the author of the devotional book "Traveling Through The Gospels."

Also by Paul Verhoeven

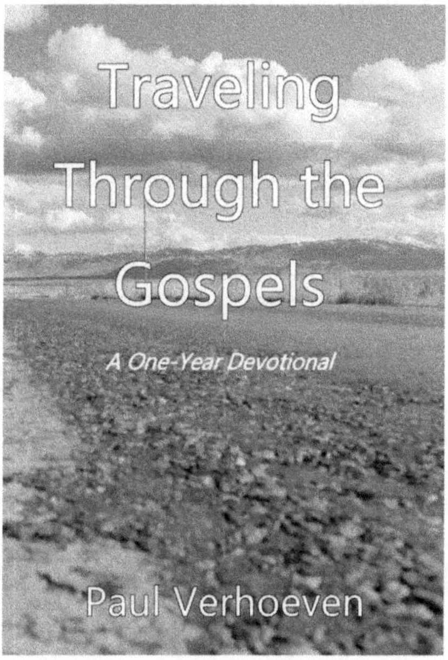

Traveling Through the Gospels, a one-year devotional, 2022

When Jesus was here on earth He was ridiculed by the religious leaders for teaching in parables and in ways the common person was able to understand. This was one of the reasons why the average person loved to listen to Jesus teach, and to follow Him. Parables often used common, ordinary, and daily events to explain spiritual truths. *Traveling Through The Gospels* is written in the same simple and easy way for everyone to understand. Through Jesus' life and ministry on earth we find application to our daily lives today from the books of Matthew, Mark, Luke, and John.

www.ingramcontent.com/pod-product-compliance
Lightning Source LLC
Chambersburg PA
CBHW070015100426
42740CB00013B/2501
* 9 7 9 8 2 1 8 3 7 1 7 9 1 *